ROUTE 28

ROUTE 28

A Mile-by-Mile Guide to
New York's
Adventure Route

ROB SCHARPF

PUBLISHING COMPANY

MELBOURNE, FLORIDA

Route 28

A Mile-by-Mile Guide to New York's Adventure Route

Rob Scharpf

© 1998 Rob Scharpf. All rights reserved.

Library of Congress Catalog Card Number: 98-93247.

ISBN 0-9663426-0-7

Printed in the U.S.A.

Photos by the author and by Glenn DeWitt.
Copy editing by Thomas E. Witherspoon.
Cover by Foster and Foster.
Cover photo of Route 28 sign by Glenn DeWitt.

1   3   5   7   9   8   6   4   2

Big Pencil Publishing
P. O. Box 410675
Melbourne, Florida 32941-0675
(407) 752-6715

Table of Contents

Foreword

Seagulls floated over the shoreline, silver rapiers of road glare pierced our eyes, and cars ahead of us shimmered in the heat as I drove my black car through the white-hot afternoon southward through Florida toward a beach destination. The air-conditioning compressor was sweating so my sweetheart Jodi and I wouldn't. Lunch was a memory, we still had many miles to go, and I was dreaming of an ice cream cone. How could we find one? The only advertising signs along the road were for restaurants and motels, not ice cream stands. Our maps showed us where the towns were, but nothing about what was in those towns, and certainly not the location of the nearest ice cream stand. Jodi had her cellular phone along, but after a short discussion we decided against calling 911 for help. We realized the only way we were going to find an ice cream stand was to hunt for one. Finally, after 30 minutes of criss-crossing a town in a military search pattern, success. I indulged in two scoops of black raspberry on a sugar cone, while Jodi, the sensible one, had a one-scoop cup of vanilla frozen yogurt.

As we searched for an ice cream stand, I thought how helpful it would be to have a travel guide which contained directions to everything a traveler could possibly want. Most travel guides present only the biggest and the best that a particular area has to offer, focusing specifically on lodging, restaurants, and attractions. And most travel guides describe only the attractions which are famous or nearly so. But how do you find an ice cream stand in an average town? Where is the beginning of the trail to the highest mountain in the Catskills? Where can you find, in a little mountain hamlet, a sub sandwich to take along on your hike? Where do you find the postcards your friends expect you to send? And where can you replenish your energy by dining on prime rib once you've returned from the mountaintop?

In my hometown of Kingston, New York, there begins a state road that I have loved all my life. It is a three-dimensional road, constantly turning left or right or going up or down, and many adventures line its route. It makes a large, open, 282-mile-long clockwise loop between Kingston and its junction with NY 9 just north of Warrensburg. Route 28 is the only road which goes through the middle of both the Catskill Park and the Adirondack Park, and as an added bonus, it goes through Cooperstown and crosses the Mohawk Valley. When I lived in Woodstock I used Route 28 to travel to and from work. I also used it to get away from it all, to travel to the mountains for hiking, fishing, skiing, and camping. For decades I had driven it only from Kingston to Andes, and through parts of the Adiron-dacks. I had always wondered what was beyond Andes, what lay to the west of Eighth Lake, and what it would be like to drive Route 28 from one end to the other. My desire for a comprehensive travel guide while searching for ice cream in Florida, and my decades-old interest in driving Route 28 in its entirety, led me to the idea that resulted in this book. Two years of work, several hundred interviews, and thousands of miles of driving later, you are reading these words. May they help you find the ice cream cone of your dreams—and anything else you could ever want along New York's adventure route.

Preface

New York's Route 28 is known by many people, be they local residents who travel it every day, neighborhood folks who travel it for fun and adventure, or distant tourists who travel it on holiday and vacation. But few people know it from beginning to end. Few people know that it bisects both the Catskill and Adirondack Mountains. Few people know all the wonderful adventures that its 282 miles offers. And few of its travelers know where on Route 28 they can find an ice cream cone on a hot day or a hot bowl of homemade soup on a cold day, where they can rent a canoe for an afternoon paddle or a snowmobile for an afternoon ride, where they can find the perfect souvenir to bring home with them, or where they can find an ATM to withdraw the cash to pay for it all. This book removes the mystery from Route 28, revealing mile-by-mile its wonderful attributes to you, the reader.

Route 28: A Mile-by-Mile Guide to New York's Adventure Route covers the entire length of the road, from Kingston to just north of Warrensburg. It also covers the towns bypassed by a rerouting of Route 28 in the 1960s, plus a number of interesting locations off Route 28 such as Woodstock. Included are short descriptions of attractions, amusements, natural wonders, lodging establishments, restaurants, merchants, and more. I hope this book will enhance your enjoyment of this wonderful road and the joys and adventures that it offers.

The author and the publisher make no warranty regarding the accuracy of the information contained in this publication. The information was as valid and accurate as humanly possible when the book was published.

Acknowledgments

Heartfelt thanks go to Diane Meleski, who faithfully nudged me off the fence and urged me to follow my dreams and write this book. Loving thanks go to Jodi Algeri, who sustained and supported me in body and spirit through two years of research and writing. And warm thanks go to Richard Schaefer, who watered to life my withering writing seedling 37 years ago.

Thank you to David Anderegg, Angelo Fasano, Bob Mallory, and Gordon Wright, whose friendships helped me sharpen the dream.

Thank you to Richard Bothen, Bruce Catlin, Debbie Clough, Georgiana Fairley, Carl Ferullo, Richard Frisbie, Judy and John Gregg, Barbara Haspiel, Jim Hazener, Chester G. Krom, Esq., Gary Livingston, Dominick Mercurio, Pete Molinari, John Nemjo, Susan R. Perkins, George Profous, Elsie Saar, Nancy Smith, Deborah J. Taylor, Joyce Urtz, Kristin Von Eiff, and to the hundreds of merchants, shop keepers, restaurateurs, and other fine people whom I interviewed who are, in fact, the essence and substance of *Route 28: A Mile-by-Mile Guide to New York's Adventure Route*.

1

Introduction

If you were to drive Route 28 in its entirety from Kingston to Warrensburg, then drive I-87 (New York's Northway and part of the Thruway) from Warrensburg to Kingston to close the loop, you would travel 400 miles, excluding side trips. From Manhattan, the total would be 600 miles, including the round trip from Manhattan to Kingston.

On one level the format of this book presents useful information for the traveler who is driving Route 28 to go somewhere as a means to an end. On a higher level, this book offers unique information for the traveler who is driving Route 28 to be immersed in new places, new experiences, and new lives. On the one hand, you can transit the entire length of the route in one long day and say you have driven Route 28. Or, you can take your time, stopping often along the way to wander the sidewalks of Woodstock, hike a mountain trail in the Catskills, stop for lunch at the park in Big Indian, attend an auction in Fleischmanns, shop at an antique shop in Colliersville, and dine at an excellent restaurant in Cooperstown. Or, you can prospect for "diamonds" in Herkimer, ride down the water slide in Old Forge, go for a float plane flight in Inlet, canoe Raquette Lake, take an excursion boat ride on Blue Mountain Lake, camp with the ducks at Lake Durant, play a round of golf in Indian Lake, raft the Hudson River white water in North River, and relax at a bed and breakfast in North Creek. Then, perhaps, you can say you have experienced Route 28. But what about snowmobiling in Old Forge, skiing at Gore Mountain, fly fishing in the West Canada Creek, experiencing a scenic rail ride in Arkville or Thendara, mountain biking down Plattekill, viewing fall foliage from the Belleayre Mountain chairlift, horseback riding in Inlet, experiencing the world's largest kaleidoscope in Mt. Tremper, and, well you get the picture, eh? Then you will *really* have experienced Route 28!

Savor the Charms

Route 28 is a 282-mile charm bracelet with Kingston at one end and Warrensburg at the other. Its forests, lakes, ponds, mountains, rivers, streams, views, vistas, ski centers, snowboard half pipes, skating ponds, bike paths, hiking trails, parking areas, horse corrals, fishing spots, hotels, motels, restaurants, shops, ice cream shops, water slides, scenic railroads, sightseeing boats, and so much more, are its charms. Of and by itself a charm bracelet is only a trinket to adorn a wrist. Its charms are special only when they are turned between the fingers, reflected upon, and memories shared with others. So it is with Route 28. On its surface, it is no different from other scenic roads, a pretty gold bracelet from here to there. But if you take the time to experience its charms along its full length, you'll remember it always.

Walk away from the main streets and onto the back streets and lanes where the architecture, construction, and manner of living are unique to the area and different from your own neighborhood.

Spend an hour at a local snack bar where the kids hang out.

Sit at the counter at a breakfast diner and rub elbows with the natives.

Engage your dinner waitress in conversation.

Dig through the local history books in a small-town library.

Talk to the librarian.

Peruse the shelves of a rural general store.

Play darts with the locals at a neighborhood watering hole.

Chat with the owner of your motel or bed and breakfast.

Ask the campsite ranger about local wildlife.

Watch the sunset over an Adirondack lake.

Hike into the forest and listen to the birds.

Climb a mountain and be awed by the view.

One of my most unforgettable hiking experiences was an evening climb up 3,140' Overlook Mountain in Woodstock. You can duplicate it. Select a day with a full moon, or a day or two just before full moon. Pack a picnic dinner and hike the two and one-half miles to the summit of Overlook Mountain from the trail head at the top of Meads Mountain Road. Depart the parking lot three hours before sunset, or earlier depending upon your physical condition, so you arrive at the summit an hour and one half or so before sunset. When you arrive at the summit, enjoy your dinner, then watch the sunset over the Catskills. After sunset, turn your attention to the east and southeast and watch the moon rise as the Hudson Valley lights up with electricity as darkness falls. Then walk down the mountain after dark with the use of good-sized flashlights powered by fresh batteries. It is recommended that each person carry two flashlights in case batteries expire or if one flashlight is dropped and the bulb breaks. The entire trip will require about five hours, and the memories will last a lifetime.

No Equipment? No Problem!

Not having necessary equipment is a poor excuse for not having the fun you want. Bikes, kayaks, canoes, sailboats, motorboats, snowmobiles, skis, snowboards, showshoes, and more are all for rent somewhere along Route 28. You can even rent a guide and go off for days at a time on a canoe trip across the Fulton Chain of Lakes or take a pack-horse trip into the Adirondack Mountains. Just grab your toothbrush, drive on up, and have a good time. Don't forget to reserve ahead to ensure the equipment will be available when you want it. See Appendix B for equipment rental sources.

Traveling Tips

There are times during the peak summer tourist season, the fall leaf-peeping period, and the winter snowmobile time frame, when spur-of-the-moment lodging along Route 28, especially in the Cooperstown area and the Adirondacks, may be difficult to find. Most bed and breakfasts are in private homes and do not accept walk-ins. Also, many lodging establishments, especially bed and breakfasts, do not allow smoking indoors. Smokers would be best served by inquiring of the establishment's smoking policy prior to making reservations. Reservations are always suggested, by the way.

Housekeeping (no maid service) cottages are usually rented for a full week from Saturday to Saturday in season, and for a minimum of two days off season. Guests set up house and do their own housekeeping and cooking. Everything for living, sleeping, and cooking is provided; guests need bring only personal effects and food. Linens and towels are usually included in the Blue Mountain Lake and Indian Lake areas, but not in the Old Forge and Inlet areas. If staying longer than a week, you will usually be offered a change of linens once a week. Know what is included before making the reservation.

Many business along Route 28 are seasonal, open only in the summer or only in the winter. Many other businesses have seasonal schedules, open seven days during the summer but open only on weekends during the winter. Other businesses are open at the whim of the owner. Therefore, a phone call to the establishment to determine its schedule is always useful.

I include all post offices along the way. If you are traveling for extended periods and you need to receive mail, have it sent to you, general delivery, at a post office where you expect to be at the time you expect the mail to arrive. For example, if you expect the sent mail to take four days in transit, determine where you expect to be in four days' time (e.g., Phoenicia), and have the mail sent to:

> Your Name
> General Delivery
> Phoenicia, NY 12464

Then go to the post office on Mt. Ava Maria after the four days have elapsed and request the general delivery mail sent in your name. Expect to show identification to prove you are who you say you are.

How this Book Works

Route 28: A Mile-by-Mile Guide to New York's Adventure Route follows New York's Route 28 clockwise from its junction with Broadway and Albany Avenue in Kingston to its intersection with NY 9 just north of Warrensburg. Stated Route 28 mileage is based upon New York State highway reference markers and my own odometer, and is relative to Kingston. Your mileage may be different. Right or left directions off Route 28 are oriented for a clockwise drive of Route 28, with the counter-clockwise-drive directions in parenthesis.

For example:

050.0   **Middletown/Andes** town line.

052.3   Left(right) **Hot Rod Farmer** (914-676-3477). Auto repairs.

055.5   Right(left) Junction with **Gladstone Hollow Road**:

   003.2   Bobcat Ski Center (914-676-3143). On Mt. Pisgah, the highest peak in Delaware County.

   End of Gladstone Hollow Road coverage.

   Entering(leaving) village of **Andes**, founded 1819.

055.8   Right(left) **Bear Hugs & Busy Hands** (914-676-3266). Finished and unfinished ceramics, gifts, paints, supplies, kiln firing, glazing, classes.

In this example:

   At mile 50.0, if traveling in a clockwise direction (Kingston to Warrensburg) you are crossing the line from the town of Middletown into the town of Andes. If traveling in a counter-clockwise direction (Warrensburg to Kingston) you are crossing from the town of Andes into the town of Middletown.

At mile 52.3, Hot Rod Farmer's repair shop is on the right if you are traveling in a clockwise direction and on the left if you are traveling in a counter-clockwise direction.

At mile 55.5, you encounter Gladstone Hollow Road on the right if you are traveling in a clockwise direction.

Three and two-tenths of a mile up Gladstone Hollow Road is Bobcat Ski Center.

Just beyond Gladstone Hollow Road, still at mileage 55.5, you enter the village of Andes.

As you travel Route 28 with this book, you can easily find what you need. Determine which page of the book covers the location along Route 28 where you are at the moment. Find in the index the service or activity (gas, camp-ground, fishing, etc.) you are seeking. The page number under the index topic which is closest to the page number covering your present location is usually the closest location of the service or activity you are seeking.

New York's Route 28 is always written as Route 28. Interstate highways are written as I- followed by the route number, e.g. I-87. United States highways are written as US followed by the route number, e.g. US 9. New York State roads, other than Route 28, are written as NY followed by the route number, e.g. NY 30. County roads are CR followed by the route number, e.g. CR 8.

Prices for lodging and food are usually quoted as a range from the lowest to the highest. A cottage colony described as having a price range of $300-$850 means that the smallest cottage off season costs $350/week while the largest cottage in season costs $850/week. Therefore, just as you wouldn't expect to pay the highest price for a cottage in mid-May, you shouldn't expect to pay the lowest price between Memorial Day weekend and Labor

Day. Also, most food prices have been rounded to the nearest dollar, so an establishment's luncheon prices of $3.25 to $6.50 would be listed as $3-$7.

The South End at Kingston

New York's Route 28 follows I-587 along its one-and-one-half mile distance from NY 32, bending behind Kingston Plaza and crossing the Esopus Creek to the Thruway traffic circle by Thruway Exit 19. On clear days first Roundtop Mountain and then Overlook Mountain in the southeastern Catskills are visible as you leave Kingston and drive the first two-tenths of a mile of Route 28/I-587.

000.0   Beginning of coverage of **Route 28** at junction of **NY 32** at intersection with Broadway,   Albany Avenue, and St. James Street in Kingston.

000.6   Crossing **Esopus Creek**.

001.2   **Thruway traffic circle**. Exits from the traffic circle are the New York State Thruway (I-87) Exit 19, Route 28 west, Washington Avenue to Kingston Plaza and uptown Kingston, and Route 28/I-587 east, also to uptown Kingston. See Chapter 3, *Kingston to NY 375*, for continued coverage of Route 28.

Kingston's Washington Avenue and Kingston Plaza

The Washington Avenue exit of Kingston's Thruway traffic circle offers access to many services for travelers, including gasoline, food, lodging, and ATMs. The route I shall describe follows Washington Avenue for one half mile, turns left onto Schwenk Drive for three-tenths of a mile, then turns left again into Kingston Plaza, home to more than 30 merchants.

The city of Kingston has much to see and do, from the uptown stockade area to the downtown Rondout Landing alongside the Rondout Creek. Along the way, there are the Senate House State Historic Site and Museum, the Old Dutch Church, Ulster Performing Arts Center, the Hudson River Maritime Museum with its boat rides to the Rondout Lighthouse and across the Hudson River to Rhinecliff, the Trolley Museum, the Fireman's Museum, and much, much more, all beyond the scope of this book. Stop at the Ulster County Tourist Information Caboose on Washington Avenue for information about Kingston and Ulster County, or call the Ulster County Public Information Office at 914-340-3566.

000.0   Thruway Traffic Circle at **Kingston, Washington Avenue** exit.

Right. **Tourism Information Caboose** (914-340-3766, 800-342-5826). Tourist information on Kingston and Ulster County. Open May through October.

Left. **Davenport's Circle Farm Stand** (914-334-9004). Farm-fresh produce, vegetables, and herbs. Great source of pumpkins in October.

Left. **Fill-'n-Shop** (914-338-6570). Mobil gas station, convenience store, deli, and an ATM. Open 24 hours.

000.2   Right. **Szymkowicz Service** (914-338-5650). Auto service and towing.

Right. **BP** gas station (914-339-0108). Auto service and snacks.

Left. **Gateway Diner** (914-339-5640). Greek specialties, open 24 hours.

Left. **Value-Thru Wine and Liquors** (914-338-4199).

Left. **Circle Beverages** (914-331-2935). Discount beer and soda.

Crossing the **Esopus Creek**.

Right. **Mike Sirni Tire and Auto** (914-331-4525). Tires, auto service, and radiator repairs.

Right. **Holiday Inn** (914-338-0400, 800-HOLIDAY). Motel and restaurant, lounge, conference rooms, indoor pool, sauna; a full-service hotel with the nicest accommodations in the area. $84-$139/two.

Right. **Super 8 Motel** (914-338-3078, 800-800-8000). Eighty-four rooms within walking distance of uptown Kingston with its shops, restaurants, and historical buildings, $52-$57/two.

Right. **Fleet Bank** (800-228-1281). 24-hour ATM.

Left. **Ulster Savings Bank** (914-338-6060). 24-hour ATM.

000.5   Traffic Light at junction with **Schwenk Drive** on left and **Hurley Avenue** on right.

Coverage and mileage continue left onto Schwenk Drive.

000.6   Right. Junction with **Frog Alley**, down which a few hundred feet are:

> *Left. The **Louw-Bogardus House**, also called the ruin in Frog Alley, was built in 1676 by Pieter Cornelissen Louw. Its ruins are enclosed by a chain-link fence.*
>
> *Right. **Deising's Bakery and Coffee Shop** (914-338-7503) at the intersection with North Front St. A superb, full-service bakery, and a coffee shop which serves breakfast seven days and lunch Monday through Saturday. Visit this goody heaven and give your eyes, nose, and mouth an exceptional, sensuous experience.*

Right. **Ulster County Sheriff's Office** (914-338-3640).

000.7   Right. **Century Buick Pontiac** (914-338-4000). Dealership.

000.8   Traffic Light at junction with **Kingston Plaza** on left, Clinton Avenue Extension straight ahead, and Fair Street on right.

Right. **Elena's Ice Cream & Sandwich Shop** (914-331-2767). Texas hot wieners, souvlaki, gyros, subs, Greek salad, and breakfast.

Coverage continues left into Kingston Plaza. Merchants, from left to right, include:

Nail Studio (914-340-4241).
Ames (914-331-0591). Discount department store.
Plaza Pizza (914-331-4451).   Pizza, Italian dinners, calzones, strombolis, pasta, hot and cold heroes, subs, Philly hoagies, sandwiches, appetizers, salads, soup, party pizzas, and six-foot subs. Take-out and deliveries. Pizza $7-$17, dinners $7-$9.
Radio Shack (914-331-3837).
Payless ShoeSource (914-338-6884).
Resnick's Mattress Outlet (914-334-8100).
Cutting Crew (914-339-2981). Men's and women's hair salon.
B' n B Bagels (914-338-7912). Bagels, gourmet cream cheeses, sandwiches, salads, danish, coffee, and soda.
Judy's ½ Off Cards (914-338-6005). Greeting cards, gifts, gift wrap, etc., at half-price.
Goodwill Travel (914-338-1100).
Fashion Bug (914-338-0233). Ladies fashions.
The Party Experience (914-339-9323). Party supplies.
Plaza Laundromat.
Plaza Liquors (914-331-6429).
Just a Buck (914-340-1341). Variety dollar store.
Sunshine Tees and Embroidery (914-339-4455). T-shirts, sweat-shirts, and logos.
The Bank of New York (914-339-5300). ATM.
Artcraft Camera and   One Hour Photo (914-331-3141). Cameras, supplies, and film developing.
Flower Nest (914-331-4440). Florist. Plants, dried and silk flowers, gifts, cards, and Teddy bears.
Blimpie Subs and Salads (914-331-3888). Sandwiches.
Plaza Barber Shop.

Walgreen's Pharmacy (914-331-2070).
Chic's Restaurant and Sports Bar (914-331-1537). Family restaurant serving Italian and American food. Salads and sandwiches, $3-$7, dinner entrees $5-$11. Large-screen TV and pool table.
Fantasy Video (914-338-1409). Videotape sales and rentals, CD sales, and used CDs bought and sold.
Style Fabric Center (914-338-1793). Fabrics, notions, etc.
H&R Block (914-339-1640). Income tax preparation.
Off-Track Betting. New York State OTB betting parlor.
Parts America (914-339-1480). Western Auto store.
Grand Union (914-339-7480). Supermarket and ATM. Open 24 hours except for Saturday and Sunday nights.

Other, free-standing businesses scattered about Kingston Plaza parking lot include:

Federal Express (800-GO-FEDEX) kiosk, at east end of plaza beyond Grand Union.
Herzog True Value Home Center (914-338-6300). Hardware, home accessories, gifts, and garden center.
Plaza Tire & Auto (914-338-1155). Tires, batteries and auto repairs.

Kingston to NY 375

001.2 **Thruway traffic circle**. Exits from the traffic circle are the New York State **Thruway (I-87)** Exit 19, **Route 28** west, **Washington Avenue** to Kingston Plaza and uptown Kingston, and **Route 28/I-587** east, also to uptown Kingston.

001.4 Exit from Thruway traffic circle onto **Route 28** west. You are now entering Catskill Park, established in 1904 and encompassing more than 700,000 acres of public and private lands. The Catskill Forest Preserve, established in 1885, constitutes 300,000 acres of state land within Catskill Park and is designated as forever wild. Among the creatures living within the park are deer, bear, raccoons, porcupines, skunks, marten, coyote, copperheads, rattlesnakes, and many species of birds. You may see a deer or a hawk as you drive, but you will improve your chances of spotting local wildlife if you hike one of the many trails in the park.

001.5 Crossing New York State **Thruway (I-87)**.

001.6 Traffic light. Right(left) turn for:

> ***Ramada Inn*** *(914-339-3900, 800-2-RAMADA). Motel, indoor pool. $65-$105/couple.*
>
> ***Roudigan's*** *(914-339-3500). Restaurant at Ramada Inn, open for breakfast, lunch, and dinner, serving American and Mexican cuisine. Wings, mozzarella sticks,*

sandwiches, burgers, salads, fajitas, quesadillas, flounder, salmon, chicken, ribs, steak, lobster tails, more. Soup and salad bar. Entrees $12-$25. Saturday night entertainment, Sunday karaoke.

***Camper's Barn** (914-338-8200). R/V store. New and used recreational vehicles, accessories, supplies, parts, repairs, and propane by weight and volume.*

***Johnson Ford** (914-338-7800). Dealership.*

Left(right) turn at traffic light for:

***Superlodge** (914-338-4200, 800-578-7878). Motel, indoor pool, and sauna. $55-$70/two people.*

***Kingston Family Restaurant** (914-331-3700). Open for breakfast, lunch, and dinner. Dinner entrees $5-$9.*

Right(left). **Thruway Nissan** (914-338-3100). Dealership.

001.7   Cloverleaf intersection with **US 209**:

US 209 north goes toward US 9W and shopping malls, and to NY 199 and the Kingston-Rhinecliff Bridge ($.75 toll) across the Hudson River toward Rhinebeck and Red Hook.

001.9   **US 209** south goes to **Hurley, Ellenville**, and **Port Jervis**:

*002.4   Right. Junction with **Wynkoop Road** in **Hurley**, down which a couple hundred feet is a stop sign at the junction with **Main Street**.*

Founded in 1662 as Nieuwe Dorp (Dutch for New Village), Hurley was for two months in 1777 the capital of New York State, immediately after Kingston, the first capital, was burned by the British.

At the junction with **Main Street**, *on the near left corner is the* **Hurley Country Store**. *On the far left corner is the* **Hurley Mountain Inn** *(914-331-1780), a locally-famous restaurant, watering hole, and gathering place where part of the Dustin Hoffman movie "Tootsie" was filmed. On the near right corner is the* **Hurley Post Office** *(914-338-9310), ZIP 12443, and a* **Stewart's Shoppe** *(914-338-3707), a convenience store. On the far right corner is a* **State Police** *barracks (914-338-1702).*

Making a right here takes you past the old church and through the middle of old Hurley with its 300-year-old stone houses. The owners of these houses generously open them to public tours on the annual Hurley Stone House Day, the second Saturday in July. (Write to Stone House Day, Hurley, NY, 12443, for a brochure.) The town also hosts the Hurley Corn and Craft Festival, featuring colonial craft demonstrations and many corn-based foods, every year on the third Saturday in August.

End of Hurley coverage.

002.1   Traffic light at junction of **Forest Hill Road**.

Left(right) **19 Roma Inn** (914-331-1919, 800-325-2525). Fifty-nine unit motel, $44-$55.

Left(right) **Acropolis Diner** (914-331-8799). The best kept dining secret in the area. Serving breakfast, lunch, and dinner. Diner menu; plus four pages of specials of beef, pork, poultry, pasta, and seafood; and meals made to order. Sandwiches $2-$5, dinner entrees $10-$17. Five-dollar lunch specials are delicious bargains. This is a gourmet restaurant masquerading as an inexpensive diner. Open until ten, eleven on weekends.

Right(left) turn at traffic light for **Forest Hill Road**:

000.0   Right. Junction with **City View Terrace**. *Turn right for:*

000.2   Left. **Potter Brothers Ski Shops** *(914-338-5119). Skis, snowboards, ski clothing, accessories, rentals, etc., plus a full-service ski shop. Patio furniture in the summer. A family ski shop for many decades.*

End of City View Terrace coverage.

000.1   Right. **Skytop Motel** *(914-331-2900). Seventy-room motel with an outdoor pool, $75-$90/two. Free continental breakfast.*

End of Forest Hill Road coverage.

002.6   Left(right) Junction with **Hurley Mountain Road** (CR 5) to **Hurley**:

000.1   Right. **Kenco** *(914-340-0552, 800-341-4103). Leisure, work, safety, optical, and sporting apparel. Mostly noted for quality work clothes and safety accessories, but also for quality outdoor recreational clothing and accessories. Everything to protect you on the job, such as safety shoes, durable clothing, hardhats, hearing protection, work gloves, high-visibility vests, overalls, union suits, and even prescription safety glasses. Also men's, ladies', and children's outdoor clothing, boots, rain gear, large-sized clothing, backpacks, fishing vests, and much more.*

001.1   Right. A scenic glen, with a 40-foot waterfall in the spring and a 40-foot trickle in the summer.

002.3   Left. Junction with **Wynkoop Road***, down which 0.6 mile are a state police barracks, a convenience store, post office, and the Hurley Mountain Inn. Again turning left by the State Police unit takes you through the center of Hurley with its old stone houses dating from the late 1600s through the 1700s. Some of them are opened for public tours every year on the second Saturday of July. Call the Hurley Heritage Society on 914-338-1661 for details.*

*003.8   Right. **Gill's** (914-331-8225, 338-0788). Genuine farm
stand run by the farmer and his family on their farm,
offering fruits, vegetables, flowers, plants and, of course,
sweet corn. Weekend hayrides in October. Seasonal.*

End of Hurley Mountain Road coverage.

Route 28 west from Kingston follows a valley through the mountains
which the Mohawks called Onteora, meaning "Land in the sky." Route 28
through this part of the Catskills was therefore often called the Onteora
Trail. Early Route 28 was a plank road, traveled by stagecoaches from
Kingston to Delhi.

002.7   Right(left) **Lock, Stock & Barrel** (914-338-4397). Specializing
for 40 years in early-American furniture of the period, with early
paint and original surfaces. Furniture, accessories, paintings, folk
art, glass, and playing marbles.   Open by chance or by
appointment.

003.1   Right(left) **Hess** gas station.

Left(right) **Horn of Plenty** (914-331-4318). Fruits, vegetables,
homemade breads, cider, maple syrup, honey, plants, and ice
cream.

003.3   Right(left) **Pine & Pewter** (914-331-8880). Unfinished furniture.

003.4   Right(left) **Royal Diner** (914-338-9680). Open 5:30 AM to 4 PM,
seven days a week. Sandwiches, burgers, roast beef, pot roast,
fried chicken, cold platters, and more. Entrees $5-$8.

Right(left) **Dietz Plaza:**
Dietz Auto Supply (914-331-3270). NAPA auto parts.
Bryant's(914-338-4545). Auto repair shop. Light and heavy 24-
hour towing. Propane by weight and volume.
Lee Myles Transmissions (914-339-7575). Repair shop.

Right(left) **S-D Feed World II** (914-339-2287).   Pet food and
feeds for other animals.

003.5   Right(left) **Catskill Mountain Antique Center** (914-331-0880). Two-story, gambrel-roofed, rough-sawn, barn-like building housing an eclectic collection of quality antiques and collectibles. Offered by 15 dealers, items range from jewelry to artwork to large pieces of furniture. Nicely presented. Closed Wednesdays.

Next door is **Craft Artique** (914-331-2645). More than 60 crafts people displaying handmade crafts, 80 percent locally produced. Americana, miniatures, wooden dolls, paper-twist dolls, lap trays, cats, unique bird houses, Halloween and Christmas items, much more.

003.6   Right(left) **K & W Carwash.**

004.0   Left(right) **Sunoco** gas station.

004.1   Right(left) **Parking** area.

004.2   Left(right) **Buster Dunn Sales & Service** (914-339-5500). Kawasaki, Suzuki, and John Deere dealer. Motorcycles, jet skis, lawn and garden tractors, utility vehicles, ATVs, etc.

Left(right) **Greenwald's Travel** (914-331-0816). Travel agency.

Right(left) **Steve's Pizza** (914-340-4219). Pizza, strombolis, calzones, Philly cheese steaks, and more. Deli and free delivery. Open seven days.

Right(left) **Trail Liquor Shop** (914-331-8750). Wines and liquors.

Left(right) **Price-Rite Transmissions** (914-331-4900). Repair shop.

004.3   Left(right) Junction with **NY 28A**. NOTE: LEFT TURN FROM ROUTE 28 ONTO NY 28A PROHIBITED HERE. Left turn to NY 28A allowed via left turn lane 0.2 mile west at top of hill.

004.4   Left(right) **Doll House Miniatures** (914-338-0641). More than 2000 square feet of dolls (both toy and collectible), doll houses, and accessories. Doll house building components, electrical kits, wallpaper, flooring, etc.

Left(right) **Stony Hollow Taxidermy**.

004.5   Left(right) **Gene's Place** (914-331-3151). Used Saab sales and service.

004.6   Left(right) **Pizza Pantry** (914-338-3776). Rustic restaurant and bar open for lunch and dinner. Pizza, pasta, and Italian dinners. Hot and cold sandwiches, subs, appetizers, burgers, and finger foods. Dinner entrees $6-$9. Take out and delivery available. Also,
Ampro Sports (914-331-9440). Camping, fishing, hunting, boating equipment, and supplies. Guns and ammo, black powder arms and supplies, archery equipment and supplies. Live bait and licenses. Comprehensive, well-stocked sporting goods store.

Left(right) Junction with **NY 28A**, the main road from Kingston to Oneonta before Route 28 was built in the late 1940s:

000.0   Turn right at bottom of hill to follow NY 28A.

*000.6   Left. Junction with **Morgan Hill Road**:*

> *001.0   Left. Junction with **Schildknecht Road**. Turn left for:*

> > *000.4   Right. **New York Conservatory for the Arts** (914-339-4340). Dance, theater, music, and art. Performances and education.*

> *End of Schildknecht Road and Morgan Hill Road coverage.*

000.8   Right. *Junction with* **Basin Road**, *up which 0.4 mile is the Reservoir Inn on the right (see description later in this chapter).*

001.5   Right. *Junction with southern end of* **Dike Road**, *up which is the Ashokan Reservoir (description to come).*

002.0   Left.   **Betty's and Ray's Pantry** *(914-331-2877). Groceries, sandwiches, beer, soda, and food, across from a lovely little pond.*

002.6   Left. *Junction with* **Spillway Road**. *Make left for:*

   001.2   Right.   **Terrapin Restaurant** *(914-331-3663). Fine dining on contemporary American cuisine in a romantic, country setting. A former New York City chef's imaginative dinner creations are available Thursday through Monday. Brunch is served on Saturday and Sunday. Dinner entrees $10-$20. Early bird specials, 4:30-6:00 PM.*

   001.3   Right.   **Crafts People** *(914-331-3859). Large, four-building complex housing an eclectic collection of quality crafts, some produced by the proprietors and others by local artisans. Jewelry, toys, lamps, pottery, glass, clothing, cards, soaps, food, weaving, leather, wood, iron, furniture, baskets, wind chimes, candles, more. Open Friday through Monday. Well-known and well-respected.*

End of Spillway Road and NY 28A coverage.

005.3   Left(right) **Woodstock Harley-Davidson** (914-338-2800). Motorcycle sales, service, clothing, and accessories.

005.5   Left(right) **Fireside Warmth** (914-331-5656). Woodstoves. Propane tanks filled by weight.

Right(left) **Bluestone Wild Forest**. This is a New York State Department of Environmental Conservation area on the site of an old bluestone quarry and encompassing **Onteora Lake**. Current offerings are three hiking, mountain biking, and cross-country ski trails; a boat launching site for small boats; and a few lakeside camp sites. In the lake are largemouth bass, pickerel, and various panfish you may be able to coax into your frying pan. Since there are no trout in this lake, ice fishing is allowed. Grooves worn into stone by iron-rimmed bluestone wagon wheels can still be seen.

Right(left) **Lilly K's** (914-331-2880). Family restaurant. Breakfast, lunch, and dinner. Eggs, pancakes, French toast, omelettes, hamburgers, sandwiches, subs, Philly steaks, pizza, and pasta. American-style dinners from $7-$10.

Right(left) **La Bella Pasta** (914-331-9130). Pasta store. Fresh, homemade pasta products including ravioli, tortellini, lasagna, linguini, spaghetti, sauces, Italian cheeses, more. Weekly specials.

Right(left) **E & S Discount Beer and Soda** (914-339-7164).

Right(left) **Weider Realty** (914-338-0480).

Left(right) **Cake Box** (914-339-4715). Pastries, cakes, cookies, and rolls.

Right(left) **Hobo Deli** (914-339-3452). Deli and food market.

Right(left) **Wine Hutch** (914-334-9463). Wine and liquor, with the emphasis on wine.

Right(left) **Alternative Video Shop** (914-334-8105). Big selection of foreign films, director films, gay and lesbian films, documentaries, and British TV shows.

Right(left) **Artco Printing** (914-339-2336). Printing, copying, stationery supplies, etc.

005.6   Right(left) **Judy's Flower Box** (914-331-4342). Fresh flowers, plants, dried flowers, baskets, fruit baskets, balloons, gifts, and wire service.

Right(left) **A & W Repair** (914-339-5657). Foreign and domestic car repairs.

005.8   Left(right) **Myers Auto Repair** (914-331-9368). Foreign and domestic car repairs.

006.0   Entering(leaving) **West Hurley**.

The West Hurley, Woodstock, and Saugerties area was, from the mid-1800s to the early 1900s, the bluestone capital of the Northeast. As you drive around you will see many bluestone walls, sidewalks, curbing, building foundations, fireplaces and chimneys, and gravestones. Miles and miles of sidewalk and curbing in New York City, Albany, and other eastern cities were laid with Ulster County bluestone.

006.2   Right(left) **Corner Store** (914-679-9436). Convenience store and Mobil gas.

006.3   Right(left) **Westwood Farmers Market** (914-679-7841). Fruits, vegetables, seasonal flowering plants, gardening supplies, and local products (Hudson Valley mustard, Woodstock vinegars, etc.). Some outdoorsman supplies, including live bait and tackle, guns and ammo, camping, archery, and trapping supplies. Good variety of apples in the fall.

Left(right) **BP** gas station.

Traffic light at junction with **Zena Road** to the right(left) and **Basin Road** to the left(right). Zena Road is a pretty country road past rural homes and a Kingston reservoir, and offering views of Overlook Mountain, the southeast cornerstone of the Catskills. Basin Road offers magnificent views of the Ashokan Reservoir.

Making a right(left) onto Zena Road takes you to:

001.3   Right. Kingston Water Supply Reservoir No. 4.

*001.8   Right. **New World Home Cooking** (914-679-2600). This comfortable cafe and restaurant in an old stone tavern serves new American cuisine and is nationally-known and highly-praised by the media. Everything is made fresh, with 100 percent fresh ingredients, much of which is locally grown. Lunch $5-$10, dinner $9-$19. Children's menu, wood grill, dining terrace, full bar with emphasis on micro-brewed beers, and wines. Open for lunch on weekdays and dinner every day. Weekend dinner reservations suggested.*

End of Zena Road coverage.

Turning left(right) onto **Basin Road**:

*NOTE: RAILROAD UNDERPASS AT BEGINNING OF BASIN ROAD HAS A **VERTICAL CLEARANCE OF ONLY 11'5"**. To avoid this low bridge, use NY 28A, 1.7 miles to the east on Route 28.*

*000.7   Left. **Reservoir Inn** (914-331-9806). European and American cuisine, from pizza and pasta to poultry, veal, beef, pork, lamb, and seafood, with delectable daily specials, served in a roomy and cozy, wood and bluestone, 1890s roadhouse, with high ceilings, glassed-in terrace and wonderful, country-gentleman atmosphere. Home-grown herbs, southern Italian pasta dishes, fall game specials, and winter hearty specials. Lunch Wednesdays through Saturdays, dinner seven days. Lunch $3-$6, dinners $9-$19. Popular with locals and tourists alike.*

*Right. Junction with **Dike Road**:*

*000.3   Right. Grand views of the **Ashokan Reservoir** and the **Catskill Mountains**. The imposing mountain on the right is **Overlook Mountain**, the southeast cornerstone of the Catskills. The huge* *notch in the side of Overlook is the result of bluestone quarrying. Sunsets across the reservoir can be magnificent.*

*The **Ashokan Reservoir**, built between 1907 and 1916, provides drinking water for residents of New York City 100 miles away. It is 12 miles long and three miles wide, and when full holds 130 billion gallons. It contains an upper and lower basin separated by a dividing weir. The town of West Hurley used to lie where the lower basin is now, but most of the buildings and even the cemeteries were moved northward to higher ground between the reservoir and Overlook Mountain.   For an excellent account of the building of the reservoir, read Bob Steuding's book,* The Last of the Handmade Dams *(see Appendix C,* Additional Information*).*

Note: Do not enter the woods, go down to the water, or in any way trespass on Ashokan Reservoir property. Entry is not allowed by New York City Department of Environmental Protection Bureau of Water Supply for any reason other than fishing under permit. If you do not have such a permit, or have a permit but are not fishing, you may be arrested. The reservoir police are vigilant. For information on the free fishing permits call 914-657-2663 or 212-643-2172.

End of Dyke Road coverage.

*001.7   Junction with **NY 28A**.   See coverage earlier in this chapter.*

End of Basin Road coverage.

006.4   Right(left) **Stewart's Shoppe** (914-679-2268). Convenience store, gas, and ATM.

006.5   Right(left) **Williams Lane**, down which are:

000.2   Numrich Arms (914-679-2417), Auto-Ordinance (914-679-7225) and Gun Parts Corporation (914-679-4533). Three gun-related businesses at the same location. Large selection of new and used rifles, shotguns, handguns, shells, holsters, gun parts (stocks, butts, handles, barrels), and accessories. Billed as the largest supplier of gun parts in the world.

End of Williams Lane coverage.

006.7   Right(left) **West Hurley Post Office** (914-679-6760). ZIP 12491.

007.1   Right(left) **Soho West** (914-679-9944). A serious, five-room art gallery focusing mostly on Asian, African, and Pacific art, artifacts, sculpture, furniture, and more, ranging from native African art to very contemporary art. Something for everyone, from $20 vases and $50 jewelry boxes, to serious art costing much more. A most interesting place to browse.

007.2   Right(left) **Many Feathers Books** (914-679-6305). Bookstore focusing on used, hard-cover literature. Approximately 20,000 titles.

Right(left) **Brookline Gallery and Gift Shop** (914-679-4992). Fine art and curiosities. Paintings, etchings, pre-Columbian replicas, jewelry, beads, fabrics, rugs, books, frames, more.

007.3   Right(left) Junction with **NY 375** to **Woodstock**. For coverage of NY 375 to Woodstock, see Chapter 4, *NY 375 from Route 28 to Woodstock*. For coverage of Woodstock, see Chapter 5, *Woodstock*. For continued coverage of Route 28 to Phoenicia, see Chapter 6, *From NY 375 to Phoenicia*.

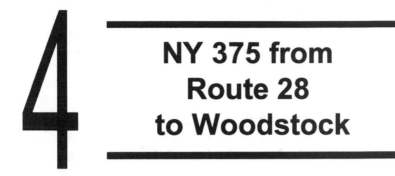

NY 375 from Route 28 to Woodstock

From **Route 28**, turn right(left) at the traffic light in West Hurley onto **NY 375**, which snakes left and right, up and down three miles to **NY 212** in **Woodstock**. **Overlook Mountain** is visible during much of the drive, and it becomes increasingly imposing the closer you get to town. (There is a hiking trail from Woodstock's **Meads Mountain Road** to the top, which offers magnificent views of the **Catskill Mountains, Hudson River Valley,** and **Ashokan Reservoir.**) Because of Woodstock's location, cradled between Overlook Mountain to the north and **Ohayo Mountain** to the south, it often can be snowing in Woodstock while it is raining, or even sunny, in Kingston.

000.0   Southern end of **NY 375** at junction with Route 28.

000.1   Left. **Westwood Home and Garden** (914-679-9961). Home and garden supplies, landscaping, and florist.

Right. Junction with **Cedar Street**. Driving up Cedar Street for 0.1 mile, then turning left onto **Clover Street,** and driving a few hundred feet takes you to the **West Hurley Library** (914-679-6405) on the left.

000.4   Right. **West Hurley Garage** (914-679-2811). Auto repairs and Getty gas station. Closed Sunday.

000.6   Right. **Langer Drug World** (914-679-5205). Pharmacy.

Right. **Hurley Ridge Market** (914-679-8121). Market, fresh meats, deli.

Right. **Hurley Ridge Wines and Spirits** (914-679-8444).

Right. **Governor Clinton Cleaners and Tailors** (914-679-2722).

Right. **Video Plus** (914-679-8993). Videos and VCR rentals. VCR, TV, monitor, CD player, stereo, and video camera repairs. Video Plus also sells Jane's homemade ice cream.

002.7 Left. Intersection with **Riseley Lane**:

*000.1   Right.   **Woodstock Lodge** (914-679-2814).   A rustic lodging colony built on nine acres of dense pine forest, plus a cafe and lounge. Lodging for one to six people in various configurations. Summer prices are $79-$109 for rooms, $119-$129 for efficiencies, and $139-$149 for the cabins, with lower rates off season. The Cafe at Woodstock Lodge, with a glassed-in porch and a fireplace, is open for breakfast, brunch, and lunch April through October, with luncheon entrees of basic Americana, grilled and fried fare, pasta entrees, and freshly baked breads; $4-$10. The lounge has a bar and fireplace and is a local night spot, open seven days year-round, with occasional live jazz. Huge swimming pool, barbecue area, game room, and horseshoes. Pets welcome.*

End of Riseley Lane coverage.

002.8 Left. Challenging playground for young children to the left of Woodstock Elementary School.

002.9 Northern end of **NY 375** at junction with **NY 212**. See Chapter 5, *Woodstock*, for coverage of the hamlet.

Woodstock

An old adage says too many cooks spoil the pot. The coiner of that phrase probably never experienced Woodstock. This famous town, an artist's colony since 1902, is an ever-changing, never-quite-finished bouillabaisse of people, places, shops, restaurants, and experiences like no other in the world, an ever-bubbling stew of life, the quintessential town with something for everyone. Its many flavors range from serious music and art to whimsical moon worship and self-adornment. Its residents include natives, artists, musicians, left-over hippies, executives, professionals, college students, drop-outs, merchants, and drifters. Its homes range from converted summer cottages to middle-American tract units to architectural-masterpieces. Activities in Woodstock are boundless, from hiking and biking mountains, to attending concerts and performances, shopping in eclectic shops, eating at ethnic restaurants, mining antique stores, or just sitting at the Village Green and tasting Woodstock's many rich flavors as they waft by.

Annual events in Woodstock include a Renaissance Faire in May, a Memorial Day parade, the Maverick Concert series throughout the summer, the Library Fair in July, a Shakespeare Festival in July and August, a crafts fair in September, Christmas Open House, the arrival of Santa Claus on Christmas Eve (a Woodstock tradition since the 1930s), and more. Stop at the Tourist Information Booth on Rock City Road or call the Woodstock Chamber of Commerce and Arts on 914-679-6234 for more information.

Woodstock lodging accommodations are scarce. Information on lodging and dining is available by calling 914-679-8025.

Almost all visitors to Woodstock arrive via NY 375. Therefore, the following section on Woodstock will be described using the junction of NY 375 and NY 212 as the starting point.

002.9   Northern end of NY 375 at junction with **NY 212.**

Turning right onto **NY 212** east yields the following:

000.0   Left. Formerly the Clermont. Also formerly Margaret's, and before that O'Callaghan's, and Deanie's, and in the 60s the Town House. A restaurant, bar, and gathering place for decades, the building was closed at the time of publication. But who knows what the future may bring.

Right. **Woodstock Golf Club** *(914-679-2914). Private golf club. Also* **Tavern on the Stream** *(914-679-3749). Public restaurant in a 1760s gristmill overlooking the Sawkill Creek and the golf course. Serving a lighter, Italian-American cuisine including pasta, seafood, and vegetarian dishes. Lunch $4-$7, dinner $10-$16.*

000.5   Right. Just after the "End 35 Mile" sign is an old driveway which now offers foot access through the tall pine forest to **Big Deep**, *a locally-popular swimming hole in the Sawkill Creek.*

End of NY 212 east coverage. NY 212 continues east approximately eight miles to New York State **Thruway (I-87)** *Exit 20 and the village of* **Saugerties***.*

Turning left onto **NY 212** west (**Mill Hill Road**) presents **Woodstock**:

000.0   Right. **Blue Mountain Villager** (914-679-4118). In a beautiful old barn: tasteful home furnishings, most with a country flavor. Lamps, furniture, curtains, gifts, etc.

Right. **Playhouse Park.** The former site of the famous Woodstock Playhouse. Built in 1938, the playhouse was mysteriously destroyed in a pre-dawn fire on Memorial Day of 1988, leaving to this day a smoke-black scar in the hearts of many of Woodstock's natives, weekend residents, and visitors. At the time of publication a new playhouse was being constructed.

Left. **Woodstock Earth** (914-679-2527). A save-the-earth-oriented shop featuring air-brushed artwork on silk, fabric, shirts, T-shirts, and more. Also, **Cut and Dry**, a barber shop.

Left. **Pat's Tats** (914-679-4429). Tattoos, body piercing.

Left. **Teran Realty** (914-679-7391).

Left. **The Seasoned Traveler** (914-679-7271). Travel agency.

Left. **Brugnoni Frames** (914-679-2717). Framing gallery.

Left. **Wheat Fields** (914-679-3200). International gourmet specialty foods, mostly from the Mediterranean. A sampling: fresh pastas, gnocci, cheeses, pates, stuffed grape leaves, focaccini, onion sourdough ficelle, taleggio, montasio, Mediterranean olives, olive oil, creamy tomato basil, basil pesto, hearts of palm, Italian peeled tomatoes, capers, peppercorns, pignolli nuts, mustards, polenta, proscuitto, mortadella, cappuccino, much more. The only such store for many miles.

000.1   Right. **Christy's Restaurant** (914-679-5300). In an old brick building, this Woodstock landmark serves fine food in a warm, cozy, rustic atmosphere. International dinner menu selections include roast duck, prime rib, pasta, chicken, and fresh fish of the day. Seafood (broiled or baked only) a specialty. Entrees usually $9-$14. Well rated by the media. Closed Monday.

Left. **Woodstock Haircutz Day Spa** (914-679-7171). Full-service salon. Hair, facials, massage, manicures, pedicures, and steam room. Hair care, skin products, and make-up.

Right. **Bradley Meadows Shopping Plaza**, housing from right to left:
Fleet Bank (914-679-2465). 24-hour ATM.

Woodstock Video (914-679-9359) At the left rear corner of the Fleet Bank building.
Eckerd Drugs (914-679-2222).
Overlook Liquors (914-679-7500).
Sunflower Natural Foods (914-679-5361). Largest natural food store for many miles.

Left. **Woodstock Building Supply** (914-679-2516). Lumber and building supplies.

Left. **First Union Bank** (914-679-2900). 24-hour ATM.

000.2   Right. **Cumberland Farms**. Convenience store and Gulf gas.

Right. **Grand Union** (914-679-5811). Supermarket.

Right. Junction with **Elwyn Lane**, down which 0.2 mile on the right is the **Hawthorne Gallery** (914-679-2711). Antique furniture, mostly of teak and rosewood, accessories, and architectural details from India. Also periodic art shows. Open April through December or by appointment.

Right. **Before & After** (914-679-1233). Full service salon.

Right. **Woodstock Post Express** (914-679-8360, fax 679-8832). UPS and Fedex shipping, packing, gift wrapping, and shipping supplies. Desktop printing, copying, fax, scanning, computer access for e-mail, and computer classes.

Right. **Woodstock Meats and Deli** (914-679-7917). Fresh prime meats, groceries, and newspapers.

Left. Junction with Pine Grove Street.

Right. **Woodstock Vital Foods** (914-679-4440). Freshly-made contemporary vegetarian foods, desserts, and juices. Take-out and catering.

000.3   Right. **Mama Mia's Pizzeria and Pastaria** (914-679-7969). Heroes, salads, and appetizers, $4-$7; pizza, $7-$16; and Italian dinners of pasta, eggplant, chicken, veal, and seafood, $6-$11.

Left. **Wok'n Roll Cafe** (914-679-7760). Chinese restaurant with sidewalk tables. Entrees $6-$12.

Left. **Wok'n Roll West of Japan** (914-679-3484). Tokyo-style, Japanese cuisine restaurant and sushi bar, open for dinners and weekend lunch. The wall decor is a collection of tributes to artists, authors, and other famous people who reside in Woodstock. Large selection of rice wines. Extensive menu offers numerous tasting adventures. Appetizers $4-$9, entrees $11-$21.

Left. **Joyous Lake.** Historically one of Woodstock's defining gathering places. Many famous singers and musicians have graced Joyous Lake with their performances as they climbed the thorny stems to the roses of success. Unfortunately it was closed at the time of publication.

Left. Junction with **Deming Street.** A few steps up Deming Street is:

> *Right.* ***Mountain Gate*** *(914-679-7858). Cozy restaurant featuring fine Indian dining which has received accolades from local media. Extensive vegetarian menu. Open for lunch and dinner. Dinner buffet for $9.95.*

Right. **Woodstock Automotive** (914-679-6822). Mobil gas and auto service.

Left. **Bookmart** (914-679-4646). Books, books on tape, gifts, puzzles, classical music and jazz CD's and cassettes, cards, stained glass, chess sets, and games.

Left. **The Fletcher Gallery** (914-679-4411). Art gallery focusing on the paintings and sculpture of artists who have worked in and around Woodstock over the past century.

Left.   **Print Express** (914-679-2354).   Commercial printing, graphics, advertising design, word processing, mail merge, first class mailings, papers, labels, envelopes, fax service, and color and black and white copies.

Right.   **Catskill Art & Office Supply** (914-679-2251).   Artist materials, office supplies, maps, books, copies, fax, and shipping.

Right.   **Sacred Space** (914-679-5539).   Statuary, art, artifacts, and used spiritual books.

000.4   Right.   **Mirabai Books**   (914-679-7819).   Spiritual and metaphysical books.   Books on all the major religions, men's and women's spirituality, health, vegetarian cooking and alternative diets, and astrology.   Audio tapes of relaxing, meditative, and alternative music. Also crystals and oils.

Left.   **Woodstock Chocolate & Fudge Factory** (914-679-3750). Molded, hand-dipped and filled chocolates homemade on the premises using Belgian milk, semi-sweet and white chocolate; fudge and other candies, some of which you haven't seen since you were a kid; and sugar-free chocolates and candies.

Left.   **Bread Alone** (914-679-2108).   Bakery, breakfast and lunch. Breads, muffins, cookies, cakes, brownies, tarts, sandwiches, vegetable salads, coffee, and drinks.

Left.   Junction with **Maple Lane**, a few steps down which are:

> *Left.   **Mower's Saturday Market** (914-679-6744). Outdoor, Woodstock-flavored flea market on Saturdays, and on Saturdays and Sundays on holiday weekends, May through October. Spend an hour, wander through, and taste another flavor of Woodstock.*

> *Left. **Pieces of Mine** (914-679-4289). Gems, gemstones, rocks and minerals, crystals, hand-crafted jewelry, and energy and healing stones in a warm, welcoming space.*

Left.   Glorious   Health   (914-679-0202).   Discount vitamins, supplements, herbs, and teas.

End of Maple Lane coverage.

Right.   **Shiek's** (914-679-7187).   Casually stunning women's apparel in cotton, velvet, silk, etc., in regular and plus sizes. Also ladies' accessories.

Right.   **holiday haus of Woodstock** (914-679-XMAS (9627)). Well-stocked holiday shop offering gifts and collectibles for Valentine's Day, Easter, Halloween, Christmas, and more.

Right.   **Maria's Bazar** (914-679-5434).   (Behind holiday haus.) Specialty and gourmet foods, delicious homemade, ready-to-eat salads, pastas, and more.   Indoor and outdoor tables, take-out. Forget cooking; let Maria cook it for you. A Woodstock landmark for many years.

Right.   **Landau Grill** (914-679-8937).   Contemporary American dining in a casual, airy atmosphere accented by local modern artwork.   Wholesome lunch and dinner menus of sandwiches, pastas, seafood, and more made from fresh ingredients. Even the ketchup, mayonnaise, and dressings are all homemade.   Raw bar seafood grill on the patio. Children's menu available. Open seven days during the summer. Dinner entrees $10-$15.

Left.   **Candlestock** (914-679-8711).   Candles handmade by the owner as well as candles and accessories from many other suppliers. A myriad collection appropriate to Woodstock. A great place to Christmas shop. Don't miss the man-sized years-old drip candle.

Right.   **Just Alan** (914-679-5676).   Beautifully different things from beautifully different places around the world. Gifts for yourself and others. Exotic, eclectic, and extraordinary.

Right. **Comfort Zone** (914-679-2028). Casual clothing, mostly in natural fibers, for men and women. Also jewelry and accessories.

Right. **tinker toys too!** (914-679-8870). Toys, toys, and more toys.

Left. **Pegasus** (914-679-2373). Comfort footwear and leather goods and Birkenstock products.

Right. **Letters and Lace** (914-679-3369). Cards, stationery, wrapping paper, ribbons, notebooks, photo frames, writing supplies and pocket telescopes.

Left. **Irving Kalish Real Estate** (914-679-6013).

Left. **Aviva** (914-679-9232). Electrolysis and waxing.

Right. **Clouds** (914-679-8155). Exquisite glass and ceramic gifts and crafts, jewelry and more, all imaginatively inspired, perfectly executed and beautifully presented. Simply heavenly.

Right. Junction with **Rock City Road**, which takes you to:

> *Right.* ***Milagro*** *(914-679-7001). Oaxacan wood carvings and pottery, ladies clothing, novelty hats, jewelry, ladies accessories, cards, and gifts.*

> *Right.* ***Changes*** *(914-679-2076). Fine, contemporary men's clothing and accessories. Suits, sports jackets, silk shirts, more.*

> *Right.* ***Village Green Realty*** *(914-679-2255).*

> *Right.* ***Woodstock Images*** *(914-679-7871). One-hour film developing, photo finishing, and electronic imaging. Film, batteries, disposable cameras, photo supplies,and darkroom services. Black and white services, enlargements, copying, etc.*

Left. **Katheryn Love** *(914-679-6595). Custom-fitted, off-the-rack ladies' dresses and hand-decorated straw hats.*

Left. **Tibetan Emporium** *(914-679-3808). Tibetan artifacts, clothing, jewelry, rugs, scarves, accessories, and books.*

Left. **Woodstock Framing Gallery** *(914-679-6003). Mostly-local Woodstock and Hudson Valley art. Framing.*

Left. **Occasions of Woodstock.** *Accessories for the home. Americana, collectibles, and gifts.*

Right. **Chamber of Commerce Tourist Information Booth** *(914-679-6234).*

Right. **Public restrooms.**

Right. Entrance to public **parking lot.**

Left. **Elephant Emporium** *(914-679-8833). Outdoor clothing, hats, sweatshirts, hiking boots, sleeping bags, backpacks, and more.*

Left. **Vasco Pini Frame Shop** *(914-679-9428).*

000.1   Left. Entrance to public **parking lot.**

000.5   Stop sign at intersection with Glasco Turnpike. Continue straight across onto **Meads Mountain Road.** *This road switchbacks its way up the steep mountain, climbing approximately 1000 feet in two miles.*

000.8   Right. Junction with California Quarry Road.

002.5   Top of pass between **Guardian Mountain** *to the left and* **Overlook Mountain** *to the right, at 1730' above sea level.*

*Right. Trailhead parking for **Overlook Mountain** (3140', 2.5 miles), **Echo Lake** (4.0), **Devil's Kitchen Lean-to** (5.6), and **Indian Head Mountain** (8.0). Because Overlook Mountain is the southeast corner of the Catskills, it offers to the east views of the Hudson River, Saugerties, Connecticut, Massachusetts and the Berkshires; to the southeast views of Kingston and the Hudson Valley; to the southwest the Ashokan Reservoir, and to the west and north the peaks of the Catskill Mountains. The trail is an abandoned road all the way to the top. At the summit is an old steel firetower which is currently closed to visitors, but which may be reopened in the future.*

*Left. **Karma Triyana Dharmachakra** (914-679-5906). Tibetan Buddhist Retreat Center and Monastery. The inner shrine of the monastery is home to a 14-foot-high golden Buddha. Open to the public and offering Saturday and Sunday tours at 1 PM. Meditation; instruction; book and gift shop open weekends offering books, tapes, statues, incense, practice materials, etc.*

End of Rock City Road and Meads Mountain Road coverage.

Ahead of you lies Woodstock's Village Green, a tiny triangular park ringed by shops and a church. It is Woodstock's arena. Benches provide the box seats and the steady stream of car and foot traffic along the encircling streets provide the performances. Local young people come here to play hackie sack, eat pizza, and to see and be seen. Local musicians sometimes give impromptu performances. Tourists stop to change the film in their cameras and finish their ice cream cones. And the bus from New York City periodically deposits another knot of arrivals to freshen the scene. It is a kaleidoscope of moving people whose time in the center of the scope is brief, but without whom the image would be colorless. The Green is Woodstock personified.

The Woodstock spirit may dim, but it will never die.

Left. **H. Houst & Son** (914-679-2115). Hardware, general store, auto tires, and kerosene. Trailways bus depot. Open seven days.

Right. **Flying Watermelon** (914-679-5766). Woodstock memorabilia, T-shirts, children's clothing, pocketbooks, hemposphere (hemp products: lip balm, caps, draw-string pouches, jewelry, chokers, rings, bracelets, small tobacco pipes, etc.), incense, sunglasses, fragrances, fine essential oils, and more.

Right. **Woodstock Pizzeria** (914-679-7416). Pizza, whole or by the slice. Deliveries after 5 PM.

Right. **Stoned Peaces** (914-679-8856). Wiccan supplies, herbs, smoking accessories, hair wraps, body piercing, incense, oils, T-shirts, decals, bumper stickers, license plate frames, water pipes, women's clothing, jewelry, sandals, and Woodstock memorabilia.

Left. **Corner Cupboard** (914-679-8228). Donut shop and deli.

Left. **Crossroads** (914-679-2391). Guitars and amps.

Left. **Eichhorn Real Estate** (914-679-8022). Century 21 real estate office.

Right. **Modern Mythology** (914-679-8811). New Age gifts. Eclectic collection of alternative personal expressions: gargoyles, angels, figurines, jewelry, pendants, necklaces, talismans, sun faces, buddhas, stones, crystals, wind chimes, oils, T-shirts, cards, folkways and astrology items, aromatherapy items, homeopathy items, books, tarot cards, runes, and more.

Right. **Pondicherry** (914-679-2926). Handcrafted gifts, candles, silks, jewelry, embroidery, and Woodstock spirit.

Left. **Freewheel Pottery** (914-679-7478). Moderately-priced, American and international crafts, silver, markasite and amber jewelry, sterling watches, leather items, lamps, clocks, hand-blown glass, wind chimes, and kaleidoscopes.

Left. **Woodstock Trading Post** (914-679-7431). Women's clothing, sunglasses, T-shirt, leather goods, and jewelry.

Left. **Woodstock Design** (914-679-8776). Finer ladies clothing, shoes, and accessories.

Left. **Jean Turmo** (914-679-7491). Fragrances, essential oils, cosmetics, body and hair care products, and jewelry.

Left. **Rashers** (914-679-5449). Cafe. Homecooked and home-baked foods, breakfast and lunch. Brunch on weekends. Also catering.

Left. Driveway to public **parking**.

Left. **Jarita's Florist** (914-679-6161).

Left. **Wild and Sweet** (914-679-1163). Boutique with an emphasis on natural-fiber clothing. Fancy ladies apparel, intimate clothing, jewelry, accessories, hats, scarves, handbags, children's wear, and gifts. Complete, unique ensembles.

Left. **Heaven** (914-679-0011). Specialty food market. Bakery, deli, specialty foods, prepared foods, sandwiches, salads, soups, desserts, etc. Kitchenware, housewares, gifts. Breakfast, lunch and dinner items, eat in or take out. Catering. The heavenly brownies are a specialty.

000.5   Right. **Chez Grand'mere** (914-679-8140). A French general store. Antiques, gifts, coffees, candy, women's clothing, and home furnishings.

Left. **Changes II** (914-679-2076). Contemporary, casual men's clothing. Sweaters, shirts, pants, fine sweatshirts, shoes, socks, underwear, and more.

Left. **The Jewelry Store** (914-679-4000). Quality jewelry at reasonable prices; one-of-a-kind pieces; and beautiful, hand-crafted custom work.

Right. **Woodstock Artists Association Gallery** (914-679-2940). Displaying and supporting local artwork since 1922. Permanent collection, juried and non-juried solo and group exhibitions, Christmas holiday show and sale. Woodstock artist's archive, gallery store. A "must see" while in Woodstock.

Left. **The Golden Bough** (914-679-8000). Wind chimes, china, plates, cups and saucers, pots, flatware, books, cards, gifts, watches, wooden eggs, jewelry, picture frames, wrapping paper, games, puzzles, musical instruments, and musical instruction tapes.

Left. **The Golden Notebook Store for Children** (914-679-8000). A cornucopia of children's books.

Left. **The Golden Notebook** (914-679-8000). A great thing in a small package, this overflowing bookstore reflects the eclectic nature of Woodstock's residents and visitors. A natural high for all readers. Open late on Saturdays.

Right. **Crabtree and Evelyn** (914-679-2040). Toiletries and specialty foods. Soaps, bath gels, body lotions, and talcum powders. Marmalades, jams, jellies, cookies, and teas. Bath accessories and men's traditional shaving accessories.

Right. **The Craft Shop** (914-679-2688). The Woodstock Guild crafts store featuring crafts and gifts made by local artisans.

Left. **Taco Juan's Mexican Food** (914-679-9673). Tacos and burritos, ice cream, and a wall of photographic portraits of local people. Spend an hour eating an inexpensive lunch and savoring the local color. One of the defining locales of Woodstock, especially for the young folks.

Left. **Woodstock Wines and Liquors** (914-679-2669).

Right. **Kleinert/James Arts Center** (914-679-2079). The gallery for the Woodstock Guild. Works of local and resident artists, concerts, performances, literary programs, and classes.

Left. **Vida Kafka** (914-679-9139). Intimate women's apparel and accessories.

Right. **The Rare Bear** (914-679-4201). Specialty gifts, plush toys, collectible bears, figurines, wind chimes, bird feeders, cards, posters, children's books, T-shirts, throw blankets, and baby accessories.

Left. **Pleasures** (914-679-2085). Ladies' clothing and jewelry.

Left. **Jitters** (914-679-1205). Coffees, teas, tisanes, espresso, cappuccino, bagels, lox, nova, whitefish, pasta, meat sauce, pasta deli, vegetable lasagna, etc.

Left. **Joshua's Cafe** (914-679-5533). Woodstock's oldest restaurant. Four-star dining in the heart of the hamlet. Joshua's serves lunch, brunch, and dinner. Serving cutting-edge international cuisine, the three-course dinners include an appetizer, salad, and an entree such as Bedouin mixed grill, vichyssoise vegetable strudel, filet mignon, and paella cous-cous, $12-$19. Consistent raves by local, national, and international media.

Left. Junction with **Tannery Brook Road**:

> *Right.* **Timbuktu** *(914-679-1169). A lifestyle store featuring global home furnishings and accessories. Pottery, jewelry, international carvings and crafts, tapestries, rugs, linens, ladies clothing, and accessories. Aromatherapy and personal care products, CD's and tapes from around the world, cards, and more.*

> *Right.* **Birchtree** *(914-679-7585). Ladies fashions, accessories, jewelry, and shoes.*

> *Left.* **CD Video** *(914-679-4303). Video rentals.*

> *Right.* **Sweetheart Gallery** *(914-679-2622). A wonderful collection of fine arts and crafts, home furnishings, unique clothing, and ladies' accessories. Also the gallery for the beautiful ceramic art work of owners Lila and Norman Bacon. Lovely.*

> *000.2 Right.* **Woodstock Inn on the Millstream** *(914-679-8211, 800-697-8211). Bed and breakfast motel tucked under pines and maples alongside Tannery Brook. Eleven motel units and seven efficiencies. Roomy, comfortable, and nicely furnished. Freshly baked gourmet breakfast, stream swimming in a natural pool, and a five-minute walk to the village green. Motel units $79-$89/two, efficiencies $99-$124.*

End of Tannery Brook Road coverage.

Right. **Tannery Brook.** Pedestrian walkway behind the Old Forge building:

Dharmaware (914-679-5417). Women's, men's, and children's clothing, jewelry, gifts, Tibetan art, incense, drums, books, meditation materials.

Bluestone Country Foods *(914-679-5656). Sandwiches, baked goods, drinks, and specialties.*

Anatolia (914-679-5311). Tribal rugs, weavings and pillows from Turkey, Afghanistan, Azerbaijan, Iraq, Bulgaria, Armenia, etc.

Left. Sidewalk to the rear of the Tinker Street Cafe:

Center for Photography at Woodstock (second floor) (914-679-9957). Always an exhibit, always interesting. Contemporary works and educational programs.

Tinker Village (914-679-2568):
Garden Oasis. Garden center selling perennials, annuals, hanging house plants, tropical plants, cactus, and succulents. Dish gardens, patio plants. Also old and almost-new used books, antiques. A beautiful display of nature's botanical jewels.
Treasure Chest Antiques. Collectibles, tchatchkas, glass, pottery, paintings, and more.
Also an apartment with a full kitchen, two sleeping areas, a deck overlooking a waterfall, a grill, and cable TV, for $85/couple/night or $150/weekend.

Right. **Woodstock Bead Emporium** (914-679-0066). Beaded necklaces and bracelets, macrame jewelry, and silver jewelry. Things made out of beads, plus anything and everything from which to make beaded jewelry. An eye-opening collection of beadwork.

Right. **Slick** (914-679-7039). A leather goods store which also sells cigars. Leather clothing, boots, motorcycle helmets, and briefcases.

Left. **Tinker Street Cafe** (914-679-2487). Casual restaurant, bar, sidewalk patio, evening entertainment. This location has been a gathering place for many of Woodstock's unknown, almost famous, and famous for decades. Lunch and dinner of soups, salads, sandwiches, burgers, and vegetarian items, $3-$10; chicken, pasta, seafood, and steak entrees, $11-$17.

Left. **Ann Leonard Gallery** (914-679-2112). An impressive, varied collection of fine art, sculptures, jewelry, and paintings from all over the world as well as from Woodstock. Ms. Leonard, a sculptor, offers art directly from her fellow artists. This serious gallery has been a Woodstock landmark for more than 30 years.

Right. **Woodstock Cottage and Camp Antiques** (914-679-6499). Decorative home furnishings and accessories for country living. Chests, cupboards, chairs, benches, lamps, china, ornamentation, and more.

000.6   Right. **New Age Hemp** (914-679-0036). Hemp and hemp-blend products. Shirts, jeans, sweaters, T-shirts, ties, kerchiefs, purses, knapsacks, bags, shoes, and more. Also glass art objects and tobacco products.

Left. **Ben & Jerry's** (914-679-6527). Great ice cream and yogurt.

Left. **Catskill House** (914-679-8819). Gifts and collectibles, pewter and glass figures, hundreds of unique kaleidoscopes, exotic musical instruments, and Richie Havens' artwork.

Right. **Woodstock Sportscards and Comics** (914-679-2178). Sports cards, collectible gaming cards, and comic books. New and pre-owned.

Right. **Walkabout** (914-679-8288). An eclectic collection of imported women's clothing, accessories, gifts, collectibles, and antiques. Trousers, jackets, blouses, sweaters, jewelry, musical instruments, masks, carvings, deity and ikon candles, quilts, walking sticks, and much more. Many things you've probably never seen before.

Right. **Rhythms** (914-679-4349). Eclectic selection of new and used CD's, tapes, and LP's.

Right. **Woodstock Real Estate** (914-679-6880).

Left. **Not Fade Away Tie Dye Co.** (914-679-8663). Tie-dyed T-shirts and other products, and smokers' supplies.

Right. **Annie's Down Home Stitchin'** (914-679-2963). Boutique and tailor shop. Resale clothing for men and women. Tailoring, hems, zippers, repairs, and leather work.

Right. **Readers Quarry** (914-679-9572). A wall-to-wall, floor-to-ceiling bookcase filled with yesterday's books.

Right. **Baby Toes Clothing** (914-679-7989). Hand-painted clothing for adults and children.

Left. **Twin Gables** (914-679-9479/5638). A Woodstock landmark, this 1930's-style, non-smoking guest home in the center of town within walking distance of everything has been serving visitors for more than 50 years. Nine rooms with private and shared baths, living room, and reading areas. $50-$70.

Right. **Polka Dot Penguin** (914-679-9550). A happy, fun, play store for all ages, full of puppets, novelties, jewelry, toys, glow-in-the-dark paints, inflatables, Groucho get-ups, hand buzzers, whoopee cushions, rubber chickens, masks, bumper stickers, hopping spiders, and much more. You won't want to miss a store with such a great sense of humor.

Right. **Woodstock Police and Town Hall.** (914-679-2422).

Left. **Weathervane Studios** (914-679-6948). Antiques.

Right. **Woodstock Hardware.** (914-679-2862).

Left. Junction with driveway to the town offices and:

Municipal parking.

Woodstock Historical Society Museum *(914-679-2265, 6744). In a former 1920 artist's home, three rooms of exhibits including a standing tools exhibit, plus exhibits which change annually. Open 1-5 PM on weekends July through October, or by appointment.*

Bird-on-a-Cliff Theatre Company's *(914-679-5979) outdoor stage on which is presented the* **Woodstock Shakespeare Festival** *from late June through August. Two plays a season, curtain is at 5 PM on Fridays, Saturdays, and Sundays. Blankets, chairs, picnic dinners welcome; refreshments available.   Admission free but donations cheerfully accepted.*

000.7   Right. Junction with **Library Lane**:

Left. **Woodstock Library** *(914-679-2213).   A profes-sionally-run, small-town library with a great staff. Strong concentration of books on art and local history. Activities include a Library Forum sponsoring speakers on topics of local and global interest (usually one Saturday a month), occasional hamlet walking tours sprinkled with local history, and the Library Fair on the last Saturday in July, a tradition since the 1920s.*

Right. **Woodstock Laundry.**

End of Library Lane coverage.

Left. **Christian Science Reading Room** (914-679-9534).

Left. **Overlook Mountain Bikes** (914-679-2122). Bicycle sales, service, and rentals.

Left. **Woodstock Doll House** (914-679-2607).   Dolls, toys, miniatures, educational toys, and children's amusements.

Left. **Gilded Carriage** (914-679-2607). Fine kitchen and tableware, linens, baskets, dolls, toys, cards, stationery, and wrapping paper.

Left. **Basil Garden Supply** (914-679-8137). Garden supplies and accessories, garden furniture, bird feeders, plant bulbs, etc.

Left. **Melody's Hair Station** (914-679-5754). Hair salon in old railroad station.

Left. **Woodstock Post Office** (914-679-2116). ZIP 12498.

000.8   Left. **Once Possessed** (914-679-3243). Antique and new, local and imported furniture, home furnishings, and decorative accessories. One-of-a-kind items, hand-painted items, and reproductions.

Left. **Third Eye Sights** (914-679-6111). Photography gallery.

000.9   Left. **Side Porch Studio** (914-679-2993). Watercolors by Bernice M. Hoyt.

Right. **Tinker Street Cinema** (914-679-6608). Movie theater.

Left. **Morning Glory Bed & Breakfast** (914-679-3208). Family operated, four-room, two-bath, bed and breakfast in an old house within walking distance of the village green. Decorated in wicker and Woodstock art. Full breakfast of authentic Belgian waffles and more. $63-$75. Pets allowed.

001.0   Left. **Lily Ente Gallery** (914-679-6064). Sculptures of wood, stone, metal, and clay. Spring through fall weekends or by appointment.

Left. **Woodstock Undiscovered** (914-679-4308). A gallery showing the works of not-yet-famous Woodstock artists.

001.1   Left. Site of new Post Office (under construction at time of publication).

001.3   Left. **Jeffery Gallery** (914-679-6871). Serious, beautiful oil paintings mostly of landscapes, with some marine subjects and seascapes. The artists depiction of snow is especially striking. June through October, by chance or appointment.

001.6   Left. **Sunfrost Farms** (914-679-6690). Fruits and vegetables.

002.0   Left. **Gypsy Wolf Cantina** (914-679-9563). A casual, California-Mexican restaurant decorated with carved wooden masks depicting wolves, chickens, and lizards from Guatemala, Mexico, and El Salvador, creating a folk-art museum. Serving fajitas, chimichangas, grilled chicken and fish, vegetarian burritos, etc. seven nights a week. $9-$15.

002.2   Right. **Bearsville Garage** (914-679-2110). Auto repairs.

         Right. **Moving Body Fitness Center** (914-679-7715).

002.3   Entering **Bearsville**.

002.4   Left. **The Petersen House** (914-679-8990). Contemporary restaurant with marble tabletops and natural wooden furniture in an old farmhouse open only for Sunday brunch from 10:30-2:30. Eggs Benedict, lemon ricotta-stuffed crepes, Grand Marnier-spiced brioche French toast, steak sandwich, etc., $4-$11. Also on- or off-site catering. Closed a few months in winter.

         Left. **Bear Cafe** (914-679-5555). Fine dining and cafe. Well-regarded, Woodstock-style, gourmet restaurant serving new American cuisine in a casually elegant setting overlooking the Sawkill Creek. Fine dining dinner menu serving the likes of filet mignon with Stilton cheese and port garlic sauce, and ravioli with arugula and radicchio. Also a cafe menu serving interesting sandwiches, pastas, burgers, and more. Entrees $7-$23. Extensive wine list. Closed Tuesdays.

         Left. **Little Bear** (914-679-8899). The Woodstock version of a fine Chinese restaurant. Bright and airy with large windows overlooking the Sawkill Creek. Open for lunch and dinner. Dinner entrees usually $8-$15.

Left. **Bearsville Theatre** (914-679-4406). Various musical and other performances, mostly on weekends, from Memorial Day to Labor Day. Call for upcoming events.

Junction with **Bearsville-Wittenberg Road**. **NY 212** turns to the right toward **Shady, Lake Hill, Willow**, and **Mt. Tremper**. **Bearsville-Wittenberg Road** continues straight ahead toward **Wittenberg, Wilson Public Campground**, and **Mt. Tremper**.

End of Woodstock and Bearsville coverage.

From NY 375 to Phoenicia

You are now passing through bluestone country. As you drive through the rock cuts west of NY 375 you can see the bluestone jutting out from the sides of the cuts. West Hurley and Woodstock held many bluestone quarries in the mid-to-late nineteenth century. The bluestone was quarried and moved by horse-drawn wagon to the Rondout Creek in Kingston, where it was loaded onto barges for the trip down the Hudson River to New York City. Much of the curbing and sidewalks in Manhattan came from here.

007.3   Right(left) Junction with **NY 375** to **Woodstock**. See Chapter 4, *NY 375 from Route 28 to Woodstock*.

Right(left) **Eichhorn Realty** (914-679-8600). Century 21 office.

Right(left) **Watson Memorials** (914-679-9075). Also bluestone for sale.

007.4   Right(left) **Elusive Butterfly Antiques** (914-679-2521). Antique oak furniture from the turn of the century and before which has been beautifully and carefully restored to like-new condition by an old-world craftsman. Open weekends and by appointment.

008.4   Right(left) Junction with **Maverick Road.**

*Immediately on the right on Maverick Road is **Catskill Forest Sports** (914-657-8311). Outdoor equipment, clothing, accessories, and parts. Snowboards,* *skateboards, in-line skates, archery pro shop, camping supplies, snowshoes, and more.*

Right(left) **Mountainside Family Style Restaurant and Motel** (914-657-7133). Newly-refurbished, family-style restaurant and motel. Restaurant serves Italian and American cuisine for lunch ($4-$6) and dinner ($5-$13). Daily specials, sandwich board, children's menu, bar and party room, open seven days. Twelve motel units with all new furnishings, set back from road, $50 per couple, reservations suggested.

010.9   Right(left) **Kenozia Lake.** During the peak fall color season around the second weekend of October this lake doubles the beauty of the colorful trees on the far shore and the mountains beyond.

011.5   **Hurley/Olive** town line.

011.6   Right(left) **Editions** (914-657-7000). New, old, rare, first edition, and out-of-print books.

Entering(leaving) **Ashokan.**

Right(left) **Reservoir Delicatessen & Dairy** (914-657-8113).

011.8   Right(left) **Fleet Bank** (800-228-1281).

012.0   Right(left) **Just Alan** (914-657-6773). Cafe, antiques, and gifts. Cafe serving cappuccinos, hot chocolates, ice cream, malts, sundaes, etc., surrounded by an eclectic collection of antiques, crafts, and gifts. Chocolates to diamonds, cigars to antique furniture, children's items to adult games, magic to pianos, sculptures to Judaica. Open weekends in winter, Friday through Monday in summer.

012.1   Right(left) **Walts Auto Repair** (914-657-6959). Auto repairs, towing.

012.2   Right(left) **The Olive Branch** (914-657-2600). Florist.

012.5   Right(left) **Hickory Hill Antiques** (914-657-2879, 6252). Barn sale. Antiques, furniture, primitives, cupboards, blanket boxes, farm tables, handmade pillows, and more. Fresh, estate-sale merchandise; nothing from auctions; new items every day, all at wholesale prices.

Right(left) **Winternight Gallery** and **Sunlight Studio** (914-657-6982). Two artists with two studios. Nancy Winternight, whose theme is flying women and angels, offers paintings, carved folk art, and handmade greeting cards. Robert Selkowitz creates art images for healing and renewal, in the form of relaxing landscapes as seen from porches or verandas. His works include oils, pastels, silkscreens, posters, photo prints, and note cards.

012.6   Right(left) **The Berry Patch** (914-657-2075). Purple building with gifts, outdoor statues, cat corner, angel corner, pig corner, bears, candles, rubber stamps, stickers, nautical corner, corner for men, T-shirts, bird houses, handmade baskets, handmade jewelry, and free gift wrapping.

Right(left) **Memorabilia** (914-657-6366). Antique chinaware, glassware, kitchenware, crockery, jewelry, linens and lace, textiles, furniture, paintings, clocks, lamps, Christmas items, and more. Weekends April through October, plus Mondays in July and August.

Right(left) **Paula J. Kitchen Real Estate** (914-657-2133).

012.8   Left(right) **Olive Plaza**:

Sheldon Hill Forestry Supplies (914-657-6658). Forestry, logging, outdoor power equipment, safety equipment, and small engine repair.

Get the Scoop (914-657-2125). Ice cream and miniature golf. Ice cream parlor in a 1950's and cartoon characters motif, with a miniature electric train and cable car. Hard and soft ice cream and yogurt, egg creams, hot dogs, pizza, pies and cakes, coffee, soda, etc. Also 18-hole miniature golf. Mid-April through October.

The Meat Wagon *(914-657-7223). Butcher shop featuring prime and choice meats, natural chickens, organic beef, homemade sausage, etc. Also vitamins.*

RK's Video *(914-657-8676). Video rentals.*

012.9   Right(left) **J & J Automotive** (914-657-2299). Automobile repair.

Right(left) **Shokan Square:**

Fill'n Station *(914-657-8959). Country store, cafe, and Mobil gas. Sandwiches, burgers, daily specials, soups, subs, Jane's ice cream, bulk foods, coffee bar, baked goods, and deli. Also automotive supplies and ice.*

Shokan Post Office *(914-657-8477). ZIP 12481.*

013.0   Left(right) **Dependable Energy Services** (914-657-8225) . Gas station.

013.2   Right(left) **Steve's Foreign Car Service** (914-657-2530). Specializing in Mercedes-Benz.

013.4   Left(right) **Ashokan Artisans** (914-657-8772). Fine crafts. Six rooms of crafts in wood, pottery, brass, silver, fiber, glass, and leather, created by more than 100 local and national artisans. Home and personal accessories, jewelry,   watercolors, and photographs. Planters, wind chimes, walking sticks, hummingbird houses, porcelain creatures, lizards, and more.

013.5   Left(right) **Winchell's Pizza** (914-657-3352). Pizza, pasta bar, calzones, barbecued chicken, desserts, and ice cream.

Left(right) **Winchell's Corner Antiques Market** (914-657-2177). Multi-dealer antiques and collectibles, pottery, tableware, planters, glassware, perfume bottles, jewelry, furniture, paintings, prints, kitchen supplies, and more.   Also greeting cards, post cards, homemade fudge, and magazines. This building was moved here from the planned reservoir site during the building of the Ashokan Reservoir.

013.6   Left(right) Junction with **Reservoir Road**. at Winchell's Corners. Turning left(right) at this intersection for a two-and-one-third-mile side trip to the Ashokan reservoir fountain offers you magnificent views of the **Ashokan Reservoir** (especially at sunset), the **Catskill Mountains**, and a perfect place to park and rest.

> *001.3   Beginning of dividing weir, the dam which separates the Ashokan Reservoir's upper basin (to your right) from its lower basin (to your left).   The reservoir offers good fishing for trout, smallmouth bass, perch, crappies, and pickerel, but only with proper permit (free). Call 914-657-2663 or 212-643-2172 for details.*

> *Construction of the reservoir was begun in 1907 and completed in 1915.   For an excellent account of the building of the reservoir, read Bob Steuding's* The Last of the Handmade Dams *(see Appendix C, Additional Information).*

> *001.7   Make a left at the stop sign at* **Monument Road** *at the end of the dividing weir, overlooking the fountain.   To the left as you start down the hill is the old dike road which is now closed to vehicular traffic and dogs.   It is used by the public as a one-and-one-half-mile walking/jogging/biking lane.*

> *002.0   At the bottom of the hill, bear right at the fork to the parking area and the fountain. (Bearing left puts you on* **NY 28A**, *which takes you, after a windy and scenic drive of many miles, back to* **Route 28** *at mile 004.3 west of* **Kingston**.*)*

The fountain at the Ashokan Reservoir.

New York City's water supply is kept safe among the Catskill Mountains.

02.1   Turn right into the parking area. The fountain, constructed about 1980, sends water 80 feet into the air. Leashed dogs are allowed but you must pick up after them. Rest rooms are to the left, across the fountain circle from the parking area.

Upon leaving the parking area by car, make a left and then make the next left to leave NY 28A and return to the road which climbs the hill back to the dividing weir. At the top of the hill turn right to cross the dividing weir and continue back to Route 28.

End of Reservoir Road coverage.

013.7   Right(left) **Reservoir Motel** (914-657-2002). Eight motel units and two efficiencies, recently renovated by new owners. Clean, comfortable, air-conditioned lodging at a moderate price of $45/couple.

013.8   Right(left) **Pet Fare Feeds & Needs** (914-657-2500). Pet food and supplies.

014.6   Right(left) **Shokan Bend Bait and Tackle** (914-657-9852). Live bait of all kinds, fishing tackle, coffee, ice, cigarettes. Local fishing information. April through November.

014.7   Right(left) **Pine View Bakery and Cafe** (914-657-8925). Bakery, snack bar. Breads, cakes, desserts; breakfast and lunch.

Descending long hill into Boiceville offers scenic views of the valley and the mountains to the west.

016.6   Entering(leaving) **Boiceville**.

016.7   Right(left) **Fabulous Furniture** (914-657-6317). Awesome, hand-crafted furniture made from wood and 1950's car parts, and metal sculptures made from old metal scraps. Some of the furniture boards are up to 50 inches wide and are sawn from specially-selected trees 250-300 years old, while other uniquely grained and patterned boards come from decaying or diseased trees. Steve Heller's eyes and hands transform these trees into beautiful, unique, and truly fabulous furniture.

017.1   Right(left) **Bread Alone** (914-657-3328).   Cafe and bakery. Homemade breads from a wood-fired brick oven, cookies, cakes, pies. Coffee, juices, sodas.

Right(left) **Boiceville Inn** (914-657-8500).   Rustic restaurant serving Italian and American dinners. Pizza, spaghetti, ravioli, tortellini, ribs, chicken cordon bleu, shell steak, pork, shrimp, scallops, and more, $6-$15. Weekend specials. Bar with pool table, video games, TV and jukebox. Popular with outdoors folks from fishermen to hunters to skiers.

Right(left) **Catskill Produce** (914-657-6705).   Produce, plants, home-baked pies, maple syrup, local honey, pumpkins, Christmas trees, firewood.

Right(left) **Crackerbarrel Country Store** (914-657-6540). Fireplaces, pellet stoves, cook stoves, gas stoves, inserts, accessories. Also country-style kitchen supplies and home accessories, gifts, collectibles, miniatures, jellies, candies, sheepskin slippers, postcards, souvenirs, more.

017.6   Left(right) Junction with **NY 28A** to **Ashokan Reservoir**.

017.7   Right(left) **Boiceville Florist and Gifts** (914-657-6763).

Right(left) **Landmark Inn** (914-657-6287).   Comfortable and homey, family-style restaurant with country atmosphere, serving lunch and dinner. Usually steaks and seafood, with Italian night on Wednesdays and Mexican night on Thursdays. Daily specials, salad bar, home baking. Lunch specials $4-$7, dinners $9-$14. Happy hour with hors d'oeuvres on Wednesdays and Fridays.

Left(right) **Trail Nursery and Garden Center** (914-657-8638). Greenhouse.

017.8   Left(right) **Trail Motel** (914-657-2552). Comfortable motel for non-smokers with six rooms and two efficiencies, $60/couple. No credit cards. Also, **DeBaun Art Gallery.** Displaying the works of two artists. Portraits, landscapes, and still lifes in oils and watercolors, and limited-edition prints.

Right(left) **Mountain Business Services** (914-657-2455). Tax preparation, financial services, copies and fax.

017.4   Right(left) **Onteora Cafe** (914-657-8799). Cafe and country store serving short order breakfast and lunch. Daily specials, snacks, beverages, soft and hard ice cream, yogurt, gifts.

Left(right) Shopping plaza housing the following:
Boiceville Pharmacy (914-657-6511). Pharmacy and videos.
Boiceville Wines and Spirits (914-657-6262).
Boiceville Supermarket (914-657-2695).
Stucki Embroidery Works (914-657-2308) and **AM-Best Emblem and Trim** (914-657-2336). Two separate but related commercial embroidery companies. Patches, emblems, logos, banner and clerical embroidery. Main supplier of embroidered stars to flag companies, and of embroidered presidential seals, armed forces eagles, etc. for banners and flags. Artwork by thread.

017.9   Left(right) **Singer-Denman Home Care Center** (914-657-8040). Service Star Hardware store, lawn and garden supplies, lumber, etc.

Left(right) Small shopping plaza containing the following:
Boiceville Post Office (914-657-2226). ZIP 12412.
Reservoir Natural Foods (914-657-7302).
Spectrum Video (914-657-8804).
J & J Pizza (914-657-2005). Pizza parlor serving real Brooklyn pizza, Italian dinners, sandwiches, hot and cold subs, etc.

Left(right) **Boiceville Garage** (914-657-2033).   Sunoco gas station, repair garage, carwash, 24-hour towing.

018.0   Left(right) **Wilber National Bank** (914-657-8733).

018.2   Left(right) **Coldbrook Canoes** (914-657-2189). Canoes, kayaks, paddles, life vests, helmets, wetsuits, sailing rigs, accessories, automobile roof racks, books, magazines.

Right(left) Junction with **Piney Point Road**:

*000.7   Right.   **Onteora Mountain House** (914-657-6233). A magnificent bed and breakfast on 25 forested acres on the side of a mountain with a 220-degree panoramic view of the Catskills. This elegantly-rustic home with a bluestone foundation, bluestone and tree-trunk pillars, and cedar shake shingles was built in 1928/29 by Richard Hellmann of mayonnaise fame. Inside are cathedral ceilings, wainscoting, and American and Korean antiques. One guestroom has a private bath, and the other four guest rooms, each with a sink in the room, share two-and-a-half baths. Sleeping porch, game room with the original Hellmann billiard table, bar, deer and caribou trophies, sauna, gazebo, hiking trail. Full gourmet breakfast served on the dining porch enclosing three pine trees. Eight miles to Woodstock and 20 to Belleayre. This Adirondack-styled summer home offers relaxed living and outstanding views. $95-$155/couple.*

018.8   **Olive/Shandaken** town line.

019.4   Right(left) Site of the planned state **Catskill Interpretive Center**, currently a day-use area offering picnic tables and an interpretive trail.

019.6   Right(left) **Car Craft Body Shop and Towing** (914-688-5858, 5666). 24-hour towing.

Right(left) **Alyce and Roger's Farm & Fruitstand** (914-688-2114). Locally-grown fruits, vegetables, flowers, plants. Also local cider, eggs, honey, maple syrup, and preserves. April through October.

019.9   Left(right) **Lazy Meadows Cottages** (914-688-9950). On the Esopus Creek, two-bedroom/two-bath cabins, efficiencies, fireplaces, $55-$75.

020.1   Right(left) Junction with **NY 212** to **Mt. Tremper, Wittenberg,** and **Woodstock:**

> *000.1   Left. **Mt. Tremper Post Office** (914-688-7378). ZIP 12457.*

> *000.5   Junction with **Bearsville-Wittenberg Road (CR 40)** to the right and **Old Route 28** to the left. Turn left for **Phoenicia**. Continue straight ahead for **Willow, Lake Hill, Bearsville,** and **Woodstock**.*

> *Turn right at this intersection onto **Bearsville-Wittenberg Road (CR 40)** for:*

> *000.0   Left. **La Duchesse Anne** (914-688-5260). A casually elegant, 1850s French inn set on a large lawn under pines, oaks, and maples, with a wonderful French restaurant serving delectable poultry, fish, and red meats. Hors d'oeuvres $7-$8, soups $4-$6, entrees $14-$24. The inn houses 14 spacious rooms furnished in antiques at $60-$90/couple, continental breakfast included. Sunday brunch open to the public. For a unique French dining experience, have your name added to their mailing list for their quarterly, seven-course, six-wine, prix fixe dinner. One of my favorites.*

> *003.6   Left. **Kenneth L. Wilson Public Campground** (914-679-7020, 800-456-CAMP (2267) for reservations). Seventy-six sites, picnic area, swimming beach, baseball field, volleyball net, boat rentals, one-mile nature trail, four-mile mountain bike trail, cross-country ski trails, one-mile marked run (green arrows painted on the*

road, beginning by the beach parking lot), ice skating. Showers, dump station. This campsite and day-use area are nestled in the valley of the Little Beaver Kill, a stream which empties into the Esopus Creek, which, in turn, empties into the Hudson River at Saugerties. Far from the glow of any city lights, the beach area and the fields within the campground offer wonderful stargazing and meteor watching on cloudless and moonless nights.

For those of you interested in meteors, The World Almanac *discusses four significant meteor showers throughout the year. These are the Perseids around August 12, the Orionids around October 21, the Leonids around November 17, and the Geminids around December 13. The best time to view meteor showers is after midnight (when you are facing earth's forward direction) and on nights without a moon for a darker background sky. Happy hunting.*

End of Bearsville-Wittenberg Road (CR 40) and NY 212 coverage.

020.2   Left(right) **Mt. Tremper Pine Cottages** (914-688-7368). Owned by the same proprietor for more than 40 years, these four, old-fashioned, efficiency cabins with screened porches, and a mobile home, are neat and clean and sit under a tall, mixed grove on eight acres alongside the Esopus Creek with a long, gentle pool perfect for swimming.   Sleeping up to six, they are open from May or June through October. $60-$70/night.

Crossing Esopus Creek, one of the Catskills' famous fly fishing streams.

020.5   Entering(leaving) **Mt. Pleasant**.

020.8   Right(left) **Catskill Corners** (914-688-2451, 888-303-3936). A new attraction center devoted primarily to the kaleidoscope, and offering many hours of entertainment, browsing, and shopping. Attractions and shops include:

Kaatskill Kaleidoscope (914-688-5300). Certified by the 1997 *Guinness Book of Records* as the world's largest kaleidoscope, this 60-foot-high tube offers a unique audio and visual experience.

Spotted Dog Firehouse No. 1 Eatery (914-688-7700). Restaurant with a fire truck theme, fire truck booths, fire truck back bar, life nets hanging from the ceiling, and serving hot dogs, burgers, chili, dinner specials, and more. Lunch $2-8, dinner $8-$15. Children's menu.

Catskills A La Cart (914-688-9700). Gourmet deli and soda fountain. Sandwiches, quiches, salads, Jane's homemade ice cream, kitchenware, and umbrella-table dining on the patio.

Enchantments (914-688-9700). A home decor shop.

Scentsations (914-688-9700). A shop featuring aromatherapy and spa accoutrements.

Into the Woods (914-688-9700). Nature adventure store focusing on the Catskill Park.

Kaleidoworld. Featuring the Dondoakahedron, the world's second-largest kaleidoscope; and the Crystal Palace, a darkened room housing sixteen, large, unique, hands-on, interactive kaleidoscopes. Candy for the eyes.

Spotted Puppy Gift Shop. Fire and fire-fighting-oriented gift shop offering Dalmatians, fire trucks, hot sauces, more.

Kaatskill KaleidoStore. The quintessential kaleidoscope store, including science and nature items.

020.9   Right(left) **The Lodge at Catskill Corners** (914-688-2828). Log buildings on the banks of the Esopus Creek featuring 27 lodging units from rooms to suites with various amenities such as Jacuzzi's, whirlpools, refrigerators, wet bars, in-room modems, balconies overlooking the stream, and more. A conference center is also available. $95-$250/two, continental breakfast included. Open all year.

Also, the **Catamount Cafe.** Fine dining in a log cabin setting with fireplaces, twig furniture, naturally-shed-elkhorn chandeliers, deck overlooking the creek, lounge and bar, dance floor, and entertainment. Serving international farmhouse cuisine for dinner, most entrees are $15-$20. Extensive wine list. Saturday lunch and Sunday brunch.

021.1   Right(left) **Town Tinker Tube Rental** (914-688-5553). Eastern terminus of Town Tinker's Esopus Creek tubing rides. Ride the bus or the train upstream to begin the three-mile, 1 2/3-hour novice run down the Esopus to here. Or, go to the Phoenicia location for a more challenging, exciting, white water ride with bigger and faster rapids, which starts three miles above Phoenicia. Ages 12 and up; May through September .

021.2   Right(left) **Shandaken Tourist Information Caboose** (914-688-2012) and **parking** area.

021.5   Right(left) **Catskill Mountain Railroad** (914-688-7400). Scenic, six-mile, 40-minute, round-trip train rides. Also one-way return-to-Phoenicia rides for tubers. Trains also stop at the Empire State Railway Museum at the former Ulster and Delaware Railroad depot built in 1899.   Weekends and holidays only, Memorial Day weekend through mid-October.

022.4   Left(right) **Phoenicia Plaza**:
Village Pizzeria (914-688-5052).   Pizza parlor offering pizza, calzones, mozzarella sticks, wings, hot subs, etc.
Phoenicia Antique Center and Auction Service (914-688-2095). Multi-dealer shop offering general antiques and collectibles, jewelry, books, much more. Monthly auctions in summer, tag sales in winter.

022.6   Left(right) Forest access **parking**.

022.7   Right(left) **Sleepy Hollow Camp Site** (914-688-5471). Grassy tent and RV sites in the sun and shade along the Esopus Creek. Showers, dump station.   Creek fishing, swimming, tubing, kayaking. May through September, $15-$17/night/four.

023.0   Left(right) **Phoenicia Diner** (914-688-9957).   Family-run diner offering home cooking, beer, wine. Open 24 hours on weekends.

023.3   Right(left) Junction with **High Street** to **Phoenicia**. This is the easternmost exit for the hamlet of Phoenicia. Coverage of the hamlet begins at the junction of Route 28 and **NY 214**, one mile to the west.

023.6   Right(left) Junction with **Bridge Street** to **Phoenicia, Rubber Ducky Tube Rentals, Town Tinker Tube Rentals,** etc. Full coverage of the hamlet begins at the junction of Route 28 and **NY 214**, one-half mile to the west.

023.8   Crossing the **Esopus Creek**.

024.0   Right(left) Junction with **NY 214** to **Phoenicia** and **Tannersville**. See Chapter 7, *Phoenicia*.

Phoenicia

Phoenicia was founded shortly after the U.S. revolution, developing slowly as a farming and tanning community. In 1870, the Ulster and Delaware Railroad began opening the area as a resort destination, bringing visitors to boarding houses and grand hotels. Simpson Ski Slope, with the first towered ski tow in the state, opened in 1935, bringing weekend ski trains from New York City. Automobiles slowly replaced trains as the preferred means of personal transportation, reducing the railroad's presence to the current Catskill Mountain Railroad tourist attraction in Phoenicia and the Delaware and Ulster Rail Ride in Arkville.

Today the region is a popular destination for weekend tourists. Phoenicia marks the eastern edge of local ski country, with Belleayre Mountain Ski Center just twelve miles west on Route 28. Phoenicia sits in the lap of the rugged mountains where Stony Clove Creek joins Esopus Creek, and is as authentically Catskills as the Catskill Mountains are known to be.

At first glance Main Street appears to have remained virtually unchanged for the past half century, but a closer look reveals it is lined with shops, restaurants, and services which today's residents and visitors need. I like to think of it as a rural, outdoor mall, a few blocks long, in the heart of the Catskills, with a real creek instead of a fountain and real mountains instead of wall-painted murals. On any weekend you will find a steady parade of tubers, hikers, backpackers, campers, fisher folks, hunters, snowshoers, skiers, canoeists, kayakers, ice climbers, or leaf peepers shopping or dining along Main Street.

Phoenicia hosts two serious white water races annually. On the first full weekend in June are the Esopus Slalom canoe and kayak races, and in September or October are open canoe races. In addition, the Phoenicia Rotary Club sponsors an annual Crazy Quacker Race on Sunday of Columbus Day weekend, the same weekend that Belleayre Mountain holds its annual Fall Festival. The race is an event in which for ten dollars you can rent a rubber duck. Your duck, along with 500 to 1000 others, gets dumped into the Esopus Creek at Woodland Valley bridge. The sponsor of the first duck to float its way to Phoenicia wins $1000. Ducks can be rented that weekend at various Phoenicia businesses and by the Woodland Valley bridge.

For information about Phoenicia and the area, write to the Phoenicia Business Association, P.O. Box 391, Phoenicia, NY 12464, or call 914-679-8057. For assistance in finding lodging along the Route 28 corridor between Kingston and Delhi, call Lodging and Tourist Information for the Central Catskill Mountain Region, 800-431-4555.

Coverage of Phoenicia begins at the junction of Route 28 and NY 214 at the Shandaken Eagle, an eagle statue which used to spread its wings above Grand Central Terminal in New York City. Coverage continues east along Main Street and Old Route 28 (CR 40) to its intersection with NY 212 in Mt. Tremper, and includes a side trip up NY 214 to Devil's Tombstone Public Campground.

000.0   Junction of **Route 28** and **NY 214**.

Right.   **Al's Restaurant and Lounge** (914-688-5880). A Phoenicia tradition since 1940, this family restaurant specializes in seafood and steaks, including surf and turf, $12-$25. Vegetarian dishes also available. Early-bird specials featuring seventeen entrees plus soup and salad for $10. Sunday brunch, steak and shrimp buffet on Mondays (Tuesdays in summer). Also summer outdoor clambakes with live music, open bar, two lobsters per person, and all the steak, clams, mussels, corn on the cob, shrimp, sausage and peppers you can eat for $40.

000.2   Left. Junction with **NY 214** north to **Devil's Tombstone Public Campground, Tannersville,** and **Hunter**. See coverage later in this chapter. Coverage of **Main Street (CR 40)** continues:

Right. **Ruth M. Gale Real Estate** (914-688-5610).

Left. **Phoenicia Pharmacy** (914-688-2215). Pharmacy, variety store.

Right. **Phoenicia Wine and Liquors** (914-688-7280).

Right. **Phoenicia Delicatessen** (914-688-5125). Made-to-order sandwiches, home-made salads. Baked goods from Diesings in Kingston, Schaller & Weber cold cuts, imported gourmet items.

Left. **the tender land** (914-688-2001). An eclectic collection of personal and living accessories including gifts, home furnishings, home accessories, jewelry, bric-a-brac, chests, benches, natural sapling furniture, hand-carved canoes, and more. An alluring shop made even more so by the great jazz background music. The best of Soho in Phoenicia.

Left. **Sweet Sue's** (914-688-7852). Breakfast and lunch featuring two dozen varieties of specialty pancakes and French toast; lunch specials, gourmet salads, hot spinach and feta pasta, soups, sandwiches, homemade breads. Also **Lanesville Kitchen,** serving dinner Friday through Sunday, all made from scratch using many organic and local ingredients, with a different menu every week, $8-$17.

Right. **Phoenicia Library** (914-688-7811).

Left. **Key Bank** (914-688-7000). 24-hour ATM.

Right. **Morne Imports** (914-688-7738). Sporting goods; fishing tackle; hunting, camping, and hiking equipment, and supplies. Maps, newspapers, ceramics, tobacco, cigars. Also children and adult clothing, T-shirts, sweatshirts, blankets, moccasins, jewelry, perfumes, greeting cards, candles, plush toys, hand-made wreaths, and more. Fly fishing school. Trailways bus stop.

Right.   **Ricciardella's Restaurant** (914-688-7800).   Italian cuisine, seafood, lobster tank. Lobster and early bird specials.

Left.   **Phlebus Book Shop** (914-688-2744).   East Village-type, literary bookstore in the Catskills. Focusing on regional books, outdoor books, trail guides, books from local publishers, alternative fiction, classics, and poetry.

Left.   **Phoenicia Hotel** (914-688-7500).   First opened in 1853, this hotel offers lodging, food, and drink. Upstairs are twenty rooms with A/C and private and shared baths, $45-$55/couple. The tavern looks much as it did in 1936, with a fireplace, pool table, games, dart board, an outdoor deck, and horseshoe pits, plus live entertainment on Friday nights and occasional karaoke. Snowshoes can be borrowed and fishing rods rented.   A great place to experience Phoenicia.
Also **PhoHo's**, serving lunch and light dinners with an emphasis on homemade. Charcoal grilled burgers, steak sandwiches, sliced steak, fish and chips, batter-dipped shrimp, homemade salsa, homemade rolls, specials with a Mexican flavor, and more. Dinner entrees up to $7. Closed Wednesday and Thursday. Open Friday and Saturday until midnight.

Left.   **Acorn Antiques** (914-688-7978).   Antiques, pottery, and gifts; country, Victorian, and Mission Oak furniture, plus contemporary furniture in the arts and crafts style.

Right.   **Phoenicia Auto Parts** (914-688-5786).   Parts Plus auto parts.

Left.   **Ricciardella Realty** (914-688-7233).   Real estate, tourism information, copies, fax.

Right.   **To Your Health** (914-688-7771).   Health foods, vitamins, herbs, natural and bulk foods.

Right. **A Divine Idea** (914-688-2101). Cards and gifts, many of which are created by local artists. Greeting cards, cassettes, clothing, accessories, antiques, jewelry, pottery, hand-blown and hand-etched glassware, copper angels, candles, kaleidoscopes, wind chimes, dried flower arrangements, and more.

Around the corner to the right, behind A Divine Idea, is **The Boardwalk**:
Dueling Spoons (914-688-7753). A gourmet shop featuring a line of gourmet food dressings for accenting meats and salads, making sauces and dips, etc. Also jams, jellies, sauces, seasonings, hot sauces, honeys, coffee, and organic coffee. Table linens, cook books, cutting boards, knives, gadgets, tea kettles, gifts, and more. Two TV monitors tuned to the Food Channel all day. It also has a cooking crisis hot line, 888-459-DUEL, offering cooking tips, recipes, how-to-use and how-to-make information, etc. Taste and toys for people who love to eat and love to cook.
The Peanut Gallery. An art gallery.

Left. Junction with **Church Street**:

> *Right. Home of the **Shandaken Theatrical Society** in the old IOOF 1887 building. Its spring production is always a musical and is held the last two weekends in May, and its fall production is either a comedy or light drama and is held the two weekends prior to Halloween. Always looking for new on- and behind-stage talent. Write P.O. Box 473, Phoenicia, NY 12464, for more info.*

> *Left. **F.S. Tube Rental** (914-688-7633). The original Phoenicia tube rentals. Rides start at the top of the rapids at the portal for a five-mile run. Tubes, rafts, tubes with seats, and transportation. $13 buys tube, helmet, life preserver rental, and transportation. $2 extra for sneaker rental. Memorial Day through Labor Day.*

End of Church Street coverage.

Left. Country Store and Kitchen (914-688-7283). Convenience store, Exxon gas, deli, home-cooked foods, out-of-town newspapers, ATM. Hot foods to go such as egg and bacon on English muffin, soup, chili, kielbasa, barbecued beef, macaroni and cheese, fried chicken, etc. Dinner specials, $4-$7, include chicken Parmigiana, spaghetti, roast beef or turkey with mashed potatoes and vegetable, etc.

Right. Brio's Pizzeria and Restaurant (914-688-5370). Wood-fired gourmet pizza plus a full menu offering breakfast, lunch, and dinner. Homemade breads and desserts, frozen yogurt. Burritos, pita, hot dogs, chili dogs, sandwiches, subs, burgers, etc., $2-$7. Dinners include rigatoni and sausage, prime rib, shell steak, $7-13.

Right. Sportsman's Bar and Grill (914-688-9922). Pool table, live entertainment.

Right. Phoenicia Films (914-688-7705). Video rentals.

Right. Ice Cream Station. Ice cream parlor, miniature golf. Memorial Day through Labor Day, weekends through Columbus Day.

Left. Modern (914-688-7226). Outlet store for children (newborn to size 14) and adult clothing designed and crafted in Phoenicia. Also gifts and post cards.

Right. Debra Jo's Unisex Hair Styling (914-688-5312). Wednesday through Saturday.

Left.   Kirk's Market (914-688-9932).   Groceries, meats, homegrown fruits and vegetables.

Right. Nest Egg (914-688-5851). Two floors of knick-knacks, collectibles, souvenirs. Woodstock Chimes, T-shirts, coon-skin caps, toys, waterproof cameras, sunscreen, post cards, maps, much more. Also holiday store.

000.3   Junction with **Bridge Street** on the right and **Mt. Ava Maria** on the left.

Turning left up **Mt. Ava Maria** yields:

Right. **Phoenicia Post Office** *(914-688-2224). ZIP 12464*

Left. **Benedictine Hospital Phoenicia Health Center** *(914-688-7513). Walk-ins usually accommodated; call first. Monday, Wednesday through Friday, 8-5; Tuesday 9-7; Saturday 9-2. X-ray available on Tuesday and Thursday.*

End of Mt. Ava Maria coverage.

Turning right onto **Bridge Street** yields the following:

Right. **Town Tinker Tube Rental** *(914-688-5553). Outfitters for tubing the Esopus Creek for either a three-mile, 1 ½-hour mellow run (good for beginners) or a three-mile, 1 2/3-hour rough ride for more excitement. Upstream travel is by bus, except that the return ride from the downstream mellow run is by train on weekends. Age 12 and up; Mid-May to Mid-September.*

000.1   *Right.* **Rubber Ducky Tube Rentals** *(914-688-2018). Tubing on the Esopus on either a mellow run for novices or an exciting run for the experienced tuber. Tubes with seats and handles, life jackets, and helmets, $10. Tube taxi is free. Picnic tables, stream side barbecue. Age 12 and up; May through September.*

Left. **Phoenicia Trailer Park** *(914-586-4109). Mostly seasonal travel trailers used by Esopus Creek fisher folk.*

*Left. Junction with **High Street**, down which is:*

000.2   *Left.* **Empire State Railway Museum** *(914-688-7501). Beautifully restored 1899 Ulster and*

Delaware Railroad station now on the National Register of Historic Places. Antique railway cars, photographs, artifacts, memorabilia, annually-changing historical exhibit. The station is a stop on the Catskill Mountain Railroad rail ride. An antique, 1910 Alco Consolidation-type steam locomotive is currently being restored in Kingston for future operation along the banks of the Ashokan Reservoir. Open weekends and holidays, Memorial Day through Columbus Day, 11:00-4:00. Donation suggested.

End of High Street coverage.

*000.3   Junction of Bridge Street with **Route 28**.*

End of Bridge Street coverage.

000.5   Left. **Phoenicia Forge Art Center** (914-688-2262). Non-profit art center and gallery showroom for bronze casting, blacksmithing, and welding, now closed due to snow-weight collapse of a building. Planned re-opening date unknown. Donations accepted.

000.7   Left. **Terrace Farm Nursery & Greenhouse** (914-688-7110). Flowers, plants, and garden supplies.

001.5   Left. Trailhead to summit of **Tremper Mountain** (2740'). This is a short but steep trail up the southern slope of Tremper Mountain. At the summit is an old steel fire tower which is currently closed to visitors, but which may be reopened in the future.

002.4   Right. **Uncle Pete's Recreation Park** (914-688-5000). On the banks of the Esopus Creek, 80 sites with water and electrical hookups. Trout fishing in the Esopus, playground, baseball field, volleyball, basketball, and horseshoes. Reservations taken. No pets. $21 for two adults. Additional charges for hookups, extra people, creek sites, etc.

003.7   Left.   **Zen Mountain Monastery** (914-688-2228).   A Zen Buddhist monastery in a bluestone and natural wood building. Public tours are available on the second Sunday of every month by advance request. Newcomers to Zen Buddhism can be introduced to and participate in meditation and services via a range of programs of a couple of hours, a weekend, or a week-long retreat. Call for information and reservations.

Crossing the **Beaver Kill**.

003.8   Junction with **NY 212** and **Wittenberg Road**. Turning left onto NY 212 takes you to **Willow, Lake Hill, Shady, Bearsville**, and **Woodstock**. Going straight across onto Wittenberg Road takes you to **Kenneth L. Wilson Public Campground, Bearsville**, and **Woodstock**. Turning right onto **NY 212** west takes you back to Route 28 in **Mt. Tremper**.

End of Main Street (CR 40) coverage.

NY 214 to Devil's Tombstone Public Campground

One of only two roads which charge north from Route 28 through the heart of the Catskills, NY 214 slowly climbs from an elevation of 800' in Phoenicia to 2,100' in the **Stony Clove Notch** ten miles ahead. The notch, just north of **Notch Lake**, passes between 3,855' **Plateau Mountain** to the east and 4,025' **Hunter Mountain** to the west. This is a beautiful drive anytime of the year, but especially during the first two weeks of October when the valley bursts with color.

Driving up **NY 214** takes you to the following:

Left. **Simpson Mini-Park**. Benches and picnic tables along the creek.

Right. **Craftsmen's Gallery** (914-688-2100). Mission oak furniture and accessories. Open weekends or by chance.

000.1   Right. **Claude's Bistro** (914-688-2561). French restaurant, cafe, bistro, and bed and breakfast. Comfortable restaurant with fireplace serves breakfast, lunch, and dinner. Dinner entrees include pork tenderloin peppercorn, beef bourguignon, rack of lamb with herbs, calves' liver raspberry vinegar, etc., $6-$19. In summer lunch (generally $5-$6) is served on a lovely porch cheered by fresh flower boxes. Cafe serves desserts and snacks. Bistro with fireplace serves late-night bistro menu. Upstairs are five rooms sharing two baths, $35-$45/couple including breakfast. A touch of France in Phoenicia.

000.2   Right. **Cobblestone Motel** (914-688-7871). Walk to Phoenicia's restaurants and shops from this fourteen-unit complex with rooms, efficiencies, and a three-bedroom cottage on three quiet acres surrounded by mountains. Big lawn; private, in-ground pool hidden by cedars; fresh flowers in the rooms in a quiet, country setting. Motel $49/couple, efficiencies $59, cottage $85. Weekly rates. Comfortable, accommodating, and personable. Joe and Michelle are my friends, so if you stop in, please give them my regards. Thanks.

000.9   Entering **Chichester**.

001.6   Left. **Hot Stuff** (914-688-7720). Blown-glass studio. Clear and colored glass vases, perfume bottles, glasses, pitchers, bowls, plates, candelabra, paper weights, Christmas ornaments, and custom work. The working studio is open from September through December; other times by appointment.

Left. Junction with **Park Road**, down which immediately on the right is **Maplewood Bed and Breakfast** (914-688-5433). A colonial house on a shady lawn under huge maple trees. Three guest rooms with traditional furnishings share two and one-half baths. TV lounge, swimming pool, large porch overlooking flower gardens. Open weekends and holidays all year. $65/couple with full breakfast.

Right. **Chichester Post Office** (914-688-7300). ZIP 12416.

002.0   Right. **Silver Creek Cottages** (914-688-9912). Five one- and two-bedroom, fully-supplied, housekeeping cottages on three acres on the creek offering peace and quiet, $55/two. Open year-round.

003.4   **Ulster County/Greene County** line.

004.2   Entering **Lanesville**.

         Right. **Timbercraft**. Chain saw-carved figures, bears, Indians, woodsmen, etc.

004.8   Right. **Lanesville Post Office** (914-688-5244). ZIP 12450.

005.0   Left. Junction with **Diamond Notch Road**. Trail to **Diamond Notch** (ascent 1,310', 3.0 miles), **Hunter Mountain Tower** (7.4), **West Kill Mountain** summit (5.8). At the summit of Hunter Mountain is an old steel fire tower which is currently closed to visitors, but which may be reopened in the future.

007.7   Right. Junction with **Notch Inn Road**:

         *000.1   Right. **Steve's Campsites** (914-688-7062). Fifty-seven grassy and wooded sites for tents, pop-ups and vans. Fireplaces, picnic tables, and showers. $5/person/night. Open Memorial Day through Columbus Day.*

         End of Notch Inn Road coverage.

008.8   Right. **Devil's Tombstone Public Campground** (914-688-7160). Twenty-four sites for tents and R/Vs in the forest at the height of the pass between Hunter Mountain and Plateau Mountain. Picnicking, hiking; fishing in Notch Lake.

009.1   Right. Trail to **Plateau Mountain Lookout** (1.2 miles), **Mink Hollow Lean-to** (4.5), **Prediger Road** (10.3).

         Left. Parking lot at **Notch Lake**. Trail to **Devil's Acre Lean-to** (ascent 1,600', 2.2 miles), **Hunter Mountain** (ascent 2,029', 3.8 mi.), **Diamond Notch Falls** (4.4), **Spruceton Road** via **Westkill**

Mountain (7.2). In the wintertime this parking lot may be full of cars when people are ice climbing on the mammoth icicles which cling to the rock faces of the notch.

End of NY 214 coverage.

Phoenicia to Big Indian

As you head west from Phoenicia on Route 28 you plunge deeper into the Catskills. The mountains become higher, the countryside becomes more rugged, and the towns become smaller. Pre-revolutionary settlers in this area engaged in logging, furniture making, and leather tanning. After 1875 the Ulster and Delaware Railroad contributed to settlement and tourism. The Catskill Forest Preserve was established in 1904 to preserve the land and its natural resources. Encompassing over 274,000 acres and growing, the forever-wild lands of the preserve comprise more than one-third of the land within the Catskill Park, the other two-thirds being privately owned. Route 28 bisects the preserve, crossing its "blue line" boundary at Kingston on the east and at Highmount on the west. Phoenicia is almost perfectly centered within the preserve.

024.0   Right(left) Junction with **NY 214** to **Phoenicia** and **Tannersville**.

024.4   Left(right) **Ray's Cabins** (914-688-5410). A cluster of six nostalgic one- and two-bedroom tourist cabins set under tall pine trees. Built in the early 1900's, these seasonal cabins provide clean, basic lodging. (Closed after deer-hunting season in the fall.) Laundry room. Prices range from $40 to $80 per night, $200-$300 per week.

Left(right) Junction with **Woodland Valley Road** to **Romer Mountain** (site of the old Simpson Ski Slope) and **Woodland Valley Public Campground**:

000.1   *Crossing the* **Esopus Creek** *where you can "tube the Esopus" (see Chapter 7,* Phoenicia *and Appendix B,* Equipment Rental Sources, *for tube rental information), and where annual canoe and kayak races are conducted twice a year.*

000.2   *"T" junction with High Street Extension to the left. Coverage continues to the right on* **Woodland Valley Road.**

Left. **Saddle Up in Phoenicia** *(914-688-7336, 800-258-2624). Horseback riding on 85 acres on Romer Mountain Park (the old Simpson Ski Slope). One-hour trail rides along logging and ski trails, $25; pony rides for children, $4. Weekends Memorial Day through Fourth of July, then daily through Labor Day, then weekends through Columbus Day.*

000.3   *Right.* **Woodland Valley Public Fishing Stream** *parking.*

000.8   *Left.* **Woodland Valley Public Fishing Stream** *parking.*

001.8   *Left.* **Bethken's Antiques** *(914-688-5620). A little five-room house full, full, full of little things that have been collected over twenty-five years. China, vases, lamps, flatware, kitchenware, glassware, depression glass, stoneware, postcards, cards, books, and more, some of which is second hand, some old, and some antique. Almost a museum. Ring the bell for service.*

002.8   *Right.* **Hideaway Campsite** *(914-688-5109). Forty-eight tent and R/V sites with full hook-ups deep in the forested wilderness, away from phones, traffic, and the typical family camping environment. Quiet, basic, rustic camping; showers planned. Tents, $10; full hook-ups, $15. May through September.*

004.4   Left. Trailhead to Terrace Lean-to (3.2 miles), Wittenberg Mountain (3.4), Cornell Mountain (4.3), and Slide Mountain (5.9).

004.5   Right. Trailhead parking for hiking trails to Giant Ledge (3.8 miles), Panther Mountain (5.6), Slide Mountain (7.4), and Fox Hollow (10.5).

004.7   Left. Woodland Valley Public Campground (914-688-7647). A state campground since the early 1930's. Seventy-two tent and trailer sites near the end of the road nestled in the clove of the mountains. Picnic area, showers, and dumping station. Activities include hiking, fishing, and wading in the stream.

End of Woodland Valley Road coverage.

Left(right) **The Inn at Woodland Valley** (914-688-5711). Fine dining in a warm and cozy restaurant with fireplace. The chefs' varied cuisine features pasta, pork, filet mignon, seafood cassalet, lobster, escargot, ostrich, and more, $10-$23. Homemade breads and desserts, outdoor dining by the water garden. Open seven days for dinner, Friday through Sunday lunch and brunch, Sunday breakfast. Serving town and country since 1933.

024.5   Left(right) **Phoenicia Motor Village** (914-688-7772). Motel and cottages open year-round. Five-unit motel ($45/double) plus five efficiency cabins ($250-$325/week).

026.0   Right(left) **Tackle Shack** (914-688-7780). Live bait, guns, ammo, fishing, and hunting supplies. Large collection of dry flies, wet flies, and streamers. Custom rods from ultra light fly rods to offshore salt water rods. Entrance on back porch. Seasonal.

Left(right) **Yvonne's** (914-688-7340). Homemade, mostly French country cuisine with all natural ingredients served in a simple, country casual setting. Order from the menu or enjoy the buffet. Entrees usually $14-$17; buffet $15; early-bird buffet (4-5:30 PM) $10. Inside and outside dining, plus take-out. Open May through

October (weekends only spring and fall) or by special request. Also catering.

026.3   Right(left) **Margo's Hungarian/German Restaurant and Sports Bar** (914-688-7102). Authentic Hungarian and German home cooking by Margo and her sister Maria, who each have over forty years of cooking experience. Good meals with good gravies at a good price in an immaculate, varnished-pine restaurant. Sports bar has beautiful mahogany bar, pool table, games, large TV. Dinner $8-$14. Daily special from 5 to 6 PM at $11. Open every day.

026.6   **Allaben/Shandaken** line.

026.7   Left(right) **Esopus Creek Public Fishing Stream parking**.

Right(left) **Forest Preserve Access parking**.

026.8   Left(right) **Copperhood Inn & Spa** (914-688-2460). A country inn and spa on forty acres along the Esopus Creek with a pedestrian swing bridge to a private island, hiking trails, and tracked cross-country ski trails. Thirteen rooms and seven suites, some with balconies overlooking the creek, some with Jacuzzis, all with private bath, and furnished with charming antiques and reproductions. Heated indoor 60' pool, sauna, Jacuzzi, tennis court, and a dining room with the famous open fireplace and its copper hood. Other amenities include outdoor dining, a bar, conference room, library, gym, and treatment rooms. Open all year by reservation only, $150-$300/couple, including breakfast and dinner of international cuisine. Spa services are open to the public and include massage, herbal rubs, body scrubs, reflexology, and more. Country elegance and sophistication along the Esopus.

027.0   Left(right) **Blue Barn Country Shops** (914-688-2161). Furniture, home interiors, accessories, and antiques. Custom upholstery, draperies, and slipcovers. Made-to-order country furniture. Closed Wednesday; closed Tuesday through Thursday in winter.

027.3   Left(right) **Allaben Ray's Service Station** (914-688-5155). Auto service, towing.

Crossing the outlet of the **Shandaken Tunnel**. Called the **portal** by local fisher folks, this is the outlet of the eighteen-mile-long aqueduct which brings water from the **Schoharie Reservoir** beneath the Catskill Mountains to the **Esopus Creek** for eventual flow into the **Ashokan Reservoir** and on to **New York City**.

027.6 Left(right) **Loretta Charles' Natural Wood Grill** (914-688-2550). Fine dining in a rustic setting with a corner fireplace and pretty, welcoming, rustically elegant decor accented by fresh flowers. The blackboard menu lists an ever-changing selection of mouth-watering American-contemporary appetizers and entrees such as Prince Edward Island cultivated mussels with garlic red sauce; warm goat cheese salad; hickory-wood-grilled rib eye steak with green peppercorn sauce; wood-grilled and lightly smoked duck roast with lemon, honey, peach sauce, and many more. Dinner (entrees $14-$18), Saturday and Sunday lunch ($4-$8).

028.5 Left(right) Junction with **Fox Hollow Road**:

*001.6   Right. **Fox Hollow Trailhead Parking Area**. Trail to Fox Hollow Lean-to (.4 mile), Panther Mountain (4.9), Giant Ledge (6.6), Woodland Valley Parking Area (10.1).*

End of Fox Hollow Road coverage.

Right(left) **R & R Auto Supply** (914-688-5031). NAPA auto parts.

028.6 Entering(leaving) **Shandaken**.

028.8 Left(right) **Mechanic on Wheels** (914-688-7109). Automobile air conditioning repairs.

029.0 Left(right) **Ford's Garage** (914-688-5474) . Automobile repairs.

Right(left) **Lamp Lite Motor Lodge** (914-688-7130). Well-kept motel with four rooms ($40) and three efficiencies with kitchenettes ($50). Clean, modest, comfortable lodging. Cable TV.

029.1   Right(left) Junction with **NY 42** to **Hunter**. NY 42 follows **Bushnellsville Creek** north, and is one of only two roads to go north through the center of the northern Catskills, passing through **Deep Notch** at 1,900' above sea level, with 3,537' **Halcott Mountain** to the west and 3,565' **Balsam Mountain** to the east. NY 42 yields the following:

*000.1   Right. **Shandaken Post Office** (914-688-5220). 12480.*

*000.3   Right. **Glenbrook Park** alongside **Bushnellsville Creek**. Picnic tables, swing set, baseball diamond.*

*000.8   Right. **Auberge des 4 Saisons** (914-688-2223). A French country restaurant and inn with 28 rooms in three buildings. Three-story chalet houses sixteen rooms, each with balcony. Bar, fireplace, volleyball court, tennis court, and in-ground pool on sixty acres of lawns and forest nestled in a sharp mountain valley. French proprietor has been a chef in Paris, London, and New York. First-class menu served on Limoges china. Dinner $15-$23, rooms $65-$225. Wonderful French atmosphere.*

*002.6   Right. **Mountain Brook Inn** (914-688-2755). Friendly bar with lounging area, pool table, and dart board, whose motto is "Come as a stranger, leave as a friend."*

*002.7   Right. **Ramble Brook House** (914-688-5784). Bed and breakfast in country setting with trout stream and mountain view adjacent to state lands. Two rooms share a bath and one suite has a large, private bath. Some private decks. Full country breakfast. $55-$85/couple. Gracious, understated elegance.*

*002.9   **Ulster/Greene** county line.*

*003.7   Right. **Forest Preserve Access Parking**.*

End of NY 42 coverage.

029.9   Right(left) **Shandaken Inn** down **Golf Course Road** (914-688-5100). Refined quietude and privacy on forty acres of lawns and forest along the Esopus creek. Built in the 1870s as a dairy barn, and formerly a golf club and then a ski lodge, this graciously rustic inn houses eleven guestrooms, most with private bath, and is open Friday through Sunday only. Swimming pool, tennis, and fishing on the property. Per-day price of $195/couple includes breakfast and dinner. Closed April and December.

031.9   Left(right) **Forest Preserve Access Parking**.

032.0   Left(right) **Big Indian Trading Post** (914-254-4238). Native American crafts, much locally made. Tepees, kachinas, moccasins, blankets, artwork, pottery, jewelry, beads, music, and dream catchers. Chain saw bears, souvenirs, and gifts.

032.1   Left(right) Junction with **Oliverea Road** (CR 47) to **Oliverea**. See Chapter 9, *Oliverea Road (CR 47)*.

Oliverea Road (CR 47)

Turn left(right) onto **Oliverea Road (CR 47)** from Route 28 at **Big Indian**.

000.0   Left. **Morra's Market** (914-254-4649). Grocery store, deli, cold cuts, and fax service.

000.5   Right. Junction with **Lost Clove Road**:

   *000.1   Left. Junction with **Cruikshank Road**, down which 0.3 mile on the right is **Big Indian Springs** (914-254-5905), a large, sprawling, older bed and breakfast on 37 peaceful acres with a swimming pool, tennis court, and pond with a rowboat. Usually there are five guest rooms with shared and private baths, but with other rooms a total of 40 people can be accommodated. Wrap-around porch, fireplace; full breakfast; $85/two. Children and pets welcome.*

   *001.3   **Lost Clove Trailhead parking** area. Trail to **Belleayre Mountain Lean-to** (1.4 miles), **Belleayre Mountain**, (3,420', 1.8), **Hirschland Lean-to** (2.3), **Balsam Mountain** (4.0), and **Belleayre Mountain Ski Center** (2.6). The Lost Clove Trail also provides access to the **Big Indian Wilderness**, 33,500 acres of Catskill Forest Preserve lands in northwest Ulster County offering hiking, primitive camping, snowshoeing, hunting, fishing, and trapping. Camping permits are required if staying more than three* *consecutive nights at the same site, or for groups of ten for any number of nights.* Contact *the New York State Department of Environmental Conservation in New Paltz on 914-256-3000 for information.*

End of Lost Clove Road coverage.

002.0   Entering(leaving) **Oliverea.**

002.4   Right.   **Cold Spring Lodge** (914-254-5711).   Quaint and charming, family-run lodging on forty acres.   Individual rooms with private baths in renovated barn, $50/two; plus two- and three-bedroom cabins with fireplaces, $60-$35/person/night in winter, $575/week in summer.   Restaurant with fireplace and A/C offers contemporary American selections such as steaks, chops, veal, seafood, and fresh lobster from the tank; $9-$16.   Also child-friendly menu and dining by the waterwheel on a screened deck.   Bar, rec room, pool table, games, and swimming pool.

002.8   Right.   Junction with **McKinley Hollow Road**:

*000.9   Left.   **Trailhead parking** for hiking trails into the **Big Indian Wilderness**, and to **McKinley Hollow Lean-to** (.4 mile), **Balsam Mountain** (2.6 miles, 3,600'), **Rider Hollow Lean-to** (3.1).*

*Right.   **Mountain Gate Lodge** (914-254-6000, 800-733-0344).   An Indian restaurant and lodge on forty acres at the end of a dead-end road, nestled in a hollow with forested mountains rising steeply on all sides.   Large lawns, heated swimming pool, pavilion, and game room.   The Indian restaurant is open to the public and serves breakfast, lunch, and dinner, with dinner entrees $7-$17.   Belleayre Mountain ski packages available.   Lodging $105/two, including breakfast and dinner.   Remote, secluded, and truly a gate to the mountains and Catskill wilderness.*

End of McKinley Hollow Road coverage.

003.5   Left. **Slide Mountain Forest House** (914-254-5365). Alpine-style chalets and rooms and the **Forsthaus Restaurant and Cafe** in a manicured country setting. Outdoor swimming pool, tennis, volleyball, shuffleboard, basketball half court, trout ponds, bar, lounge, and beautiful lawns. A dance hall is available for private parties. The three housekeeping chalets (one-, four-, and five-bedroom) have kitchens and are open year-round. The twenty rooms, most with private bath, are operated as a country inn bed and breakfast. The restaurant serves German continental cuisine, with dinner entrees $10-$15. Open Memorial weekend through the middle of October, with the exception of the chalets, which are open all year. Flexible lodging/meal arrangements. Chalets are $130-$350/night, and the rooms are $50-$75/couple/night, full breakfast included. Traditional German lodging and dining in the forest.

003.7   Right. Junction with **Burnham Hollow Road**:

000.2   *Left. **Alpine Inn** (914-254-5026). A Swiss-style inn on a Catskill mountain side. With its commanding views of the mountains and valley, and its sixty years of Swiss family ownership, this squeaky clean inn is well named. The perfectly manicured grounds, chalet-style buildings with large decks, Swiss/German dining and often European clientele add to the Alpine flavor. Twenty-two air-conditioned rooms with private bath, TV and phone; large sitting room with fireplace; and swimming pool. Lodging rates are $67-$97 per room, without meals, or $61-$80 per person, breakfast and dinner included. The restaurant is open to the public by reservation, offering $22-$28 prix fixe dinners. Alpine elegance in the Catskills.*

003.9   Right. **Brookside Cottages** (914-254-6003). Office on left side of road. Thirteen housekeeping cottages (bring your own towels and soap) with fireplaces and outdoor fire rings on seven acres, with large lawn, large swimming pool, horseshoes, handball wall, swing set, basketball, volleyball, shuffleboard, and bacci ball. Pets welcome. $80/couple, $335-$355/week.

005.2   Right. **Valley View** (914-254-5117). Quiet and home-like lodging with great lawns, huge trees, swimming pool, and farm animals (horses, goats, chickens, ducks, and geese). Twenty-six rooms with private and shared baths in three buildings, plus two housekeeping cabins. Main building has a large front porch, cuckoo clocks, a community TV, a fireplace, and a pool table. The dining room serves three home-style meals per day. (Lunch in September through June is a pack lunch, popular with hikers and skiers). Proprietress says her husband is "famous for his mashed potatoes." $90/couple/day including three meals. Closed for the month of March.

007.4   Right. **Giant Ledge Trailhead Parking** for hiking trails to **Giant Ledge** (1.5 miles), **Panther Mountain** (3.3), and **Woodland Valley Public Campground** (3.4). Giant Ledge is one of the best hiking values in the Catskills, providing breathtaking views from 3,200 feet of many mountains and requiring only one and one-half miles of moderately strenuous (mostly at the beginning) hiking.

008.0   Left. Lake Winnisook. Private property. Just north of this lake, at an elevation of 2,648 feet, Oliverea Road passes over the high point in the notch between Slide Mountain on the east and Hemlock Mountain and Spruce Mountain to the west. This notch marks the divide between the Hudson River basin and the Delaware River basin.

009.3   Left. **Slide Mountain Trailhead Parking** for hiking trails to **Slide Mountain** (2.7 miles, 4180', the highest in the Catskills), **Denning Lean-to** (4.4), **Cornell Mountain** (4.9, 3,860') and **Wittenberg Mountain.** (5.8, 3,780'), **Terrace Lean-to** (8.0), and the **Woodland Valley Campground** (9.7).

End of Oliverea Road coverage.

Big Indian to Pine Hill

032.1   Junction with **CR 47**:

To the left(right), **CR 47** is also known as **Oliverea Road** and goes to **Oliverea**. See Chapter 9, *Oliverea Road (CR 47)*.

To the right(left), **CR 47** is also known as **Firehouse Road**, and takes you to:

*000.4   Left. **The Weyside** (914-254-5484). This is a spotless, white, Victorian guest house with black trim on beautifully manicured lawns that you can see across the Esopus Creek from Route 28 as you round the bend south of Big Indian. Efficiency cottages and a private lake complete the pristine setting. Swimming, trout fishing, basketball, badminton, lawn furniture, table tennis, swings, and bicycles. Five rooms with private baths, $40-$50/couple; two-bedroom cottage $300/week; three-bedroom cottage $400/week. May through October.*

End of Firehouse Road (CR 47) coverage.

Right(left) **Val D'Isere Inn and Restaurant Francais** (914-254-4646). Fine French dining and lodging. Four guest rooms with private baths, $65/two/night including continental breakfast. The restaurant serves mixed classic French and nouvelle cuisine with a comprehensive menu plus daily specials, $14-$22, with a ten percent discount before 6 PM. Refined yet relaxed and comfortable ambiance. Authentically French. Closed Monday and Tuesday. Also Trailways bus stop.

Right(left) **Big Indian Service Center** (914-254-4000). Gulf gas, auto service, emergency road service, towing. Open until 5 PM. Closed Thursdays.

Left(right) **Big Indian Post Office** (914-254-4036). ZIP 12410.

032.2   Left(right) **Big Indian Park.** Parking area, pavilion, picnic tables, basketball hoop, playground, and portable toilet. A perfect place for a picnic lunch break.

Crossing **Esopus Creek.**

032.5   Left(right) Former Jake Moon restaurant and cafe, closed at time of printing.

033.3   Left(right) **Remember the Past** (914-254-5034). A general line of antiques with an emphasis on oak, mahogany, and walnut furniture; silver; and collectibles.

033.6   Right(left) **Starlite Motel** (914-254-4449). Efficiencies, cable TV, and gifts. Eight units, two of which are efficiencies, $44-$49. Neat, tidy, and clean, with chairs out front. Pets permitted. Driveway off Rose Mountain Road.

033.7   Right(left) **Mystical Visions** (914-254-4714). "All Things Spiritual". Tarot cards, readings, candles, oil, books, and accessories. Open Thursday through Sunday.

033.8   Right(left) **Alpine Delicatessen** (914-254-5827). Deli and groceries. Homemade soups, salads, and sandwiches; hot breakfasts and lunches. Inside tables. Open every day, 6-6.

034.1   **Big Indian/Pine Hill** line.

Left(right) Junction with the eastern end of **Friendship Manor Road** to **Belleayre Mountain Day Use Area** (914-254-5600). On stocked Pine Hill Lake, this park offers rowboat rentals, beach swimming, picnicking, volleyball courts, horseshoe pits, and fishing for brook, brown, and rainbow trout. A new covered bridge spans the entrance. Pine Hill Lake is only one-third of its former size, the dam to the former lake having been washed out in a flood in 1951.

034.4   Left(right) Junction with the western end of **Friendship Manor Road** to **Belleayre Mountain Day Use Area** as described in previous paragraph.

034.7   Left(right) Junction with south end of **Main Street** (another section of old Route 28) of hamlet of **Pine Hill**. See Chapter 11, *Pine Hill*.

The covered bridge at the entrance to Belleayre Mountain Day Use Area stands faithfully through the winter awaiting next summer's visitors. (DeWitt)

11

Pine Hill

Like Phoenicia, the hamlet of Pine Hill was settled by loggers and tanners just prior to 1800. It straddles old Route 28, which replaced the plank road from Kingston. An Ulster and Delaware Turnpike stage coach stop was located at the site of the Colonial Inn, and tourists endured the seven-hour ride from Kingston to bask in the clear mountain air. In 1872 the Ulster and Delaware Rail Road brought more people to the area. Pine Hill was incorporated as a village in 1895, when local employment focused on tanning, quarrying, and serving the guests of about thirty hotels in the area. At the time Pine Hill had a population of 800, large enough to support two newspapers, the *Pine Hill Sentinel* and the *Pine Hill Optic*. In 1987 the village of Pine Hill disincorporated into the town of Shandaken.

Pine Hill is tucked beneath Belleayre Mountain and offers access to hunting, fishing, hiking, biking, skiing, snowboarding, antiquing and leaf peeping. It is usually a sleepy place, but comes awake in the fall during the foliage and hunting seasons, and in the winter during ski season. Belleayre Mountain Ski Center, one of New York's three state-owned ski areas, is just ten minutes away, and an old ski trail comes down from the mountain to Pine Hill behind the Colonial Inn. Plattekill Mountain, offering skiing and chair-lift-supported mountain biking, is only ten miles away.

000.0   Junction of **Route 28** and the east end of **Main Street** in **Pine Hill**. Turn left(right) onto Main Street.

000.2   Right.   **Target Transmissions** (914-254-5938).   General automobile service, specializing in transmissions. Towing.

000.3   Right. **Pine Hill Arms Hotel** (914-254-9811, 800-932-2446). Accommodations, restaurant, saloon. A country inn more than 110 years old which has 25 rooms with private baths, some with Jacuzzi. Hot tub, sauna, fireplace, in-ground pool, and greenhouse dining room. Dinners to $15, Sunday brunch, and early-bird specials. Package plan for skiers. Rooms are $45-55 off-season. Weekend ski packages with and without lift tickets from $110/person for two nights and three meals. Other packages available. Entertainment and dancing on Saturday nights.

Left. **Parking lot.**

Left. **Bellayre Hostel** (914-254-4200). Up the hill to the left at the rear of the parking lot. Bunk beds, $9-12/night; private, lockable rooms with double beds, $20 per night; cabins, $35. Guests provide own housekeeping. Communal kitchen house, recreation hall, pool table, pin-ball machine, piano, barbecue pits and grills, and bicycles.

Left. **Cafe Belleayre** (914-254-5911). Breakfast and lunch. Omelettes, pancakes, French toast, home-baked muffins, sandwiches, burgers, melts, grilled sandwiches, and more. Daily breakfast and lunch specials.

Right. **Pine Hill Post Office** (914-254-4756). ZIP 12465

Right. **La Pequena Shoppe.** Gift shop. Fine needlework, antique linens, creative crafts, and hand-painted cards.

000.4   Right. **Pine Hill Indian Restaurant** (914-254-6666). Tastefully decorated Indian restaurant with comprehensive menu of appetizers, soups, and vegetarian and non-vegetarian entrees; $7-$17. Sunday brunch buffet, $7; Monday through Thursday lunch special; Tuesday all-you-can-eat dinner buffet. Bar, and take-out service. Also motel with rooms with shared bath from $45.

Right. Junction with **Elm Street**:

*Left. **Morton Memorial Library** (914-254-4222). In a beautiful, old, gray stone building which appears as if it will last forever. Open Tuesday, Thursday and Saturday, 2-6 PM.*

*000.1   Left. **Cloud Spinners** (914-254-4838). Antique furniture for sale plus custom hardwood furniture built. Custom furniture created along the styles of Shaker arts and crafts, Greene and Greene, and more. Open seven days, but call ahead if coming from afar.*

*000.2   Junction with **Route 28**.*

End of Elm Street coverage.

Left. **The Colonial Inn** (914-254-5577). The oldest building in Pine Hill, with the original part having been constructed just prior to 1800, with a number of expansions carrying it through an inn to a hotel. In the 1860s it was a toll booth for horse and carriage, and has been offering rooms and food to the public ever since. Currently it houses eight rooms with private baths and three adjoining rooms with a central bath. Spring and summer, $45/two with breakfast.   Fall and winter, two-night weekend packages including three meals, $170/couple.   Restaurant open to public, Saturday buffet includes shrimp, fish, roast beef, ham, chicken, pasta, and more, $9. Lodging and Belleayre lift ticket packages. Popular with skiers, hunters, fishermen, leaf peepers, hiking clubs, and antique hunters.

000.5   Right. Junction with **Academy Street**:

*000.1   Right. **Town of Shandaken Historical Museum** (914-254-4460). In the old schoolhouse at the corner of School Lane, this building is on the National Register of Historic Places. It is a depository of many artifacts of past life in the Pine Hill area and Delaware County. (The Ulster/-Delaware county line is only a mile west of Pine Hill.). Local history is retained in old books, maps, postcards, photographs, and newspaper articles. The collection of* *photographs of the old Delaware County hotels is amazing, as is the tome, "A Commemorative Biographical Record of Ulster County, New York, containing biographical sketches of prominent and representative citizens and of many of their early settled families. Illustrated. 1896." This book is five inches thick and deserves its 27-word title! Substantial genealogy section. Open Thursday and Friday, 11-4; Saturday and Sunday, 1-4. Admission is free.*

End of Academy Street coverage.

001.0   Junction of west end of **Main Street** with **Route 28**.

End of Pine Hill coverage.

Pine Hill to Fleischmanns

Between Pine Hill and Fleischmanns Route 28 climbs up and over the pass between Belleayre Mountain and Rose Mountain, leaves Ulster County for Delaware County, and leaves the Hudson River watershed and enters the Susquehanna River watershed. At the top of the pass a road goes off to the left to Belleayre Mountain Ski Center, one of only three state-run ski areas in New York, the other two being Gore Mountain in North Creek (see Chapter 36, *North Creek to Warrensburg*) and Whiteface Mountain in the northern Adirondacks. Belleayre was established in 1949 and was the site of the first chair lift in the state. In early 1998, five million dollars of improvements and expansions to the ski area, including a new quad chair, were announced. And in 1999 Belleayre will celebrate its fiftieth birthday with various celebrations. For more information, call the ski center on 914-254-5600. For lodging information in the Belleayre area, call the Lodging and Tourist Information Service at the Belleayre Mountain Ski Center on 800-431-4555.

034.7   Left(right) Junction with south end of **Main Street** (another section of old Route 28) of hamlet of **Pine Hill**. See Chapter 11, *Pine Hill*.

034.9   Right(left) **Belleayre Plaza Shopping Center** (914-254-4753). A miniature department store with a little bit of everything. Beer, soda, grocery, deli, pizza, cold and hot sandwiches, New York newspapers, video rentals, video games, hardware, fishing supplies, auto supplies, greeting cards, T-shirts, and more. Also Mobil gas, a liquor store, and the **Plaza Laundromat**.

035.1   Junction with **Elm Street** to **Pine Hill**. Coverage of the hamlet of Pine Hill begins at south end of **Main Street** 0.3 mile to the south.

Turn right on **Elm Street** for:

> *Right.* ***Rosemount Real Estate*** *(914-254-5454).*

> *000.1   Left. Junction with Academy Street. Continue straight ahead.*

> *000.5   Left.* ***Birch Creek Bed and Breakfast*** *winter entrance. See description at Route 28 entrance below.*

End of Elm Street coverage.

035.7   Right(left) **Birch Creek Bed and Breakfast** (914-254-5222). Formerly the private residence of local architect Henry Morton, this powerful and proud 100-year-old house is virtually an architecture and antiques museum. The interior is voluptuously warm with wood. The seven bedrooms with private baths and the common areas are furnished in 18th-century antiques, including a 150-year-old billiards table and an upright piano. The grandest bedroom even has a spa bath. A full gourmet breakfast is served each morning either in the impressive dining room or on the large porch. Twenty-three acres of grounds include hiking trails and trout streams. Two mortarless keystone bridges are noteworthy. $75-$125. In winter the Route 28 entrance is closed; enter from Birch Creek Road in Pine Hill.

035.8   Left(right) Junction with north end of **Main Street** of hamlet of **Pine Hill**. See Chapter 11, *Pine Hill.*

Pine Hill/Highmount town line.

036.1   Right(left) Junction with **Highlands Road**:

> *000.1   Left.* ***Gateway Lodge*** *(914-254-4084). Seven-room bed and breakfast just across Route 28 from road to Belleayre Mountain Ski Center. Great views, woodstove, piano,*

seasonal above-ground swimming pool, and private baths. $65/couple. Pets allowed.

End of Highlands Road coverage.

036.4   Left(right) Junction with **CR 49A** to **Belleayre Mountain Ski Center** to the left and **Owl's Nest Road** to the right. At this point Route 28 crosses the divide between the Hudson and Delaware River basins.

Turning left(right) onto **CR 49A** takes you to:

000.0   Right. **Highmount Post Office** *(914-254-4754). ZIP 12441.*

00.1   Right. **Belleayre Ski Shop** *(914-254-5338). Downhill and cross-country skis, boards, boots, clothing, accessories, ski and snowboard rentals, etc. October-April.*

000.2   Left. Junction with entrance to **Belleayre Mountain Cross Country Ski Center** *(914-254-5600, 800-942-6904). Free novice to expert cross-country skiing on four trails totaling nine kilometers. X-C skis can be rented at the Belleayre Mountain Ski Center lodges' ski shops.*

000.4   Left. **Belleayre Mountain Ski Center** *(914-254-5600, 800-942-6904). Lower parking lot of this family-oriented, New York state-owned ski center, providing access to the excellent and long novice slopes and the Discovery (lower) Lodge. The upper parking lot and lodge are one-half mile farther up the road. Belleayre offers 33 slopes and trails, eight lifts, cross-country trials, a snowboard obstacle park, and half-pipe. Each lodge has a cafeteria, cocktail lounge, ski shop, rental shop, ski school, and fireplaces. The Sunset Lodge at the 3,429' summit has a snack bar.*

Right. Junction with **Gunnison Road:**

*000.4   Left.   **Wild Acres Hotel and Motel** (914-254-9868). Continue up the 0.3-mile-long driveway. Originally built in 1905 as a summer "cottage" for $135,000, a 90-year-old mansion on 88 mountainside acres houses the living room and dining room for the 27 motel rooms in the carriage house and two newer buildings. The exquisite mansion is beautifully constructed throughout, with chestnut paneling, pocket doors, and natural wood floors. The view from the large porch and lawns is breathtaking. A swimming pool is available for seasonal use. Room rates are $70-$75/couple without meals, and $65-$70/person including two meals a day. A lovely country retreat.*

End of Gunnison Road coverage.

*000.9   Left.   **Belleayre Mountain Ski Center** (914-254-5600, 800-942-6904). Upper parking lot provides access to all slopes, snowboard obstacle park and half-pipe, and the Overlook (upper) Lodge. First opened in 1949, Belleayre had the first chairlift in New York State and is the oldest surviving ski area in the Catskills. Today Belleayre's slopes and trails are 91 percent covered by snowmaking. Belleayre also hosts a summer concerts series, and an Octoberfest on Columbus Day weekend with sky rides, a huge crafts fair, and more. Call for details.*

End of CR 49A coverage.

Turning right(left) onto **Owl's Nest Road** takes you to:

*000.5   Left.   **The Owl's Nest** (914-254-5917). Rustic restaurant, bar, and chalet with one of the greatest mountain views in the Catskills, on the site of the 1881 Grand Hotel. Old stone walls can still be seen about the grounds. Around the turn of the century this old hotel had portable liquor bars which were moved back and forth across the Dela-*

ware/Ulster county line to take greatest advantage of the constantly-changing county temperance laws. Today the restaurant is open for dinner Friday and Saturday evenings, and Sunday afternoons and evenings. Menu of American cuisine features steaks, chops, chicken, pasta, and seafood, $12-$18, including the salad/soup/shrimp bar. The housekeeping chalet sleeps four in two bedrooms, $80/two, $120/four.

End of Owl's Nest Road coverage.

036.6   **Ulster/Delaware** county line and **Shandaken/Middletown** town line.

Delaware County is home to hills and mountains, rivers and streams, lakes and reservoirs. Its terrain is so varied that every mile of every road offers the traveler a different vista. Delaware County is rural, the largest settlement being county seat Delhi (population 3,064), 31 miles to the northwest.

037.6   Entering village of **Fleischmanns**.

037.8   Right(left) Junction with east end of **Main Street** into the village of **Fleischmanns**. See Chapter 13, *Fleischmanns*.

A solitary motorcyclist descends the long Route 28 hill from Highmount to Fleischmanns.

Fleischmanns

Formerly known as Griffin Corners in honor of a local lawyer and businessman, the name was changed in 1913 to honor another local resident and benefactor of a village park, Julius Fleischmanns, of yeast and whiskey fame. The village straddles old Route 28, a plank road continuation of the plank toll road that stretched all the way from Kingston. In the late 19th century Fleischmanns developed into a summer boarding town. During the 1940s, the wintertime population of 500 exploded to a summertime population of 10,000. As automobile travel increased, rail travel decreased, and summer vacationers flew to Europe, the boarding houses closed, many having been burned by arsonists. Two old houses which are still active today are the Highland Fling Inn and Oppenheimer's Regis Hotel. Today Fleischmanns is a popular summer resort area for second-home owners and Hasidim.

Fleischmanns appears to be a sleepy little village, but occasionally big things happen here. On January 19, 1996, many inches of rain quickly followed a three-foot snowfall, creating the flood of '96. Many buildings in Fleischmanns, as well as Margaretville and Andes, were flooded. Many people lost many of their possessions. Then, in the summer of 1996, Fleischmanns was the setting for the filming of "The Tears of Julian Poe," with Christian Slater. Who knows what events over the next few years will make their way into Fleischmanns' history books.

Fleischmanns is a walker's village, having most of its lodging and businesses housed in old Victorian buildings. Park benches are abundant along the length of Main Street. And the village maintains a heated swimming pool, a softball field, soccer field, basketball court, tennis courts, and playground on Wagner Avenue.

Junction of Route 28 and the east end of Fleischmanns' **Main Street**. The village of **Fleischmanns** is described in a westerly direction from this east end of Main Street.

Right. **Belleayre Realty** (914-254-4111).

Left. Village **parking lot**.

000.1   Left. **Fleischmanns Realty** (914-254-4848).

000.4   Right. Junction with **Lake Street**. Turn right for:

*000.4   Right. **Oppenheimer's Regis Hotel** (914-254-5080, 800-468-3598). Large, family hotel with many activities overlooking Lake Switzerland. Ninety-seven rooms with private and shared baths, heated swimming pool with scheduled swimming, children's playground, basketball, tennis, volleyball, and handball. Lodging includes three strictly kosher meals daily. $70-$90/person. Children's and weekly rates. April through November.*

End of Lake Street coverage.

Right. **Sayde's Country Store and Citgo Food Mart** (914-254-4010). Convenience store with many kosher items, e.g. kosher frozen yogurt. Citgo gas, Trailways bus stop.

Right. **Northland Resort Motel** (914-254-5125, 800-696-5294). Motel, restaurant, and pizzeria. Twenty-six hotel rooms, efficiency rooms, and two-bedroom apartments, $52-$85. Dining room serves sandwiches, pizza, and burgers to complete dinners such as souvlaki platter, calves liver, veal bratwurst, chicken cordon bleu, and shell steak. Dinners $6-$13. Dining room, bar, big fireplace, video games, pool table, dart boards, and horseshoe pits.

Left. **Main Street Automotive** (914-254-4308). Automobile repair and service. 24-hour towing.

000.5   Right. **Flagstone Inn** (914-254-5101). Twenty-eight efficiencies with private baths, $48-63/two. Lounge, fireplace, and pool table.

Right. **Delaware Court Motel** (914-254-5090). Motel rooms, efficiencies, and one- and two-bedroom cabins, all with private baths, $40-$80. Large swimming pool. Pets welcome.

Right. **This + That.** Second-hand store featuring clothing, accessories, and more.

000.6   Left. **Wilber National Bank** (914-254-5252).

Left. **Fleischmanns Liquor Store** (914-254-4909). Wines and liquors.

Left. **Fleischmanns Supermarket** (914-254-4919).

000.7   Right. **Skene Memorial Library** (914-254-4581). A charming building with cedar-shake siding and an octagonal tower, the library was built in 1901 as a memorial to Dr. A. J. C. and Mrs. Skene, summer residents of the Fleischmanns area. Through the efforts of Mrs. Skene after the death of her husband, $5,000 was donated for the library by Mr. and Mrs. Andrew Carnegie. The library has an expanding collection on the resort Catskills, plus a "vacation reading collection" containing the great books you may have time to read usually only while on vacation. Open hours expand to include weekends in summer. The library also functions as the **Visitor Information Center.**

Right. **Fleischmanns Museum.** Behind the library, contains memorabilia of Fleischmanns. Photos, postcards, history, artifacts, etc.

Left. **La Cabana Mexican Restaurant and Motel** (914-254-4966). Motel, restaurant, and bar. Mexican and American entrees to $9.95. Motel units, some with kitchenette, range from $40 to $55/night. Pool table and arcade in restaurant.

Left. **Fleischmanns Theaters** (914-254-4666). An Art Deco movie theater built in 1929 before the stock market crash.

000.8   Left. **Fleischmanns Post Office** (914-254-5661). ZIP 12430.

Right. **Highland Fling Inn** (914-254-5650). A smoke-free bed and breakfast with a Scottish flair, including freshly-baked blueberry scones served with a full breakfast. Comfortable sitting room with library, TV, fireplace. Rooms are distributed among two Victorian homes (private and shared baths, some refrigerators). The inn also sponsors quilting seminars. Children and well-behaved pets welcome. $60 to $65 per night per couple.

Left. **Valkyrian Motel** (914-254-5373). Clean, quiet all-efficiency motel, set back from road. $40/day/couple. Weekly and seasonal rates available.

Left. **River Run Bed & Breakfast** (914-254-4884). A comfortable, Victorian bed and breakfast with eight guestrooms, most with private bath. Also a suite with private baths and kitchen. The hexagonal front parlor has stained-glass windows, a fireplace, and a piano. In the dining room are stained-glass windows and lace tablecloths, and in the library are lots of books, a TV, VCR, and stereo, and a soft, comfortable couch and chairs. The large, wrap-around porch with Adirondack chairs and the lawn with riverside picnic area complete the home-like accommodations. Warmly welcoming. Pets also accommodated. $55-$105/couple.

Left. **Gales Luncheonette and Gift Shop** (914-254-4466). Home-cooked breakfast and lunch. Gift shop carries T's and sweats, toys, novelties, greeting cards, and more. Closed Tuesdays.

Left. Junction with **Bridge Street**:

One-tenth of a mile down Bridge Street is the junction with **Wagner Avenue**. *Making a right from Bridge Street onto Wagner Avenue yields:*

Left. **Village Pool**. *Public swimming pool.*

Right. **Village Park** *offering a softball field, soccer field, basketball court, tennis court, and playground.*

End of Bridge Street and Wagner Avenue coverage.

Left. **Roberts' Auction Service** (914-254-4490). An interesting and fun place to spend Saturday evenings. Viewing of the eclectic stock is permitted all day Friday and Saturday, with the auction commencing at 7 PM Saturday evening. The inventory, including antiques, home furnishings, furniture, tools, farm implements, perhaps a sleigh or a buggy, and much, much more, is fascinating, exciting, and amusing, and the auction bursts with activity and surprises. Great fun.

001.2   Left. Junction with **Depot Street**, down which 0.2 mile is **Route 28**.

Right. **Linden Hill** (914-254-4333). Six heated, two-bedroom, housekeeping cottages, each having four beds, a full bath and full kitchen; $70/two/night, plus $15/extra adult. Pretty, grassy setting 100 feet above Main Street.

002.7   Junction of west end of Main Street with **Route 28**.

End of village of Fleischmanns coverage.

Fleischmanns Through Arkville to Margaretville

037.8   Right(left) Junction with east end of **Main Street** into village of Fleischmanns. See Chapter 13, *Fleischmanns*, for a description of Fleischmanns in a westerly direction beginning at this intersection.

039.0   Right(left) Junction with **Depot Street** to **Fleischmanns**:

> *Left.* **West Wind Motel** *(914-254-4421). Twelve rooms, six with efficiencies, all with private bath. $38-$45/two.*

> *Left.* **Hasay Realty** *(914-254-4040).*

> *000.1   Left.* **Elizabeth House & Motel** *(914-254-5280, 4006). Lodge and motel offering accommodations since 1955. The main lodge has eleven units with kitchens, bedrooms, and private baths, plus common lounging and dining rooms; open in summer, hunting season, and ski season. The nine-unit motel is open year-round, and each unit has a bedroom, full kitchen, and full bath. $38-$60/two.*

> *000.2   Junction with* **Main Street** *in Fleischmanns.*

> *End of Depot Street coverage.*

040.4   Right(left) Junction with **Old Route 28**, western entrance to **Fleischmanns**.

040.5   Right(left) **Crystal Brook Plaza**:

Lou-Jon Auto Parts (914-254-4950). Auto parts and hardware.

Peabody's Pets (914-254-6172). Pet foods and supplies.

Left(right) **Ray's Sports Shop** (914-254-4951). Hunting, fishing, archery, camping equipment, and supplies. Also licenses and toys. Open seven days all year.

040.8   Right(left) **Charming (but Cheap and Possibly) Antiques** (914-254-9969). Twelve rooms full of a ten-year collection of old, interesting, handmade and beautiful merchandise. Ladies' handwork, lots of books and records, a cornucopia of tasteful, small items, and more. The coffee and the wood stove are always hot. Stop in, browse around, and be spoiled. Open weekends, and by appointment during the week.

041.3   Right(left) **Tinkers Village Flea Market** (914-586-1528). An indoor flea market comprised of fifteen rooms of anything and everything both old and new. Antiques, jewelry, collectibles, sporting goods, and much, much more. A treasure hunter's paradise.

Right(left) **Redmond Real Estate** (914-586-2696).

042.0   Right(left) **McDaniel's Tavern.**

043.0   Entering(leaving) **Arkville.**

Right(left) **ABC Auto Service Center** (914-586-3598). Auto service, propane tanks filled, kerosene, and 24-hour towing.

Right(left) **Arkville Country Store** (914-586-2442). Grocery store, deli, subs, sandwiches, breakfast. Also Coastal gas.

043.1   Left(right) **Delaware and Ulster Rail Ride** (914-586-3877, 800-225-4132). Catskill scenic rail ride, museum, and souvenirs. One-and-three-quarter-hour round-trip rides in open flatbed cars or closed passenger cars to Roxbury and either Halcottsville or Highmount. The tracks are clickety-clackety, providing genuine railroad motion and excitement as you ride through forests, over bridges, and along streams. A 1963 diesel engine pulls 90- to 100-year-old cars along an 1866 right-of-way. The rail ride also holds mock train robberies and other fun runs. And there is a visitor information rack inside the train station. Memorial Day weekend through October.

DURR train pulled by engine 5017 about to depart.

Left(right) **Betz's Sport Shop** (914-586-3699). Hunting and fishing supplies, live bait, and licenses. Guns and ammo, shooting accessories, fishing tackle, and used guns bought and sold.

Right(left) **Erpf House** (914-586-3326). Home of the **Catskill Center for Conservation and Development** and the **Erpf Cultural Institute**. Representing a vision for the quality of life in the Catskills, this private, not-for-profit organization is committed to the balance of environmental conservation and economic development of the area. Cultural activities include local art shows and photo exhibits; a lecture series on the Catskills; children's educational programs; and educational hikes. Tourists are welcome to visit the center, view the exhibits, and participate in programs. Call for latest schedule of events.

043.3   Right(left) Junction with **CR 38 (Arkville Cut-Off Road)** to **Roxbury** and **Ski Plattekill**:

000.2   *Right.* ***Erickson's Automotive (914-586-2242).*** *Body shop, auto repairs, and 24-hour towing.*

001.0   *Junction with **NY 30**. Turn right onto **NY 30** north for **Hanah Country Club**, the **Pakatakan Farmer's Market** at the **Round Barn of Halcottsville**, **Roxbury**, and **Ski Plattekill**.*

001.6   *Left. **Hanah Country Club** (914-586-2100, 800-752-6494). Also **Hanah Country Inn and Resort** and the **Hanah International Golf School**. Fine, public eighteen-hole golf course, restaurant, lodging, and golf school. The 7,052-yard golf course has many water hazards, and five holes are on the mountainside; $42-$55/two for eighteen, including cart. Motel units are available without golf for $45-$95/two, or $60-$89 per person with breakfast and dinner included. Many golf/lodging/dining packages available. Tennis courts, swimming pool, driving range, putting green, spa, steam room, sauna, hot tubs, pro shop. Restaurant and bar are open for all three meals, with dinner selections including shrimp scampi, pasta prima-*

*vera, chicken chardonnay, salmon, filet mignon, etc, $10-
$20. Open April through October, weather permitting.
Lodging open through hunting season in November.*

003.8   Right.   **Round Barn of Halcottsville** *(800-586-3303).
Home of **Pakatakan Farmer's Market**. Locally-produced
fruits, vegetables, honey, maple syrup, jellies, jams,
flowers and plants, crafts, and more. Saturdays, 9 AM to
3 PM, mid-May to October.*

004.5   Left.   **Parking** *area with picnic tables and scenic views.*

005.6   *Entering town of **Roxbury.***

007.1   Left.   *Junction with **Cold Spring Road** to **Ski Plattekill**:*

   000.0   *For **Ski Plattekill**, make left turn onto Cold Spring
Road. Beyond here road signs are rare, so follow
signs for Ski Plattekill and these directions.*

   000.4   *Left. Make very sharp (about a 160-degree) turn
to the left which leads to **Lower Meeker Hollow
Road.***

   001.2   *Stop sign. Bear left and continue down hill.*

   004.4   **Ski Plattekill** *(607-326-3500). Family skiing,
snowboarding, and biking center. One thousand
feet vertical drop with 27 slopes and trails, three
lifts including triple chair, with a two-mile novice
run, the longest and steepest double black
diamond expert slope in the Catskills, and a
snowboarding trail with jumps and tabletops.
Snowmaking covers 75 percent of the mountain.
Lodge with fireplaces, cafeteria, hot carving
station, nursery, bar, and apres ski entertainment.
Ski, snowboard, and shaped ski rentals.
Withworth Ski Shop (607-326-2845). December
through March. May through November is*

mountain biking and skyride season via the triple chair. Bike shop, bike rentals, cafeteria, and bar.

End of coverage to Ski Plattekill.

NY 30 north follows the foothills of the western Catskills north past Schoharie Reservoir, crosses I-90 at Amsterdam, passes Great Sacandaga Lake, plunges north through the middle of the Adirondacks, joins Route 28 again between Indian Lake and Blue Mountain Lake, and continues north through Malone, to its end at Trout River on the Canadian border. Like Route 28, NY 30 is a scenic, less-traveled route through mountain and meadow, covering 300 miles from its southern end at East Branch to its northern end at Trout River.

End of CR 38 and NY 30 north coverage.

Right(left) **Mary's Cookin' Again...** (914-586-4141). Dining in a caboose. Lunch Tuesday through Saturday consisting of various preparations of grilled chicken, sandwiches, burgers, salads, and daily specials, $5-$10. Dinner on Friday evenings featuring steaks, seafood, weekly specials, and more, $12-$20. Also outdoor dining. Open mid-April through November.

Left(right) **Antiques & A Little Bit of Everything** (914-586-3786). Mostly local antiques, paintings, jewelry, books, magazines, knick-knacks, kitchen items, silverware, clothing, old magazines, crafts, glassware, an oil can collection, and much more, all displayed in an original, century-old building. Arkville's unofficial local history museum.

Right(left) **Railway Laundry** (914-586-9838). Laundry and dry cleaning.

Right(left) **LaRosa Pizza** (914-586-2552). Pizza parlor offering pizza, calzones, salads, heroes, etc. Closed Tuesdays and Wednesdays.

043.4   Right(left) **Rocko Minerals & Jewelry** (914-586-3837). Jewelry, crystals, beads, and fossils.

043.5   Left(right) **Maine Black Bear Seafood Market, Restaurant, and Lobster Deck** (914-586-4004). Live lobster, shrimp, clams, fresh fish, etc. Market open late Thursday through Saturday, restaurant open Friday and Saturday for lunch ($4-$8) and dinner ($10-$15), late April through New Year's Eve. Fresh seafood in the middle of the Catskills.

043.6   Left(Right) Junction with **Pakataken Road** (sic):

> *000.2   Left. **Pakatakan Motel** (914-586-4911). Comfortable, contemporary, and tidy twelve-unit motel on a quiet hillside with valley views. A welcome plus is the full bathtub. $35-$40/two.*

Leaving(entering) **Arkville**.

Right(left) **Arkville Flea Market**. An outdoor, multi-vendor flea market active on weekends from April through Columbus Day.

Right(left) **Indoor Flea Market**. Stemware, glassware, dishes, jewelry, sterling silver, books, tools, and auto parts. Open seven days all year.

043.8   Right(left) **Discoveries.** Past and present, antiques and collectibles, furniture, odds and ends, repairs. Closed winters. Sister shop of the Discoveries on Main Street in Margaretville (914-586-3990).

Left(right) **Country Plaza**:
Sanford Auto Parts (914-586-4600). All-Pro autoparts.

044.0   Left(right) **Red Barrel Food Stores** and Getty gas (914-586-2526). Convenience store.

044.1   Right(left) **The Meadows** (914-586-4104). Nine-hole, par 3 golf course, driving range, 18-holes of miniature golf. Golf: $7 for nine holes, $11 for eighteen; miniature golf: $3; driving range: $2 or $4. April through mid-October, weather dependent.

Left(right) **H&H Motors** (914-586-2493). Complete auto service specializing in foreign cars.

Right(left) **E & D Spirit Shop** (914-586-2835). Liquors and fine wines.

Left(right) **Merritt's Motel** (914-586-4464). Ten-unit motel with proprietor on premises. Neat, clean, and comfortable. $36/double.

044.2   Right(left) **Catskill Mountain Real Estate** (914-586-4255).

Right(left) **Country Cutting Gallery** (914-586-3838). Hair salon.

Right(left) **The Inn Between** (914-586-4265). A cozy, casual, and popular restaurant with a varied menu of steaks, chops, ribs, veal, chicken, seafood, and more. Salad bar, homemade soups, daily specials, and early-bird specials. Dinner entrees $9-$18. Open for dinner Wednesday through Monday, and for breakfast and lunch on weekends. Also riverside dining overlooking the East Branch of the Delaware River.

Left(right) **Wayman's Auto Body** (914-586-4882). Body shop, auto repairs, and discount auto glass.

044.3   Left(right) **Margaretville Bowl** (914-586-2695). Bowling alley.

Left(right) **Michelle's Hair Designs** (914-586-1887). Hair salon.

Entering(leaving) village of **Margaretville**.

Right(left) **Radio Shack** (914-586-3624).   Electronics and computers.

044.4   Right(left) **Brookside Home and Hardware** (914-586-2345). Lawn and garden supplies, tractor sales and service, auto tire sales and service, and road service.   Also, propane by weight and volume.

Right(left) **Dr. Gigabyte** (914-586-3804).   Computer sales and service.   New and used systems, upgrades, software, and troubleshooting.

044.5   Left(right) **Margaretville Memorial Hospital** (914-586-2631). 24-hour emergency room and 24-hour ambulance service. **Emergency Hotline** (914-586-2929).

044.7   Right(left) Junction with **NY 30** north into Margaretville.   See Chapter 15, *Margaretville.*

Margaretville

Margaretville, formerly Middletown Center, was named for Margaret Lewis, great-granddaughter of Robert Livingston, the owner in the mid-eighteenth century of a half-million acres of the Catskill Mountains. Today, a large percentage of the homes in the area, most only three hours from Manhattan, are second homes of weekend visitors. Therefore, many of the shops in Margaretville have a New York City flavor, offering products not found elsewhere along Route 28, except for perhaps Woodstock. But Margaretville is no suburb of Manhattan: at the time this was written, coin telephones still required only a dime for a local call.

Margaretville was flooded on January 19, 1996, caused by more than three feet of snow, followed by heavy rains. The combination of the heavy rains and the snowmelt was overwhelming. The East Branch Delaware River, which normally is just a stream flowing under Bridge Street as you enter town, pumped itself up beyond overflowing and turned into a river which flooded Main Street by more than four feet. A number of shops have the flood level marked by high-water signs. And, when the water receded, the mud remained. Some business never recovered. Then, on November 9, 1996, the village was flooded again, but not as severely as in January.

Notable activities and attractions in the area include hiking, skiing, mountain biking, trout fishing, hunting, antiquing, shopping, and the Farmer's Market at historic Round Barn of Halcottsville (pronounced HALL-cotts-ville) seven miles north of the village on NY 30. Margaretville hosts the Fire Department Field Days during the Fourth of July holiday, with rides, games, food, fireworks, and more. The Margaretville Memorial Hospital Auxiliary Antique and Flea Market is the first Saturday in August, and the Margaretville Street Fair, with an emphasis on arts, crafts, and food, is usually held on the Saturday of the weekend before Labor Day weekend. For more information, call the Margaretville Chamber of Commerce (914-586-3300, 800-586-3303).

Many of the shops in Margaretville are open six days during the summer months, and usually only on weekends and holidays other times.

Margaretville is entered from Route 28 via Bridge Street (NY 30 north), which forms a short upright of the letter "T" with Margaretville's Main Street. The description first goes north along Bridge Street (NY 30, the upright of the "T") from Route 28 to Main Street, then east along Main Street and NY 30 north (the right part of the "T"'s horizontal top), and then west along Main Street (the left part of the "T"'s horizontal top).

Junction of **Route 28** with **NY 30** north (**Bridge Street**) into **Margaretville**. Heading north on **Bridge Street**:

Crossing the **East Branch Delaware River.**

000.1   Left. Junction with **Granary Road** to a shady municipal parking lot.

Right.   At the right side of the shopping plaza is a driveway to **Village Park,** with a baseball field, a soccer field, and a pavilion with picnic tables.

Right. **Soap 'n' Suds.** Coin laundry.

Right. **A & P** (914-586-9859). Supermarket.

Right. **Revco Pharmacy** (914-586-2955).

Right. **Now and Then Video** (914-586-2666). Video rentals, copies, and fax service.

Right. **Expressions** (914-586-3344). Unusual gifts, T-shirts, candles, pot pourri, cards, rag dolls, picture frames, Woodstock

Chimes, jewelry, gift baskets, sun catchers, Teddy bears, flags, and books. Photo development and copy machine.

Left. Along the north side of Granary Road is **The Granary**, housing:
Timberland Properties (914-586-3321). Real estate.
Natures Offerings (914-586-4006). Natural and organic foods. Closed Thursday.
Buswell's Bakery (914-586-3009). Bakery, restaurant, sweet shop, and take out. Breakfast, lunch, Thursday steak night, and Friday and Saturday night dinner by reservations only. Reservations may be needed for weekend breakfast, especially after church. Mr. and Mrs. Buswell have been married for more than 50 years. He does the baking, she does the cooking. Everything is cooked on premises; they don't serve anything they don't make, and even salads, such as chicken salad, are made fresh when the sandwich is ordered.

Right. **The Bun & Cone** (914-586-4440). Rebuilt new since the flood, this restaurant, open 5 AM to 9 PM, serves breakfast all day, plus sandwiches, burgers, soups, salads, hot sandwiches, and dinners such as veal Parmigiana, spaghetti and meatballs, eggplant, chicken, and more. Also ice cream. Prices to $6.

Junction of **Bridge Street** with **Main Street**. Main Street is described first by turning right and going east on Main Street (**NY 30** north), then by turning left and going west on Main Street.

Margaretville's Main Street (and NY 30 north) east of Bridge Street

000.0   **Right. The Cheese Barrel & Gourmet Shop** (914-586-4666). Gourmet shop, fine foods, sandwich shop, deli, coffees and teas, gourmet ice cream, more.

Left.   Mr. Toad (914-586-2962).   Decoratives and home accessories.

Right. **Main Street Jewelers** (914-586-4413). Jewelry. Watch, clock, and jewelry repairs.

Left. **Margaretville Antique Center** (914-586-2424). Twenty-seven dealers in an old movie theater. This antique center has the proverbial little bit of everything, something for everyone, to fit everyone's wallet. You could spend hours browsing and never see the same thing twice.

Right. **Briteway Realty** (914-586-4442).

Right. **The Village Pub** (914-586-2627). Bar, bar menu of burgers, grilled sandwiches, etc. Dartboard and video games.

Left. **Del-Sports** (914-586-4103). Hunting supplies, firearms, scopes, fishing tackle, outdoor supplies, and topographical maps. Beautiful commemorative guns, collectors' guns, and gun smithing. About 600 wet and dry fishing flies.

Right. **Margaretville Gift and Frame** (914-586-3444). Eclectic variety of nicely-presented, reasonably-priced gifts, home accessories, and decoratives. Also custom framing.

Right. **Lauren's Closet** (914-586-1877). Ladies consignment boutique. Quality vintage clothing, shoes, accessories, fur and leather coats, hats, more.

Right. **Village Kids** (914-586-1880). New and gently used children's clothing and accessories.

Right. **Royal Cleaners** (914-586-4414). Dry cleaning. Also **Sportacus, a** soccer outfitting shop offering shorts, T-shirts, caps, shin guards, socks, soccer balls, etc.

Right. **Village Cobbler** (914-586-1771). Shoe and leather repairs.

Right. **At Wit's End** (914-586-1799). Department store. Clothes, toys, housewares, baby supplies, yarn, and so much more.

000.1   Left. **B & D Motors** (914-586-3253). Used car dealer, new and used R/Vs, repairs, and car and trailer rentals.

000.3   Right. **Bodyworx** (914-586-3101). Massage therapy.

001.2   Leaving **Margaretville**.

001.9   Right. Junction with **CR 38**, the **Arkville Cut-Off Road** to Arkville.

Continue straight ahead on **NY 30** north for **Hanah Country Club**, the **Pakatakan Farmer's Market** at the **Round Barn of Halcottsville, Roxbury**, and **Ski Plattekill**. See description in Chapter 14, *Fleischmanns Through Arkville to Margaretville.*

End of Main Street east and NY 30 north coverage.

Margaretville's Main Street West of Bridge Street

000.0   Right. **The Commons**. A former department store which has been rejuvenated into several shops, some of which front on the street while others are inside:
Franklyn Footwear & Clothing (914-586-1633). Better-quality casual country clothing. Jackets, coats, pants, shirts, socks, caps, hiking and work boots, and shoes. Workwear, casual cottons and woolens; ski wear; snowboard boots and clothing.
Cafe on Main (914-586-2343). Breakfast, lunch, dinner, and Sunday brunch. The Milanese proprietor and chef presents osso buco, rabbit, lamb shank, polenta, fresh pastas such as bluecorn ravioli stuffed with black beans and Monterrey jack, zuppa de pesce, and more, $11-$17, all in charming ambiance.
Bookmark(914-586-2700). General book store, but also carrying "seconds", and new books with minor imperfections at deeply discounted prices.
Home Goods (914-586-4177). New and vintage kitchenware, cookware, bakeware, yellowware bowls, glassware, teapots, cookie jars, gadgets, linens, antique bathroom accessories, and more. Gift and bridal registry.

Wildflowers (914-586-2444). Fresh flowers and arrangements. Also unusual gifts, antiques, and artwork.

Kicking Stones (914-586-1844). Antiques, collectibles, and art. Wide range of antiques, country furniture, mission furniture, hand-painted cupboards, primitives, rugs, and more, presented in an open and gallery-like setting. Customer service emphasized. Special orders encouraged. Also four annual art exhibitions.

Country Treasures (914-586-4656). Antiques and gifts.

Enid's One of a Kind (914-586-1888). Handmade clothing and home furnishings made from leather, wool, and fur. One-of-a-kind dresses, jackets, and coats for men, women, and children, as well as quilts and pillows for the home. Also hand-crafted silver jewelry and pottery by local artisans. Every piece is different.

Frog's Leap (914-586-4446). Handcrafted home furnishings and unique gifts made by area and regional artisans. Furniture, home furnishings, pottery, glassworks, lamps, jewelry, musical instruments, pillows, and more.

House of Chaos (914-586-1477). Computer, hobby, artist, and office supplies.

Catskill On Line (800-444-9338). Internet service provider. Also internet access for visitors to Margaretville needing to check their E-mail while away from home or office.

Left. **Greenbery Hair** (914-586-1688). Full-service unisex salon. Hair styling, massage, facials, manicures and pedicures, makeup application, etc. Open Sat-Mon.

Left. **Miller's Drug Store** (914-586-4212). Pharmacy. Cards, post cards, magazines, out-of-town newspapers, photography supplies, and gifts.

Left. **Margaretville Liquor Store** (914-586-4314). Wines and liquors.

Right. **Hourglass Shoppe** (914-586-2111). New, used, and antique clocks, and clock repairs. Open Saturdays. Saturdays and Sundays in summer, Saturdays only in winter.

Left. **Frank Lumia Real Estate Plus** (914-586-4486).

Left. **Chamber of Commerce** (914-586-3300, 800-586-3303). Tourist info and calendar of events.

Right. Junction with **Walnut Street**. Turn right for:

000.0   Right. Public parking lot.

*000.2   Continue straight onto **Margaretville Mountain Road** (also called New Kingston Road) for:*

*001.6   Right. **Margaretville Mountain Inn** (914-586-3933). A large, solid, Dutch turret house bed and breakfast on six open, hilltop acres with outstanding mountain views. The 1886 house features Queen Anne Victorian doors, oak trim, stained-glass-edged windows, period furniture, brown family portraits, and wholesome breakfasts. Seven guest rooms with private and shared baths, $65 to 95/couple, including full breakfast. Dogs welcome on a case-by-case basis, $10 per night. The quintessential, historic, grandmother's house in the country.*

End of Walnut Street and Margaretville Mountain Road coverage.

Left. **Binnekill Square:**
The Square Restaurant (914-586-4884). Restaurant whose Swiss proprietor/chef serves genuine Swiss dishes with German, French, and Italian influence. Casually elegant dining room plus a dining terrace overlooking a duck pond. Sirloin steak, filet mignon au poivre vert, rack of lamb, pastas, salmon, duckling, and similar entrees are $13-$25. Schnitzel night on Thursdays and Sundays, $13. A great place to relax, unwind, and sate oneself after a long trip or a hard day.
Look-N-See Apparel (914-586-2099). A clothing store featuring men's, women's and children's clothing. Women's regular and larger sizes. Fashionable, upscale clothing at reasonable prices.
Shampoos Beauty Salon (914-586-3787) and **Karen's Hair Place** (914-586-3212). Unisex hair salons. Also piercing.
East Branch Art Gallery (914-586-2190). Displays artwork of local artists. Also color copying and graphics work.

Discount Frames, Candles, Etc. (914-586-1444). Discount frames, candles, gifts, and more.
Barber shop (914-586-2322).

Right. **Village Homemaker** (914-586-3620). Country gifts, locally-made and other crafts, Teddy bears, plush cats, handmade wooden furnishings, baby quilts, fabrics, and notions.

Right. **Hairport Haircutters** (914-586-3341). Hair stylists.

Right. **Margaretville Pizzeria** (914-586-1441). More than just pizza, this new restaurant serves pizza, calzones, heroes, subs, appetizers, burgers, and salads, as well as Italian dinners such as spaghetti and meatballs, baked pasta, eggplant parmigiana, veal parmigiana, chicken parmigiana, sausage and peppers, and more. Dinners $7-$10. Closed Monday and Tuesday.

Left. **J. C. Penney** (914-586-2688). Catalog sales office.

Left. **Margaretville Memorial Hospital Auxiliary Thrift Shop** (914-586-3737).

Right. **NBT Bank of Margaretville** (914-586-2623). 24-hour ATM.

Left. Walkway to Granary Road parking lot.

Left. **Terra Real Estate** (914-586-4499).

Left. **Ming Moon Kitchen** (914-586-2188). Chinese restaurant. Entrees $5-$11. Take-out.

000.1   Left. **Discoveries** (914-586-3990). Antiques and collectibles. Furniture, china, glassware, jewelry, home accessories, lamps, clocks, bric-a-brac, and more.

Left. **Bull Run Tavern** (914-586-9833). Saloon. Bar menu of burgers, hot dogs, sandwiches, etc., to $5. Shuffleboard, bowling machine, and pool table. Summer weekend barbecues, $6-$11.

Right. **Great American** (914-586-4102). Supermarket.

000.2   Right. **Country Store** (914-586-4222). Groceries, Sunoco gas, and a cash machine.

End of Main Street west coverage.

Margaretville Through Andes to Delhi

044.7   Right(left) Junction with **NY 30** north into **Margaretville**. See Chapter 15, *Margaretville.*

045.0   Left(right) **RK's Flea Market** (914-586-1854). New and used items. Antiques, jewelry, much more.

045.1   Right(left) **Bruce Country Farms** (914-586-2643). Farm and home store, True Value hardware.

046.5   Right(left) **Old School House**. A one-room schoolhouse, built in 1820 and used as a schoolhouse until 1940, is now a museum. Open Saturday afternoons in July and August. Even if the schoolhouse is not open, a peek through the windows will put you a century back in time.

047.2   Crossing the **East Branch Delaware River** and leaving(entering) **Catskill Park**.

Ever since Fleischmanns, Route 28 has been following the East Branch Delaware River or one of its tributaries. The East Branch joins the Delaware River at Hancock. The Delaware forms the state line between New York and the northeast corner of Pennsylvania. It then makes a hard right at Port Jervis, where New York, Pennsylvania, and New Jersey meet. The river then becomes the western boundary of all of New Jersey, eventually forming Delaware Bay between New Jersey and Delaware and entering the Atlantic Ocean at Cape May.

Like the Esopus Creek, the East Branch is part of New York City's water supply. Damming the East Branch at Downsville created the Pepacton Reservoir, from which the East Delaware Aqueduct pipes water to the city. The Pepacton was completed in 1954 and holds 140 billion gallons of water (about 14 percent more than the Ashokan).

047.8   Right(left) **New York State Police** (914-586-2681).

048.1   Left(right) Junction with **NY 30** south to the **Pepacton Reservoir** and **Downsville**. NY 30 south follows the fingers of the reservoir like a glove, constantly turning and twisting its way to Downsville and eventually to its end at its intersection with **NY 17** at **East Branch**. The ride around the reservoir is through beautifully remote foothills of the Catskills. No towns or commercialism mar the 20-mile drive. During the fall foliage season the drive becomes doubly scenic as the reservoir waters reflect the vivid autumn colors.

Route 28 between Kingston and here was rebuilt in the early 1960's. The old, narrow, often stream-following road was replaced by a wider, straighter road which bypassed towns and allowed higher cruising speeds. That rebuilt road is now behind us, and it reverts to its old stream-following ways, with many curves calling for a reduction in speed to 25 or 30 miles per hour. The terrain also begins to change. On this western side of the Catskills, the mountains fade into big hills dappled with the remnants of dairy farming.

050.0   **Middletown/Andes** town line.

052.3   Left(right) **Hot Rod Farmer** (914-676-3477). Auto repairs.

Top of the pass between Margaretville and Andes offering outstanding views southbound. Northbound, a road sign suggests the use of low gear for the one-and-one-half-mile descent to Andes. As you descend you will be treated to broad views of hills, pastures, and cultivated farms. Maple trees abound in this area west of the Catskills, producing much maple sap and also producing bright and fiery oranges and reds during the foliage season in early October. In early spring, many local folks fire up their sugar shacks to reduce maple sap to maple syrup, and then hang out shingles advertising the syrup for sale.

A weathered barn, with an entrance on each of two levels, stands straight and tall as it awaits a new owner.

055.5   Right(left) Junction with **Gladstone Hollow Road**:

> *003.2   **Bobcat Ski Center** (914-676-3143). On **Mt. Pisgah**, the highest peak in Delaware County, Bobcat offers eighteen slopes and trials plus a glade on 1,050 vertical feet serving novice to expert skiers and snowboarders. Two T-bars, lodge, cafeteria, rental shop, and ski accessories shop. Open Friday through Sunday and holiday periods. Bobcat also hosts an annual state **lumberjack competition** on the Sunday of Labor Day weekend. This show features amateur (anyone can enter) and professional lumberjacks, and decides the New York State lumberjack champion of the year. Bobcat also hosts nature walks during fall foliage season.*

End of Gladstone Hollow Road coverage.

Entering(leaving) village of **Andes**, founded 1819.

The village of Andes, an old dairy center which used to ship milk and cheese via rail to places as far away as Washington, D.C., is tiny, with a population of only 150, but is increasingly the center of a second-home community which fans out to the hills and valleys beyond the village. The village has many interesting old frame buildings, some of which have been restored. *Tin Horns and Calico* by Henry Christman (See Appendix C, *Additional Information*) relates the "thrilling unsung story of the American revolt against Serfdom", commonly called the anti-rent wars which took place here in 1845. Differences of opinion exist to this day, with the people of Andes usually supporting the former tenants, and the people of Delhi usually supporting the former landowners.

In the Andes area are unique, hillside barns having entrances on two floors. On the low side of the hill there is ground-level access to the ground floor, while further up the hillside there is a stone-ramp providing access to the first floor above. One of these barns is along Tremperskill Road past the Andes Post Office, and another is on Bovina Road toward Bovina Center.

Andes is a charming stop for food, refreshment, and antiques, or just to rest and chat with the friendly residents who seem to love visitors. On my visits to Andes I felt a tangible attachment to the village, its people, its bucolic setting, and the period architecture. I felt as if I had just returned after many years to my old hometown. Everyone looked me in the eye and seemed to treat me as a friend. I felt warmly safe and comfortable here, and I can't wait to go back. A local real estate agent summed up Andes' virtues perhaps best: fresh air, fresh water, no traffic, and no crime. That's perfect.

055.8   Right(left) **Bear Hugs & Busy Hands** (914-676-3266). Ceramics, unfinished ceramics, finished gifts, paints, and supplies. Kiln firing, glazing, and classes.

056.0   Left(right) **National Bank of Delaware County** (914-676-3115).

056.1   Left(right) **The Hunting House**. A restoration project of the Andes Society of History and Culture. When completed, it will house a small museum, and provide a meeting place for local groups, educational programs, and cultural activities. Next door is the **Andes Society of History and Culture Thrift Shop**, whose business proceeds fund the restoration of the Hunting House.

Left(right) **Andes Public Library** (914-676-3333) in **Bohlmann Memorial Park**. The library is a wonderful repository of local history books. War memorial and park bench in the park.

Right(left) **Timberland Properties** (914-676-4600). Real estate.

056.2   Left(right) **Andes Hotel** (914-676-4408). Restaurant ($10-$15 for dinner entrees, $8 Sunday and summer Friday buffet). Flexible chef not limited to menu, so don't be afraid to ask for your favorite meal. Also, **Temming's Colonial Room** cocktail lounge, a ten-unit motel ($45/double), and a liquor store. Hotel run by the Temming family for more than 50 years.

Right(left) **Conrad's Service Station** (914-676-3470). Gas, groceries, and propane cylinder exchange.

Right(left) **Appletree Realty** (914-676-3377).

Right(left) **Cassie's Kitchen** (914-676-4500). Breakfast and lunch seven days. Omelettes, pancakes, overstuffed sandwiches, hot sandwiches, burgers, soups, salads, and homemade pies and cakes, $2 to $6. Parlor-style ice cream creations. French toast and soups are customer favorites. Breakfast served all day. Pine Hill Trailways Bus stop.

Left(right) **Mercantile** (914-676-4477). Recycled vintage and contemporary goods for the home and garden. Garden and patio furniture, linens, kitchenware, vintage drapery, Adirondack twig furniture, children's furniture, bathwares, greeting cards, etc.

Left(right) **Brooke's Variety** (914-676-3123). Collection of antiques, toys, Delaware County history books, contemporary-patterned oilcloth, candles, baseball cards and memorabilia, local baked goods, farm-fresh eggs, candies, jellies, nuts, herbs, topiaries, plants, plant materials in the spring, forced bulbs in the fall, license plate birdhouses, holiday items in season, and Americana kitchen accessories, with a constantly-changing inventory.

0056.3 Right(left) **Paisley's Country Gallery** (914-676-3533). Imported collection of inexpensive but stylish home and personal accessories. Pottery from Portugal, glassware from Spain, textiles from India, hand-painted napkin rings from Indonesia. Baskets, rugs, batiks, broomstick skirts, precious stones, jewelry. Many second-home owners shop here for Christmas presents. Open Thursdays through Sundays.

Route 28 makes a hard right under the watchful eye of the Andes General Store. (DeWitt)

Flashing traffic signal at junction with **Delaware Avenue**. **Route 28** turns right(left) while Delaware Avenue goes straight ahead (is to the right) and takes you to:

*000.0   Left. Junction with **Tremperskill Road (CR 1)** at triangle:*

*000.2   Left. **Andes Post Office** (914-676-3211).   ZIP 13731.*

*000.3   Right. **Park** with benches alongside the Trempers Kill.*

*The next few miles pass through pretty, hillside pastures which remind me of the dairy regions in the foothills of the Swiss Alps. Along the way you will pass **Upper Dingel Hill Road** on the left, at which intersection is a sign marking the site of the murder of Undersheriff Osmon N. Steele during the anti-rent wars. Tremperskill Road continues on to the **Pepacton Reservoir**.*

End of Tremperskill Road and Delaware Avenue coverage.

Left(right) **Andes General Store** (914-676-3228). A general store since 1863, the first floor now houses both the general store, offering groceries, ice cream and a delicatessen, and **Andes Pizza Place** (914-676-3703), a charming, quaint, casual restaurant serving fresh, homemade breakfast, lunch, and dinner, as well as pizza. This building was inundated during the January 19, 1996, flood which followed heavy rains and the rapid melting of four feet of snow.

056.4   Left(right) **Village Pool** (914-676-4703). Public swimming pool.

Left(right) **Tennis courts** at Andes Central School.

Summer's grazing cows have been replaced by winter's smattering of snow on this hillside pasture. (DeWitt)

056.6   Leaving(entering) the village of **Andes**.

058.4   Left(right) Junction with **Damgaard Road**, down which one-tenth of a mile is **Mid-County Printing & Used Furniture & Antiques** (914-676-4706). Antiques and collectibles.

058.6   Right(left) **Dana's Place** (914-676-3464). Family restaurant serving home cooked foods. One menu offering lunch and dinner all day. Sandwiches, burgers, pastas, chicken, fish, etc. Steaks a specialty. Closed Mondays. Dinner entrees $9-$17.

059.1   **Andes/Bovina** town line.

The thickly-forested mountains of the Catskills are replaced by naked pastures on broad hillsides offering distant views. A former colleague from Texas and I once discussed the treed New York countryside versus the open grasslands of central Texas. I complained of Texas's not having any trees taller than I was. "Yeah," he said, "but in Texas you can see!" Being from New York I had never considered his perspective. We are all most comfortable with the familiar. He opened my eyes to the ubiquitous grassland views which treed mountainsides can't offer. Here in Delaware County pasture land the views outnumber the trees.

061.1   Right(left) Junction with **Bovina Road** (**CR 6**) to **Bovina Center**, a loose grouping of B&Bs, a motel, a museum, an antique shop, a contemporary cafe and general store, a gourmet specialty food shop, a fishing stream, an auto repair shop, and one gas pump. The hamlet offers country tranquility, pretty views, friendly people, historic homes of character with no visible neighbors, and a bit of heaven on earth. Along the road are old homes, barns, and cemeteries, and probably ghosts of old bovines. Turn right(left) onto Bovina Road for:

001.0   *Entering **Bovina** township, established 1820.*

001.5   *Left. Junction with **Bramley Mountain Road**:*

000.3   *Left. **The Country House** (607-832-4371). An 1840 farmhouse bed and breakfast on 600 acres perfect for hunting, fishing, and hiking. Three guest rooms, each with a high bed and a private bath. The house is largely original, with wide-board floors, high-stepped staircase, a stone fireplace, and a woodstove, and is furnished with colonial antiques, an organ, and some uniquely framed paintings on the walls. Outside are broad lawns, a wide porch, a gazebo, and a pond. Open year round, $60-$65/two, including full breakfast. A simply lovely colonial home.*

Bear left at "Y" just beyond The Country House and continue on Bramley Mountain Road for:

001.6   *Right. **The Swallow's Nest** (607-832-4547). An 1850 farmhouse bed and breakfast with colonial furnishings and four guest rooms with private and shared baths. A large family room offers a pool* *table, card table, and TV. Activities include hiking the property, swimming in the pond or sitting by the brook. $65-$70/couple, including old-fashioned, family-style breakfast of seasonal fruit, homemade breads, pancakes, eggs, and bacon. Comfortable, quiet, and quaint.*

End of Bramley Mountain Road coverage.

001.7   *Right.   Creamery Road to* **McIntosh Auction** *(607-832-4829, 832-4241) in an old creamery, which hosts an auction every Saturday evening at 6:30 from April through November.   Antiques and a little bit of everything.*

001.8   *Left.* **Main Street Bovina** *(607-832-4300). A bright and cheerful, upscale cafe and general store. Bakery, butcher shop, fresh produce, fresh baked goods, deli, prepared foods, groceries, coffees, teas, juices, specialty foods, bulk spices, pastas, health foods, and ice cream. Also serving breakfast; lunch; and early dinner and dinner take-outs such as Beltie meatloaf, pork and pasta dishes, and more, $10-$11. Open 8-5.*

001.9   *Right.* **Bovina Museum**. *Artifacts, books, photos, old clothing, a miniature carved circus, and more, plus an old firehouse next door.   Open Saturdays from July fourth through Labor Day or by appointment by calling 607-832-4360.*

Left. **Bovina Motorworks** *(607-832-4295). Auto repair shop.*

Left. Junction with **Maple Avenue***:*

Left. **Bovina Center Library** *(607-832-4884).*

Right. **Playground***.*

End of Maple Avenue coverage.

Left. **Russell's Store** *(607-832-4242). Country store and gas. Dry goods, groceries, hardware, sandwiches, and coffee.*

002.1   *Right.* **Churchside** *(607-832-4231). Bed and breakfast in an 1840 Greek Revival farmhouse with period furnishings on two-and-one-half acres with its own private Little Delaware River. Two guest rooms, each with private bath. Amenities include a gazebo, hot tub, and an open fire in the family room. $65/two first night, $60 additional nights, including a hearty, country breakfast.*

Left. Junction with **Pink Street** *(CR 5):*

001.2   *Right. Junction with* **Jim Lane Road,** *up which about one-half-mile is the* **Carriage House Bed & Breakfast** *(607-832-4209). On a 145-acre farm with accommodations for up to six in one two-bedroom apartment, one one-bedroom apartment and a studio. Each has a kitchen or kitchenette with full cooking facilities, and a private bath; breakfast on request. A suite, with a king-sized, four-poster bed, sleeps four in two rooms, continental breakfast included. All accommodations are $50/couple.*

002.2   *Left.* **Suits Us Farm** *(607-832-4369, 4470). A family farm on 350 acres with twenty-two rooms, a heated swimming pool, and tennis courts. Lodging in one- and two-room units with private baths can accommodate from single hunters to vacationing families. Lodging includes three family-style meals a day. Open Memorial Day through Labor Day, and the first two weeks of big game hunting season for hunters only. $295-$360 per adult per week (including twenty meals), with lower rates for teens and children. Special rates for holiday weekends; daily rates available. Chickens, rabbits, lambs, goats, and pigs are on* *the premises. Feed the animals, play softball, wander the pastures, roast marshmallows, and count the stars at this real farm in the western foothills of the Catskills.*

End of Pink Street coverage.

*004.9   Right. **Delaware River Public Fishing Stream parking** area.*

*005.3   Right. **Mountain Brook Chalet** (914-832-4424). Eight efficiency motel units with living room, bedroom, kitchenette and bath, sleeping up to seven, $52/two. Catering largely to hunters, the chalet is open from early May through mid-December.   During deer season breakfast and dinner are available on request.*

*Left.   **Mountain Brook Antiques** (607-832-4871). Antiques and gifts. General line of furniture, collectibles, cookie jars, more. Also gifts. Usually open in summer or by chance.*

*005.7   Right.   **Plain and Fancy** (607-832-4457).   Gourmet specialty items.*

End of Bovina Road (CR 6) coverage.

062.1   Crossing **Little Delaware River**.

062.3   Entering(leaving) town of **Delhi**.

063.3   Right(left) **Walt's Taxidermy Studio** (607-746-7399) Taxidermy, maple syrup.

067.4   Left(right) Junction with **Arbor Hill Road** to **State University of New York College of Technology at Delhi** (607-746-4111).

067.5   Left(right) **County Tire Company** (607-746-3003). Goodyear tire dealer.

067.7   Left(right) **Buena Vista Motel** (607-746-2135).   Thirty-three clean, orderly rooms that virtually shine, with views of the village and the college campus across the valley. $49-$58/two, continental breakfast included.

067.9   Entering(leaving) village of **Delhi.**

Delhi

The county seat of Delaware County, Delhi has a permanent population of only 3,064. It is a rural village surrounded by cows and corn and is home to the two-year State University of New York College of Technology at Delhi, and is peppered with history. Charles Evans Hughes, chief justice of the U. S. Supreme Court from 1930-1941, studied law here (1881-1882) while teaching school at the age of 19 at Delaware Academy on the east end of the village. Two miles north of Delhi on NY 10 is the Delaware County Historical Association Museum which bursts at the seams with two centuries of history. If you slowly walk on Main Street from Kingston Street north to Meredith Street you will see many of Delhi's interesting, historic buildings, and you'll taste the flavor of the village's past.

Tourist information can be obtained from the Greater Delhi Area Chamber of Commerce at 607-746-6100.

067.9   Entering(leaving) village of **Delhi**.

068.0   Left(right) **Mary Imogene Bassett Hospital** (607-746-2130). **Emergency Room**.

068.5   **Route 28** makes a left(right) turn onto(from) **Kingston Street**.

Right(left) **Sunny Dale Flower Shoppe** (607-746-7300). Florist.

Crossing **West Branch Delaware River**.

Left(right) Junction with **Elm Street**, down which one-tenth of a mile on the right is the **Cannon Free Library** (607-746-2662).

Right(left) **Parts Plus** (607-746-6973). Auto parts store.

Right(left) **Presto Pizzeria** (607-746-2090).   Pizza, calzones, strombolis, hot and cold subs, mozzarella sticks, fried ravioli, salad, etc. Free delivery.

Left(right) **Quickway** (607-746-3353).   Convenience store and Citgo gas.

Right(left) **Presto Country Store** (607-746-6287).   Groceries, Sunoco gas, Trailways bus stop, propane cylinder exchange, and cash machine.

068.6   Left(right) **Great American** (607-746-6684). Supermarket.

Right(left) **Express Mart** (607-746-7722).   Convenience store, Mobil gas, ATM. Also **Subway** (607-746-8848). Sub sandwiches and more.

Traffic light at junction with **NY 10** (**Main Street**). Making a left (or going straight if traveling south on Route 28) puts you onto **NY 10** and **Main Street** south toward **Fraser** and **Walton**, and takes you to:

000.0   Right. **Parker House** *(607-746-3141). Room after room of upscale gifts, accessories, and antiques. A wide range of elegantly displayed merchandise for the lady, for the man, for the office, and for the home. Jewelry, linens, tableware, glassware, silverware, flatware, pewterware, vases, linens, candles, frames, clocks, door knockers, desk sets, walking sticks, gourmet products, and more. A lovely shop.   Also* **Smith's Jewelry Store** *(607-746-2285). Diamonds, gems, and estate jewelry bought and sold, and custom jewelry designed. Also jewelry and watch repairs.*

Right. **Ray's Fine Wines and Spirits** *(607-746-3775).*

Right. **Nonie's Beauty Shop** *(607-746-6680).*

Left. **Shearing Shed** *(607-746-3528). Barber shop, and* **V S Dry Cleaning** *(607-746-3528).*

Left. **Delhi Liquor Store** *(607-746-2321).*

000.1   *Right.* **CVS Pharmacy** *(607-746-6817).*

Left. Four related businesses under one roof (607-746-6562):
Quarter Moon Cafe. *Made-from-scratch wholesome foods including vegetarian and meat dishes.*
Good Cheap Food. *A food co-op selling health foods, coffee, gourmet foods, local produce, and organically-grown produce. Open to members and non-members.*
United Book Guild. *Children's books, cook books, eccentric selection of remainders, second-hand books, and more.*
Allegro CD's and Tapes *. Celtic, new age, jazz, classical, and more.*

000.3   *Right. Entrance to* **SUNY Delhi College of Technology** *(607-746-4111).*

Left. **Bagels -n- Cream** *(607-746-8100). Deli. Closed Sunday.*

Left. Junction with western end of **Elm Street***, down which two-tenths of a mile on the left is the* **Cannon Free Library** *(607-746-2662).*

000.5   *Left.* **Pizza Hut** *(607-746-7773).*

000.6   *Left.* **McDonald's** *(607-746-7489).*

Left. **Ames Plaza***, housing the following, from left to right:*
Ames *(607-746-2352). Department store.*

Rite-Aid Pharmacy (607-746-7110).
Plaza Laundromat and Cleaners (607-746-2680).
Style for You (607-746-3333). Beauty and tanning salon.
Ming Moon (607-746-6650). Chinese restaurant.
La Bella Pizzeria (607-746-3311).
Grand Union (607-746-7347). Supermarket.
Delaware National Bank of Delhi 24-hour ATM in kiosk in middle of parking lot.

000.7   Left. *Junction with* **Sherwood Road** *to* **Wilber National Bank** *(607-746-2162). 24-hour ATM.*

000.9   Right. *Entrance to* **SUNY Delhi College of Technology** *(607-746-4111).*

End of NY 10 south and Main Street south coverage.

Route 28 turns right from **Kingston Street** onto **NY 10** and **Main Street** north.

Left(right) **Delhi Dance and Performing Arts Center** (607-746-7181). Performing arts classes. Acting, singing, tap dance, jazz dance, and ballet classes.   Also occasional performances throughout the year at various Delaware County locations including a yearly recital the first weekend in June at Delaware High School.   Call the Center or Chamber of Commerce for details.

Left(right) **Timberland Properties** (607-746-7400).   Real estate.

Left(right) **Uncle Buck's Dollar Store** (607-746-2252).

Left(right)   **Village   Seafood   Restaurant**   (607-746-7170). Restaurant open seven days for breakfast, lunch, and dinner. Dinner entrees of seafood, ham, steaks, Italian specialties, and more, $9-$13 for most; combination platters, twin lobster tails, and more.

Left(right) **Sunrise Video** (607-746-3000).

Right(left) **Dairy Delight** (607-746-6484). Soft ice cream and ice cream cakes.

Left(right) **Dubben Brothers Hardware** (607-746-2229). Hardware, plumbing, and heating.

Left(right) **Kulaski Realty** (607-746-7377).

068.7   Right(left) **Stewart's Department Store** (607-746-2254). Piece goods, dry goods, notions, ladies' and men's clothing; Delaware Academy, Andes High School, and SUNY Delhi memorabilia. This department store has not been modernized and retains the look and layout of fifty years ago. A visit is a refreshing departure from the same-look, same-store syndrome found in so many villages, towns, and cities throughout the country, which causes people to be able to travel a thousand miles and feel they are still in their hometown with all the same-look restaurants, banks, fast-food vendors, department stores, and specialty "shoppes". Refreshingly nostalgic.

Left(right) **Mortar and Pestle Card Shop** (607-746-6763). Hallmark card and gift shop.

Right(left) **Delaware Business Systems** (607-746-3533). Fax and copier service.

Left(right) **The Cardio Club** (607-746-7050). Fitness club.

Right(left) **Delhi Diner** (607-746-2207). Breakfast and lunch.

Left(right) **Delaware County Chamber of Commerce** (607-746-2281). Tourist info.

068.8   Left(right) Junction with **Court Street**. A few steps down Court Street on the left is the **Delhi Post Office** (607-746-2256). ZIP 13753. Inside is a 1940 mural by Mary Earley depicting the anti-rent wars which took place in Delaware County.

Left(right) **Courthouse Square**. The center of town, bounded by Main Street, Court Street, and Church Street, and site of the Delaware County War Memorial. You can feel the history of Delaware County by just standing in this square. It is fronted by the post office, town office building, two churches, and the county office building, all old and architecturally interesting. Further along Main Street on the left is the beautiful St. John's Church, dating from 1818.

Right(left) **Delaware County Office Building.**

Right(left) **Delaware National Bank of Delhi** (607-746-2356). 24-hour ATM.

Right(left) **Shire Pub and Restaurant** (607-746-6202). Casual dining for lunch and dinner. Appetizers, soups and salads, over-stuffed and specialty sandwiches, and burgers, plus the chef's dinner menu of various steaks, pork Milanese, chicken Florentine, char-grilled trout, garden-style salmon, and more, $7-$12. Nightly dinner specials such as all-you-can-eat buffet on Tuesday. Outdoor patio, pool table, bowling machine, foosball, etc.

068.9   Junction of **Route 28** and **NY 10**. **Route 28** turns left onto **Meredith Street**. (If traveling south, Route 28 turns right onto **Main Street**.) Route 28 coverage continues in Chapter 18, *Delhi to Oneonta.*

NY 10 north continues straight on Main Street toward **Bloomville** and **Stamford,** yielding the following:

*000.0   Right. **Wickham Pontiac Oldsmobile and Ford** (607-746-2148). Dealership.*

*Right. **Coin laundry** (607-746-3769).*

*000.1   Left. **D&D of Delhi** (607-746-2168). NAPA auto parts.*

*Left. **Delaware Discount Tires** (607-746-6866).*

Right. **Wood's Gas Station Groceries Etc.** *(607-746-3159). Gulf gas, convenience store.*

000.2   *Right.* **Delhi Community Park.** *Soccer and Little League fields, playground, picnic tables, charcoal grills.*

000.4   *Right.* **Mid County Auto Body and Glass Inc.** *(607-746-6476).*

000.7   *Right.* **Winter's Flower Shop and Greenhouses** *(607-746-7000). Greenhouses, flowers, balloons, and gifts.*

Leaving village of Delhi.

001.6   *Right.* **Parking area** *with picnic table overlooking stream.*

002.2   *Left.* **Delaware County Historical Association Museum** *(607-746-3849). Housed in the federal-style Frisbee House built in 1797, the Historical Association operates a museum and library with Delaware County as its focus. Gideon Frisbee, one of the early founders of Delaware County, was a lawyer, judge, tavern keeper, and farmer, and many historically significant Delaware County activities occurred here. The Frisbee family lived here and worked the farm for more than 160 years. The house also served as a way station for people from places such as Albany, Kingston, and New York City traveling along the turnpike which eventually became NY 10. The library is awash in books, letters, and photographs. Other attractions include a nature trail, a four-seater outhouse (no longer used), and four buildings (toll house, blacksmith's shop, gunsmith's shop, and schoolhouse) that were moved here from other locations. The museum also hosts various events and programs throughout the year. A perfect Delaware County time machine.*

Left. **Webb & Sons** *(607-865-7413). Hardware store, home center, garden and building supplies. Propane cylinders filled.*

*002.7   Right.   Side road with **covered bridge**.*

End of NY 10 north coverage.

Delhi to Oneonta

068.9   Junction of **Route 28** (**Meredith Street**) and **NY 10** (**Main Street**). Heading north toward **Meridale** and **Oneonta**.

Right(left) **R. H. Lewis and Son** (607-746-2187).   Buick, Chevrolet, and GMC truck dealership.

Left(right) **Delhi Motor Company** (607-746-2181).   Chrysler, Plymouth, Jeep, Eagle, and Dodge truck dealership.

As you climb the hill and drive north from Delhi wide open spaces and steeply rolling pastures will greet you. This is cow and hay country, a remnant of the former robust dairy industry. The paintless, teetering, old barns now house only drafts, creaks, and mice. Nearest neighbors can be a ten-minute walk away. Peace, quiet, and tranquility are as thick as a down comforter. Hilltop views are long and magnificent. After sunset the bright stars contrast sharply with the black night. The current crop of for-sale signs prompts thoughts of trading crowds, crime, and croissants for cows, clods, and corn muffins. There may not be gold, but there's peace in them thar hills.

An old barn sits with only memories of cows to keep it company.

071.1   Right(left) **Archery 28** (607-746-7055). Archery shop.

075.7   Entering(leaving) **Meridale**.

076.4   Right(left) Junction with **CR 10**. Turn onto this road for side trip to the **Hanford Mills Museum**:

     *000.0   Right. **Meridale Market** (607-746-6657).   Gas, groceries, cold cuts, sandwiches, beer, soda, ice, kerosene, greeting cards, videos, etc.*

     *Right. **Meridale Post Office** (607-746-6440).   ZIP 13806.*

     003.6   Long keyhole view from crest of hill, beginning one-and-one-half-mile descent.   Once through the keyhole, the view broadens to encompass pastures, corn fields, and wooded hillsides.

005.2 Stop sign in **East Meredith**. Make left turn, following **CR 10**.

*Right. Junction with **CR 12** immediately after making the above left turn. Turn right toward the **Hanford Mills Museum**:*

000.0 Left. **East Meredith Post Office** *(607-278-9938). ZIP 13757.*

000.2 Left. **Hanford Mills Museum** *(607-278-5744, 800-295-4992). Parking on the right. Interpreting rural life and water-powered industry, this working museum on an 1846 mill site features sawmill and gristmill demonstrations, a hardware store, an ice house, farm house, barns, and other buildings with numerous exhibits. Also, a museum store and a snack shop. Annual events include an Ice Harvest in February, Heritage Craftsmen Days in June, a July 4th celebration, a Lumberjack Festival in August, and an Antique Engine Jamboree in September. On the New York State and National Registers of Historic Places. A wonderful step back in time. May through October.*

End of CR 8 and CR 10 coverage.

076.5   Right(left) **Maggie & Mike's Antiques** (607-746-7410). Furniture, photos, paintings, and more.

076.6   Leaving(entering) **Meridale**.

080.5   **Meredith/Franklin** town line.

084.0   **North Franklin.** Junction on the left(right) with **NY 357** to **Unadilla**.

If you are driving a motor home you will probably develop a line of cars behind you as you climb the two-mile hill that begins here. If you are driving any model Porsche you will probably develop a snicker and a heavy foot as you drive the same hill. But even if you are driving a company car or a delivery truck, you are bound to enjoy the scenery and the views between here and Oneonta five miles ahead.

085.6   Left(right) **G & K Auto & Truck Service** (607-432-8419).

086.1   Right(left) **John F. Ross Gunsmith** (607-432-5999).   Guns, ammo, supplies, and repairs. Shooting range available.

086.2   **Delaware/Otsego** county line and **Franklin/Oneonta** town line at the crest of the hill.

Otsego County is mostly rural, with Oneonta and Cooperstown the county's two major oases. Major places of interest along and near Route 28 in Otsego County include Hartwick College, SUNY Oneonta, the National Soccer Hall of Fame, Goodyear Lake, the National Baseball Hall of Fame, the Farmers' Museum, the Fenimore House Museum, Otsego Lake, the Glimmerglass Opera, Glimmerglass State Park, Hyde Hall, and Canadarago Lake. There are also many minor places of interest scattered between Oneonta and Richfield Springs for travelers to discover and explore.

As you descend the two-mile hill into **Oneonta** you will see fleeting views of the valley through the trees. The views become broader and more frequent as you approach Oneonta.

088.5   Right(left) **Kountry Living Bed and Breakfast** (607-432-0186). Homey, 125-year-old farmhouse with green lawns, a spring-fed brook, neighboring cows, direct access to Oneonta, and second-story views across the valley to Hartwick College. Four guest rooms share a bath and a half. Screened porch, wood-burning stove, full breakfast with homemade sweetbreads and fresh fruit, and homemade candies on your bed stand. $60/couple, tax included.

088.8   Left(right) Junction with **Main Street** into **Oneonta**. See Chapter
19, *Oneonta*.   Route 28 north continues straight ahead; see
Chapter 20, *Oneonta to Cooperstown*.

Route 28 bypasses the city of **Oneonta** and continues north via a short
stretch on **I-88** to **Colliersville** five miles to the northeast. For a taste of
Oneonta while continuing your way north, turn left here onto **Main Street**
in Oneonta and follow it (which becomes **NY 7**) east five miles to
Colliersville, where you will rejoin Route 28.

At Oneonta Route 28 signage changes its east and west orientation to north
and south.

19 | Oneonta

Oneonta, whose accepted meaning is "City of the Hills", sits on the banks of the Susquehanna River and used to be called Klipnockie. Initial settlement can be traced to 1780, while today it has a population of 14,000. Oneonta was once a major trolley and railroading town, having had the largest roundhouse in the world. Various lines serving the city were the Albany and Susquehanna; the Ulster and Delaware; the Delaware and Hudson; the Oneonta and Otego Valley; the Oneonta, Cooperstown and Richfield Springs Railway; the Oneonta and Mohawk Valley; and others. Today Oneonta is home to the State University of New York (SUNY) at Oneonta, Hartwick College, the Oneonta Yankees Class A baseball team, and the National Soccer Hall of Fame. The city offers historic and cultural attractions, entertainment, many restaurants and places of lodging, and all the usual merchants and services found in a small city.

Walking along downtown's Main Street feels like visiting an old friend. The sidewalks are brick-paved, park-bench-studded, and replica-gas-lamp-lighted. Shops, eateries, and watering holes stand shoulder to shoulder like spectators watching a parade, offering a warm and comfortable backdrop to the mixture of smiling people scurrying along. Busy-ness without stress seems to be the prevalent local mental attitude.

Because Oneonta is home to a college and a state university, it is a cultural center. Hartwick College, a private liberal arts college with spectacular valley views off West Street, offers museums, performances, visiting artists' programs, lectures, and more, all open to the public. SUNY Oneonta offers the Science Discovery Center, an art gallery, and the Goodrich and Hamblin Theaters. The city also has a semi-professional theater company called Orpheus Theater, which performs at the Goodrich Theater at SUNY Oneonta. See the Chestnut Street section below, and call ahead to learn what events are scheduled for the time of your visit.

While Oneonta is large enough to offer a variety of interests and small enough to explore on one's own, the best and fastest way to learn Oneonta's and Otsego County's secrets is to visit either the Otsego County Chamber of Commerce office (607-432-4500, 800-843-3394) on Carbon Street or the Otsego County Tourist Information Booth in Colliersville. Each of these locations distributes a free comprehensive tourism guide called "Otsego County Central Leatherstocking Region."

Oneonta is only 22 miles from Cooperstown. Lodging in Cooperstown is usually sold out during the National Baseball Hall of Fame's Game and Induction weekend, leading people to stay in Oneonta and making lodging in Oneonta also scarce that weekend. The Game and Induction activities are usually the last weekend in July or the first weekend in August.

Route 28 through Oneonta is covered in Chapter 18, *Delhi to Oneonta*, and Chapter 20, *Oneonta Through Milford to Cooperstown*. This chapter covers the city of Oneonta in three parts:
Main Street North from Route 28: Oneonta's Main Street north from its junction with Route 28 south of I-88 Exit 14, for five miles east to Route 28 in Colliersville.
Chestnut Street (NY 7 and NY 23) West from Main Street: Selectively from its intersection with Main Street to Hartwick College and SUNY Oneonta.
NY 23 East Through Oneonta's Southside: Covering that section of Southside not on Route 28 in Chapter 20, *Oneonta Through Milford to Cooperstown*, coverage begins at the junction of Route 28 and NY 23 east, at the south end of the James F. Lettis Highway.

Main Street North from Route 28

000.0   South end of **Main Street** at its junction with **Route 28** south of **I-88** Exit 14.

Crossing the **Susquehanna River**.

000.1   Junction with **I-88** Exit 14. Westbound entrance toward **Bing-hamton** and eastbound exit from Binghamton only.

Left. **Golden Guernsey Ice Cream** (607-432-7209). Dozens of flavors of hard ice cream, soft yogurt, sugar-free and dairy-free hard and soft products, candies for blending into ice cream, frozen bars, frozen cheese cakes, fried ice cream, slush puppies, etc. Also, hot dogs, burgers, sandwiches, homemade salads, fresh daily homemade soups, $4 lunch specials, more.

000.2   Right. **First Choice Discount Laundromat and Cleaners** (607-432-4141). Wash and fold service.

Right. **Alfresco's Italian Bistro** (607-432-8466). A family-style restaurant with unique Italian atmosphere with garden furniture, stone tables, statuary, tile houses, and a deck under an arbor, complemented by roses, grapevines, and fresh herbs. Predominantly northern Italian cuisine of imported pasta, homemade sauces and breads, seafood specials, and pizza, all with child portions, too. Open for lunch and dinner, with dinner entrees $6-$15. Seasonal outdoor dining deck. Closed Sundays.

Right. **Silver Screen Video** (607-432-5713).

000.3   Right. **Classique** (607-431-9747). Family hair and skin care.

Left. **Doll Artisan Guild & Seeley's Doll Center** (607-432-4977). Antique doll museum. Open weekdays.

Left. **Country Store** (607-432-0173). Convenience store, Sunoco gas. Deli and pizza. Open 24 hours.

Traffic light at junction with **River Street** to the left and **Neahwa Place** to the right.

Turning left onto River Street takes you to:

*000.0   Right. **India House of Tandoori** (607-432-6445). Indian lunch and dinner cuisine served Indian style, surrounded* *by Indian decor, and, if you like, washed down by Indian beer. Dinner entrees range from $8 to $15, including dessert. Closed Monday.*

Left. **Seeley's Doll Center** *(607-433-1240). A doll crafts store. Parts and products for the hand-crafting of antique-style and modern porcelain dolls, including molds, paints, brushes, porcelain slips, clothes patterns, and much more. Open weekdays 9-5.*

000.3   Left.   Traffic light at intersection with **Wilcox Avenue.** *Turn left for:*

    000.1   Right. **Swart-Wilcox House.** *Mostly-restored two-story, clapboard house originally built in 1807 by Revolutionary War soldier Lawrence Swart from Schoharie, NY. The oldest standing wooden structure in the city of Oneonta, the house was built in accordance with German Palatine vernacular architecture. Representing the beginnings of a living history museum, it contains an 1840 working melodion (a foot-pump-operated, five-octave, organ-like instrument), a child's high chair, 1870's wallpaper, a dry sink, and other period furnishings and household antiques. Viewing by appointment by calling 607-432-8417.*

End of Wilcox Avenue and River Street coverage.

Making a right onto **Neahwa Place** takes you to:

000.0   Left. Junction with **Carbon Street***:*

    000.1   Right. **Otsego County Chamber of Commerce** *(607-432-4500, 800-843-3394). Tourist information.*

End of Carbon Street coverage.

*Entrance to **Neawah Park**, containing softball fields, tennis courts, pavilions, picnic tables, restrooms and the **Railroad Brotherhood Union Caboose**, a shrine to the founding in 1883 of the Brotherhood of Railroad Trainmen. Also Damaschke Field at far end of park.*

End of Neahwa Place coverage.

Left. **Stewart Shoppes** (607-431-9359). Convenience store, gas, ATM.

000.5   Left. **Ross's Market** (607-432-3243). Old-time grocery store.

Left. **Oneonta Police** Department (607-432-1111).

Right. **Red's Filling Station** (607-432-4570). Bar that also serves food such as wings, burgers, etc. Pool table and foosball.

Right. Junction with **Market Street**:

Right. ***Uncle Buck's Dollar Store*** *(607-433-0399).*

Right. Junction with **Clinton Plaza Drive**:

Right. ***Wolf Wilde Goldsmith*** *(607-432-4862). Jewelers.*

Right. ***Domino's Pizza*** *(607-432-3033).*

Right. ***Jreck Subs*** *(607-432-8638).*

Left. ***Plaza Annex**, on the lower level in the rear of **Clinton Plaza**:*
General Clinton Pub *(607-432-9592). Lunch specials, burgers, and wings.*
Cahill's One-Hour Photo *(607-432-6203). Passport and ID photos, and portrait studio.*
Clinton Plaza Specialty Market *(607-432-5855). Fresh fruits and vegetables.*

Hober Packaging (607-432-2597). Fax, copies, and shipping.
Fin and Feather (607-433-0183). Small animals, fish, birds, and reptiles.
Silks and Treasures Consignments (607-432-0587). Clothing consignment shop.
Clinton Plaza Dry Cleaning and Laundromat (607-433-1640). Drop, wash, and fold.
Froot Loupes (607-432-5507, 888-FRO-FROO). Mexi-Greek experience. Breakfast, lunch, appetizers, and dinners. Enchiladas, chimichangas, burritos, gyros, and more. Free delivery.
Down Under Hair Design (607-432-7753). Walk-ins welcome.
Elly's Island (607-432-8947). Tanning.

*Right. **Public parking.***

End of Clinton Plaza Drive coverage.

Left. **Salvation Army Thrift Store** (607-432-0952).

000.6   Left. **Vic's Service** (607-432-3162). Auto repairs, Citgo gas.

Right. **Clinton Plaza:**
Village Music (607-432-7055). Buyers and sellers of new and used CD's and tapes, and sellers of used vinyl records. Also sheet music and Ticketmaster tickets.
OPT, the Bus Store (607-432-7100). Oneonta Public Transportation bus terminal.
Gary's Flowers & Gifts (607-432-0138).
Clinton Plaza. Stairway to the Plaza Annex through **Fin & Feather** (607-433-0183) pet shop.
Drury Lane Bakery and Cafe (607-433-2293). Cookies, rolls, bagels, breads, pastries, muffins, coffees, soups, salads, sandwiches, cream cheese spreads, lunch specials, pizzas, and more.
Little Panda (607-432-8244). Chinese food.
CVS Pharmacy (607-432-4445).

Traffic light at intersection with **Chestnut Street**, carrying **NY 7** west and **NY 23** west, to the left, and **Chestnut Street Extension** to the right. See **Chestnut Street (NY 7 and NY 23) West from Main Street** coverage later in this chapter.

Left. **Scorchy's Metropolitan Diner** (607-432-2154). Old-fashioned, nostalgia-evoking, modestly-priced diner adorned with photos of old movie stars. Famous for its Big Apple Breakfast of three pancakes, three eggs, three pieces of bacon, three links of sausage, and coffee, all for $4.

Right. **Kitty Gordon's** (607-432-9410). Pub-styled sports bar with green, brass, and oak interior. TV, billiards, soup, sandwiches, wings, etc.

Left. **Maxwell's** (607-432-4731). Buy and sell used CDS and movies. Adult room. Also candles, incense, smoking accessories, and a small, young folks boutique.

Right. **Measure for Measure** (607-432-0200). Barber shop. Also **Alice Blue Gown** (607-436-9762). Unisex lingerie; intimate apparel; ballet, tap, and jazz dancewear.

Right. **Black Oak Tavern** (607-432-9566). Imported and domestic beers, darts, foosball, and pool tables which are refelted every six weeks. No juke box, but a good collection of jazz for your listening pleasure.

Right. **Tino's Pizza** (607-432-8975). Downstairs. Pizza, calzones, Italian dinners ($4-$6), sausage and peppers, salads, subs, etc. Open for lunch and dinner. Closed Sunday. Main entrance on Water Street.

Left. **Indelible Ink** (607-432-6924, 432-6854). One talented man's art gallery, studio, and tattoo parlor. Oils, acrylics, sculptures, air-brushed custom T-shirts, and more.

Right. **Zim's Shoes** (607-432-0480).

Left. **Novelty Lounge** (607-432-6671). Bar, cocktail lounge, and topless dancers.

Right. **Razzle Dazzle** (607-432-0042). The store with affordable panache.   Ladies' and children's clothing, jewelry, stuffed animals, toys, home furnishings, kitchenware, picture frames, candles, piece goods, books, gifts, greeting cards, and more.

Left. **Steven's Hardware and Sporting Goods** (607-432-2720). Hunting, fishing, camping, archery, outdoor supplies, canoes, and basic hardware.

Right. **Alpine Ski Hut** (607-432-0556). Skis, bicycles, sporting goods, golf clubs, etc.

Left. **Bresee's** (607-432-6000). Home furnishings, and kitchen appliances, cabinets, and furniture.

Right. **China 19** (607-433-8888). Chinese restaurant, $5-$11.

Right. **Bookends & Beginnings** (607-433-1523). Books for children and young adults.

Right. **Once Upon a Time** (607-432-5325). Antiques. Upstairs.

000.7   Right. **Sport Tech** (607-432-1731). Sporting goods, clothes, tennis racquets, shoes, soccer balls, skis, snowboards, etc.

Right. **Artware** (607-432-0679). Discounted art materials and supplies. Framing, cards, and giftwrap.

Left. **Oneonta Bagel Company** (607-433-0162). Bagels. Closes at 3:30 PM.

Left. **Delaware Guitar** (607-432-6103). New and used musical instruments.

Right. **Hummel's Office Plus Business Centre** (607-432-3010). Office equipment and supplies.

Left. **The Lifestyle Centre** (607-432-6133). Natural body-care products. Vitamins, minerals, supplements, cosmetics, oils, balms, sports nutrition, coffees, books, tapes, homeopathic remedies, and gifts. Cafe with entertainment on Friday evenings.

Left. **McPhail's Pharmacy** (607-432-6111). Cosmetic center. Prescriptions.

Right. **Brass Rail Billiards** (607-433-2609).

Left. **Galinns Jewelers** (607-432-2462).

Right. Walkway to parking garage.

Left. Junction with **Dietz Street:**

000.0 Left. ***Wedding Gallery*** *(607-432-8655). Wedding gowns, tuxedos, etc.*

   Left. ***Main Street Flea Market.***

   Left. ***Ed Teleky Jeweler*** *(607-432-0770). Jewelry and watch repair.*

   Left. ***Total Body Salon.*** *Hair, nails, etc.*

   Left. Junction with ***Wall Street:***

   Left. ***Monser Brothers Tire Sales*** *(607-432-4060).*

   Right. ***Carhart Camera*** *(607-432-4846). Camera shop.*

   Left. ***Huntington Memorial Library and Park*** *(607-432-1980). Rear of Chestnut Street library property, with large lawns and park benches.*

000.1 *Left.* ***Astoria Federal Savings*** *(607-433-0274). 24-hour, drive-up ATM.*

End of coverage of Dietz Street.

Right. **Subway** (607-433-4782). Sandwiches and salads.

Right. **Pentacles New Age Shoppe** (607-436-9427). Books, crystals, jewelry, candles, incense, and oils.

Right. **Video to Rol** (607-432-1884). Video rentals.

Left. **Tina Marie's Salon** (607-431-9919). His and her hairstyling.

Left. **Downtown Deli Company** (607-432-1929). Fresh bread daily. Specialty sandwiches. Soups, salads, subs, and burgers.

Right. **Key Bank** (607-432-2500). 24-hour ATM.

Left. **Saratoga Trunk** (607-436-9208). Antiques, vintage clothing, textiles (linens, lace, early fabrics), jewelry, and furniture.

Left. **Old Spanish Tavern** (607-432-9574). Old local bar with passageway to the Downtown Deli (same operators) through which bar patrons can get food to go with their drink.

Right. **Circle Park**. You can sit here on a bench under the trees and watch Oneonta move. Your personal Oneonta front porch. Also steps down to parking lot.

Left. **Building 203** (607-431-9461). Variety store.

Left. **Otsego Outfitters** (607-432-8395). Sporting goods, sleeping bags, backpacks, canoes, canoeing supplies, sweatshirts, sporting clothing, hiking boots, sandals, more.

Right. **J & B Subs and Catering** (607-432-4132). Muffins, bagels, subs, sandwiches, hot sandwiches, homemade soups and salads, burgers, etc.

Left. **The Wearhouse.** Clothing outlet. Open Thursday through Saturday.

Right. **Joe Ruffino's Pizzeria Restaurant** (607-432-7400). A quarter century of pizzas from scratch. Subs, strombolis, and Italian dinners. Famous for their roniroll (macaroni & cheese). Rear dining deck; free delivery; closed Sundays. Difficult to resist the wonderful pizza aroma bathing the sidewalk in front of this serious pizza shop.

Left. **Harold's Army Navy Store** (607-432-7672). A clothing store for young people. Brand name wide-legged jeans, shirts, jackets, shoes, work boots, etc.

Right. **Ruffino Mall**, housing, among others, the following:
The Laundry Chute. Self-service laundry.
Pathfinder Center (607-432-0405). A soft, comfortable, feel-good, new age store. Books, candles, incense, body oils, jewelry, calendars, cards, astrological cards, local artwork and jewelry, chimes, crystals, music tapes, posters, and more.

000.8   Right. **Autumn Cafe** (607-432-6845). Restaurant in period storefront with high, tin ceilings, large overhead fans, sturdy oaken furniture, and a large outside deck. Lunch and dinner, beer and wine, blues bands. Varied menu (including vegetarian and non-dairy items) with interesting specials. Dinner specials up to about $13.

Right. **Kubiak Gallery** (607-432-1393). The gallery of the Upper Catskill Community Council of the Arts (UCCCA, 607-432-2070), presenting mostly local artists. Art shows, juried exhibitions, music concerts, art programs, and more. Art shows change monthly.

Left. **Wilber National Bank** (607-432-1700). 24-hour ATM.

Intersection with **Ford Avenue** on the left and **South Main Street** on the right.

Turning left and walking a few hundred feet up **Ford Avenue** takes you to:

> *Left.* ***National Soccer Hall of Fame*** *(607-432-3351, 800-545-3263). Established in 1981, the NSHOF houses a museum of memorabilia, photos, and film. However the Hall of Fame is more than just a museum. Every weekend from early June to the end of August, the Hall of Fame hosts soccer tournaments for up to 36 teams at a time on four soccer fields in Oneonta's west end. Participants include youth, high school, college, and adult teams. Every year the NSHOF hosts an annual induction match that features an Olympic soccer team. Future plans call for a multi-faceted national sports center on a 61-acre campus. Call for schedule of events. Adults $8, children twelve and under $4.*

End of Ford Avenue coverage.

Turning right and going down **South Main Street** takes you to:

> *Left.* ***Chicorelli's Barber Shop***.

> *Left.* ***The Rail*** *(607-432-9617). A bar.*

> *Right.* ***The Eighth Note*** *(607-432-0344). Musical instruments from small to large, used instruments, and repairs.*

> *Right.* ***Parking lot***.

End of South Main Street coverage.

Right. Oneonta **City Hall**.

Left. **American Sports Works** (607-432-4880). New and used, mostly ladies, clothing and accessories.

Left. **The Rose and Laurel Bookshop** (607-432-5604). New and used books.

Left. **Palace Cigar Store** (607-432-8385). Cigars, cigarettes, newspapers, magazines, paperback books, and beer.

Left. **Sweet Indulgence by Elena** (607-431-9140). Pastry shop and cafe serving European-American foods. Pastries, croissants, breads, cakes, pies, desserts, prepared Italian entree specialties, gourmet deli items, flavored coffees, cappuccino, and more. Also **Elena's Rosticcerie** catering.

Left. **Sal's Pizzeria and Restaurant** (607-432-6766). Pizza, calzones, subs, Italian dinners, etc.

Left. **The Paper Chase** (607-432-6741). Office supplies and fax.

Left. **Shakedown Street** (607-436-9776). New Age consignment shop and boutique featuring new, used, and homespun clothing. Also hemp clothing, jewelry, locally-blown glass, candles, drums, and hackie sacks.

Left. **Adventure Travel** (607-432-1114).

Left. **Mane Street Cutters** (607-432-8740). Hair salon.

Left. **Mama Nina's Pizzeria and Restaurant** (607-431-9800). Cozy, comfortable pizza parlor with soft lighting, wooden booths, and a pool table. Free delivery.

000.9   Left. Junction with **Elm Street**:

> *Left.* ***Good News Center*** *(607-432-2181). Bibles, books, and gifts.*

> *Left.* ***The Green Earth*** *(607-432-7160). Natural food store. Vitamins, power foods, organic foods, bulk foods, fresh herbs, and spices.*

> *Left.* ***Showcase Cinema*** *(607-432-7131, 432-5689). Movie theater.*

End of Elm Street coverage.

Right. **Town House Motor Inn** (607-432-1313). Comfortable rooms with vaulted ceilings, tall windows, bedside thermostats, and full bathtubs. Usually $50-$75/double, up to $100 on special weekends.

Right. Junction with **Grand Street**. Turning right onto Grand Street and obeying the following directions takes you to Neawah Park and Damaschke Field where you can watch the Oneonta Yankees play baseball:

*000.1   Right.   Intersection of **Grand Street** with **Division Street**. Turn right onto Division Street.*

> *000.1   **Division Street** flows directly into **Market Street**.*
>
> > *Left.   Intersection of **Market Street** with **James Georgeson Avenue** to **Neawah Park** and **Damaschke Field**:*
> >
> > > *Right.   **Damaschke Field**, home to the **Oneonta Yankees** (607-432-6326), a New York Yankees-affiliated Class A minor league baseball team in the NY-Penn League. Evening games are held from mid-June to the beginning of September. Game time is 7 PM, except for Sundays when games start at 6 PM.*
> > >
> > > *Continuing into Neawah Park, you'll find pavilions, picnic tables, restrooms, and the **Railroad Brotherhood Union Caboose**, a shrine to the founding in 1883 of the Brotherhood of Railroad Trainmen.*
> > >
> > > *You can also get to Neawah Park and Damaschke Field from Neawah Place at the southeast end of Main Street.*

End of coverage to Neawah Park and Damaschke Field.

Left. **Red Barrel Food Stores** (607-432-1123). Deli, subs, pizza, and Getty gas.

001.0   Junction of **Main Street** with **Maple Street** on the left and **James F. Lettis Highway** (**NY 23** east) on the right.

Making a left onto **Maple Street** gives you access to **Wilber Park**:

> *Wilber Park is tucked away in a residential area of Oneonta. It offers a large swimming pool, a children's wading pool, children's playground, full basketball court, two handball courts, eight tennis courts, two pavilions, picnic tables, charcoal grills, all on grassy lawns under monstrous pine trees. One way to get there is to drive up Maple Street a couple blocks, make a right onto Center Street, then drive five or six short blocks and make a left opposite Taft Avenue into the park. This takes you to the playground, basketball court, a pavilion, picnic tables, and charcoal grills. To get to the handball and tennis courts and the swimming pool, drive up Maple Street past Center Street and make a right turn onto Spruce Street, drive a few short blocks, then make a left onto Albert Morris Drive, which dead ends in the park at the pool.*

End of Wilber Park coverage.

Making a right turn onto **James F. Lettis Highway** and driving a half mile takes you to **I-88** Exit 15, with **Albany** to the east and **Binghamton** to the west.

Right. **Oneonta Post Office** (607-432-6100). ZIP 13820.

001.1   Right. **Kentucky Fried Chicken** (607-432-5700).

Right. **Dunkin' Donuts** (607-436-9269).

Left. **Friendly's** (607-432-0361). Bright, family restaurant with large menu of breakfasts, sandwiches, burgers, munchies, finger foods, dinners, and ice cream. Dinners $6-$9. Open 6 AM to 11 PM.

001.2   Left. **Pyramid Liquors** (607-432-0055). Discount wine and liquor.

Right.   **A. O. Fox Memorial Hospital** (607-432-2000). **Emergency room.**

001.4   Right. **Ritchko's Pharmacy** (607-432-6742).

Right.   **Higgins Jewelers** (607-432-4236). Gemologist and diamond dealer.

001.6   Right. **Taylor's** (607-433-0576). Gas, candy, cigarettes, etc.

001.7   Right. **Tiger Lily Antiques** (607-436-9588). Vintage textiles, linens, clothing; art, architecture, jewelry, furniture, and home accessories.

001.8   Left. **Rainbow Wok** (607-433-8885). Chinese restaurant.

Right. **Coach's Corner.** Sports bar.

Left. **Burger King** (607-432-7161).

001.9   Right. **East End Coin Laundry.**

Right. **Robo Automatic Car Wash** (607-432-5965).

002.0   Leaving the city of **Oneonta.**

Left. **Monroe Muffler and Brake** (607-433-1080).

Right. **Oneonta East End Liquors** (607-436-9040).

Right. **Bob's Auto & Truck Repair** (607-432-6413). Auto and truck repairs, and propane system repairs.

002.1   Right. **Quickway Foodstores** (607-432-0559). Convenience store and Mobil gas.

Right. **The Pine Shop** (607-432-1124). Unfinished and finished furniture.

002.2   Right. **Interstate Oil** (607-432-7749). Gas station.

Right. **Annutto's Farm Stand** (607-432-7905). Large farm stand offering fresh fruits and vegetables, honey, marinades, hot sauce, maple syrup, chocolates, fudge, candies, baked goods, apple cider, flowers, bulbs, garden supplies, garden statuary, ceramic ware, and more.

002.4   Right. **Wilber National Bank** (607-432-6910). 24-hour ATM.

002.6   Right. **Pizza Hut** (607-432-9004).

002.8   Right. **Oneonta Plaza**, housing:
         Parts America (607-433-7391). Auto parts.

Right. **Arby's** (607-432-9821). Roast beef.

002.9   Right. **Morey's Family Restaurant** (607-432-6664). Breakfast, lunch, and dinner in a family restaurant displaying a family member's outstanding miniature creations. The menu offers eggs, pancakes, omelettes, hot and cold sandwiches, grilled sandwiches, salads and sides, plus dinner entrees such as steaks, pork chops, roast turkey, fried clams, chicken Florentine, and more, $7-$10. Children's menu, soup and salad bar, and dessert carousel. Some of the miniatures are awesome.

003.0   Right. **Brook's House of Bar-B-Qs Drive-in** (607-432-1782). Large, friendly, family-run barbecue with a history spanning three generations serving lunch and dinner. Restaurant seats 300 in booths, at tables, and in a banquet room, plus an outdoor picnic area. Barbecue entrees include pork spare ribs, pork sampler, beef, tenderloin steak, with chicken a specialty, $6-$14. Salad bar. The restaurant's own barbecue sauces are also for sale.

003.3   Traffic light at entrance to **Price Chopper Plaza** on the right: **Eckerd Drugs** (607-432-0434).
Perrucci's Pizza (607-433-2505). New York and Sicilian-style pizza, white and stuffed pizzas, strombolis, calzones, hot and cold subs, salads, and pasta dinners. Dinners $5-$7.
Price Chopper (607-432-8905). Supermarket, pharmacy, and ATM. Open 24 hours.

Left. **Farmhouse Restaurant** (607-432-7374). Fine country dining in a cozy farm house with awnings and shutters, sun porch, dining deck, fireplace, and many Tiffany lamps. Varied menu features hearty dinners of beef, seafood, chicken, and veal; filet mignon, shrimp scampi, teriyaki sirloin, etc. Shrimp/salad/soup bar features dozens of hot and cold items. Salad bar as a dinner, $10; entrees $13-$18. Children's and senior citizen's menu.

003.4   Right. Traffic light at junction with **CR 47** south, down which one-tenth of a mile is **Route 28/I-88** Exit 16.

003.5   Right. **Munsons True Value Hardware and Building Supplies** (607-432-8756).

003.7   Right. **Master Hosts Inns** (607-432-1280, 800-446-7871). Twenty-eight-room motel on beautifully landscaped grounds. The rooms are spotless, and some feature sitting rooms, powder rooms, water beds, comfortable couches, whirlpool tubs, satellite TV with private channels, and more, $58-$158. Sundeck, barbecue, and eighteen-hole mini-golf. Closed January and February.

004.6   Entering town of **Milford**.

005.3   Left. **Lost and Found Antiques** (607-432-9094). A serious antique shop offering a general line with an emphasis on furniture and accessories from the 1840s through the 1940s. Fancy oak and walnut Victorian furniture, some largely impressive and some impressively large.   Also clocks, silver, oriental rugs, paintings, and decoratives.

005.6   Entering **Colliersville.**

Left. **Colliersville Cottage Antiques** (607-432-7427). Sixteen spaces displaying antiques and collectibles offered by 14 dealers. Blue Ridge pottery, sports memorabilia dating to the 1880s, ephemera (paper items such as magazines, advertisements, etc.), furniture, glassware, toys, wall decorations, paintings, miniatures, kitchenware, and much more.

005.7   Left. **Elaine's Coffee and Deli** (607-432-8349). Open for breakfast and lunch Monday through Saturday, and serving eggs, pancakes, sandwiches, subs, burgers, etc.

005.8   Right. **Country Cabin** (607-433-1122). Ice cream stand and snack bar in a new log cabin. Hard and soft ice cream, sundaes, shakes, burgers, subs, wings, and more. Open April through October.

Left. **Colliersville Post Office** (607-432-0282). ZIP 13747.

005.9   Right. **Agway Energy Products** (607-432-1903). Gas, and propane by weight and volume.

Left. **Lorenzos Motel** (607-433-2770). Modest motel with swimming pool, $39-$75/couple.

Left. **The Homestead** (607-432-0971, 800-782-8248). Fine dining from a menu featuring prime ribs, steaks, seafood, chicken, and more. Daily specials, Friday and Saturday night buffets, shrimp on the salad bar on Sundays, children's and senior's menus. Most entrees $13-$19. Knotty pine interior, multiple dining rooms, cozy atmosphere. Closed Mondays.

Flashing traffic signal at junction with **D.K. Lifgren Drive** on the left. See coverage of **NY 7 along D.K. Lifgren Drive to Route 28** later in this chapter.

Continuing straight ahead following **NY 7** east takes you to:

000.1   Right. **Colliersville Fishing Access Site** *parking area.*

Leaving **Colliersville.**

Left. **Vintage House Antique Center** *(607-433-4772). Seventeen multi-dealer showcases in 15 rooms featuring furniture, home accessories, china, glassware, jewelry, clothing, fabrics, artwork, dolls, railroad memorabilia, and much more. A browser's delight.*

000.2   Left. **Redwood Motel** *(607-432-1291). Eight clean and cozy country-style motel units offering easy access to Oneonta and Cooperstown, $39-$85. Also two mobile homes which sleep four to six and are rented as efficiencies, $50-$90/night; weekly rates available.*

000.6   Entering **Cooperstown Junction.**

000.8   Left. Offices of the **Leatherstocking Railway Historical Society** *(607-432-2429) and a depository for old rolling stock. Plans for this location include a Leatherstocking Railway Museum and a rail ride to Cooperstown.*

001.0   Left. **Falco's Junction** *(607-433-0140). A cozy, restored, 1926 Susquehanna Railroad passenger car serves as an Italian restaurant emphasizing fresh ingredients, imported pasta, and home baked breads and desserts. The cocktail lounge is decorated with a large, upside down airplane, musical instruments, a lobster pot, and other antiques. The rail car's charming interior evokes the nostalgic romance of earlier days. Great atmosphere and a mouth-watering menu promise an enjoyable dining experience. Entrees $8-$15; take-out service available. Closed Mondays.*

End of NY 7 east coverage.

End of Main Street and NY 7 east coverage. See Chapter 20, *Oneonta Through Milford to Cooperstown,* for coverage of Route 28 north from Oneonta.

NY 7 along D.K. Lifgren Drive to Route 28

006.3   Left. **Otsego County Tourist Information Booth** and **parking** area.

006.4   Junction with **Route 28** north to **Cooperstown** and south to **I-88** and **Oneonta**.

End of D.K. Lifgren Drive coverage.

Chestnut Street (NY 7 and NY 23) West from Main Street

Chestnut Street carries NY 7 and NY 23 west from Main Street to the West End of Oneonta. Along the way are a number of shops, restaurants, car dealers, and other amenities. Coverage of Chestnut Street is selective, focusing on a few places of interest immediately off Main Street, plus trips to Hartwick College and SUNY Oneonta. The coverage path is Chestnut Street to a right turn onto West Street to Hartwick College, and then continue on West Street to a right turn onto Ravine Parkway to SUNY Oneonta.

000.0   Right. **Ray's Baseball Card Store** (607-436-9693).

Left. **Oneonta Movie Theater** (607-432-2820). Twin theaters. Also box office for the **Orpheus Theater** acting company (whose performances occur at the Goodrich Theater at SUNY Oneonta).

Right. **Huntington Memorial Library** (607-432-1980).

000.3   Traffic light at intersection with **West Street**.

Coverage and mileage continue to the right onto West Street for Hart-wick College and **SUNY Oneonta:**

000.6   Left. Junction with **Clinton Street**:

*000.1   Right. An entrance to **Hartwick College** (607-431-4200) which provides access to the **Anderson Center for the Arts** and **Yager Hall**.*

*Hartwick hosts performances, programs, musical events, sporting events, lectures, discussions, exhibitions, and a film series, all open to the public. For information on these events, call the **Campus Events Hotline** on 607-431-4225. To be put on a mailing list for a monthly events brochure, call 607-431-4415.*

*Turning right from Clinton Street into the college and then making an immediate right puts you in the parking lot for the **Anderson Center for the Arts**, which houses the **Foreman Gallery** (607-431-4663). From the parking lot, follow the sidewalk around to the right to the doors off the patio on the opposite side of the building. The Foreman Gallery presents professional and student shows with exhibits changing every few weeks. The lobby and hallways in the Anderson Center display student art. A visiting artists program offers art lectures by visiting artists and art historians. The center also hosts a themed film series each semester. Open daily, noon to 9 PM, September through May.*

*Up the hill and to the left from the parking lot is **Yager Hall**, which houses the **Yager Museum**, the **Stevens-German Library**, and **Slade Theater**:*

***Yager Museum** (607-431-4480). Seven galleries on the first floor serve the students, the community, and the public. Changing every two to three months, these galleries display art, sculpture and cultural artifacts, as well as regional, national, and international items. The museum's 6000-item permanent collection of Susquehanna Valley Indian artifacts is one of the best collections of regional American Indian material in the country. Other*

important   collections   include   nineteenth   century
landscapes,   American   Indian   baskets,   Mexican   and
Central American masks, and South American artifacts.
And, for miniature lovers, there is a nine-foot-long, four-
story, 28-room, $50,000 doll house. Closed Mondays.

***Stevens-German Library** (607-431-4440). Fourth floor.*
College library of more than 280,000 volumes, plus
collections of Native American history and culture;
sixteenth century first-edition texts by Martin Luther; and
the largely-theological, eighteenth-century collection of
college founder John Christopher Hartwick. The library
archives have papers of the college; of J. C. Hartwick;
and of Judge William Cooper, founder of Cooperstown
and father of James Fenimore Cooper.

***Slade Theater**. (607-431-4925). Call the Campus Events*
Hotline (607-431-4225) or the Office of Special Programs
(607-431-4415) for performance and ticket information.

End of Clinton Street coverage.

000.8   Left.   Main   entrance   to **Hartwick   College** (607-431-4200).
Hartwick College is a liberal arts college founded as Hartwick
Seminary by John Christopher Hartwick's will in 1797.   The
campus dates from 1928 and is terraced up the hillside, ensuring
from each building spectacular views of Oneonta, the Susquehanna
Valley, and the hills beyond.   Hartwick hosts many cultural
activities which are open to the public.   See information on
***Anderson Center for the Arts** and **Yager Hall** above for details.*

001.0   Right. **Ravine Parkway** to **SUNY Oneonta** campus:

000.2   *Entering **State University of New York (SUNY) Oneonta***
        (607-431-3500).

000.4   *Right. **Science Discovery Center** (607-436-2011). Fun*
        with science for visitors both young and old. The center,
        whose philosophy is "You're never too old to have a

happy childhood," provides science fun through hands-on brain teasers, puzzles, and challenging demonstrations. Great fun! Enter the Physical Science Building through the side door down the sidewalk on the left side of the building. The center is downstairs and to the right. The parking lot on the right just beyond the Physical Science Building has some visitor parking spots. Open Noon to 4 PM; Thursdays through Saturdays from September through June, Mondays through Saturdays in July and August.

*000.5   Right. **Fine Arts Building** housing the following:
Fine Arts Gallery (607-436-2445), just inside the front door on the left.   Four or five exhibits of national professional contemporary artists annually, plus the student exhibit every April to May.   Gallery is open Monday through Friday, 11-4, except during college breaks. Admission free, tours available by appointment.*

***Goodrich Theater** and **Hamblin Theater**. SUNY Oneonta hosts various student, faculty, and professional performances including musicals, opera, dance, classic and modern plays, children's programs, concerts, and lectures. Programs are produced September through June and occasionally in summer by the university as well as by professional companies from Oneonta and New York City. Academic productions admission is usually $4-$5. For information call the **Hunt Union Information Desk** (607-436-3730). The Public Relations Office (607-436-2748) produces a monthly calendar of events.   Call the **Performing Arts at SUNY** box office (607-436-3100, staffed at production times) for tickets for performances by the student producing company. Call the **Hunt Union Box Office** (607-436-3722) for tickets for outside productions.*

*Also using the Goodrich Theater is an Oneonta semi-professional theater company called **Orpheus Theater** (607-432-1800, box office 607-432-9392), which produces* *primarily musicals, but also occasionally drama, comedy, thrillers, and concerts, four or five times a year. Orpheus also hosts a two-week summer children's theater workshop culminating in a public performance. The box office is in the **Oneonta Movie Theater** on **Chestnut Street** (described earlier in this chapter) and is open for two weeks prior to a performance. Tickets are usually $14-$18.*

End of Ravine Parkway, West Street, and Chestnut Street coverage.

NY 23 East Through Oneonta's Southside

Following **NY 23** east from its **Oneonta** intersection with **Route 28** at south end of **James F. Lettis Highway** south of I-88 Exit 15:

000.0   Right. **McDonald's** (607-432-7608). Burgers, etc.

Right. **Southside Autoparts** (607-433-1140). NAPA autoparts. Behind Red Barrel.

Right. Self-service car wash.

Right. **Red Barrel Food Stores** and **Taco Bell Express** (607-432-8880). Convenience store, gas, pizza, subs, tacos, ATM.

Left. **Getty** (607-433-9963). Gas, convenience store, car wash.

Left. **Super 8 Motel** (607-432-9505). Sixty rooms, VCR rentals, coffee and donuts in the morning, pets with permit; $77-$93/two.

000.1   Left. **Perkins Family Restaurant** (607-432-5290). Modestly priced family restaurant open weekdays until midnight, 24 hours on weekends.

Left. **Midas Muffler and Brake Shop** (607-432-0287).

Left. **Neptune Diner** (607-432-8820). Steaks, chops, seafood, and cocktails. Everything homemade, all baking done on premises, well-regarded soups, daily specials, with most dinner entrees $8-$13. Open 24 hours.

000.2   Traffic light at entrance to **South Side Mall** (607-432-5478) on the right:

Office Max (432-1091).
J. C. Penney (607-432-0262). Department store.
Restrooms
Radio Shack (607-432-1600). Electronics and computers.
Foot Locker (607-432-0907). Athletic footwear.
NRM Music (607-432-8546). Tapes, CDs, etc.
Waldenbooks (607-432-7842).
etc, etc (607-432-8172). Cigarettes, newspapers, magazines; T-shirts, and T-shirt printing.
Kay-Bee Toys (607-432-1200).
Payless ShoeSource (607-433-8829).
Schatz Stationery (607-433-1800).
GNC Nutrition Center (607-433-0504).
Cellular One (607-433-2878).
Hoyt's Cinema (607-432-3750). A four-screen movie theater.
Nail Trix (607-433-5200).
K-Mart (607-433-1600).
Little Caesar's Pizza Station (607-433-4690). In K-Mart.
Astoria Federal Savings (607-432-1149). ATM.
Cutting Crew (607-432-9851). Hair salon.
Gino & Joe's Pizza (607-433-2195).
Label Shopper (607-431-9291). Men's, women's, children's and plus-sized clothing.
Empire Vision (607-436-9200).
Afterthoughts (607-433-1879). Personal accessories for the young. Jewelry, candles, mood rings, sunglasses, ankle bracelets, novelties, cosmetics, hair products, etc.
S & S Liquor (607-433-1361).
Dream Machine (607-432-2574). Arcade.
Wilber National Bank (607-432-2343). ATM.
Gentry (607-432-3829). Hair salon.
Michael's Food Court (607-433-6601).

Littman Jewelers (607-432-4885).
Fashion Bug (607-432-7060). Ladies clothing boutique.
Candles Unlimited (607-433-1946).
Sunburst Reflect (607-433-0236).
Piercing Pagoda (607-432-1246). Jewelry, ear piercing, etc.

000.3   Left. **Enterprise rent-a-car** (800-RENT-A-CAR, 800-736-8222).

Left. **Smokers Choice**. Cigars and cigarettes.

000.4   Traffic light at entrance to **Wal-Mart Supercenter** on the right (607-431-9557).   Department store, tire and lube service, pharmacy, supermarket, one-hour photo, vision center, **McDonald's**, ATM. Open 24 hours.

Left. **Riverview Motel** (607-432-5301). On the banks of the Susquehanna River, this pretty and homey motel has a basket of flowers hanging by every room. Nicely maintained, waterbeds available, children 12 and under are free. $35-$99/couple.

000.8   Right. **Roger Karns** (607-432-7300). Ford Lincoln Mercury dealership.

001.0   Right. **Quickway Foodstores** (607-432-2144). Groceries, deli, fresh bakery, sandwiches, soups, hot meals, etc. Also Mobil gas.

Left. **Interskate 88** (607-432-0366). Roller rink.

Right. **Holiday Lanes** (607-432-2540). Bowling alley.

Left. **Rua & Sons** (607-432-0601). Truck and auto service, tires.

001.1   Right. **Holiday Inn** (607-433-2250). Some 120 rooms, restaurant, outdoor pool, exercise room, and lounge. Room rates are seasonal, $57-$148. Also efficiencies. **Abbey's Garden Restaurant** is bright and cheery with mountain views, and serves three traditionally American meals a day. Dinner entrees of veal, steaks, seafood, poultry, and nightly specials, $11-$17. Ski packages with

Scotch Valley Ski Area in **Stamford**, monthly murder mysteries, and dancing in the lounge.

001.3   Right. **Susquehanna Valley Bookmart** (607-433-1034). New and used books and comics.

001.6   Entering town of **Davenport** and **Delaware County**.

012.0   Left. **Beaver Spring Lake Campsites** (607-278-5293). Mountain views, beautifully manicured lawns, and a lily-pad-adorned fish pond provide the setting for 19 tent sites and 104 R/V sites with full hook-ups. The grassy sites are adjacent to trees, providing both sun and shade.   Amenities include boating, fishing, swimming pool, boat and canoe rentals, playground, game room, store, laundry, and propane. Planned activities for children and adults, bands and fishing contests on holiday weekends, and more. Mid-April through October, $16-$19/night.

End of NY 23 coverage.

Oneonta Through Milford to Cooperstown

088.8   Left(right) Junction with **Main Street** into **Oneonta**. See Chapter 19, *Oneonta*.

088.9   Left(right) **Metro Cleaners** (607-436-9613).

089.1   Left(right) **Shop and Save** (607-432-0012). Food and drug superstore. ATM.

089.2   Right(left) **Christopher's Restaurant and Country Lodge** (607-432-2444). Ruggedly rustic and casually elegant restaurant and motel with Adirondack north-country decor. Rough-hewn beams, barnsiding, elk horn chandeliers, hunting trophies, and a fireplace adorn the restaurant. Continental lunch and dinner menu features chicken, veal, Italian specialties, pizzas, sandwiches, vegetarian items, and daily specials; usually $4-$8 for lunch, $8-$16 for dinner. Homemade desserts, sandwich bar. Penny-a-pound dinner for children 10 and under. Motel rooms and suites, some with whirlpools, offer north-country Adirondack and western cowboy decor. Rooms $50-$99, suites $120-$160.

089.3   Right(left) **Sabatini's Little Italy** (607-432-3000). Pre-World-War-II-Italy-styled restaurant displaying photos of local luminaries. Open kitchen serves made-to-order, northern Italian, Tuscan-influenced cuisine with homemade pastas and fresh herbs and spices, brick-oven pizza, and homemade desserts. Godfather booths and a fireplace add to the ambiance. Individual menu, $7-$13; family-style menu with papa-sized platters, $10-$19. Large cigar selection for an after-dinner smoke. Plans call for a 20-room villa in 1998. Tuscany in Oneonta.

Right(left) **BJ's Wholesale Club** (607-431-1111).

Left(right) **Aldi Food Store**. Supermarket.

089.4   Right(left) **Wendy's** (607-433-0940). Burgers, etc.

Traffic light at junction with **NY 23**. **Route 28 north turns left onto NY 23/James F. Lettis Highway west for 0.2 mile. (Route 28 south turns right.)**

If you don't make this left turn but continue straight onto **NY 23** east, you will go through a section of **Oneonta** called **Southside**. See *NY 23 East Through Oneonta's Southside* in Chapter 19, *Oneonta.*

089.6   Junction with **I-88** Exit 15. **Route 28 north makes a right turn onto I-88 east. (Route 28 south makes a left from I-88 onto NY 23/James F. Lettis Highway.)**

If you don't make this right turn but continue straight on **NY 23/James F. Lettis Highway** west, in one-half mile the road intersects with **Main Street/NY 7** in **Oneonta**. See Chapter 19, *Oneonta,* for details.

091.6   **Route 28/I-88** Exit 16 to **CR 47** north to **NY 7** by the Farmhouse Restaurant.

094.0   **Route 28/I-88** Exit 17 at Mile 60. **Route 28 north leaves I-88 at this exit.**

094.4   End of exit ramp. **Turn left to follow Route 28 north. (If traveling south, make a right turn to follow Route 28 onto I/88 west.)**

Route 28 follows a meandering stream through flat cow pastures surrounded by soft, lumpy hills. While not always visible, the cows' recent presence is occasionally confirmed by the lingering fragrance of the by-product of their milk production process.

095.7   Left(right) Junction with **D.K. Lifgren Drive** to **NY 7** in **Colliers-ville**:

> *000.1   Right.* ***Otsego County Tourist Information Booth*** *and* ***parking*** *area.   Open 9-4 daily   during the summer, weekends only in May and September.*

> *End of D.K. Lifgren Drive coverage.   See Chapter 19, Oneonta, for coverage of Colliersville.*

Route 28 approaches **Colliers Dam**.   Built in 1907, it dams the **Susquehanna River**, creating **Goodyear Lake**.   The lake is large enough to support boating, fishing, water skiing, sailing, and more.   You can launch your canoe or motorized rowboat at either of two places on the Susquehanna River above the lake.   The first launching site is Riverside Trailer Park in Portlandville.   The second is off CR 35 on the east side of the river, northeast of Portlandville and southeast of Milford.   See CR 35 in Portlandville or NY 166 in Milford for directions.

096.4   Right(left) **Knott's Motel** (607-432-5948).   A charming place to stay and with all the toys you need to play on Goodyear Lake. Fresh and tidy two-bedroom apartments, small efficiencies, and 15 rooms, $55-$92/couple, set back from the road on manicured lawns sloping down to the lake.   Canoe, rowboat, and sailboat rentals plus a waterskiing towboat for hire.   Swimming area, tennis court, picnic pavilion with charcoal grill, and an impressive arrowhead collection behind the front desk, all in a north country, Adirondack-like setting.

096.7   Left(right) **Taylors Mini Mart** (607-432-8018).   Convenience store, Mobil gas.   Subs, pizza, ATM.

097.5   Left(right) **Poje's Auto Repair** (607-432-5698).   Auto and truck repairs.

097.6   Left(right) **Summer Joy** (607-432-1350).   Hard and soft ice cream, fast food. Seasonal.

098.8   Entering(leaving) **Portlandville** above Goodyear Lake, where the narrow Susquehanna River still supports boating behind the old houses lining the east side of Route 28.

099.1   Right(left) **Blue Bonnet Antiques** (607-286-7568). Big red barn and other buildings housing refinished antique (pre-1850) country furniture. In business for almost 50 years.

Right(left) Junction with **CR 35** (**Cliffside Road**) to boat launching and fishing access site:

000.0   *Crossing the **Susquehanna River** on a bridge so low to the water that only small boats can pass beneath it.*

000.3   *Make a left at the bend, continuing to follow CR 35.*

002.7   *Right. **Susquehanna State Forest** of 422 acres.*

002.8   *Left. Entrance to New York State **boat launching** and **fishing access** site on the Susquehanna River. Follow dirt road 0.2 mile to parking area and cartop boat launching site. You can also stand on the small pier and fish among the lily pads.*

End of CR 35 coverage.

099.2   Right(left) **Portlandville Post Office** (607-286-9838). ZIP 13834.

099.3   Right(left) **Jerry's Bait and Tackle** (607-286-7514). Fishing and hunting supplies.

099.4   Leaving(entering) **Portlandville**.

099.6   Right(left) **Riverside Village** (607-286-7100, 800-477-9898). Forty-two R/V sites with partial or full (including cable and telephone) hookups,   20 tent sites, fireplaces, picnic tables, bathhouse, and showers. Some sites have private boat dock on the Susquehanna River, providing access to over 12 miles of river between Goodyear Lake and Cooperstown. Tent sites $12/couple, full hookups $25, boat launch ramp, $3. Camping season May through September.

Corn fields and cow pastures surrounded by soft, lumpy hills.

102.9   Right(left) **Red   Barrel   Food   Stores**   (607-286-3313). Convenience store. Subs, pizza, and Getty gas.

Right(left) **Valley Recreation** (607-286-7207). Boats, outboards, snowmobiles, ATVs, personal water craft, and trailers. Sales and service.

103.2   Right(left) **Jackie's Restaurant** (607-286-7843).   Family restaurant open for breakfast, lunch, and Friday night dinner. Varied dinner menu plus a weekly special, $7-$9.   Closed Tuesdays. Chicken Parmigiana, seafood platter, sirloin steak, ham steak, breaded pollack, etc.

Right(left) **Milford Lanes** (607-286-9910). A six-lane bowling alley with a beer and snack bar.

Entering(leaving) village of **Milford**.

Milford hosts a French and Indian War re-enactment and the Leatherstocking Railway Historical Society hosts the Milford Railroad Day celebration each year in late May or early June. Centering on the Upper Susquehanna Cultural Center and the Milford Depot Museum, activities include the re-enactment program, an antique car show, a village-wide yard sale, bake sales, entertainment, a dance, and more. Call either the historical society (607-432-2429) or the cultural center (607-286-7038) for details.

Right(left) **Dick's Auto Service** (607-286-7518). Automobile repair shop.

103.3   Right(left) **Wilber Park**, with a full-sized baseball field, a Little League field, a playground, and a concession stand.

103.6   Right(left) **Milford Free Library Association** (607-286-9076). Established in 1927, the library has a local history section, including *Time Once Past*, a history of Milford recently published by the Greater Milford Historical Association. In this book is an account of Eva Coo, who, in 1934, was the first woman in the United States to be executed in an electric chair. Open Monday and Thursday evenings, and Tuesday and Friday afternoons.

Left(right) **Crowley's Corner Store** (607-286-9901). A food market established in 1944.

Right(left) **Milford Post Office** (607-286-7512). ZIP 13807.

Traffic light at junction of Route 28, **CR 44** and **NY 166**. Turning left at traffic light onto **CR 44** takes you to:

000.6   *Right. **1860 Spencer Inn Bed and Breakfast** (607-286-9402). An imposing Victorian building on 20 acres with stately pines, a manicured lawn, and magnificent views of the Susquehanna River valley. This perfectly-kept home* *has guest rooms with private or shared bath, a suite, and an efficiency apartment, all tastefully furnished with antiques; a dining room with a raised-hearth fireplace; and a breakfast deck. Cable TV and A/C. Popular with Glimmerglass Opera fans and other Cooperstown visitors. $65-$95/couple, full breakfast included. Open April through October. Lovely.*

End of CR 44 coverage.

Making a right at the light onto **NY 166** north yields the following:

*000.0   Right. **Elm Inn** (607-286-9903). A 100-year-old, quaint, and charming inn with a dining room, a tap room, and a liquor store. Breakfast, lunch, and dinner Tuesday through Saturday, and breakfast on Sunday. Lunch about $4, dinner $10-$13. Daily specials, salad bar on Wednesday through Saturday. Saturday salad bar includes shrimp. The inn, warm and cozy like an old flannel shirt, serves as Milford's town square, pot-bellied stove zone, and watering hole all in one.*

*Left. **Wilber National Bank** (607-286-3361).*

*Right. **Furniture Doctor** (607-286-7038). Mission furniture, antique restoration, and refinishing.*

*000.1   Left. **Murdock and Murdock Galleries** (607-286-9941). Fine art and antiquities in restored house. Old and contemporary European and American artwork, bronzes, and lamps. An eye-opening experience.*

*Right. **Beau's Bed and Breakfast and Giftshop** (607-286-9167). Old two-story country house with front porch and two guest rooms with private bath. A third bedroom is rented as a second bedroom for families or parties willing to share a bath. $70/couple for first night, including large country breakfast; additional nights less. Open May through October. Also a gift shop.*

Right. **Milford Depot Museum.** *The restored 1869 Milford Depot, a station on the old Cooperstown and Charlotte Valley Railroad, is now a museum with artifacts and memorabilia in the station agent's office, the waiting room, and the baggage room. Visitors can also ride around the station property on a working, 18" gauge, passenger train. The museum is run by the Leatherstocking Railway Historical Society (607-432-2429), which is progressing with its plans for a nine-mile rail ride from here to Cooperstown in the fall of 1998, and a 16-mile rail ride from Cooperstown Junction to Cooperstown in 1999. Gift shop. Open weekends, June through October.*

000.2   *Right. Junction with* **River Street***:*

000.0   *Right.* **The Cooperstown Brewing Company** *(607-286-9330) in a restored creamery. Brewers of "Old Slugger Pale Ale", " Nine Man Golden Ale", "Benchwarmer Porter", and "Strike Out Stout". Tours of the brew house, fermentation deck, conditioning room, bottling room, and the public tasting room. Closed Sunday mornings.*

End of River Street coverage.

000.9   *Right. Junction with* **CR 35***. Turn right for a Susquehanna River fishing access and boat launching site.*

000.2   *Turn right to continue following* **CR 35** *south for a Susquehanna River fishing access and boat launching site.*

002.8   *Right. Entrance to New York State* **boat launching** *and* **fishing access** *site on the Susquehanna River. Follow dirt road 0.2 mile to parking area and cartop boat launching site. You can also stand on the small pier and fish among the lily pads.*

The boat launch and fishing access site along the stress-reducing Susquehanna River.

End of CR 35 south and NY 166 north coverage.

Left(right) **Upper Susquehanna Cultural Center** (607-286-7038). This circa 1805 former Presbyterian church, administered by the Greater Milford Historical Association, is now a cultural center hosting performances, music programs, lectures, and exhibits. Hours by chance or appointment.

Left(right) **David Sayre House** (607-286-7038). Also circa 1805, a largely-original historic house museum representing the early 19th-century history of Milford and the area. Hours by chance or appointment.

103.8   Right(left) **Milford Flea Market** (607-286-9839, 607-286-9350). Indoor flea market featuring furniture, antiques, collectibles, handcrafts, leathers, jewelry, and more. This and that and old and new. Open Friday through Sunday.

Right(left) **Country Meadow Inn** (607-286-9496). Bed and breakfast in a 200-year-old farm house adjacent to a farm. Four air-conditioned guest rooms with private and shared baths, library, 24-hour coffee, and resident cats. Children welcome. Pet kennels. Homey, relaxed, and comfortable. $65-$75/couple, including full breakfast.

104.1   Left(right) **Brookside Motel** (607-286-9821). Just what the name says, a brookside motel set back from the road on a broad, green lawn under tall pine trees. Nine units, $50-$60/couple, quietude included. End of May through early November.

Leaving(entering) village of **Milford**.

104.2   Right(left) **Wood Bull Antiques** (607-286-9021). A "museum" with no admission charge. Huge, one-of-a-kind, must-see, four-floor barn housing a 20-year collection of antiques. Dozens of furnished room settings, each one a different Hollywood set. Reportedly 2000 chairs (no, I didn't count them), 48 stoves, beds, tables, harvest farm tables, cupboards, cabinets, pinball machines, radios, microscopes, typewriters, globes, tools, strange electronic items, a mannequin, and much, much more. All surrounded by fields sown with crocks and pots, garden furniture, weather vanes, and deer. A wonderful place to browse for a couple of hours.

Route 28 runs northward here, high along the east side of a hill, presenting broad, pastoral views of the corn fields in the valley and the treed hillsides beyond.

104.7   **Milford/Hartwick** town line.

106.3   Right(left) **Pop's Place** (607-286-7219). Ice cream and fast food stand with pavilions, picnic tables, and a large parking lot. May through mid-October.

106.9   Left(right) **Cat's Pajamas Bed and Breakfast** (607-286-9431). Well-kept, century-old, old-fashioned farmhouse with interesting floors and doors. Four guest rooms, each with its own bath, cable TV, and A/C. Warm, cozy and comfy, just like Grandmother's house, and patrolled by Henrietta the cat. Full breakfast. $60-$90/couple.

107.2   Right(left) **Cooperstown Dreams Park** (704-630-0050). Bring your team and play in baseball-famous Cooperstown against other teams from around the country. Week-long, Saturday to Saturday, baseball tournaments for girls and boys 12 years old and under on 10 lighted baseball fields. On-site lodging and dining; free admission for spectators. June through August.

Left(right) **Brockmann's Antique Center** (607-547-9192). Large, multi-dealer shop in two buildings. Collectibles, curiosities, early Americana, new unfinished furniture, new but old-looking weather vanes, and baskets, baskets, baskets. Closed January.

107.3   Left(right) **Maple Shade Bed & Breakfast** (607-547-9530). Tall, stately, 120-year-old former mansion of a hops grower houses three lovely guest rooms with antique furnishings and brass beds and sharing two baths. Sitting room with TV in the sun-drenched tower with pretty views. Thermostat and ceiling fan in each room. $65-$95/couple. Outdoor swimming pool. Big arrowhead collection downstairs.

107.4   Left(right) Junction with **Seminary Road**:

*001.5   Stop sign at "T" at **Towers Road**. Turn left:*

*000.8   Left. **Beaver Valley Campground** (607-293-8131, 800-726-7314). A warm, friendly, family-oriented campground on 276 acres of forest, meadows, ponds, and fossil pits. One hundred sites, camping cabins, bunk houses, large rec hall, playground, swimming pool, and activities. Partial hook-ups, dump station, and propane. $24-$27/night/family, cabins $45/night. Also two-bedroom modular homes rented by the week.*

*Left.   **Cooperstown Baseball Camp** (607-293-8131, 800-726-7314).   An instructional, adult-coached, one- to six-day baseball camp for children aged 8-17.   Play on a little league or a full-sized field, and participate in nightly baseball-oriented outings to the National Baseball Hall of Fame, an Oneonta Yankees baseball game, and more.*

End of Towers Road and Seminary Road coverage.

107.7   Right(left) **Ingalls Farms** (607-547-5481).   Home-grown flowers, plants, fruits, vegetables, and produce. In season, pick your own strawberries, blueberries, and raspberries. Open Mother's Day to Halloween. Closed Sundays.

107.9   Right(left) **Central National Bank** (607-547-8301).   Drive-thru ATM.

Left(right) **Fox Den Guide Service** and **Coulman's Taxidermy Studio** (607-547-5004).   Gun and bow hunting guide service for the Cooperstown area and upstate New York, including the Adirondacks, for turkey, predator, small game, deer, and bear.

108.0   Traffic light at **The Commons** on the right.   Shopping Plaza. Left to right:
Edmund's Barber Shop.
A.S.A.P. etc (607-547-2834).   Printing, copies, and shipping.
Shear Intrigue (607-547-4173).   Unisex hair salon, nails, and waxing.
Video to Go (607-547-7167).
Family Dollar Store (607-547-5531).
China Wok (607-547-5888).   Chinese restaurant open for lunch and dinner.
P&C Foods and Pharmacy. (607-547-5956).   Supermarket.

Right(left) **Best Western Inn at the Commons** (607-547-9439, 800-528-1234).   Sixty-two rooms, heated indoor pool, whirlpool, and exercise room.   Free continental breakfast.   The inn, sitting pretty on a ridge, offers scenic views of the valley to the east. $75-$200/double.

Right(left) **Pizza Hut** (607-547-1000).

Right(left) **McDonald's** (607-547-1110).

108.1   Right(left) **Kaleidoscope** (607-547-1852). Gifts and cards. Six rooms, each with its own theme. Jewelry, incense, and fragrance and massage oils. Gardening, pottery, and seasonal gifts. Gourmet foods, teas, and cookie and scone mixes. Toys, plush animals, puzzles, and gifts for infants to teenagers. Outdoor-themed gifts for fisherfolk, hunters, sailors, campers, etc.   Christmas ornaments, cards, gift wrap, stocking stuffers, decorations, oil candles, tapers, and much more.

108.2   Left(right) **Dandy-Li Inn** (607-547-5700). A bright yellow, non-smoking bed and breakfast with family-style atmosphere, four guest rooms sharing two baths, and a suite for up to four with private bath. Living room, full dining room, patios, porches, gas grills, and picnic area.   Full sit-down breakfast with fresh homemade muffins and fresh fruit in season. Rooms $100-110, suite $160-170. Children welcome. Open May through October.

108.7   Left(right) **Bella Cibo's** (607-547-1359). Family-style pizzeria and restaurant offering a full Italian menu of fresh salads, homemade lasagna, hand-tossed pizzas, etc. Open for lunch and dinner, with dinner entrees $5-$8.

108.8   Right(left) **Cooperstown Fun Park** (607-547-2767). Go-carts, bumper boats, golf driving range, arcade, picnic area, information center, hot dogs, drinks, and ice cream. Memorial Day through Labor Day.

Left(right) **Pit Stop** (607-547-9572).   Convenience store, groceries, subs, and Citgo gas.

Right(left) **Cooperstown Putt'n Around** (607-547-2767). Miniature golf. Seasonal.

Right(left) **Hamburger Hall of Fame** (607-547-4113). Menu has two dozen different flame-broiled burgers ($3-$5), plus steaks, seafood platters, sandwiches and hot sandwiches, sides, soups, salads, and more. Serving breakfast, lunch, and dinner. Dinners $5-$11.

Left(right) **Wayman's Antiques** (607-547-8693). Antiques and handmade wares. Almost an entire two-story house full of antiques tastefully presented.

Right(left) **The Wildwood Gift Emporium** (607-547-5151). An eight-room collection of gifts, some local and some from the far corners of the world: specialty foodstuffs, cookie and scone mixes, women's jumpers, T-shirts, handcrafted baskets; locally-crafted Victorian gifts; children's toys, plush toys, jigsaw puzzles, kites; Americana, pillows, coffee mugs, tins, candles, potpourri; baseball first day covers and baseball cards; wind chimes, hummingbird feeders, watering cans, flags; fishing and nautical items; and a Christmas room.

108.9   Left(right) **Lonesome Whistle** (607-547-8439). Toy train shop. "HO", ".027" and "G" gauge trains and accessories. Active, two-line layout. Also used trains including Lionel and American Flyer. Train fans of all ages should stop, look, and listen.

Left(right) **J and J Wine and Liquor** (607-547-1125).

Left(right) **First Choice Dry Cleaners** (607-547-1351).

109.1   Left(right) Junction with **CR 11**:

*000.2   Left. **The 1819 House** (607-547-1819). Fine dining with historical ambiance in a largely-original, four-columned, eyebrow colonial house. Formerly a brothel and an underground railroad stop, the restaurant has three dining rooms and is decorated with prints of impressionistic* *masters.   Dinner is also served in the family-friendly tavern with its smooth, varnished, honey-colored furnishings, dark, rough stone walls, and a two-sided fireplace. The seasonal menu offers European, American, and regional cuisine, with selections of fresh seafood, veal, chicken, beef, and vegetables, as well as children's selections.   Personal requests and casual attire are welcomed.   Entrees are $11-20.   Open 5-9 PM, reservations suggested.*

001.0   *Left. **Whispering Pines Chalet** (607-547-5640, 888-547-5650). A luxurious, European-styled bed and breakfast nestled in Chase's Gorge. Secluded and quiet, with its own brook in a wild and forested setting, the chalet has a huge deck, balconies, vaulted ceilings, and skylights. The newly-renovated interior boasts four suites, each with a queen or king canopy bed, sumptuous furnishings, and a gas or wood fireplace. The honeymoon suite has a marble bath and an awning-covered private balcony, while the VIP suite has a whirlpool bath, a bidet, and a wood-burning fireplace.   Luxurious accommodations in the forest. $110-$135/couple, with full breakfast.*

003.9   *Right. Junction with unnamed road to:*

000.2   *Left. **Cooperstown Famous Family Campground** (607-293-7766). Rustic campground with more than 100 sites accommodating tents to RVs with full hook-ups including cable TV. General store, recreation hall, in-ground pool, and fishing pond, $18-$24/two.   Also the **Lolly Pop Farm and Petting Zoo**. Farm, petting zoo, hay rides, and cow milking. Mid-May to mid-October.*

End of CR 11 coverage.

109.6   Left(right) **Smith-Cooperstown** (607-547-9924). Ford, Mercury, Jeep, and Eagle car dealership.

110.0   Left(right) Junction with **CR 26**. Up this road is:

> ***Adelaide Country Inn*** *(607-547-1215).   Bed and breakfast.   From Route 28, drive CR 26 one mile to left turn onto CR 59, 1.4 miles to right turn onto Bush Road, then 0.7 mile to Adelaide Country Inn on the right.   A family-oriented bed and breakfast in an almost two-century-old center-hall colonial house on more than 100 acres with walking/cross-country ski trails.   Two guest rooms have a private bath and two more share a bath. $75-$90/couple, including full buffet breakfast.*

End of CR 26 coverage.

111.0   Right(left) **Trolley Parking. The Blue Lot.** One-tenth of a mile down this road.   Trolley runs every 20 minutes; $.75 a ride or $1.50 for an all-day pass.

Right(left) **Wilber National Bank** (607-547-7222).   24-hour ATM.

111.1   Right(left) **Haggerty Hardware** (607-547-2166).   Ace Hardware store.

Right(left) **Church & Scott Pharmacy** (607-547-1228).

111.2   Right(left) **The Peppermill** (607-547-8550).   A family restaurant with a casual atmosphere and a sun room.   Open for dinner only, serving steaks, seafood, pasta, and ribs.   Happy hour is from 4 PM to 5 PM daily with half-priced beverages and 10 percent off dinners.   Mid-week specials include $11 lobsters on Tuesdays, a $10 fish fry on Wednesdays, and $11 prime rib on Thursdays.   Lite menu, children's menu.   The Peppermill is well-regarded by locals. Closed January through March, during which time a local organization operates the restaurant in teaching mode and serves lunch and dinner to the public.

111.3   Right(left) **Kirn's Body Shop** (607-547-8784).   24-hour towing.

Right(left) **Staffin Realty** (607-547-8221).

Entering village of **Cooperstown**. Route 28 follows **Chestnut Street** to **Glen Avenue**.

111.4   Left(right) **Rose & Thistle** (607-547-5345). A lovely rose and white, three-story, bed and breakfast with wrap-around porch and pretty accent flowers, and furnished with Victorian antiques. The circa-1905 home's amenities for guests include three rooms, one of which has a private bath, a fireplace room, a living room with a large-screen TV, central air conditioning, and brookside benches in the backyard. The proprietress emphasizes hospitality with a personal touch including robes and slippers, coffee and juice brought to your room, dinner prepared upon request, special touches for special occasions, etc. Open April through November, and at other times upon request. Smoking allowed on the porch; children aged eight and up welcome. $85-$95/couple with full country breakfast.

Right(left) Junction with **Walnut Street,** down which one-tenth of a mile on the right is **trolley parking** in the Cooperstown Central School yard when school is not in session. Trolley runs every 20 minutes; $.75 a ride or $1.50 for an all-day pass.

111.5   Right(left) **Great American** (607-547-2527). Supermarket. Out-of-town and international newspapers.

Left(right) **Getty** gas, auto repairs.

111.6   Left(right) **Stewart Shops** (607-547-7248). Convenience store, Citgo gas, and an ATM.

Right(left) **Cooperstown Motel** (607-547-2301). Large, clean, contemporary motel with 37 rooms housing from one to seven people, $49-$109/couple. Contemporary furniture, full tub in bathroom. Well-behaved pets allowed upon approval.

Right(left) Junction with **Beaver Street:**

*000.5   Beaver Street bends left onto **Fair Street**.*

*000.6   Right. Junction with **Atwell Road**:*

> *000.1   Right.   **Bassett Hospital** (607-547-3456) and **emergency room** (607-547-3355).*

End of Beaver Street coverage.

111.7   Left(right) **Taylor's Gas Station** (607-547-8579). Full-service gas station and car wash. Also **Village Tower 2** (607-547-5570). Convenience store.

Left(right) **Mohican Motel** (607-547-5101). Nicely kept bright-white motel units with varnished wooden doors, practical furnishings, and private baths, some with tub. Thirteen units in two buildings can accommodate up to six, and feature A/C and TV with HBO. Outside are park benches and lawn furniture for relaxing. Rates are $48-$103/two. Open May through November.

111.8   Right(left) **Chestnut Street Guest House** (607-547-5624). Lovely and pleasant bed and breakfast in an 1860 home with original tin ceilings, antiques, and personal collections (antique milk glass, autographed baseball hall of fame photos, and more). Three rooms, each with private bath and each tastefully furnished in a different theme, plus a family suite for four with living room, two bedrooms, kitchen, and bath. Rooms $95/couple, suite $125, including deluxe continental breakfast. Golfers note: the proprietor also makes custom golf clubs.

Right(left) **Quickway Citgo** (607-547-2632). Full service gas.

Right(left) **Chestnut Street Grocery & Deli** (607-547-5829). Deli and grocery.

111.9   Right(left) **Cooperstown Antiques Center** (607-547-2435). General line of antiques where you can browse in an uncluttered shop. Also antique lighting and hand-painted parchment shades. Antique lighting rewired and antique lamps restored.

Junction of **Route 28 (Chestnut Street)** with **NY 80 (Glen Avenue)**. Route 28 north turns left to join NY 80 west, while NY 80 east goes straight ahead through the village of Cooperstown. See Chapter 21, *Cooperstown,* for a description of the village. See Chapter 22, *Cooperstown to Richfield Springs to Mohawk,* for continuation of Route 28 coverage.

Cooperstown

Cooperstown is famous as the birthplace of baseball and the home of the National Baseball Hall of Fame. Add Doubleday Field, Cooperstown Dreams Park, and dozens of baseball-themed attractions and shops, and Cooperstown wins the most valuable player award for the preservation and promotion of baseball heritage. But, there is much more to Cooperstown than baseball. Founded in 1786, the village sits at the southern end of nine-mile-long Otsego Lake where it feeds the Susquehanna River. Despite an 1862 fire which destroyed much of Main Street and despite over half a century of the commercialism of baseball, Cooperstown retains its colonial heritage throughout. The village is resplendent with Federal-style homes, huge maple trees, lakeside parks, walkable sidewalks, and a charming atmosphere. Even if you're not a baseball fan it's easy to fall in love with this wonderful place.

While Cooperstown's population is just over 2,000 people, it is host to almost one-half million visitors a year. In addition to baseball, attractions include the Fenimore House Museum, The Farmers' Museum, and the New York State Historical Association. Beautiful Otsego Lake offers boating, water skiing, scenic boat rides, and fishing (New York state fishing license required) for brown trout, land-locked salmon, bass, walleye, pickerel, perch, bullhead, and more. Nearby are the Glimmerglass Opera and Glimmerglass State Park. You can golf at the Leatherstocking Golf Club; shop until your credit cards wince; search for that elusive perfect antique; find the painting of your dreams at the Cooperstown Art Association Gallery; enjoy a picnic lunch by the lake at Lake Front Park; dine at many fine restaurants; stay at a motel, hotel, an inn, or one of dozens of charming

B&Bs; then work out the next morning at Clark Sports Center. The variety of activities in and around the village of Cooperstown is astonishing.

Every Memorial Day weekend the Bainbridge Chamber of Commerce hosts from Friday evening through Monday the General Clinton Canoe Regatta, a series of canoe races attracting 3,000 canoeists. Monday is an endurance race which starts at Otsego Lake in Cooperstown and ends at Bainbridge, seventy miles down the Susquehanna River. For information call the Bainbridge Chamber of Commerce (607-967-8700), or write P.O. Box 2, Bainbridge, NY, 13733.

A must stop in Cooperstown is the Chamber of Commerce Visitor Information Center (607-547-9983) for its wonderful *Cooperstown Visitor's Guide*, chock full of what to do and see, and where to stay, eat and shop in and around Cooperstown. It also contains interesting vignettes on local color and history. The Visitor Information Center is at 31 Chestnut St. (NY 80) just south of the Main Street traffic light in the center of the village.

Travelers may also call toll-free, 888-875-2969, to receive information about Cooperstown via first-class mail. Callers receive a full-color brochure featuring the Baseball Hall of Fame, Fenimore House Museum, The Farmers' Museum, Glimmerglass Opera, other attractions, calendar of events, rates, hours, phone numbers, and selected accommodations.

Cooperstown's popularity often makes lodging difficult to find, with some lodging reserved a year in advance. Prior planning and reservations are strongly suggested. Also, many of Cooperstown's restaurants and shops are open seven days during the summer, but only six or five, or perhaps not at all, during the winter. If coming from afar to visit a particular restaurant or shop, phone ahead to confirm it will be open when you get there.

Parking in the center of Cooperstown is limited, especially during peak tourist months. Cooperstown runs a trolley system from parking lots to major attractions 8:30 AM to 9:00 PM daily from the last week in June through Labor Day, and 8:30 AM to 6:00 PM on weekends from Memorial Day weekend through the second to last weekend in June, and Labor Day through Columbus Day. There are four free parking lots on the outskirts of the village where you may board the trolley. Cost for the trolley is $1.50

all day or $.75 per ride. There are public restrooms at each of the three color-coded lots. The Blue Lot (#1) is off the east side of Route 28 (Chestnut Street), 1.1 miles south of the village traffic light. The Red Lot (#2) is off the east side of Route 28/NY 80 on Glen Avenue, 0.2 mile north of the Route 28's junction with NY 80. The Yellow Lot (#3) is on the east side of NY 80 (Lake Street), 1.2 miles north of the village traffic light. There is an additional lot, available only when school is not in session, at the Cooperstown Central School 0.1 mile down Walnut Street from Chestnut Street. Walnut Street is 0.7 mile south of the village traffic light.

If you are walking around the village, easily accessible public restrooms are located at the rear of the Visitor Information Center and at Doubleday Field facing Doubleday Court parking lot.

Cooperstown has two main arteries: Chestnut Street/NY 80 north from Route 28 through the center of the village to the Alice Busch Opera Theater, and Main Street/CR 31 east and north from Chestnut Street to Glimmerglass State Park. Each artery is described below separately.

Chestnut Street/NY 80 East from Route 28

000.0   Junction of **Route 28** with **NY 80**. Route 28 north turns left to join NY 80 west (**Glen Avenue**), while NY 80 east goes straight ahead through the village of Cooperstown. Following NY 80 (Chestnut Street) east:

Right. **J. P. Sill House** (607-547-2633). An outstanding, breathtaking, and exquisite Victorian home. Built in 1864 and the subject of a purist renovation, the J.P. Sill House is listed on the National Register of Historic Places. The main house has 14-foot ceilings, marble fireplaces, 14k gold leaf wallpaper, and is full of antiques, many original to the house. A carriage house offers two country-furnished, two-bedroom suites with parlors, kitchens, and all amenities. Call for rates and availability. Open June through Thanksgiving. A one-of-a-kind, Civil War-era luxury home.

000.1   Left. **The White House Inn** (607-547-5054). A meticulously-kept, pirate-built, circa 1835 home now serving as a lovely bed and breakfast. Four guest rooms and a four-room apartment in the main house and two guest rooms (one handicapped accessible) in the carriage house. All rooms have a private bath and are tastefully furnished with either formal or country antiques. Comfortable, homey, and warm accommodations with a gathering room with fireplace, original artwork, a "wall of fame", a TV/VCR, and an in-ground swimming pool in a garden setting. Every day a different breakfast specialty with seasonal fruit and home baked muffins and breads is served on china and accompanied by stemware. Special diets accommodated; non-smoking; $85-$175 including breakfast. Casual grace and charming hospitality a short walk from Main Street.

Right. Junction with **Susquehanna Avenue (CR 52)**:

*000.8   Right. **Clark Sports Center** (607-547-2800). Private club with day passes available to the public. Indoor running track, full-sized gym floor, basketball court, bouldering wall, high climbing wall, ropes course, diving and swimming pools, racquetball and squash courts, aerobics room, Nautilus room, bowling alley, and saunas. Also soccer fields and softball diamonds, plus cross-country skiing, snowshoeing, climbing, and canoeing programs.*

*001.2   Right. Junction with **CR 33** after crossing a small bridge. Follow CR 33 for:*

> *004.8   Left. **Brewery Ommegang** (607-547-8184, 800-656-1212). A brand new Belgian-style brewery in an impressive building on a former hops farm. Ommegang's founders are importers of Belgian beers since 1982 and owners of three breweries in Belgium. The brewery currently brews two ales and will soon brew three: Ommegang, Hennepin, and Rare Vos. Brewery tours, beer tasting, and a gift shop. Open Saturdays and Sundays, 11-7; 12-5 off season. $3 admission.*

End of CR 33 and Susquehanna Avenue coverage.

Right. **Global Traders** (607-547-4439). Gifts imported from South and Central America and elsewhere. Jewelry, women's clothing and accessories, educational toys, musical instruments, rain sticks, incense and incense burners, candles, postcards, journals, statues, stationery, little boxes, hackie sacks, marionettes, and much more. A colorful, fun shop.

Right. Cooperstown Chamber of Commerce **Visitor Information Center** (607-547-9983). This information center is tied with the one in Old Forge for being the best information center along Route 28. The chamber produces a wonderful *Cooperstown Visitors' Guide*, and the friendly staff offers volumes of information on lodging, dining, activities, and attractions in and around Cooperstown. Many other guides and brochures are also available. Be sure to check the sidewalk bulletin board's calendar of events. Public restrooms.

000.2   Right. **Quickway** (607-547-7169). Mobil full-service gas station and snack shop.

Right. **Doubleday Court:**

> *NAPA Auto Care Center and Radio Shack (607-547-9929). Automobile parts and electronics.*

> *Doubleday Data Systems (607-547-2600). Computer store.*

> *Cooper Country Crafts (607-547-9247). A co-op of about two dozen local crafts people. Wrought iron, pen and ink sketches, fur animals, quilting, crocheting, wood, glass, textiles, sun catchers, items made from handspun wool from locally-raised sheep, rustic furniture, mink Teddy bears, jams, pickled vegetables, fudge, and more. A large collection of varied merchandise in a small space. Open daily May through December.*

Right. Driveway to **Plain & Fancy** (607-547-8093). Gourmet foods and gifts. Nuts, candies, dried fruits, jams, teas, coffees, hot sauces, exotic sauces, mustards, salsas, cheeses, customized gift baskets, cookbooks, and more.

000.3   Traffic light at corner of **Chestnut Street/NY 80** and **Main Street/CR 31**. See below for coverage of Chestnut Street/NY 80 north to the Alice Busch Opera Theater, and of Main Street/CR 31 east and north to Glimmerglass State Park.

Turning left onto **Main Street** west yields the following:

*000.0   Left.   **Gabriella's on the Square** (607-547-8000). Casually elegant dining on continental cuisine with a European flair. Newly refurbished and redecorated, the recently-opened Gabriella's serves lunch and dinner. The formal furnishings and table settings belie the relaxed and homey atmosphere and friendly staff. A mouth-watering dinner menu offers pan-seared herbed chicken, fettuccine carbonara, herb-encrusted rack of lamb, grilled filet mignon, tuna steak au poivre, and similarly enticing entrees, $15-$20. Reservations suggested.*

*Left. **Box Office Video** (607-547-7162).*

*Left. **Clip Joint** (607-547-1053). Hair salon.*

*Left. **Leatherstocking Travel** (607-547-5291).*

*Left. **cooperstown botanica** (607-547-7400). A personal care salon. Botanical cosmetics, manicures, pedicures, facials, massage, and more.*

*Left. **Ashley-Conner Realty** (607-547-4045).*

End of coverage of Main Street west.

Chestnut Street/NY 80 east, northward to the Alice Busch Opera Theater

Right. **The Cooper Inn** (607-547-2567, 800-348-6222). A classic inn in an 1812 Federal building set among beautiful lawns, hedges, trees, and park benches. The 10 guest rooms and five two-bedroom suites (all non-smoking) are tastefully decorated, as are the three sitting rooms downstairs. Stately touches include high ceilings, gilt-framed artwork, and beautiful fireplaces. Owned and operated by the Otesaga Hotel, guests are encouraged to use the Otesaga's dining and recreational facilities. Complimentary continental breakfast. Refined lodging at $89-$150/couple.

Left. **Lippitt's Jewelry and Gifts** (607-547-9661).

Left. **Lamb Realty** (607-547-8145).

Left. **Glimmerglass Opera Ticket Office** (607-547-2255). Ticket office for Glimmerglass Opera performances at the **Alice Busch Opera Theater** eight miles north on NY 80 east. The company produces two or three operas at a time on alternating evenings, allowing you to see multiple operas within a few days. Open July and August with matinees, evening performances, and special events. Wednesdays dark.

Left. **The Inn at Cooperstown** (607-547-5756, 800-437-6303). An 1874 hotel completely renovated in 1985. Eighteen rooms, all with private bath, furnished with antiques and quality reproductions. Floor-to-ceiling windows, functional and non-functional fireplaces, and tasteful artwork add to the ambiance. The large porch has rocking chairs which beckon the weary traveler. Recipient of media accolades, recipient of the New York State Certificate of Achievement in Historic Preservation, and listed on the National Register of Historic Places. One wheelchair-accessible room. $85-$125/couple, including continental breakfast. The quintessential Cooperstown inn.

000.4   Junction of **Chestnut Street** and **Lake Street**. Make left turn to follow **NY 80** east along the west shore of **Otsego Lake**.

000.6   Right. **The Otesaga. The Resort Hotel of Cooperstown** (607-547-9931, 800-348-6222). A stately, Colonial-styled, grand hotel since 1909 on the banks of Otsego Lake. This elegant and refined hotel offers the Leatherstocking Golf Course, lake and pool swimming, a dining terrace, gorgeous Otsego Lake views, the **Hawkeye Bar & Grill**, and the **Templeton Lounge**. Lodging in 137 rooms, $270-$400/couple/night, breakfast and dinner included. The hotel is open from the third week in April through the first weekend in November, with the Hawkeye Bar & Grill remaining open all year. Non-guest dining prices: breakfast buffet, $9.50; lunch, $13; dinner, $30; Sunday brunch, $17.50. One of the grandest hotels on or near Route 28.

Right. **Leatherstocking Golf Course** (607-547-5275). The Otesaga's 1909, Devereux Emmet-designed, eighteen-hole golf course. Open to the public, with greens fees $60 during the week and $70 on weekends; cart $16/person.

Left. **Green Apple Inn** (607-547-1080). A warm, comfortable, and cozy bed and breakfast with refreshing green and apple accents. Built in 1870 and run as a tourist home in the 1930s, current charms include four-poster canopy beds, a double rocker, a French fainting sofa, and a brass-claw-footed tub. All guest rooms have a private bath. Living room with fireplace, a sun porch, and a hot tub. $129/couple, including gourmet breakfast.

000.9   Leaving **Cooperstown** and entering the town of **Otsego**.

001.2   Left. **The Farmers' Museum** (607-547-1450). Early 19th century agricultural and rural life depicted and demonstrated in a small village of thirteen buildings. Working printing, broom making, weaving, and blacksmith's shops. Farm buildings, school house, church, and more. **Herder's Cottage Restaurant** serves food and drink, lunch $2-$5. There are also the **Farmers' Museum Shop** and **Todd's General Store**. On Saturday evenings from October through March at the **Bump Tavern** you can experience a 19th-century "Evening at the Tavern" with candlelight dinner and entertainment (advance reservations required). Special events and holiday programs. Open daily June through October; restricted hours in April, May, November, and December. Adults $9, children aged 7-12 $4. Combination tickets available with Fenimore House Museum and Baseball Hall of Fame.

Right. **Fenimore House Museum** (607-547-1400). Fine, folk, and American Indian art; photography; and artifacts of James Fenimore Cooper. Museum shop and **Fenimore Cafe**. Combination tickets available with The Farmers' Museum and Baseball Hall of Fame.

001.3   Right. **New York State Historical Association Research Library** (607-547-1470). Harboring an 80,000-volume collection focusing on American, New York State, and local history; genealogy; folk art; old maps; over 200 years of census records; church and cemetery records; much more.

001.4   Right. **Trolley Parking. The Yellow Lot.** Trolley runs every 20 minutes; $.75 a ride or $1.50 for an all-day pass.

001.9   Left. **Barkley Barn Antiques** (607-547-5339).

002.7   Right. **Sam Smith's Boatyard** (607-547-2543). Powerboat, pontoon boat, and canoe rentals; service; supplies; launching ramp; live bait; etc.
Also the **Blue Mingo Grill** (607-547-7496). On the banks of Otsego Lake overlooking Kingfisher Tower in a setting reminiscent of the Adirondacks. Fine dining on predominantly grilled seafood with a slightly Asian influence, plus chicken, steaks, ribs, etc. Blackboard menu may include entrees such as roast chicken with cider garlic, roast salmon with Asian basil pesto, black Angus strip steak with anchovy chili butter, barbecued ribs with tamarind guava sauce, and more, $16-$21. Bar, wood-burning stove, dining deck, boat dock for visiting diners. Favorably acclaimed by local and national newspapers and

magazines. Open Thursdays through Sundays, May through Labor Day.

Continued coverage of **NY 80** north to **US 20** is selective, with many restaurants, lodgings, and business establishments along the way but outside the scope of this book.

003.5   Right. **Three Mile Point Picnic Area** (607-547-2777). Lakeshore park with swimming beach, dock, handicapped-accessible fishing pier, pavilion, picnic tables, and fireplaces. Open Memorial Day through Labor Day; $5/car admission for out-of-towners.

008.5   Left. **Alice Busch Opera Theater** (607-547-5704, tickets 607-547-2255). Home of the **Glimmerglass Opera Company** in a contemporary theater with opening sides, set amid broad lawns perfect for picnicking while awaiting curtain time. The company produces two to four operas at a time on successive evenings, allowing you to see multiple operas within a few days. Open July and August with matinee and evening performances and special events. Wednesdays dark.

011.0   Traffic light at junction of **NY 80** and **US 20**. End of coverage of Chestnut Street/NY 80 east.

Main Street/CR 31 East and North to Glimmerglass State Park

000.0   Junction of **Main Street/CR 31** with **Chestnut Street/NY 80** at the traffic light in the middle of Cooperstown. Heading east on Main Street:

Right. **Schneider's Bakery** (607-547-9631). Fresh baked goods.

Right. **Hubbell's Real Estate** (607-547-5740).

Right. **Homescapes** (607-547-8425). Home furnishings, furniture, and oriental rugs.

Left.   **The Cooper Inn** (607-547-2567).   See description on Chestnut Street.

Right.   **Metro Fashion** (607-547-2749).   An upscale ladies' boutique.

Right.   **Rudy's Liquor Store** (607-547-8297).

Right.   **Muskrat Hill** (607-547-9552).   Kites, sundials, T-shirts, flags, pennants, pottery, candles, accessories, and more.

Right.   **Willis Monie Books** (607-547-8363, 800-322-2995). Some 60,000 books in all subjects amassed over more than two decades. Used and rare books, manuscripts, and papers. Also T-shirt graphics.

Right. **Collector's World** and **Gift World** (607-547-5509). Base-ball cards, autographs, souvenirs, and custom T-shirts.

Right. **Moon Dreams** (607-547-9432, 800-437-3265). Specialty shop and more. See description at Doubleday Court below.

Right. **Frog Hollow Real Estate** (607-547-7168).

Right. **The Galleria**:
Seventh Inning Stretch (607-547-7220).   Baseball cards; autographed photos, balls, bats, gloves; souvenir clothing; and other memorabilia. Open March through November.

Left. **Cooperstown Diner** (607-547-9201). Cozy diner with a small counter and four tables open for breakfast and lunch. Jumbo ham-burgers a specialty. Open seven days until 2 PM.

Right. **The Jewelry Box** (607-547-1382). Sterling and 14k gold baseball jewelry and more.

Left. **The Stables**:
Mrs. Van's Gift Box (607-547-2138). Collectibles and gifts. Baseball figurines, bobbing heads, plates, and street signs. Brand-

name collectibles, miniature houses, Teddy bears, stained-glass village pieces, and musicals.   Also crystal prisms, giftware, Christmas items, and more.

Hands of Stone (607-547-9684).   Cast your hand in stone for a permanent keepsake. May through October.

The Latest Obsession (607-547-7150).   Sports and non-sports cards, memorabilia and collectibles, comics, magic cards, gifts, ties, and jewelry.

Right.   **Around the House** (607-547-5165).   Collectibles, gifts, and miniatures.

Right.   **Cooperstown Kid Company** (607-547-1300).   Clothing, toys, and accessories.

Left.   **T.J.'s Place** (607-547-4040).   Family restaurant. Breakfast, lunch, and dinner.   Hot dogs to filet mignon.   Dinner $5-$18.

Left.   **The Home Plate** (607-547-4041).   Baseball memorabilia and souvenirs.

Right.   **Doubleday Court**, down which are the following:

*Public **parking** lot.*

***The Factory Store** (607-547-5826).   Family apparel, baseball gifts, and Cooperstown memorabilia.*

***Metro Cleaners and Coin Laundry** (607-547-2541).*

***Doubleday Dip Ice Cream Store** (607-547-2541).   Ice cream and frozen yogurt. Open May through October.*

***Baseball Nostalgia** (607-547-6051).   Baseball memorabilia.*

***Doubleday Field** (607-547-2270, 547-2411).   Built in 1939 to commemorate the birthplace of baseball. Open to the public every day from the second week in April* *through Columbus Day, the stadium hosts two to three games a day. Teams from all over the country and outside the country come here to play. Even your team can play here. Call the Cooperstown Village Clerk on 607-547-2411 to request an application to play on the field. Hall of Fame Weekend brings an admission-free minor league game with the Oneonta Yankees on Saturday, and a major league exhibition game on Monday.*

Doubleday Clubhouse Shop and Shirt Stop *(607-547-4034). Field goods, teamwear, accessories, souvenirs, and memorabilia.*

Doubleday Batting Range *(607-547-5168).*

Moon Dreams *(607-547-9432, 800-437-3265). Specialty shop in an old vaudeville theater featuring inspirational books, relaxing music, hand-crafted jewelry, gifts, fine crafts, cards, and aromatherapy. Also a tea room and cafe featuring healthful foods for lunch, a lovely garden in which to relax, a massage therapist, and lodging in a two-bedroom apartment with living room and kitchen operated as a bed and breakfast ($125/night, weekly rates available).*

Left. **Gallery 53 Artworks**. (607-547-5655). A nonprofit, multi-arts center and gift shop. Art exhibits, musical performances, poetry readings, open mike nights, and more. The gallery exhibits paintings, sculpture, photographs, and mixed media works. A gift shop offers photographs, pottery, paintings, and jewelry. Hours vary by season.

Left. **Made in the Shade** (607-547-4125). Stained glass studio on the second floor.

Left. **Tin Bin Alley Country Store** (607-547-5565). Nostalgia, gifts, country wares, folk art, fudge, candy, and cards.

Left. **"As We Were..."** (607-547-7138). Country paintings by Kittie L. Johnson. Located within Tin Bin Alley.

Right. **Key Bank** (607-547-2551). 24-hour ATM.

Left. **Sal's Pizzeria and Restaurant** (607-547-5721). Pizzas and more.

Right. Driveway, down which is the **Cooperstown Farmer's Market** which operates Saturdays 9 AM to 1 PM, mid-May through mid-October.

Left. **Cap City** (607-547-1814). Baseball and other sports caps, T-shirts, and souvenirs.

Left. **Pioneer Sports Cards** (607-547-2323). Sports cards, autographs, supplies, and more.

Left. **CVS Pharmacy** (607-547-8791). Drug store.

Right. **The American Baseball Experience** (607-547-1273). Mickey Mantle museum and baseball wax museum. The entire third floor of this building is a shrine to Mickey Mantle, with display case after display case of photographs, autographed balls, books, magazines, uniforms, and much more. Also video excerpts. The second floor houses a baseball wax museum, including Abbott and Costello and their "Who's on First?" routine. Great fun. Closed January and February.
Our National Game (607-547-1317). Gift shop. Also a virtual reality batting game for one or two (batter and pitcher) players. Closed January and February.
Shoeless Joe's Outdoor Food Cafe. Open Memorial Day to Labor Day, weather permitting.

Left. **Italy** (607-547-7499). A comfortable, contemporary-styled, and tastefully decorated Italian restaurant serving lunch and dinner. Lunch consists of Italian and traditional American dishes, $4-$10. The dinner menu features pastas, seafood, steaks, chicken, and veal, $6-$15. Beer and wine available. Seasonal dining patio.

Right. **Doubleday Cafe** (607-547-5468). Restaurant and bar serving breakfast, lunch, and dinner. Dinner entrees $7-$12.

Left. **Danny's Main Street Market** (607-547-4053). Gourmet specialties, salads, and sandwiches. Bagels, scones, Danish, deli items, squeezed juices, fresh fruit smoothies, cheeses, bulk coffees and spices, mustards, and cookbooks.

Right. **The Cupboard** (607-547-2361). Cards, stationery, chocolates, candies, gifts, gift wrap, and more.

Left. **Riverwood** (607-547-4403). A craft gallery featuring the works of local and national artists and crafts people. Furniture, pottery, glassware, leather, jewelry, and wood. Toys and games. Handmade paper-headed drums and thumb pianos. Back packs and briefcases. Garden accents, fountains, cedar birdhouses, birdfeeders, and more. Also baby and wedding gifts. A gallery to browse through slowly.

Right. **Where It All Began Bat Company** (607-547-7101). Specializing in personalized, limited edition and pro model bats.

000.1   Right. **McEwan Hardware** (607-547-8191). Plumbing, heating, clothing, tools, toys, and housewares. Camping, fishing, and hunting equipment, supplies, and licenses.

Right. **National Pastime** (607-547-2524). Baseball clothing, memorabilia, baseball cards, caps, pennants, collectibles, etc., for the serious collector.
Walker Gallery. Original art, photographs, posters, and custom framing.
Cooperstown Cigar Company. Cigar store.

Right. **Ellsworth and Sill** (607-547-9277). Women's clothing, accessories, and jewelry.

Right. **Pro Image Photo** (607-547-2287). Professional portrait of you in Major League uniform in a fan-packed stadium setting. A unique, personalized, fun memento of your Cooperstown visit.

Right. **Church & Scott** (607-547-2558). Over-the-counter drugs, beauty aids, baseball memorabilia, souvenirs, post cards, Cooperstown "T" shirts, and sweat shirts.

Left. **Pioneer Park**. Called Farkle Park by Cooperstown's young folks.

Intersection with **Pioneer Street**. North on Pioneer Street are:

> *Left.* ***The Tunnicliff Inn*** *(607-547-9611). An almost 200-year-old Federal-style, brick hotel with historic character. The 17 generously-sized rooms, all with private bath, are furnished with many antiques. One-half block from the Baseball Hall of Fame. $45-$135/room.*
> ***James Fenimore Cooper Room.*** *The restaurant at the Tunnicliff offers fine dining on American cuisine such as chicken and broccoli Alfredo, seafood primavera, filet mignon, and English mixed grille, $15-$20.*
> ***The Pit*** *(607-547-9860). The downstairs tap room at the Tunnicliff serves lunch and dinner. Lunch menu includes appetizers, fries, wings, burgers, soups, salads, sandwiches, shrimp, and specials, $4-$9. Dinner menu of beef, veal, poultry, pasta, and seafood is similar to the dining room menu upstairs, $13-$19.*

> *Right. Intersection with* ***Stagecoach Lane***, *down which is* ***Alley Antiques***. *Furniture, artwork, home accessories, and more. April through December.*

> *Right.* ***Stagecoach Coffee*** *(607-547-6229). Coffee roastery and espresso bar serving coffee, cappuccino, teas, cold drinks, bagels, croissants, scones, grilled sandwiches, specialty sandwiches, salads, ice cream, smoothies, and more.*

> *Right.* ***Purple Star Boutique*** *(607-547-8479). Fine ladies fashions and accessories.*

*Right. **A Village Bed and Breakfast** (607-547-7216). A private home built in 1867 with three guest rooms furnished in antiques and sharing two full baths. Sitting room, dining room with hand-crocheted table cloth, TV room, and guest refrigerator. One shower even has a window. Tastefully decorated, comfortable, and homey. No smoking. $65-$75/couple, deluxe continental breakfast included. Staying here is like staying at your Aunt Vera's.*

*Right. **Lake Front Park**. A grassy, sloped park dotted with shade trees and park benches on the shores of Otsego Lake.   A great place to picnic, to read a book, or to snooze. Public restrooms.*

Lake Front Marina and the lighthouse from Lake Front Park.

End of Pioneer Street north coverage.

South on Pioneer Street are:

*Left. **Don Olin Realty** (607-547-5622).*

Left. **Pioneer Street Stadium** *(607-547-6206).* *Sportswear and memorabilia.*

Right. **Pioneer Alley to Doubleday Court***:*

> *Left.* **Leatherstocking Gallery** *(607-547-5942).* *Art and crafts created by area members of the* **Leatherstocking Brush and Palette Club***.* *Open mid-June through Labor Day.*

> *Left.* **Pioneer Patio** *(607-547-5601).* *Casual, almost secluded baseball-decorated restaurant, bar, and outdoor dining patio offer restful dining. Lunch features Reubens, Monte Cristos, knockwurst, bratwurst, steak sandwiches, seafood salad, etc., $2-$7. The dinner menu offers spaghetti and meatballs, veal and chicken Parmigiana, ribs, steak, and more, $8-$13.*

End of Pioneer Alley coverage.

Right. **Straws & Sweets** *(607-547-5365).* *Chocolates, fudge, Crabtree & Evelyn products, candles, plush animals, coffee mugs, and gifts.*

Right. **Pioneer Photo** *(607-547-5211).* *Cameras and supplies.*

Left. **Pioneer Wine & Spirits** *(607-547-4048).*

Left. **The Bold Dragoon** *(607-547-9800).* *A popular local bar with a pub atmosphere, pool table, pinball, electronic darts, and a juke box. Native-Cooperstown elbow rubbing.*

Right. **Foo Kin** *(607-547-2868).* *Chinese restaurant.*

Right. **Sherman's Tavern at the Hotel Pratt** *(607-547-4000). Local watering hole with pool table, darts, and juke box. Thursday night karaoke.*

Left. **Stone House Gifts** *(607-547-2828). Americana gifts in an historic 1826 stone building. Wood carvings, pottery, pewter, prints, candles, and folk art.*

Right. **Holley Music** *(607-547-5117, 800-526-9441). CD's, tapes, baseball music, and sheet music. Also musical-themed T-shirts, coffee mugs, and gifts.*

Left. **The Smithy-Pioneer Gallery** *(607-547-8671). Step back in time as you enter the oldest building in Cooperstown, now housing a nonprofit gallery featuring paintings, sculpture, and ceramics by area artists. A sculpture garden presents outdoor and garden sculpture, and the third floor houses local Otsego County history exhibits in a museum setting. A pottery school is also offered. The building was built as a storehouse in 1786 by William Cooper, founder of Cooperstown and father of James Fenimore Cooper. The building was later enlarged to accommodate a blacksmith's shop. Still in the shop are the original forges, bellows, and blacksmith's tools. Open June to September.*

Left. **Lake Classic Designs** *(607-547-8499). Upscale ladies' apparel, accessories, and gifts, plus some men's clothing and accessories.*

Left. **Toad Hall** *(607-547-4044). Furniture, folk art, tchachkas, plush toys, and more. Almost a museum. A fascinating collection of unique, imaginative, and boldly-colored creations.*

Right. **Astoria Federal Savings** *(607-547-9971). Bank.*

End of Pioneer Street south coverage.

Left. **Mickey's Place** (607-547-5775). Baseball memorabilia, souvenirs, photographs, collectible baseballs, uniforms, caps, baseball cards, etc. Down the stairs is a shop devoted to Mickey Mantle memorabilia and souvenirs.

Right. **Augur's Corner Bookstore** (607-547-2422). Greeting cards, children's books, candles, stationery, office supplies, giftware, and local and regional maps.

Right. **Cooperstown News and Sports Memorabilia** (607-547-4477). Sports cards and autographed memorabilia. Also newspapers, magazines, candy, tobacco products, and lottery tickets.

Left. **A Cooperstown Christmas** (607-547-4438). Christmas store.

Left. **Cooperstown Bat Company** (607-547-2415). Baseball, softball, Little League, autographed, and limited-edition bats. Visit the factory in Fly Creek to see them made.

Right. **Short Stop** (607-547-9609). A family restaurant since 1921, with booths, tables, and a soda fountain. Usually open for breakfast and lunch until 4 PM, and in summer for dinner until 6 PM. A locally-popular, inexpensive eatery.

Left. **Black Bart's B-B-Q** (607-547-5656). Family restaurant serving southern and southwestern specialties for lunch and dinner. Appetizers, salads, Tex-Mex, barbecued sandwiches, ribs and chicken, with all meats smoked on the premises. All-weather, awning-covered patio dining. Beer and wine available. Dinner entrees $6-$17. Open May through October.

Right. **F. R. Woods Baseball Town Motel** (607-547-2161). Ten units, each with private bath, housing from one to six, on second floor, with off-street parking, $59-$96/couple.

Right. **F. R. Woods House of Pro Sports** (607-547-2161). Large variety of baseball memorabilia and souvenirs. Autographed plaques, baseballs, pennants, T-shirts, sweatshirts, clocks, chairs, and more.

Left. **Wilber National Bank** (607-547-9941).

Left. **Veterans Club** (607-547-8282). Open to all members of the American Legion, the VFW, and the Royal Canadian Legion.

Left. **Extra Innings** (607-547-2292). Baseball shop. Clothing; autographed baseballs, photos, baseball cards; induction cards, and souvenirs. Open March through October.

Right. **J. J. Newberry Co.** (607-547-9981). Department store.

Left. Intersection with **Hoffman Lane**. North on Hoffman Lane are:

> *Left. **Book Nook** (607-547-2578). A general book store plus books on baseball, Cooperstown baseball, and the Baseball Hall of Fame. Also books on Cooperstown and area history.*
>
> *Left. **Clinton's Dam Sandwich Cafe** (607-547-9044). Cozy, casual, and comfortable. Upstairs and covered-patio dining with a brick-floored basement bar. Open for lunch and dinner and serving sandwiches, salads, pizza, burgers, etc., $6-$9. Also dinner entrees of beef, chicken, veal, and seafood, $13-$18.*
>
> *Left. **Red Nugget Ice Cream Saloon** (607-547-8442). Ice cream.*

End of Hoffman Lane coverage.

Right. **National Baseball Hall of Fame and Museum** (607-547-7200). Founded in 1939, 100 years after Abner Doubleday was reported to have invented baseball in Cooperstown, the National Baseball Hall of Fame and Museum are monuments to the game and the players who made it America's pastime. Three floors house the Hall of Fame Gallery, a theater, museum halls, a library, a records room, a book store, and a museum shop (888-425-5633). All 232 Hall of Fame inductees, 57 of whom are still alive, are honored by a personal plaque displayed in the gallery. Exhibits include photographs, memorabilia, and artifacts of the inductees and the game, all of which have been donated by players, fans, and other individuals interested in preserving the history of baseball. Special exhibits honor Babe Ruth, Hank Aaron, the Negro League, and the women of baseball. Adults $9.50, juniors (ages 7-12) $4. Senior rates and combination tickets with the Fenimore House Museum and The Farmers' Museum are also available. Closed Thanksgiving, Christmas, and New Year's Day.

Left. **Cooperstown Post Office** (607-547-2311). ZIP 13326.

000.2   Intersection with **Fair Street**: North on Fair Street are:

*Left. **Bassett House Inn** (607-547-7001). An inn with flair. This three-storied inn, built in 1816, is delightfully furnished with antiques, gilt-framed mirrors, chandeliers, multi-colored lamps, an old piano, a grandfather clock, an 1895 billiards table with burgundy felt, and collections of antique clocks, canes, and cap pistols. The eclectic mixture of styles and stuff bursts with warmth, color, and gaiety. Outside is a park-like terrace with a fountain and umbrella tables. Five guest rooms with private baths, $115-$135/couple, including continental breakfast. Immediately across the street from the Baseball Hall of Fame. No smoking. Children 16 years of age and older welcome. April through October.*

*Left. **Lake Front Motel, Restaurant, and Marina** (607-547-9511):*
*The **Lake Front Motel** has 44 comfortable, air-conditioned rooms and deluxe rooms right on Otsego Lake and mere steps to downtown Cooperstown and the Baseball Hall of Fame. $55-$130/couple.*
***Lake Front Restaurant** (607-547-8188). Bright, many-windowed, family restaurant offering lakeshore dining.*

Breakfast, lunch, and dinner served inside or on deck. Appetizers, soups, entrees, children's and vegetarian menus. Dinner entrees $10-18. Open April through October.
Lake Front Marina *offers seasonal dockage with limited overnight dockage available. Gas dock, holding tank pumpout.*

Left. ***Classic Boat Tours*** *(607-547-5295). One-hour tours of Lake Otsego aboard the classic* Chief Uncas. *Every two hours on the hour. Rates $8.50, children 3-12 $5, under 3 free. Chartering and catering available (607-547-8238). Mid-May through Columbus Day.*

At the lake at the north end of Fair Street is a public ***boat launching ramp***.

End of Fair Street coverage.

Left. **Village Library** (607-547-8344) and **Cooperstown Art Association Gallery** (607-547-9777). Both of these are in a stately, 12-columned, two-story, stone building. The library has a general collection of books, with concentrations of large print books, books on tape, local history, mystery novels, and James Fenimore Cooper works. The art gallery has constant exhibits which change monthly. Library closed Sundays, gallery closed Tuesdays.

000.3   Intersection with **River Street**. Turning right and going south on River Street three short blocks brings you to **Atwell Road** and **Bassett Hospital** (607-547-3456, emergency room 607-547-3355).

Crossing the **Susquehanna River** as it flows out of Otsego Lake on its journey to Havre de Grace, Maryland on the upper Chesapeake Bay. A note in a bottle thrown into Otsego Lake can come to rest on any coast in the world after flowing down the Susquehanna River and the Chesapeake Bay, and entering the Atlantic Ocean at Norfolk, Virginia.

Leaving **Cooperstown** and entering the town of **Middlefield**.

001.2   Left. **Fairy Springs Park**. (607-547-2150). Down a steep drive is a lakeside park with a swimming beach, picnic tables, charcoal grills, and toilet facilities. Open Memorial Day through Labor Day; $5/car admission for out-of-towners.

007.5   Left. **Glimmerglass State Park** (607-547-8662, 888-806-CAMP). A beautiful park on 600 acres on the shores of Otsego Lake offering 39 partially-wooded campsites (no hook-ups), picnicking, swimming, fishing, biking, hiking trails, ball fields, playgrounds, horseshoe pits, snowmobiling, snow tubing, cross-country skiing, and ice fishing. Also showers and a dump station. May through September, primarily, but winter camping is allowed for self-contained units.

Entering town of **Springfield**.

007.7   Left. Driveway to **Hyde Hall** (607-547-5098). A National Historic Landmark and New York State Historic Site, this neo-classic country mansion was built by George Clarke between 1817 and 1834. Bankruptcy and time led the architecturally-significant mansion to become neglected, and in 1963 it was threatened with demolition. That same year New York State claimed 600 acres of the property and built Glimmerglass State Park. The next year an effort was organized to begin saving the deteriorated house. Restoration is expected to be completed early in the 21st century. The mansion currently houses a visitor center, exhibits, original furniture, and views of the restoration in progress. Open all year, 10-6, Fri-Mon.

End of coverage of Main Street east and CR 31.

 **Cooperstown to Richfield Springs to Mohawk**

111.9   Junction of Route 28 with **NY 80 (Chestnut Street).**

112.2   Right(left) **Trolley Parking. The Red Lot.** Trolley runs every 20 minutes; $.75 a ride or $1.50 for an all-day pass.

112.8   Leaving(entering) **Cooperstown** as you climb the hill going out of town.

113.7   Cresting the hill north of Cooperstown. Beautiful views to the north and west.

114.6   Right(left) **Cooperstown Bat Company** (607-547-2415). A baseball bat factory and store. See baseball bats made and personalized via color graphics and laser engraving. World's Champions bats, All-Star bats, bats honoring famous players, limited-edition bats, autographed bats, and other collectibles. Also Little League bats and softball bats. Interestingly, the bats are made from northern white ash grown in New York State west of the Catskills.

114.7   Entering(leaving) **Fly Creek.**

114.8   Right(left) **Major League Motor Inn** (607-293-6109). Neat and tidy motel in the country. Nine units with two double beds, HBO, and A/C each; $69 for up to a family of four. Open Memorial Day weekend through Columbus Day.

Right(left) **Staffin's Auto Repair** (607-547-8997).

115.0   Right(left) **Up the Creek Antiques Etc.** (607-547-9088). Furniture, lamps, coin-operated games, cash registers, jewelry, knick-knacks, postcards, and more. Open Wednesday through Sunday May through October, closed December through March, open weekends otherwise.

115.1   Flashing traffic signal at junction of **CR 26**. Making a left onto CR 26 south takes you to:

> *000.0   An immediate fork in the road. Bear left at fork to follow CR 26.*

> *001.2   Right. Junction with* **Fork Shop Road***:*

>> *000.0   Left.   **Creekside Bed & Breakfast** (607-547-8203). An elegant, sprawling, colonial bed and breakfast along the creek. Owned by Glimmerglass Opera founders and performers and praised in national magazines, this lovely inn has three bright rooms, two suites, and a cottage, each exquisitely furnished in a different style, with queen- or king-sized bed, private bath, and TV. The penthouse suite has two queen-sized beds, the bridal suite boasts a bridal tree and a private entrance and porch, and the honeymoon cottage has three rooms and a back porch overlooking the creek. $85-$145/couple, including full breakfast served on china and crystal. Low cholesterol breakfast by request. Gracious hospitality in the country.*

End of Fork Shop Road and CR 26 south coverage.

Making a right onto **CR 26** north takes you to the following:

> *000.4   Right. Junction with* **Goose Street***:*

000.0   *Left.* ***Fly Creek Cider Mill and Orchard*** *(607-547-9692). Watch the water-powered apple press turn apples into cider. Wheels spin, belts hum, and the floor shakes as the 1856 cider mill does its work. Sip some cider as you feed the ducks at the mill pond. Shops offer apples, cider, cheese, fudge, pies, scones, country gifts, miniatures, kitchen items, and more. Special weekend events include an antique engine show, a tractor festival, craft shows, entertainment, and more. For info, call for a copy of its* Cider Press *newsletter. Country autumn fresh air, flavors, and fun for everyone.   Open daily mid-August through November.*

Left. ***The Christmas Barn*** *(607-547-2637). An old, two-story barn loaded with Christmas decorations, accessories, gifts, brand-name collectibles, toys, plush toys, candles, books, candy, and much more.   Open May through December.*

End of Goose Street and CR 26 coverage.

Right(left) **Fly Creek General Store and Deli** (607-547-7274). Groceries and Citgo gas. Deli, fresh meats and produce, New York City newspapers, and five different coffees freshly-brewed daily. Tired of driving? Stop for a coffee break and play a tune on the player piano.

Right(left) **Fly Creek Post Office** (607-547-5111). ZIP 13337.

Left(right) **Mayhew Motors** (607-547-5302). Auto repairs.

115.2   Left(right) **Litco Farms Bed and Breakfast** (607-547-2501). A circa 1827 farmhouse on 70 acres with in-ground swimming pool and five miles of nature trails around a beaver pond. Two guest rooms with shared bath, plus a two-room family suite for four with private bath, all furnished with country antiques and hand made quilts. Rates are $79-$89/room, $109/family suite, including full country breakfast with homemade breads. Ask the proprietor about the lost trolley. Open May to November. Country warm and homey.

Left(right) **Heartworks Quilts and Fabrics** (607-547-2501). A quilt gallery offering original-design, handmade quilts for sale. Quilting materials and supplies, quilting classes, antique quilt restoration and repair. Gifts and cards, too.

Right(left) **Past Times Antiques** (607-547-8050). A general line of antiques in a red barn. Furniture, model trains, postcards, toys, stereoscopic cards, crockware, cameras, books, silver, china, glassware, and more.

115.8   **Fly Creek/Oaksville** line.

115.9   Left(right) **Cooperstown Hardware and Supply** (607-547-8328). An independent hardware store with mostly American-made products for sale at discounts. Marine hardware, hard-to-find hardware, and items from 60 to 70 years ago.

116.0   Left(right) **B & S Inn** (607-547-8390). A casual restaurant and bar with knotty pine accents, dart board, pool table, shuffleboard table, and player piano. Thursday evening spaghetti or lasagna, $2-$4. Friday evening dinners of haddock, fish platter, shrimp basket, New York strip steak, veal Parmigiana, hot beef sandwich, and filet mignon, $6-$10. Sandwiches available other evenings.

116.2   Crossing **Oaks Creek**.

116.3   Left (right) **Bennett's Motor Sales** (607-547-9332, 547-5340). Motorcycles, snowmobiles, ATVs, and go-carts. Sales, service, and parts.

Leaving(entering) **Oaksville**.

117.2   Left(right) Junction with **NY 80** west and **NY 205** south.

Route 28 runs along the east side of a hill, offering wide views to the north and east. The mountains have faded into hills and the valleys are wide, level, and green. In September the valleys are awash in bright yellow wildflowers, and the tops of the pine trees are adorned with small pine cones. This is still farm country so be on the lookout for slow moving farm vehicles.

118.7   Entering town of **Exeter**.

120.3   Entering(leaving) **Schuyler Lake**.

120.6   Left(right) **Schuyler Lake Hotel** (315-858-9910, 800-458-5822). Built in 1825, this former hotel is now a restaurant and lounge serving lunch and dinner. Dinner specialties include deep-fried seafood, homemade Italian dishes, pizza, pork chops, steaks, etc. Entrees, including the salad bar, are usually $5-$14. Children's menu $3-$4; bar menu with sandwiches and finger foods. Lunch menu features soups, salads, and specialty sandwiches. Closed Mondays.

Right(left) **The Brass Lantern** (315-858-9711).   Bar and restaurant. Burgers, jumbo wings, hot roast beef sandwich, etc., $2-$4.

Right(left) **Hand-Did-Shop** (315-858-0956). Handmade folk art, country accessories, antiques, crafts, gifts, and holiday room.

Right(left) **Schuyler Lake General Store** (315-858-1219). Convenience store, freshly-brewed coffees, Citgo gas, propane cylinder exchange.

Left(right) **Schuyler Lake Post Office** (315-858-0390).   ZIP 13457.

120.9   Leaving **Schuyler Lake**.

About a mile north of Schuyler Lake Route 28 winds along the western shore of **Canadarago** (pronounced Canada-RAY-go) **Lake**. Private homes stand shoulder to shoulder along the narrow strip of shoreline between the road and the lake, with more homes similarly lining the west side of the road.   According to *Richfield Springs and Vicinity. Historical, Biographical, and Descriptive,* by W. T. Bailey and published by A.S. Barnes & Company in 1874 (available at the Richfield Springs Public Library), there used to be two islands in Canadarago Lake where now there is only one, the western one having suddenly and mysteriously slipped below the surface of the lake at the beginning of the 19th century.

An old barn evokes spirits of cows who have long ago mooed their last moos.

122.5   Right(left) **Lakeside Bed and Breakfast** (315-858-3307).   Directly on the banks of Canadarago Lake with a breathtaking lake view. Accommodations for four people in one large room with private full bath, white spaghetti wicker furnishings, and a TV/VCR.   Also available for the guests' use are a small library, an outdoor fireplace, two docks, a paddle boat, and a rowboat.   Made-to-order hot breakfasts of fresh fruits, breads, eggs, meats, waffles with homemade maple syrup, etc., served on the patio, weather permitting. $85-$95, breakfast included.   Open May through October.   Unpretentious accommodations with warm hospitality and a beautiful view.

122.8   **Exeter/Richfield** town line.

123.6   Right(left). Junction with **Dennison Road** to:

> *000.2   Left. Junction with **Woodland Road**:*

>> *000.0   Right. New York State **Boat Launching Ramp** on Canadarago Lake. Launching fee $4 or free with Empire Passport ($39).*

End of Woodland Road and Dennison Road coverage.

124.2   Right(left) **Baker's Beach** (315-858-2043).   Community recreation area.   Public swimming and picnicking.   No pets allowed.

125.9   Left(right) Junction with **CR 25A**, a 0.6-mile bypass of **Richfield Springs** to **US 20** west and **Route 28** north.

126.0   Left(right) **Suburban Propane** (315-858-1550).   Propane tanks filled, but usually only after 3:30 PM when the route drivers are there.   See Anderson's Hardware on Main Street in Richfield Springs for propane.

126.3   Entering village of **Richfield Springs**.

126.6   Stop sign at **Monticello Street** followed immediately by junction of **Route 28** with **US 20**.   Prior to the building of the Interstate system US 20 was a major cross-country route from Boston on the east coast to Newport, Oregon on the west.

Turning right (or continuing straight ahead if traveling southbound) onto US 20 east takes you down **Main Street** through the center of **Richfield Springs**.   See description of **Richfield Springs' Main Street** later in this chapter.

Route 28 north turns left onto **US 20** west. (Southbound, **Route 28** turns right leaving **US 20** east.)

126.7   Right(left) **Curcio Realty** (315-858-0544).

126.8   Left(right) **Dari-Creme** (315-858-1490).   Mexican hots, fries, malts, and cones.

Left (right) **Tourist Information** (315-858-1050). In little booth.

Leaving(entering) **Richfield Springs**.

126.9   Left(right) **Chuck's Towing and Collision Service** (315-858-1179). 24-hour towing.

127.0   Traffic light at junction of **Route 28** with **CR 25A** to the left and **US 20** west straight ahead. **Route 28** north turns to the right. (Southbound, **Route 28** turns left onto **US 20** east.) **CR 25A** is a 0.6-mile bypass of **Richfield Springs** to **Route 28** south.

> *Immediately on the left on **US 20** west is **Skinner & Damulis** (315-858-1350).   Ford, Jeep, and Eagle dealership.*

127.5   **Otsego/Herkimer County** line. Mountains and big hills are now in the past, leaving only rolling hills on the landscape as Route 28 crosses a plateau and approaches the Mohawk Valley.

129.0   Entering(leaving) **South Columbia**.

129.1   Left(right) **Mister Shake** (315-858-0832).   Soft and hard ice cream, sandwiches, burgers, hot dogs, floats, shakes, cones, sundaes, and sodas. Also miniature golf.

129.2   Left(right) Junction with **McKoons Road**. The first house on the left is:

> *000.0   Left. **Aunt Martha's Bed and Breakfast** (315-858-1648). This former post office and general store is now a neat and trim, country B&B. Downstairs is a parlor with TV; upstairs a sitting room, three country guest rooms with private bath, and a two-bedroom family unit with bath.*

> *Clean, bright, and homey, with a crocheted Afghan on each bed. $70/couple, full country breakfast included. The proprietress also sells her homemade Afghans and jellies. Closed for the month of March.*

129.7   Leaving(entering) **South Columbia.**

134.8   Right. Exit lane for trucks, buses, and cars with trailers to a sign warning drivers about an upcoming long and steep descent of Route 28 into Mohawk.

135.2   Left(right) **Toni's Country Place** (315-866-2100). Pizza, subs, groceries, and beer.

135.5   There are great views for passengers as you descend the hill into **Mohawk**, but drivers must devote their attention to the road.

136.1   Right(left) **Shedd's Antiques** (315-866-1758). Two-car garage full of furniture, glassware, old tools, and more.

136.7   Left(right) **Schell's Automotive** (315-866-1640). Motor vehicle repair shop.

137.1   Drive carefully as you begin the steep part of the descent down **Vickerman Hill Road** into **Mohawk**. This descent offers excellent views of the **Mohawk Valley**. As you enter Mohawk, you will see under the pavement remnants of tracks which used to carry the trolleys of people to the sulphur spring resorts in Richfield Springs, to Cooperstown, and to Oneonta.

137.5   Entering village of **Mohawk** on Columbia Street. Coverage of Route 28 north continues in Chapter 23, *Mohawk.*

Richfield Springs' Main Street

The word "Springs" in Richfield Springs derives from the local abundance of mineral springs, mostly sulphurous, in the area. The combination of sulphur water and massage was once considered curative for many ailments from asthma to rheumatism. If you've never experienced sulphur water, stop by the Great White Sulphur Springs Drinking Fountain on the west side of Spring Park between the sidewalk and Main Street, across from Stewart's, and take a whiff. Such sulphur water once attracted so many visitors to the area that dozens of hotels and boarding houses sprang up and turned Richfield Springs into a resort town for 100 years, from 1820 to the 1920s. Many celebrities, politicians, and other luminaries found their way to Richfield Springs. By the late nineteenth century summer resort boarders numbered 3000, tripling the population of the village at the time. In addition to therapeutic massage, summer pastimes included tennis, area carriage rides, concerts, and polo. However, during the 1920s the increasing popularity of the automobile, the decline in the use of sulphur waters as a cure, and the stock market crash of 1929 all contributed to the decline of the resorts.

Junction of **Route 28** with **US 20**. Heading east on **US 20** (**Main Street**) yields:

000.1   Right. **Taylor's Easyway Mini Mart** (315-858-2088). Convenience store, Taylor's gas, propane cylinder exchange.

Right. **Red Apple Food Mart and KwikFill** (315-858-0279). Convenience store, KwikFill gas.

Right. **Richfield Springs Public Library** (315-858-0230). Dating from 1910, the library was built with money donated by Thomas R. Proctor on land donated by Richard Montgomery. As with most local libraries, the Richfield Springs Public Library boasts a local history section. And, in addition to expected library services, it lends Books-on-Tape, videos, jigsaw puzzles, and, from May through mid-August, fishing poles.

000.2   Right. **Fleet Bank** (800-228-1281). 24-hour ATM.

Right. **Vicky's Florals** (315-858-1009). Fresh, dried, and silk flowers; balloons.

Right. **Maneen's Village Store** (315-858-1141). Pharmacy, groceries, and greeting cards. Moneygram, fax, and UPS.

Right. **Video-Fax** (315-858-1607). Video rentals and sales.

Left. **Kinney Pharmacy** (315-858-3229). Pharmacy, groceries, greeting cards, stationery, toys, New York City newspapers, etc.

Right. **Rick Worden's Antiques & Collectibles** (315-858-9354). A huge, four-room store containing a general line of antiques offered by a dozen dealers. Furniture, collectibles, kitchen accessories and utensils, lamp globes, and much more. If you're looking for something and haven't found it elsewhere, you may find it here.

Left. **Bargain Hut** (315-858-2350). Used furniture, second-hand items, collectibles, sodas, and candy.

Left. **Anderson's Hardware** (315-858-2411, 800-379-2411). ServiStar Hardware store. Propane tanks filled by weight and volume. Western Union money transfer agency. Stop in and see the collection of old barn lanterns.

000.3   Right. **New York Pizzeria** (607-858-0405). Pizza, calzones, subs, and tunnels (hot subs with tomato sauce and cheese).

Right. **Chefs Diner** (315-858-2124). A 1947 diner with booth and counter service. Open for breakfast and lunch seven days, and for dinner Monday through Friday. Dinner $6-$7.

Right. **Silver Fox Antiques and Videos** (315-858-1289). Open Friday through Sunday afternoons or by chance or appointment.

Right. **21 West Antiques** (315-858-0206). General line of antiques and collectibles from the unusual to the bizarre and from the low end to the high end. Open by chance or appointment.

Right. **Fisher Auto Parts** (315-858-0240).

Left. **Foo Chow Restaurant** (315-858-9988). Chinese restaurant featuring Cantonese, Szechuan, and Hunan cuisine for eat-in or take-out.

Right. **Finders Keepers** (315-858-9633). Multi-dealer antique shop offering a general line including furniture; old 33, 45, and 78 rpm records; dishes; pottery; and more.

Left. **Park Inn** (315-858-2914). Bar, pool table, and bar menu. Have a beer with Chinese take-out dinner from next door.

Right. **Rick's Clothing and Footwear** (315-858-0710). As the sign says, clothing and footwear.

Left. **Stoll's Motors** (315-858-0900). Used car dealer, auto service. Tires, batteries, oil changed, brake service, etc.

Right. **Sherry's Pizza Place** (315-858-0943). Pizza, wings, hot sandwiches, etc. Eat-in or take-out.

000.4   Traffic light at junction with **NY 167 (Church Street)** to the left and **Lake Street** to the right. The clock on the far left corner dates from 1918 and used to be in the middle of the intersection. It was moved in the 1960s because it was struck too often by vehicles.

Turning left onto **NY 167 (Church Street)** takes you immediately to **Spring Park** on the right with a pavilion, a gazebo, and the Great White Sulphur Springs Drinking Fountain on its Main Street side.

Turning right onto **Lake Street** yields:

Left. ***Sounds of Yesteryear.*** *Antique phonograph museum.*

Right. ***Barber shop.***

Right. ***Richfield Springs Laundromat*** *(315-858-1670).*

Left. ***Basset Health Care. Richfield Springs*** *(315-858-0040). A health care center with a part-time doctor and a nurse practitioner, open weekdays, 9 AM - 5 PM, by appointment only.*

Right. **Big A Auto Parts** *(315-858-2442). Auto parts.*

Left. **Ssnippers 2** *(315-858-1837). Hair salon.*

Left. **Richfield Veterans Club** *(315-858-9924).*

End of Lake Street coverage.

Right. **Parkview Liquors** (315-858-0430). Wines and liquors.

Right. **Stitches N Stuff** (315-858-2744). Custom embroidery for sports clothing, hats, T-shirts, pillows, etc. Also custom sewing, alterations, and gifts.

Right. **Richfield Springs Post Office** (315-858-2884). ZIP 13439.

Right. **Tally-Ho Restaurant** (315-858-0180). Family-style restaurant serving breakfast, lunch, and dinner. Home baked muffins, turnovers, pies, and homemade soups. Specialty sandwiches, 1/3 pound burgers, dinner entrees. Dinner $6-$9.

Right. **Klem's Liquor Store** (315-858-1560).

Right. **Village Motel** (315-858-1540). Eleven units accommodating from one to five people per room, with full tiled bath, A/C, and TV. One unit is handicapped-accessible. $48-$70/two. Comfortable and spotless.

Left. **Great White Sulphur Springs Drinking Fountain**. Water from such springs each year drew thousands of people seeking relief from their ailments.

000.5 Right. **Stewart Shops** (315-858-6410). Convenience store, gas, and an ATM.

000.6 Right. **Great American Food Stores** (315-858-9975). Supermarket.

Right. **Central National Bank** (315-858-2800).

000.7   Right. **Stony Brook Motel** (315-858-9929). A neat and tidy, seven-unit motel decorated with baskets of colorful flowers. Each room has two double beds, heat and A/C, TV, telephone, a separate bathroom heater, and outside chairs and a table. $42-$67/two. Open all year.

000.9   Right. **Summerwood** (315-858-2024). A lovely, 1890 Queen Anne Victorian bed and breakfast with many large south-facing windows that bathe the interior with sunlight and breezes. A fireplace warms the sumptuous parlor and another the large dining room. A cozy window seat graces a bay window beneath the stairway. Five guest rooms, three with private full bath, period furnishings, heirloom bedspreads, and TVs. No smoking, $65-$80/two with full breakfast. Elegant and charming.

001.0   Leaving **Richfield Springs**.

Left. **New York State Police** (315-858-2726, 24-hour dispatch 315-858-1122).

001.2   Left. **Fountain View Motel** (315-858-1360). Popular 16-room motel with comfortable and attractive accommodations for one to six people. Each room has a full tiled bath, a large-screen cable TV, A/C, a refrigerator, and a microwave oven. Badminton, croquet, and frisbees. $45-$80/couple. Closed December through March.

001.6   Entering **Herkimer County**, town of **Warren**.

003.6   Left. Junction with **Little Lakes Road (CR 131)**. Make left turn for campground:

000.1   *Right. Junction with **Ostrander Road**. Make right turn for campground:*

001.5   *Left. **Cooperstown North KOA** (315-858-0236, 800-562-3402). Some 120 sites with no, partial,* *and full hookups, $19-$26/two, and cabins for up to four, $37/night. Swimming pool, game room, playground, and free movies. Open April 15 to October 15.*

End of coverage of Ostrander Road and Little Lakes Road (CR 131).

End of coverage of US 20 east and Richfield Springs.

23

Mohawk

Mohawk sits on the banks of the Mohawk River and the Erie Canal, which was built between 1817 and 1825. The 365-mile-long canal's completion connected the Atlantic Ocean with the Great Lakes and allowed commerce to flow between Europe and interior United States. It also allowed travel between Hudson River cities and Great Lakes cities, and facilitated the establishment and growth of settlements along the canal's length and the expansion of the country. Mohawk, initially settled around 1722, grew as canal traffic grew.

Today the Erie Canal is used by commercial shipping interests as well as by pleasure boaters. Even if you don't own a boat you can experience the pleasures of canal boating. Collar City Charters (518-272-5341, 800-830-5341) in Troy offers canal boats for week-long, self-captained rentals. Mid-Lakes Navigation Co. in Skaneateles (315-685-8500, 800-545-4318) offers daily canal cruises, two- and three-day canal excursions with nights spent at hotels along the way, and week-long, self-captained rentals. Cruises on other bodies of water are also available. Canal boating season is usually from May through October. For information on the New York State Canal System call 800-4CANAL4.

For information on Mohawk, Herkimer, and Herkimer County, contact the Herkimer County Chamber of Commerce (315-866-7820) on West Main Street in Mohawk.

137.5   Entering village of **Mohawk** on **Columbia Street**.

138.0   Left(right) **Mohawk Police Station** (315-866-3460).

Right(left) **Mohawk Post Office** (315-866-1720). ZIP 13407.

138.1   Right(left) **Crafty Haircutters** (315-866-6057). Hair salon.

Left(right) **Shibley's Superette** (315-866-9859).   Small supermarket.

Right(left) **The Frame Place & Art Gallery** (315-866-0933). Art studio, fine art, commercial art, signs, and framing.

138.2   Left(right) **nice n easy** (315-866-1354). Grocery store and Mobil gas.

Right(left) **Lawrence Paul Fuels** (315-866-1390). Citgo gas.

Traffic light at intersection of **Route 28** with West and East **Main Street**. Route 28 continues straight ahead onto **Warren Street** (**Columbia Street** if traveling south).

See **"Mohawk's West Main Street to Ilion"** later in this chapter for **West Main Street** coverage.

Turning right(left) onto **East Main Street** offers the following:

*000.0   Right. **Mohawk Washing Well**. Coin-operated laundry.*

*Right. **Back To Granny's Day Antiques** (315-866-8479). Furniture, Adirondack furniture and artifacts (e.g., pack baskets, fishing creels), china, silver, glassware, kitchenware, jewelry, quilts, cameras, and books.*

*000.1   Left. **Francis E. Spinner Home**.   On the National Register of Historic Places, this private home used to be the residence of Herkimer County Sheriff, Congressman and Lincoln-appointed Secretary of the Treasury Francis E. Spinner.*

*000.4   Right. **Mohawk Big M Supermarket** (315-866-6711).*

*Left.   **The Treasure Chest** (315-866-1255).   Antiques, collectibles, furniture, and jewelry.*

000.5   *Right.* **Factory Store** *(315-866-5150).   Family apparel.*

000.6   *Left.   **Mohawk Station** (315-866-7460).   Casual restaurant and cocktail lounge in an old railroad station decorated with railroad memorabilia.   Lunch ($5-8) and dinner ($7-$19).*

*Junction of **East Main Street** with **Route 28** north and south **and NY 5S** east and west.*

End of East Main Street coverage.

Left(right).   **Optima Gold Hair Spa** (315-866-PERM).   Hair salon.

Left(right).   **Warren Street Antiques** (315-866-9475).   General line of antiques.

138.3   Junction of **Route 28** and **NY 5S**. Route 28 north bears right onto entrance ramp onto NY 5S east. To follow Route 28 north, move to left lane once on Route 28 north/NY 5S east because Route 28 north makes a left turn at the traffic light 0.4 mile ahead. (If traveling south, Route 28 south turns left at this traffic light from NY 5S west onto Warren Street.)

138.7   Traffic light at junction of **Route 28, NY 5S**, and the east end of **East Main Street**. Route 28 north turns left from left lane while NY 5S east continues straight ahead from right lane. East Main Street is to the right. (If traveling south, Route 28 north turns right at this light onto NY 5S west. Move to left lane once on Route 28 south/NY 5S west because Route 28 south makes a left turn at the traffic light 0.4 mile ahead.)

Going straight ahead (or making a left if traveling south) onto **NY 5S** east yields:

000.8   *Left. Junction with* **South Washington Street** *crossing bridge to* **Herkimer***. One-tenth of a mile north of this intersection on the right is the* **Capt. Samuel Maytan Fishing Access Site***. Bank fishing along the Mohawk River, a wheelchair-accessible fishing pier, the Herkimer Fishing Derby Pavilion, and picnic tables.*

001.7   *Left.* **Parking** *area with picnic tables on the banks of the Mohawk River and Erie Canal.*

002.0   *Right.* **Guido's R/V's and Garage** *(315-866-0680). R/V sales and service. Travel trailers, fifth-wheels, and pop-ups. Pop-up rentals. R/V repairs, hitching, wiring, inspections, awning installation, re-skinning. R/V appliances, accessories, supplies, and propane.*

East of Mohawk, south of Little Falls, is **Shu-Maker Mountain** *(315-823-4470, snow conditions 315-823-1110 or 800-689-0969), a predominantly intermediate downhill ski area. The longest run is more than a mile on 750 feet of vertical drop. Twenty-two trails, three lifts, snow-making, night skiing (Tu-F), cafeteria, and lounge. From this point on NY 5S, continue east on NY 5S for approximately three miles to its intersection with NY 167. Turn right onto NY 167 south, drive approximately one mile (crossing the Thruway (I-90)) and make a right onto Cheese Factory Road. Shu-Maker Mountain is at the end of the road.*

End of NY 5S east coverage.

138.8   Crossing the **Erie Canal** and the **Mohawk River**. **Mohawk/-Herkimer** village line.

Coverage of Route 28 continues in Chapter 24, *Herkimer*.

Mohawk's West Main Street to Ilion

000.0   Right. **Collector's Corner** (315-866-6718). Gifts and gourmet items, sports cards, and collectibles.

Right. **Classic Designs** (315-866-7039). Jackets, hats, tee-shirts, custom embroidery, screen printing, and team uniforms.

Right. **Paesano's Pizzeria** (315-866-0333). Pizza, wings, subs, calzones, lasagna, and stuffed shells. Will deliver.

Left. **Mobil** gas.

Right. **Main Street Mini-Mall** (315-866-2492). Houses the following:
The Pit Arcade. Video games, pool table.
Downtown Video.
Pappy's Pizza (315-866-8228). Pizza, subs, wings, etc. Delivery.
Modern Dry Cleaners.
Gazebo News (315-866-2492). Newspapers, magazines, cigarettes, cigars, and snacks.

Left. **Burns' Pharmacy** (315-866-4930).

Right. **Betty's Beauty Salon** (315-866-5993).

Left. **The Printer** (315-866-4495). Custom mailing labels, fax, copier, resumes, mailing, and office assistance service.

Right. **Village Market** (315-866-3344). Small supermarket.

Left. **John's Barber and Styling Shop** (315-866-5305).

Right. **Herkimer County Chamber of Commerce** (315-866-7820). Tourist information.

Left. **Fleet Bank** (800-228-1281).

000.1   Left. **Weller Park**. This multi-acred village park was formerly the Weller homestead which consumed the entire block between South Richfield Street and West Grove Street It boasts green lawns, tall trees, park benches, and a new gazebo.

Left. **Weller Library** (315-866-2983) in Weller Park. Built in 1851 as a private home, the Weller Library warrants a visit just to see its beautifully appointed interior with its Austrian crystal chandelier; brass gaslight; eight-point, geometrically-laid parquet floors; ornate, wooden bookcases; and busts and statues. A library since 1914, it houses a general-purpose collection of books as well as information on the old Erie Canal and the Adirondack Mountains. A museum on the second floor displays a collection of items from the Weller family as well as from the village of Mohawk, the Spinner House, the Valley Tavern, and more.

000.3   Right. **Holt Brothers** (315-866-2120). Buick, Cadillac, and GMC truck dealership.

000.4   Right. A free R/V **dump station** at Herkimer County Wastewater Treatment Plant, at end of driveway on the left. 7:00-3:00, M-F.

000.5   Left. **Ozzie's Mohawk Valley Brake** (315-866-3700). Auto repair shop.

Left. **Lou's Dari Creme** (315-866-3408). Ice cream stand.

Right. **The Oak Barrel** (315-866-2396). Country gifts, Amish furniture, and a holiday room.

Right. **J & L Hair Designs** (315-866-5122).

Right. **Herkimer County Water Pollution Control District Mohawk River Fishing Access Site**.

000.6   Right. **Foor's Radiator** (315-866-0230). Automobile radiator, gas tank, and air conditioning service.

000.7   Entering village of **Ilion**, home of the typewriter, first manufactured here by Remington in 1873.

000.8   Right. **Whiffletree Motor Inn** (315-895-7777). Thirty bright, spotless rooms, $48-$56. Guests have access to the tennis courts, golf course, swimming pool, and restaurant of the Mohawk Valley Country Club on NY 5 a few miles east of Herkimer.

Right. **Dick's Restaurant and Cocktail Lounge** (315-894-8532). A family restaurant serving lunch and dinner. Dinner menu of chicken, steaks, seafood, Italian dishes, and more, $5-$15. Chicken riggies (rigatoni with peppers, mushrooms, and onions in a vodka pink sauce) are a favorite. Friday fish fry, $7; Saturday prime rib, $12. Open seven days. In Whiffletree Motor Inn building.

000.9   Right. **Classic Auto Wash.**

Left. **Down Under Unisex Salon** (315-895-7843). Hair salon.

001.2   Right. **Eastern Auto Mall** (315-895-7487). Ford dealership. Towing.

Right. **Clifford Fuel Company** (315-894-9664). Citgo gas and car wash.

001.3   Left. **Remington Arms Company** (315-895-3200, 800-243-9700). Remington manufactures sporting arms including rifles, shotguns, and black-powder muzzle loaders. It offers plant tours of the manufacturing line and the custom shop. A museum presents a marvelous, almost 200-year history of long arms through an array of designs, features, and artistry. Visitors can shop in the retail store. A shooting school is also offered. Engrossing, even for those not particularly interested in guns.

End of coverage of West Main Street.

Herkimer

Herkimer and Mohawk can trace their European-based history to about 1723, when the first Palatine Germans, emigrating to avoid religious persecution, settled on both shores of the Mohawk River to farm the fertile river valley, the area being at that time part of the lands of the Mohawk Indians. In 1757, French and Indian raiders attacked and burned the settlement, then known as German Flatts. More than 40 men, women, and children were massacred and 150 were taken captive.

In 1776, Fort Dayton was built on the site north of Court Street currently occupied by the Herkimer County Historical Society. In August of 1777, General Nicholas Herkimer led his men from Fort Dayton west to help the colonists at Fort Stanwix (now Rome). However, he and his men were ambushed en route. Despite being wounded in the leg early in the battle, Herkimer directed his men to victory in a decisive battle of the war. After being treated by a Dr. Petrie, Herkimer was carried back to his home in Danube, east of Little Falls, where his leg was amputated. He died on August 17, having eventually bled to death from his wounds. Dr. Petrie was later shot and wounded, and upon his death was buried in the Reformed Church of Herkimer cemetery on North Main Street. Herkimer was later chosen as the name for the German Flatts/Fort Dayton area in the General's honor.

For further enjoyment of the history of the Herkimer area, a visit to the historic four corners on North Main Street is a must. There you can tour the old jail, wander through the graveyard, see the court house and Reformed Church, and visit the Herkimer County Historical Society museum. See appropriate entries to follow.

Herkimer hosts in August a Summer Evening, with a parade, entertainment and crafters. Call 315-866-3303 for information. Herkimer also hosts an annual Fishing Derby for children 13 and under, usually the third weekend in July, at the Capt. Samuel Maytan Fishing Access Site along the Mohawk River on South Washington Street. In addition to river bank fishing, the site has a wheelchair-accessible fishing pier to enable fishing by handicapped folks. In conjunction with the fishing derby the Basloe Public Library (315-866-1733) on North Main Street (and other area libraries) lends fishing poles with a free packet of lures to first-time fishing kids. Call 315-866-2733 for derby information.

Tourist information is available from the Leatherstocking Country Tourist Information Office, P.O. Box 447, Herkimer, NY 13350 (315-866-1500). The office is located on the second floor of the 1834 Jail building at 327 North Main Street.

138.8   Crossing the **Erie Canal** and the **Mohawk River**. **Mohawk/-Herkimer** village line.

The **Erie Canal** was built between 1817 and 1825 to take advantage of the natural Mohawk River, adding channels and locks where needed, to facilitate barge traffic. The canal, in conjunction with the Hudson River, created a navigable waterway from the Great Lakes to the ocean, eventually making New York City the major seaport on the east coast.

Entering **Herkimer** on **Mohawk Street**.

139.0   Right(left) Traffic light at entrance to **New York State Thruway (I-90)**, toll road east to **Albany** and west to **Buffalo**.

Left(right) **Skinner Sales** (315-866-3530). Ford Lincoln Mercury dealership.

Left(right) **Mohawk Valley Motor Inn** (315-866-6080). Fourteen rooms, $40-$65.

Right(left) **Denny's Restaurant** (315-866-1603). Open 24 hours.

139.1   Right(left) **Herkimer Motel** (315-866-0490).   Sixty rooms (sixteen with kitchenettes), $54-$92/double.   Handicapped-accessible room, seasonal pool, and laundry.

Right(left) Junction with **Marginal Road**, which yields the following:

000.3   Right. **B & B Auto Tech** *(315-866-8500).   Auto repair shop.*

Right. **Silverado Inn** *(315-866-8835).   Bar.   Lunch.*

000.4   Right. **Ambers Field.** *Tennis courts, basketball court, baseball field, playground, jungle gym, and picnic benches.*

End of Marginal Road coverage.

Left(right) **Studio 30 Lounge** (315-866-9736).

139.2   Route 28 makes a diagonal (less than 90 degrees) left turn from left lane of **Mohawk Street** onto **South Caroline Street**.   (If southbound, Route 28 makes a right turn from South Caroline Street onto Mohawk Street.)

Continuing straight on (or, if traveling southbound, making a left onto) **Mohawk Street** *takes you to* **Friendly's** *(315-866-1406) a few hundred feet down on the left, a restaurant and ice cream shop.*

Right(left). **JT's Convenience Center** and **Subway** (315-866-0222).   Citgo gas, subs, drinks, and groceries.

Left(right). **Herkimer Bowling Center** (315-866-3013).   Ten alleys, pinball machines, and a bar.

Right(left). **Chet's Luncheonette** (315-866-2438).   Home cooked breakfast and lunch.   Home of two-on-a-roll, daily specials, and Friday night fish-fry.

Right(left). **Mr. Shake Dairy Store** (315-866-3055). Seasonal ice cream and frozen yogurt stand.

Right(left). **Tony's Pizzeria and Deli** (315-866-4593). Pizza, chicken wings, cold subs, deli meats, tenders, mozzarella sticks, etc. Open seven days until midnight.

139.3   Right(left). **T & J's Fruits and Vegetables** (315-866-7272). Produce market, fruit baskets, and flowers.

Right(left). **Toni Ann's Doll House** (315-866-3655, 800-445-3655). Dolls, miniatures, lighted villages, ceramics, and collectibles.

139.4   Traffic light at junction with **West State Street (NY 5)**. Route 28 makes a right turn from **Caroline Street** onto **West State Street (NY 5** east toward Albany). (If traveling south, Route 28 turns left from West State Street onto Caroline Street.)

> *Going straight across (or, if traveling south, turning right at) this intersection north onto **Caroline Street**, making a left after one-tenth mile onto **Park Avenue**, and continuing a short distance to the end takes you to **Harmon Playground** with its tennis and basketball courts, baseball diamond, swing set, jungle gym, and picnic table.*

> *Turning left (or, if traveling south, going straight ahead) at this intersection and driving eight miles west on **NY 5** takes you to **Elmtree Estates** (315-724-6678) on the left, a beautifully green campground in **Frankfort**. Thirty-six sites, some with partial and full hookups, children's playground, and propane by the pound and gallon. $17-$22 for two. Pets accepted with restrictions. Open April 15 to November 1.*

Left(right) **Sears** (315-866-0154). Appliances, electronics, lawn and garden supplies, and tools.

Left(right) **First Source Federal Credit Union** (315-866-2940). 24-hour drive-through ATM.

Left(right) **Pizza Hut** (315-866-3399).

139.5   Left(right) **McDonald's** (315-866-7970).

Right(left) **T.P. Drive In** (315-866-6924).   Burgers, hot dogs, Mexican hots, sandwiches, specialties, dinners, and desserts; $1-$7.

Intersection with **North** and **South Bellinger Street**:

> *A few hundred feet north on **North Bellinger Street** is **Myers Park**, a large, grassy park with tall shade trees and park benches.   Statues here honor General Nicholas Herkimer, and Francis E. Spinner, who was Herkimer County sheriff in 1834, served in the U.S. Congress from 1854 to 1860, and was appointed by Abraham Lincoln to serve as Treasurer of the U.S. from 1861 to 1875.   The Herkimer honor roll is also located here.   This is a lovely place to sit and rest during your walking tour of Herkimer.*

Right(left) **Taco Bell** and **Kentucky Fried Chicken** (315-866-3500).

Left(right) **Herb Philipson's Army Navy** (315-866-5556). Impressive stock of name brand casual clothing, footwear, T's, sweats, and team-logo clothing; western shop; hunting, camping, and fishing supplies; sporting goods; more.

139.6   Right(left) Shopping plaza, containing, from right to left:
Auto Palace (315-866-4999). Auto parts.
Dapper Dan Laundromat and Dry Cleaning (315-866-1139).
Harry's Liquors (315-866-1940).
Rite-Aid Pharmacy (315-866-4570).
Sisters' Shearin' (315-866-3071). Hair salon.

Baker's Dozen (315-866-6770). Bakery, lunch, sandwiches, and grill items. Donuts, breads, cookies, brownies, and cakes. Open 24 hours.

Right(left) **Eggers, Caryl & Corrigan Inc.** (315-866-5400). Goodyear tire store and auto service.

Left(right) **Mid-Town Pontiac** (315-866-0391). Dealership.

Right(left) **nice n easy Shoppe** (315-866-2606). Convenience store, Mobil gas.

139.7   Intersection with **Prospect Street**:

> *Making a left(right) onto **Prospect Street** and traveling one-tenth of a mile to the corner of **Park Avenue** takes you to the **Prospect Inn** (315-866-4400) on the right. Eighteen rooms, $58/double.*

Left(right) **D.J.'s Family Video** (315-866-8314).

Left(right) **Dineen's** (315-866-8148). A pub.

Right(left) **Burger King** (315-866-3160).

Left(right) **Big Jim's Subs and Casual Dining** (315-866-9914). Breakfast, lunch, and dinner.

Left(right) **Hummel's Business Centre** (315-866-3860). Office machines, office supplies, luggage, briefcases, gifts, collectibles, fax, and copy service.

Right(left) **Herkimer County Trust Company** (315-867-2500). 24-hour ATM.

Left(right) **Empire Diner** (315-866-6710).

Intersection with **Main Street**. For coverage of Main Street see **Herkimer's North Main Street** and **Herkimer's South Main Street** sections to follow.

Right(left) **Cole Muffler Shop** (315-866-1557). Pipes, shocks, and hitches.

139.8   Left(right) **Park Avenue Barber Shop** (315-866-1625).

Left(right) **OTB**. Off-Track Betting.

Right(left) **Enjem's Floor Covering Center**, and **Small Beginnings** (315-866-4550). Floor coverings and carpets. Small Begin-nings features antiques, gifts, collectibles, artwork, and new and used furniture.

Left(right) **Valley Cleaners and Laundromat** (315-866-3545).

Left(right) **Dollar Depot** (315-866-0738). A dollar store.

Left(right) **Cosmic Closet**. Jewelry, hats, candles, clothing, pipes, Tarot, incense, and piercing.

Right(left) Intersection with **North** and **South Washington Street**. Making a left(right) onto **North Washington Street** yields:

*000.0   Left.   **Deli King** (315-866-7669).   Cold cuts, cheese, breads, bagels, party platters, and freshly roasted coffee.*

*000.2   Left.   **Inn Towne Motel** (315-866-1101, 800-464-7485). Thirty-three rooms, each with a refrigerator. $38-$54/-double.*

*Right.   **Carney's Corners** (315-866-7191). Old-time gro-cery store.*

End of North Washington Street coverage.

Making a right(left) onto **South Washington Street** and driving about one-half mile takes you to the **Capt. Samuel Maytan Fishing Access Site** on the left, which offers river-bank fishing along the northern banks of the Mohawk, a wheelchair-accessible fishing pier, the Herkimer Fishing Derby Pavilion, and picnic tables.

139.9   Right(left) **K-Mart** (315-866-4910).

Right(left) **Ponderosa Steak House** (315-866-0110).

140.0   Right(left) **Monroe Muffler Brake** (315-866-2187).

Left(right) Shopping plaza:
Radio Shack (315-866-7083).
Eckerd Drugs (315-866-3855).

Right(left) **Arby's**.

140.1   Junction of **Route 28** and **NY 5** east. Route 28 north turns left toward **Poland** and **Barneveld**.

End of coverage of Route 28 in Herkimer. See Chapter 25, *Herkimer to Poland,* for continuation of Route 28 coverage.

Continuing straight ahead on **NY 5** east yields the following:

*000.0   Right. **EFK Plaza**, right to left:*
Video to Rol (315-866-7456).
A.J.'s Pizzeria (315-866-4480).
Subway (315-866-6420). Sub sandwich shop.
Jet Photo (315-866-4653). 45-minute photo finishing.

*Right. **nice n easy** (315-866-7131). Convenience store and Citgo gas.*

*Right. **Bikes 500** (315-866-6552). Bicycle sales and service.*

*Left.   **Valley Automotive Sales and Service** (315-866-7446).   Auto sales and repairs.   Facing NY 5 but really on West Albany Street with access from Protection Avenue immediately to the east.*

*Intersection with **Protection Avenue**.*

*Left.   **Baby Boomers Cookery and Lounge** (315-866-3183).   Comfortable, popular, family restaurant serving lunch ($4-$7) and dinner ($7-$14).   Daily specials. Lounge.   Where the natives go.   Facing NY 5 but really on West Albany Street with access from Protection Avenue immediately to the west.*

*Crossing **West Canada Creek**.*

*East of **Herkimer**, south of **Little Falls**, is **Shu-Maker Mountain** (315-823-4470, snow conditions 315-823-1110 or 800-689-0969), a predominantly intermediate downhill ski area.   The longest run is more than a mile on 750 feet of vertical drop.   Twenty-two trails, three lifts, snow-making, night skiing (Tu-F), cafeteria, and lounge.   From this point on NY 5, continue east on NY 5 for approximately five miles to NY 167 in Little Falls.   Turn right onto NY 167 south, drive approximately three miles (crossing NY 5S and the Thruway (I-90)) and make a right onto Cheese Factory Road.   Shu-Maker Mountain is at the end of the road.*

End of NY 5 east coverage.

Herkimer's North Main Street

000.0   Right.   **Collis True Value Hardware** (315-866-0826).

Right.   **Golden House Chinese Restaurant** (315-866-8888).

Right.   **Dan Murphy Optical** (315-866-7784).

Right. **Moretti's Barber Shop** and **Herkimer Barber and Beauty Supply**.

Left. **Pete's Tavern**.

Right. **Brian Roast Beef Deli** (315-866-3664). Pizza, wings, and subs.

Right. **Woolworth's** (315-866-3358).

Left. **Vinny's Pizzeria** (315-866-7961). Pizza, Sicilian pizza, and calzones.

Left. **Maria's Jewelry** (315-866-2674).

Left. **Ultimate Tanning** (315-866-8471). Tanning salon, tanning lotions, beauty supplies, cosmetics, T-shirts, and bathing suits.

Left. **Mykola's Ukrainian Perogi House** (315-866-6171). Perogis and candy .

Right. **Antiquity Express** (315-866-9848). Printing, typesetting, and graphics. Wedding invitations, small books, business cards, notepads, etc. Fax.

Left. **Mid-Town Tavern** (315-866-7523).

Left. **Cutting Loose** (315-866-7276). Hair studio.

Right. **Bonnie's Art & Craft** (315-866-2444). Hand-crafted gifts, floral supplies, miniatures, and Girl Scouts headquarters.

Right. **King's Court**. A collection of merchants:
Towne Crier (315-866-3087). Newspapers, magazines, cards, snacks, and smoke shop.
Last Tangle (315-866-7617). Unisex hair salon.
Steve's Jewelry (315-866-5384). Custom jewelry and repairs.
Oat's Gym (315-866-9913). Downstairs.

Right. **Smitty's Diner** (315-867-5718).

Left. **Saturday's Child** (315-866-5032). Children's clothing.

000.1   Right. **Marine Midland Bank** (315-866-7900). 24-hour ATM.

Left. **Rotunda Building**:
The Shoe Gallery (315-866-2280).   Shoes, purses, and accessories.
Desperado (315-866-2453). Western wear and dance club.

Right. **Payless ShoeSource** (315-866-8615). Shoe store.

Left. **Department of Environmental Conservation** Region Six (315-866-6330). Offices.

Right. **2 + 4 Antiques** (315-866-1861). Multi-dealer shop featuring Empire, Federal, and Sheraton furniture, glassware, stoneware, clocks, and more.

Right. **The Last Unicorn** (315-866-0510). Stereos, components, and accessories. New and used CD's, tapes, and LP's. Records, tapes, and CD's purchased.

Right. **Chateau Boutique** (315-866-4681). Fine ladies clothing.

Right. **Brownies**. Bar.

Right. **Coin-Op. Laundry**.

Right. **Weisser's Jewelers** (315-866-2544). Jewelry and watch repair.

000.2   Right. **Waverly Pub**. In old General Herkimer Hotel building.

Left. **Frank J. Basloe Public Library** (315-866-1733). Set in a small park with benches under shade trees. General library, local info, and genealogy room. A notable lending program is that of fishing poles with a free packet of lures for first time users, a program helpful to the youngsters during the local fishing derby.

Left. **Herkimer County Office Building** (315-867-1002).

Right. **Smokey's** (315-866-2641). Premium cigars, cigarettes, tobacco products and accessories, newspapers, magazines, soda, and candy.

Left. **Orchid Cleaners** (315-866-7865).

Left. **Byte-Me** (315-866-5104). Computer services.

Left. **Coffee Bar** (315-866-0409). Bagels, quiches, sandwiches, pastries, desserts, espresso, cappuccino, latte, zomby woof, and specialty non-alcoholic drinks.

Left. **Herkimer County Trust Company** (315-866-2550). ATM.

You are now approaching Herkimer's historical four corners, the intersection of North Main Street, Church Street, and Court Street. The buildings on the four corners are the 1834 Jail, the Herkimer County Court House (1873), the Herkimer County Historical Society building (the Suiter House, 1884) and the Reformed Church of Herkimer (1835). In 1834, inmates at the prior jail, which was at the time housed in the same wooden-frame building as the county courthouse, set the jail ablaze. Burning shingles from the jail blew across the street and ignited the earlier Reformed Church building. Both buildings burned to the ground and were later rebuilt.

Left. **1834 Jail** (315-866-6413). This old stone block building was built in 1834 to replace the jail destroyed when the old courthouse burned. It was used as a jail until 1977. Two of its famous residents were Roxalana Druse, a murderess, who, in 1887, was the last woman to be hanged in New York state, and Chester Gillette, the convicted murderer who killed his pregnant, 20-year-old girlfriend, Grace Brown, in what Gillette said was a boating accident on Big Moose Lake in the Adirondacks, and who was housed here in 1906 and 1907 during his trial in the courthouse across the street. The Gillette murder inspired Theodore Dreiser to write his famous 1925 novel *An American Tragedy*.

Do take the jail tour; the building, its primitive facilities, and its history and that of its inmates are all fascinating. The gift shop and book store contain many local photos and books, and a doll house and miniatures collection is upstairs. The building also houses the Leatherstocking Country Tourist Information Office (315-866-1500). Open Monday through Friday, 10 AM to 4 PM.

Right. **Herkimer County Court House** (315-867-1171). Built in 1873 and thrust into prominence by the Chester Gillette murder trial in 1906 and 1907.

Right. Building behind the court house (on Court Street) is made of deep red stone. Built in 1897 for $17,000 as the clerk's office, it now houses the county treasurer's office. Affixed to the wall just outside the main entrance is an historical plaque, placed in 1907, commemorating nearby **Fort Dayton**, built in 1776.

000.3   Left. Intersection with Church Street.

Left. **The Reformed Church of Herkimer** (315-866-1523). Re-built in 1835 after the fire that destroyed the jail and the former church. The interior was designed by Louis Comfort Tiffany.

Right. **Herkimer County Historical Society** (315-866-6413). Museum and resource center housed in the Suiter house, which was built in 1884 but never lived in by the doctor who had it built. Beautifully-carved griffins on the front doors guard the entrance while gargoyles lurk above some of the windows. The museum is comprised of four rooms which present the area's historical overview, and domestic, agricultural, and industrial life. The resource center and library on the second floor is open by appointment and at a small fee to the public for local history and Herkimer County genealogy research. Museum open Monday through Friday, 10 AM to 4 PM.

Right. **The Eckler House** (1870), under restoration. It is an extension of and attached by covered porch to the Herkimer County Historical Society. It houses exhibit rooms and a meeting room.

000.4   **North Main Street** north from the historic four corners to **German Street** is a lovely section of town with historical buildings, a church, cemetery, and older, well-kept residences. This part of North Main Street, and a block or two east and west, offer excellent architectural, historical, and cultural sights for a walking tour of old Herkimer.

End of North Main Street coverage.

Herkimer's South Main Street

000.0   Left. **Whaley's Tavern**.

Right. Intersection with **Mohawk Street**:

Left. ***Comin' Around Again*** *(315-866-0864). Clothing and jewelry consignment shop.*

Left. ***Yetty's Pizza*** *(315-866-4201). Pizza, pasta, beer, and wine. Deck with umbrella tables for alfresco dining.*

End of Mohawk Street coverage.

Left. **House of China** (315-866-7615). Chinese restaurant.

Right. **Gusto di Pileggi** (315-866-6336). Charmingly appointed Italian cafe and deli serving breakfast and lunch, and featuring homemade Italian bread, sausage, marinated sun-dried tomatoes, roasted peppers, cookies, pastries, imported pastas and oils, etc. Sandwiches, panini (stuffed roll), salads, daily hot special; $3-$5. Cappuccino, espresso, and flavored coffees. Friday evenings open for coffee, pastry, and dessert. A delightful taste of Italy.

Left.   **Reina's of Herkimer** (315-866-5044).   Fine women's fashions.

Right.   **Flower Soup Children's Wear** (315-866-7215). Children's clothing.

Right.   **Read's Girmonde** (315-866-4600, 800-522-9529). Flowers and gifts.

Left.   **Children's Exchange** (315-866-7328).   Second-hand children's clothing.

Right. **Rudy's Men's Fashions** (315-866-3270). Men's clothing, including big and tall sizes.

Left. **Sheer Pleasure** (315-866-0596). Unisex hair salon.

000.1   Right. **Villa Italia** (315-866-5002). Sicilian pizza and subs.

End of South Main Street coverage.

Herkimer to Poland

140.1 Junction of **Route 28** and **NY 5** east in **Herkimer**. Route 28 north turns left toward Poland and Barneveld.

140.8 Left(right) **Bob Kavic Chrysler Plymouth Dodge Jeep Eagle** (315-866-3030). Dealership.

141.0 Left(right) **Shopping plaza**:
Wesley's Auto Repair.
Only One (315-866-8041). Dollar store.
Pharmhouse (315-866-2990). Discount drug store.
P&C Foods (315-866-2681). Supermarket. Open 24 hours.
Citgo gas.

Designated Bike Route.

141.3 Leaving(entering) village of **Herkimer**.

141.4 Right(left) **Len Brown Chevrolet, Oldsmobile, and Geo** (315-866-5080). Dealership.

141.5 Right(left) **Heidelberg Bakery** (315-866-0999). Breads, cakes, muffins, cookies, and scones. Sausage, pepperoni, and spinach rolls; quiche. Good stuff!

141.7 Right(left) **West Canada Creek fishing access** parking.

142.6   Left(right) **Mohawk Trapping and Outdoor Supplies** (315-866-7937). Hunting, fishing, trapping, and reloading equipment and supplies.   Hides and pelts bought and sold.   Snowshoes, topographical maps, and worms.

142.8   Right(left) **P & J's Antiques** (315-866-0106).   Original and refinished antique furniture, furniture hardware, mirrors, frames, collectible glass, and books. Furniture refinishing scrapers and tools, materials, wax, and instruction for the do-it-yourselfer.

142.9   Entering(leaving) **Kast Bridge**.

Left(right) **Kast Bridge Crafts** (315-866-6313). Pre-1840s barn featuring handmade country crafts. Wooden items, dolls, pottery, candles, wreaths, and more.

143.1   Designated Bike Route.

143.4   Left(right) **Parking** area in a pretty place with picnic tables under shade trees. Across the road from West Canada Creek.

144.2   Leaving(entering) **Kast Bridge**.

The countryside along here is mostly flat with some small hills. Past and present farms checker the flat land and even drape some of the distant hills. The West Canada Creek to the east, which Route 28 follows to Barneveld, offers one scenic view after another.   The Mohawks called the creek "Kuyahoora", meaning "falling waters", for the falls known today as Trenton Falls. The creek is host to canoeing, kayaking, and fishing, and is navigable by canoe and kayak for 28 miles from Trenton Falls to its confluence with the Mohawk River in Herkimer, with two portages at the dams at Newport and just below Kast Bridge. Its personality ranges from placid to class two white water, meaning, on a scale of one to six, moving water with rapids and waves up to three feet high.

146.5   **Herkimer/Middleville** town line.

147.3   Left(right) **Crystal Chandelier** (315-891-3366).   Large family restaurant serving dinner Wednesday through Sunday, April 1 through January 1; Friday and Saturday only January through March. Italian cuisine includes appetizers, soups, salads, pastas, chicken, veal, beef, fish, combinations, and more, with most entrees $8-$14. Weddings, banquets, and outdoor bakes. Pleasant atmosphere.

Left(right) **Herkimer Diamond Mines** (315-891-7355). Prospect for "diamonds" (quartz-crystals). While the discovery of large crystals seems to be everyone's goal, the small ones are the more perfectly faceted. Prospecting with a hand pick in the diamond fields provide hours of interesting fun for the entire family. Large gem and mineral shop, and a museum. April through November.

147.4   Right(left) **Herkimer Diamond KOA** (315-891-7355, 800-562-0897). Pretty, manicured campground in a field alongside the West Canada Creek. One-hundred sites, 40 with hookups, log cabins with porches, swimming pool, recreation building, playground, creek fishing, tubing, and miniature golf. Across street from Herkimer Diamond Mines. April through November. Rates for tent sites, $19; R/V with full hookups, $26; cabins, $38/two; cottages with bath, shower, and kitchen, $95/four. Also cable TV hookups on some sites.

147.5   Entering(leaving) village of **Middleville**.

147.7   Left(right) **Ace of Diamonds Diamond Mine** (315-891-3855). Mine, campground, and a gem and tool shop. Six recreational vehicle sites and six tent sites support miners who stay for a while. Most of the big stones come in pockets, and a pocket could be worth as much as $1,500 to $2,000. Some people mine here every day for a living, polishing and selling whatever they unearth to jewelry manufacturers and gem collectors. Open April through October.

148.0   Right(left) **Werthman's Market and Deli** (315-891-3325). Groceries, hot and cold subs, hot dogs, and seasonal soft ice cream. Also videos.

Right(left) **Bev's Diner** (315-891-3220). Serving breakfast and lunch. Grill items, sandwiches, homemade soups and pies. Daily special.

148.1   Left(right) **West Canada Sport Shop** (315-891-3804). Hunting and fishing equipment and supplies. Canoes, outdoor clothing and footwear, snowmobile and motorcycle helmets, custom tied trout flies, worms, and salted minnows. Fishing, hiking and back-country hunting guide service. Free local knowledge. In same family for more than 45 years.

Right(left) **Dibble's Inn.** Bar with billiards and darts.

Right(left) **Dawn's Beauty Salon** (315-891-3082).

Right(left) **Sue's ABC Store** (315-891-3777). Birds, birds, and more birds. And bird equipment and bird supplies. And still more birds.

Left(right) **Stewarts Shops** (315-891-3432). Convenience store, gas, ATM.

Traffic light at junction with **NY 29** (**Fairfield Street**) and **NY 169** in middle of Middleville. Route 28 turns left. Turning right at this intersection onto NY 169 south toward Little Falls takes you to:

000.0   *Left.* **Middleville Free Library** *(315-891-3655). Library plus state-of-the-art computers offering Internet access.*

Left. **Middleville Post Office** *(315-891-3131). ZIP 13406.*

002.2   *Left.* **Piggy Pat's BBQ** *(315-891-3839). Carolina-styled pig roasts and barbecue in a dairy barn converted to a restaurant. Lovely setting on 225 green acres with broad views. Chicken, ribs, pulled pork, beef brisket, smoked turkey, homemade East Texas sausage, $6-$10. Homemade pit-baked beans, coleslaw, and pies. Draws regulars from many miles away. Open for dinner on*

Thursdays, and lunch and dinner Fridays through Sundays. Open Fridays and Saturdays off season.

End of NY 169 south coverage.

Going straight through this intersection and up the hill onto **NY 29** (**Fairfield Street**) toward **Dolgeville** yields:

*000.3   Left.   **The West Canada Hatch** (315-891-3642).   Custom-tied trout and classic Atlantic salmon flies and custom fishing rods.   Also guide service.*

End of NY 29 coverage.

148.2   Right(left) **Arnolds Drive In** (315-891-3434).   Bright and shiny, 1950s-themed short-order restaurant with a 1990s twist. Traditional 1950s fare such as hamburgers, fries, hard ice cream, vanilla custard, and more, plus 1990s fare such as turkey burgers, veggie burgers, and pitas.

Right(left) **Central National Bank** (315-891-7502).

Right(left) Side street, 200 feet up which is a small **park** on the left with children's playground, tennis courts, two small baseball fields, an old pavilion, and picnic tables.

Left(right) Two large plaques summarizing the history of Middleville offer interesting reading and reflection.

148.4   Right(left) **Flansburg's Antiques and Collectibles** (315-891-3032).   Glassware, stoneware, furniture, and primitives.   Also oddities such as a bear skin, old tools, 1952 army snowshoes, postcards, and more.   April-December.

Left(right) **French's Restaurant** (315-891-9440).   In an older, many-angled, and many-gabled building with a dining room and bar pleasantly evoking the past.   Monday lunch buffet, $4.50; Thursday evening all the sirloin you can eat, $9.   Dinner entrees $8-$14.

Left(right) **The Golden Drake Fly Shop** (315-891-3591). Fishing flies.

148.7   Leaving(entering) village of **Middleville**.

148.8   Right(left) **Car Connection** (315-891-3998). Auto repairs and sales.

149.2   Left(right) **West Canada Creek Public Fishing Stream** parking down a dirt road.

150.3   Left(right) **Reilly's Yankee General** (315-845-8383). Lunch, dinner, baked goods, burgers, fries, subs, pizza, wings, and fish fry.

151.1   Left(right) **Parking** area with picnic tables alongside West Canada Creek.

The creek, now on the left, is peacefully beautiful. Gone are the rocks and riffles. The water hides the rocky bottom like a comforter hides a lumpy mattress, and it just flows and flows and flows.

151.9   Left(right) **Pop's Ponderosa Campground** (315-845-8413). In a green-carpeted field with tall pines and maples, an apple tree and grapevines, and 600' of frontage on the banks of West Canada Creek. Eleven sites with water and electric hookups, $18; plus primitive tenting in the field and alongside the creek, $10. Creek stocked with trout and bass, and is so wide and shallow here you can walk straight across from one bank to the other. Dump station. Showers planned. Open mid-May to October.

Entering(leaving) village of **Newport**.

The town of Newport was first settled in 1791 by Christopher Hawkins, who came from Newport, Rhode Island. Because he and a number of other settlers also came from Rhode Island, Newport was chosen for the settlement's name. Newport's most famous resident was Linus Yale, Sr., a member of the same Connecticut family for which Yale University was named. Yale, who was a great inventor, primarily with lock devices, came to Newport early in the nineteenth century. Yale also arranged to build the Octagon House on the north side of the village.

The village of Newport is a one-crossroad town characterized by restored and unrestored large, architecturally and historically interesting homes, large lawns, and large oak and maple trees. In the fall foliage season the leaves blaze like a forest fire. The people are warm, friendly, personable and helpful, and their collective pride in their village is palpable. If thinking of moving or retiring to the country, place Newport on your list of places to consider.

152.2   Right(left) **Newport Free Library** (315-845-8533).

152.4   Left(right) **Main Street Ristorante** (315-845-8835). Old Newport preserved. Formerly the Colonial Inn and an American Legion hall, this building is more than 200 years old and boasts floor-to-ceiling front windows overlooking the large front porch. This homey restaurant serves breakfast (weekends only, $2-$5.50); lunch, $3-$5.50; and dinner $6-$15, in a dining room furnished with country crafts. Entrees include seafood, steak, chicken, pasta, and more. Even the home fries and toast for the breakfast special start the day as potatoes and flour respectively.

Left(right) **Newport Historical Center** (315-845-8434). Historical souvenirs of local interest. Operated by the Newport Historical Society.

Left(right) **Cafe Newport** (315-845-1742). Cozy cafe serving breakfast and lunch. Cakes, dinner rolls, salads, bread, pies, and bagels. Homemade breads, rolls, pies, soups, and daily specials.

Left(right) **New York Pizzeria** (315-845-8121). Pizza, wings, and subs.

Left(right) **Newport Liquor Store and Party Shop** (315-845-8782). Wines and liquors, beer and soda, groceries, snacks, party goods, decorations, etc.

Right(left) **Luigi's Pizzeria** (315-845-8350). Pizza, wings, and subs.

Left(right) **Town Tavern** (315-845-9311).

152.5   Flashing traffic light at junction with **Bridge Street** on the left and **School Street** on the right. A few steps down Bridge Street are:

*000.0   Right. **Primary Care Center at Newport** (315-845-6100). Part of Little Falls Hospital. Walk-ins accepted.*

*Left. **Majestic Acres Photography** (315-845-8997).*

*Right. **Newport Post Office** (315-845-8593). ZIP 13416.*

*Left. **Soron's Radio and Appliances** (315-845-8651).*

*Right. **Newport HPA** (315-845-8562) Pharmacy, health and beauty aids, gifts, toys, and video rental.*

*Left. **Herkimer County Trust Company** (315-845-1600). Bank with 24-hour ATM.*

*Right. **Flowers For You** (315-845-8606).*

*Left. Village **parking** lot.*

*Right.   **Handicapped-accessible fishing deck** with pavilions and picnic tables, just before crossing West Canada Creek.*

*Continuing across the bridge to the end of **Bridge Street**, making a right onto **Old State Road**, making your first left onto **Honey Hill Road (CR 139)**, and driving for a total of 2.4 miles from the flashing light in the middle of Newport, takes you to the **Golf Club of Newport** (315-845-8333), a Geoffry Cornish-designed, rolling, eighteen-hole, par 72 golf course built in the late 1960s. Driving range and Grill Room with full-service bar. Sandwiches, burgers, steaks, etc., $3-$10. Greens fees are $15 for 18 holes. Cart rental $20. Mid-April to mid-October.*

End of Bridge Street coverage.

Right(left) **Newport Hardware** (315-845-8032).   True Value hardware store. Copies and fax service.

Left(right) **Asaro's Service Station** (315-845-8082).   Power Champ gas, auto repairs.

Right(left) **Steve's Barber Shop** (315-845-8102).

Left(right) **Moody's Farm and Home Store** (315-845-8994). Snowmobiles, ATVs, garden tractors, lawnmowers, snowblowers, chainsaws, hydraulic hoses, belts, clothing, etc.   Sales, service, parts, and accessories.

152.6   Right(left) **What Cheer Hall Bed and Breakfast** (315-845-8312). A large, two-story, stone-block Federal building with a four-columned portico fronted by a large lawn and nestled among maples and pines. The house, including the three guest rooms (two with private bath), is furnished with Federal-style antiques. Fireplaces, and old clocks, china, and silver. $55-$65/couple with full breakfast.

152.9   Right(left) **Newport Service** (315-845-8079).   Gas, auto repairs, towing. Propane by weight and volume.

On the left, across from Newport Service, are two beautiful stone Italianate houses on the banks of the creek, and just beyond Newport Service is the **Linus Yale Octagon House**.   All three of these stone houses are private residences and are not open to the public, but all three houses are architecturally noteworthy. The Octagon House was built in the 1850s by Linus Yale, Sr., reportedly for his daughter upon her marriage. It is one of only a few octagonal houses remaining in New York State.

153.1   Right(left) **C & D's Market** (315-845-8526) Groceries, deli, soft ice cream, and Sunoco gas.

Left(right) **West Side Saloon and Steakhouse** (315-845-8822). Popular restaurant offering casual fine dining in a beautiful setting on the banks of West Canada Creek overlooking islands and the meadows beyond.   Rustic, varnished, knotty-pine interior with multiple dining rooms, large windows, and comfortable seating. Offerings include burgers, sandwiches, pastas, chicken, seafood, traditional steaks, prime rib, and surf & turf. Salad bar, clam tank, and seasonal outdoor dining. Most entrees $6-$17.

Leaving(entering) village of **Newport**.

153.2   Right(left) **Carousel Collection Antiques** (315-845-8053). Antique and tack shop. At Harris-Dale estate, with columned 170-year-old, Greek revival house, imposing barn, and two-acre pond. The house is listed in the National Register of Historic Places. Used clothing, small antiques, jewelry, herbal products, local crafts, unfinished furniture, and local artwork. Also horse tack.

153.4   Left(right) **Fishing access** parking.

153.9   Right(left) **Blue Rose Restaurant** (315-845-8922). Popular eatery serving breakfast, lunch, and dinner in booths and a dining room. Homemade cookies, muffins, cakes, and pies; daily specials. Dinner entrees $4-$11. Sunday afternoon dinner buffet, $8.

155.0   Left(right) **West Canada Creek Fishing Access Site** parking, across from scenic bog.

155.7   Entering(leaving) village of **Poland**.   Another village with interesting big old homes with big porches.

156.0   Left(right) **Kuyahoora Outdoor Center** (315-826-3312). Power equipment, snowmobiles, etc.

Left(right) **Irwin House** (315-826-7716). Bar, pool table, and juke box. Friday night fish fry with salad bar, $7.

156.2   Left(right) **Haver's Meats and Groceries** (315-826-3722). An old-time grocery store and meat purveyor thriving in rural New York. Fresh meats, deli, and produce.

156.3   Right(left) Junction with **NY 8** north to **Speculator**. Following NY 8 north yields:

000.0   *Right.* **Kuyahoora Inn** *(315-826-3875). Pizza, wings, and Friday fish fry.*

      Right. **Poland Post Office** *(315-826-3794). ZIP 13431.*

000.1   *Right.* **Town of Russia Kuyahoora Valley Park.** *Large, green meadows and tall trees with a pavilion, picnic tables, playground, little league field, soccer field, and nature trails.*

      Right. **Salms Auto Repair** *(315-826-7774). Auto repair shop and Citgo gas.*

000.3   *Left.* **K. F. McVoy Chrysler Plymouth Dodge** *(315-826-3143). Dealership.*

NY 8 continues north 45 miles to Speculator. End of NY 8 coverage.

Coverage continues in Chapter 26, *Poland to Barneveld.*

Poland to Barneveld

156.3　Right(left) Junction with **NY 8** north to **Speculator** (47 miles).

Left(right) **Fleet Bank** (800-228-1281).

156.4　Left(right) Intersection with **Case Place**, down which a few hundred feet on the left is a **New York State Police** station (315-866-7111).

157.0　Crossing **West Canada Creek**. **Herkimer/Oneida** county line, **Newport/Deerfield** town line, leaving(entering) village of **Poland**.

157.1　Left(right) **West Canada Creek Public Fishing Stream** parking.

Right(left) **West Canada Creek Campsites** (315-826-7390). Seventy-five sites, most with full hook-ups, and two camping cabins. Pool, game room, playground, fishing, and canoe rentals. Store, propane, fishing and hunting licenses, R/V dealer. $20-30/night, April through Mid-October.

Right(left) **Little Red Caboose** (315-826-7390). Ice cream, hot dogs, and subs.

157.2　Left(right) **The Cookie Cutter** (315-826-7620). Marketplace and museum. One-of-a-kind shop housing a large collection of cookie cutters, 500 on one wall alone, featuring different shapes, sizes, materials, manufacturing processes, age, function, etc., with some dating to before 1905. Marketplace sells cutters, cookie baking items, novelties, crafts, collectibles, gifts, fudge, and snacks.

157.3   Left(right) **Eddie's Auto Repair** (315-826-7704).

Right(left) **Blue Anchor Motel and Diner** (315-826-3444). One of the best lodging bargains on Route 28. On the banks of West Canada Creek, seven cabins, one of which is a double unit with two double beds and a porch, overlooking the creek, and two motel rooms, one of which has two double beds, all clean and tidy. Motel rooms open year-round, cabins open April or May into October. Cabins $22-28, motel $25-$30. Call for reservations. Also diner serving breakfast and lunch six days, breakfast only on Sundays.

157.4   Left(right) **Nice 'n' Easy** (315-826-7222). Convenience store and Mobil gas, ATM.

157.7   Junction with **NY 8** south. Route 28 turns to the right to cross the creek, while NY 8 south goes straight ahead.

Crossing West Canada Creek. **Oneida/Herkimer** county line, **Deerfield/Russia** town line.

157.9   Left(right) **West Canada Creek Public Fishing Stream parking**.

158.8   Left(right) **West Canada Creek Public Fishing Stream parking**.

160.2   On the right is a beautiful little pond, a sample of north country scenery to come.

160.5   Right(left) Junction with west end of **Gravesville Road**, leading immediately to **Partridge Hill Road** and **West Canada Creek Public Fishing Stream parking** on the left. Following Gravesville Road to the right leads you immediately between two beautiful forest ponds.

160.6   Crossing West Canada Creek, **Herkimer/Oneida** County line, **Russia/Trenton** town line.

163.5   Right(left) **Fisher Auto Parts** (315-896-2603).

163.6   Junction with **NY 12** at **Barneveld**. **Utica** is to the left, nine miles
         south on NY 12. Route 28 turns right. Route 28 coverage
         continues in Chapter 27, *Barneveld to Alder Creek.*

NY 12 South Toward Utica

Junction of **Route 28** and **NY 12** south of **Barneveld**.

000.1   Right. **Adirondack Lanes and Diner** (315-896-2871). Bowling
         alley and diner.

         Left.   **Hinge Hardware** (315-896-2681).   Hardware, garden
         supplies, and propane by weight/volume.

         Left.   **Wild Bird Crossing** (315-896-4608).   In Hinge Hardware
         store. A bird lover's heaven. Binoculars, bird houses, feeders and
         feed, books, magazines, barometers, audio and video nature tapes,
         and video rentals. Bird-themed and other nature gifts, T's, and
         sweats.   Also hosts occasional nature walks.   An interesting
         activity promoted by the folks at Wild Bird Crossing is
         barnstorming, a fun way to spend an afternoon touring Oneida and
         Oswego counties.   An auto jaunt similar to a casual road rally,
         barnstorming is done by following directions set forth in guides.
         Using clues, each guide directs your drive along scenic routes to
         interesting and historic places and buildings, posing questions to
         prompt exploration and investigation along the way. Barnstorming
         guides are available from Wild Bird Crossing for $5 each.

000.2   Left. **Barneytown Mini-golf and Foodstand** (315-896-6766). Ice
         cream (traditional, fat-free, and sugar-free), frozen yogurt,
         hotdogs, hamburgers, mozzarella sticks, onion rings, etc.
         Seasonal.

         Left.   **Barneytown Treasure House** (315-896-6766). Gifts and
         antiques.

         Right. **Dexter Shoe Factory Outlet** (315-896-6177).

Traffic light at junction of Mapledale Road to the west and Gage Road to the east.

Right. **nice n easy**. Convenience store and Mobil gas.

Left. **Bellinger's** (315-896-6829). Sunoco gas.

000.3   Left. **Barneveld Liquor Store** (315-896-2936).

Right. **Village Plaza**:
The Snapdragon (315-896-6139). Cards, flowers, and gifts.
Village Gallery Properties (315-896-4643). Real estate.
Modern Image (315-896-4025). Unisex hairstyling and nail and tanning salon.

The Body Shop (315-896-2330). Health and fitness center.

Left. **Sunflower Naturals** (315-896-2820). Cheese, groceries, books, crystal, and gifts.

Left. **Mapledale Market** (315-896-2617). Meats, produce, bakery, groceries, and deli. ATM.

000.5   Left. **Country Bookshelf and Video Center** (315-896-2287).

Left. **Unisex Hair Design** (315-896-6532).

Left. **Candy Kaleidoscope** (315-896-2432). Candies, fudge, and gifts.

Left. **Subway** (315-896-6000). Sandwiches and salads.

Left. **Coin laundry**.

Left. **Marine Midland Bank** (315-896-2669). 24-hour ATM.

NY 12 continues south towards **Utica**. End of NY 12 coverage.

27

Barneveld to
Alder Creek

From Herkimer to Alder Creek, Route 28 runs along a relatively flat, undulating step between the Mohawk River and the Adirondack Mountains. The area is sparsely populated with much of the land dedicated to corn fields and current or former dairy cow pastures. When compared to the Adirondacks, this area has apparently little to attract tourists, but therein lies its attraction. The West Canada Creek flows through the area and offers canoeing, kayaking and fishing, and is beautiful, pristine, and uncrowded. It is probably New York State's best-kept canoeing secret. The creek is canoe-navigable for 28 miles from Trenton Falls to its confluence with the Mohawk River in Herkimer, with two portages at the dams at Newport and just below Kast Bridge. Its personality ranges from placid to class two (on a scale of one to six) white water. Additionally, the area boasts excellent cross-country skiing. Just north of Alder Creek along NY 12 lie 50km of cross-country trails. (Free maps are available at Mountain Sports in Barneveld.) Additionally, snowmobiles can be rented at Alder Creek Snowmobile Rentals in Alder Creek.

163.6   Junction of **Route 28** with **NY 12** in **Barneveld**. **Route 28** turns right(left) and joins(leaves) NY 12 north from **Utica**, which is nine miles to the south.

Route 28/NY 12 is now four lanes, and remains four lanes until Alder Creek where Route 28 leaves NY 12. From this point until its end just north of Warrensburg, Route 28 is a designated scenic highway.

Right(left) **Stewart's Shops**. Convenience store and gas. ATM.

Right(left) **Budget Inn** (315-896-2613). Motel set back from road. Rooms, efficiencies, suites, and swimming pool. Double $38-$55, efficiencies and suites $45-$65. Snowmobilers welcome.

163.7   Left(right) **Dan Hudon's Sales & Service** (315-896-SAWS). Lawnmowers, garden tractors, chainsaws, log splitters, snowblowers, etc.

Left(right) **Adirondack Military Surplus** (315-896-2572). Hiking, hunting, and camping equipment. Clothing, boots, sleeping bags, blankets, cots, packs, canteens, cold weather gear, ammo cans, knives, paintball guns and balls, insignias, medals, etc.

Right(left) **Eckerd Drugs** (315-896-4601). Pharmacy, etc.

Right(left) **Mountain Sports** (315-896-4421). Quality outdoor equipment (discounts on high-end brands), guiding, and instruction. Canoes, kayaks, tents, backpacks, skis, mountain climbing gear, sleeping bags, clothing, and accessories. Outstanding inventory of 1500 maps. Canoe and kayak rentals. Shuttle service for canoeists and kayakers on West Canada Creek. Stop in for free maps to 50km of cross-country ski trails.

Right(left) **Touchable Memories Antiques Center** (315-896-6487). Twenty-three dealers present a typical collection of antiques, collectibles, and crafts in an atypically tasteful, uncluttered, and orderly style. This well-lighted and inviting establishment resembles a contemporary retail store more than an antique shop. Glassware to jewelry to furniture. Refreshing.

163.8   Right(left) **Northern Villa Restaurant** (315-896-4431). Freshly made New York pizza and pasta in a relaxed, casual atmosphere. Many flowers decorate the parking lot.

164.6   Flashing traffic signal at junction with **Old Poland Road (Park Avenue)** at bottom of big dip on Route 28.

Making a left(right) onto **Old Poland Road** and traveling one-quarter mile takes you to the hamlet of **Barneveld**. See **Hamlet of Barneveld** coverage below.

Making a right(left) onto **Old Poland Road** yields:

000.2   *Right.   **Sugarbush Bed & Breakfast** (315-896-6860). Three single rooms with shared bath, three double rooms with private bath, and a suite, in a smoke-free, early 1800's farm house, formerly a school house.   It is furnished with antiques and there is a fireplace in the family room.   Lunches and dinners are prepared upon request.   A pleasant touch is afternoon tea, coffee, or hot chocolate, depending upon the season. $70-120/couple. Charming and elegant.*

End of Old Poland Road coverage.

165.2   Junction, at top of hill, with **NY 365** to **Barneveld** and **Holland Patent** to the west and **Prospect** and **Hinckley Reservoir** to the east. Hinckley Reservoir, finished in the late 1920's, is seven miles long and was built to provide water to the New York State Barge Canal. Its use has since been expanded to serve as a potable water reservoir for the city of Utica.

Making a right(left) onto **NY 365** east yields:

Designated Bike Route.

000.9   *Left.   **Ward's Drive-in** (315-896-4502).   Ice cream, burgers, hotdogs, chicken dinners, fish fry, etc. Picnic tables under a pavilion. May through Labor Day.*

003.1   *Right.   **Niagara Mohawk West Canada Creek Recreational Area Prospect Site**. Public **parking** area and **boat launching ramp** for boats with motors having ten horsepower or less. Open Memorial Day until Labor Day.*

*004.3   Right. Junction with **South Side Road**. For **Trail's End Campsite**, turn right here onto South Side Road. Then drive 2½ miles, crossing **West Canada Creek** and passing a dirt pull off on the left overlooking seven-mile-long **Hinckley Reservoir**. Make a left turn onto an unnamed road, following signs for the campsite. Drive another one-half mile and make a left turn onto **Rolling Hill Road** at its junction with **MacArthur Road**. Continue down **Rolling Hill Road** to **Trail's End Campsite** (315-826-7220). Seventy-five grassy sites, from tent sites ($19) to three-way hookups ($22) for R/Vs. Beach on Hinckley Reservoir, boat launching area, fishing pond, playground, game room, store, laundry, and dump station. Open May through Columbus Day.*

End of NY 365 coverage.

166.2   Right(left). **Parking** area and **Adirondack Gateway Visitors Information Center** (315-896-3963). Open every day 8:30-5:30 during the summer; Thursdays through Saturdays 9 AM to 4 PM fall through spring.

Left(right). **Parking** area.

167.1   Right(left) **E-Z Stop** (315-831-5262). Convenience store, Sunoco gas, videos.

Right(left) **T.A.M.'s Diner** (315-831-5225). Breakfast, lunch, and dinner.

167.4   Right(left) **Crest Motel** (315-831-5315). Neat and tidy white, clapboard motel perfectly positioned between a beautiful lawn and a stately stand of trees. Four pretty units plus one family unit with refrigerator, all accented by potted flowers. Mid-May through Mid-November, $40-$50 per double.

167.5   Right(left) **State Police** (Emergency 315-736-0122, Administrative 315-831-4112).

167.9   Right(left) **Deerfield Sport Shop** (315-831-5377). Snowmobile, ATV, lawn mower, and garden tractor sales, service, and repairs. Also accessories and clothing.

168.0   Right(left) **Williams Oil Company** (315-831-5811). NAPA auto parts.

Trenton/Remsen town line.

168.1   Flashing traffic signal at junction at **Remsen** crossroads with **Fuller Road** to the left and **Steuben Street** to Remsen to the right.

> *Making a left(right) onto **Fuller Road**, driving about one-half mile to a "Y" in the road, bearing right at the "Y" onto **Starr Hill Road** and then driving another couple of miles takes you to the **Steuben Memorial** on the right. There you will find a reconstruction of Steuben's two-room summer log home. His grave site is in the "sacred grove", marked by a monument. Baron Friedrich Wilhelm von Steuben was key to our Revolutionary War effort due to his training the colony's men to become victorious military fighters. Also picnic tables. Early May through Labor day.*

Right(left) **Shufelt's** (315-831-3154). Mobil gas.

168.2   Right(left). **O.K. Corral** (315-831-8831). Diner and restaurant offering daily breakfast, lunch, and dinner specials, homemade soups. $2-$7. Open 24 hours.

168.6   **Remsen/Steuben** town line.

169.2   Right(left) **Mondi's Barbeque and Steak House** (315-831-2123). Wood-fired barbecue featuring chicken and ribs, steaks and chops, burgers and dogs. Friday fish fry. Large, family-oriented restaurant decorated with antiques, open for lunch ($2-$6) and dinner ($6-$18), and catering to the customers' special wishes. Lollipops for the kids. Closed January through March.

As you drive northward and approach the foothills to the Adirondacks you will notice the oaks and maples gradually give way to more and more pine trees.

170.6   Right(left) **Back of the Barn Antiques** (315-831-8644). Multiple dealer antique shop in big long barn. General line, from matchbox cars to Buddha, jewelry to furniture, books and glassware to artwork and architectural antiques. Adirondack furniture and furnishings, tramp art, snowshoes, skis, and taxidermy items. Gift foods, jams, jellies, and more.

171.1   **Steuben/Remsen** town line.

173.3   Right(left) **Penn Mountain Inn** (315-831-5616). Family-run restaurant in an attractively-renovated 1839 inn. Two dining rooms, one rustic with barnside interior and the other more formal in wainscoting and white. Full menu with a daily prime rib special and a fish fry, usually $4-$11

173.5   Right(left) **The Red Door Bait and Tackle**. Fishing equipment and supplies, and live minnows.

174.2   Right(left) **Kayuta Fun Park and Restaurant** (315-831-5181). Eighteen hole mini-golf, snack bar, pizza, ice cream, and take-out. Open 9:30 AM to 9:00 PM, April-October.

         Remsen/Boonville town line.

174.4   Left(right) **The Trading Post**. Antiques and collectibles.

174.5   Left(right) **Alder Creek Golf Course and Country Inn** (315-831-5222). Open to the public. Eighteen holes on nine greens. (There are two tees for each green, and two cups on each green.) Golf and lodging packages. Inn open all year, offering golf in snow-free months and cross-country skiing and snowmobiling in winter. Restaurant serves lunch ($2-$5). Greens fees range from $6 for nine holes in winter to $15 for 18 holes in summer. Rooms are $62/couple, including continental breakfast.

174.7   Left(right) **Citgo** gas and service.

Right(left) **Amerigas** (315-942-6230).   Propane by weight and volume.

174.8   Right(left) **Alder Creek Post Office** (315- 831-5986).   ZIP 13301.

174.9   Entering **Alder Creek**.

Alder Creek's location generally brings it more than adequate snow for cross-country skiing and snowmobiling. Local knowledge tells of fifty kilometers of free double-set ski track on private forested property on NY 12 north of Alder Creek. Mountain Sports in Barneveld offers free maps. Also, snowmobiles can be rented at Alder Creek Snowmobile Rentals.

Right(left) **Lil's Diner** (315-831-2186).   Short order diner open from breakfast until 11 PM. Also used book store.

Right(left) **Nice n Easy Grocery Shoppe** (315-942-3526). Convenience store and Sunoco gas. Propane cylinder exchange.

Right(left) **Northern Liquors** (315-942-3526).

Right(left) **Alder Creek Snowmobile Rentals** (888-942-3526).

Junction with **NY 12** north to **Boonville**. NY 12 goes straight ahead, Route 28 north bears off to the right. See Chapter 28, *Alder Creek to Old Forge*.

Hamlet of Barneveld

Turn left(right) onto **Old Poland Road** west toward **Barneveld** from Route 28 at the bottom of the dip one mile north of the Route 28/NY 12 junction.

000.2   Right. **Water Tub Antiques** (315-896-2083).

000.3   Junction with **Mappa Avenue**. To the right on Mappa Avenue are:

000.1   *Right. Junction with **Wicks Place**, down which behind the first building on the left is **New Dimensions Sculpture**, the studio and courtyard of an artist who works in metal. Interesting pieces from materials such as black wrought-iron and verdigrised copper.*

*Right. **Sweet Basil** (315-896-2885). Diner serving breakfast and lunch with daily specials. Eggs, omelets, Belgian waffles, homemade muffins, breads, and donuts. Friday lunch fish fry.*

*Left. **Hotel Moore** (315-896-2069).   No longer a hotel, but still a restaurant in a building more than 120 years old and not shy about its age. The dining room is reminiscent of an elderly lady from a bygone era.   Daily lunches include chicken breast, ham, Philly steak, roast beef, rib eye steak, pizza, burgers, wings, soups, salads, etc. Friday haddock fish fry dinner, $5.25. Shuffleboard table, pool, table tennis, pinball, and video games. The local Rotary Club meets here. A good place to rub elbows with the locals.*

000.2   *Left. **Wergin's Market** (315-896-2644). A German-style butcher shop and small supermarket featuring a large meat department and deli. Homemade specialties include German-style franks and wursts, knockwurst, weiswurst, leberkaese, kielbasa, meatballs, cured hams, etc.   A "Metzgerei" in Barneveld.*

*Junction with **NY 365** west to **Holland Patent** and **Rome** to the left, and **Boon Street** to the right. NY 365 east goes straight ahead to Route 28.*

*A few hundred feet down **Boon Street** are:*

*Right. **Jonah Howe Park** with playground and picnic tables.*

Left. **Barneveld Library** *(315-896-2096). In an 1877 stone building.*

Left. **Candlewyck Park** *with benches along the banks of a creek.*

Left. **Van's Tavern** *(315-896-2884). Large, rustic tavern serving spirits and food, with happy hour from 3 to 6, and a big-screen TV. Daily lunch specials, $2.95. Daily dinner specials such as steak, potato, and salad, $3.95. Monday night: 92¢ spaghetti. Tuesday night: a dozen steamed clams for $1. Friday night: fish fry buffet for $4.95. Saturday night: baked lasagna for $1.95.*

End of Boon Street coverage.

000.4   *Left. Junction with* **Fish Hatchery Road.** *Make left and drive one-quarter mile to* **Trenton Town Park** *on the left. Large parking area with access to pavilion, picnic tables, playground, basketball court, baseball diamonds, swimming beach (on the old fish hatchery pond), horseshoe pits, and 1½-mile-long Steuben Valley Creek nature trail.*

End of Mappa Avenue and hamlet of Barneveld coverage.

Alder Creek to Old Forge

174.9 Junction with **NY 12** north to **Boonville**. NY 12 goes straight ahead, Route 28 north bears off to the right.

Following **NY 12** north one-quarter mile takes you to:

*000.3 Left. **Alder Creek Inn** (315-942-9976). Family-owned, family-style restaurant serving dinner of American cuisine, including chicken, roast beef, steaks, salmon, and swordfish. Saturday and Sunday specials of barbecued pork ribs and haddock. Open Sunday afternoons serving appetizers of wings, nachos, jalapeno peppers, mozzarella sticks, onion rings, hot and cold sandwiches, etc. Entrees $6-$15.*

End of NY 12 north coverage.

175.5 Leaving(entering) **Alder Creek**.

175.9 Left(right) **Adirondack Trail Brewing Company** (315-392-4009). Restaurant and draughthouse. Learn how beer is made while enjoying lunch or dinner. An Adirondack-flavored brew pub decorated with locally-produced paintings, artwork and mounts, the majority of which are for sale, and featuring its own "Trailhouse" line of beers, lagers, and Pilsners (and flavored varieties thereof) to wash down steaks, burgers, ribs, stews, chilies, and beer-battered specialties. Friday fish fry. Lunch $3.28-$6.48, dinner $6.88-$14.48, all prices ending in 8 in honor of Route 28.

Boonville/Forestport town line.

Forestport holds a Forestport Summer Festival in late June. Events include an 11k pre-Utica Boilermaker footrace, a fishing derby (no license required), anything-that-floats-but-a-boat race, a waiter/waitress race, kids' games, a crafts fair, a chicken barbecue, a dance on Saturday night, and more. Call 315-896-3963 for details.

Right(left) **Campbell's Homestyle Cooking** (315-392-2013). Popular diner with friendly waitresses serving breakfast (to $5), lunch (to $4) and dinner (to $8). Breakfast anytime. Homemade breads, muffins, pies, soups, and roasted turkey. Large menu with daily specials. Sandwiches, subs, pizza, sides, and hard and soft ice cream. Seasonal ice cream window. Patrons sometimes arrive on cross country skis or snowmobiles.

176.7   Junction with **River Street**. Turning left and driving down River Street for one-third of a mile takes you to **Forestport**.   **Note: Five-ton, wooden-decked bridges on this road.**

000.1   *Right.* ***Black River Public Fishing Stream parking*** *and* ***boat launch*** *area.*

000.2   *Crossing twin, wooden-decked,* ***five-ton bridges****.*

000.3   *Right. Junction with* ***Woodhull Street****, the first building on the left of which is* ***Al's Diner*** *(315-392-4004). Breakfast, lunch, and Friday and Saturday dinner. Daily specials. Friday fish fry, $4.50. Closed Sundays.*

End of River Street coverage.

Left(right) **Forestport Boat Company** (315-392-4898). Classic boat shop which buys, sells and restores old wooden boats. Also builds new runabouts in the classic tradition.

176.9   Crossing the **Black River** at the lower end of **Kayuta Lake**. This lake was formed by damming the river, which flows north and west from its source in the remote southwestern Adirondacks to empty into Lake Ontario at Black River Bay west of Watertown.

Between here and North Creek, if you turn off Route 28 onto any side road you'll know for sure you're no longer in Manhattan. This far north on Route 28 there are no traces of any kind of city life. This is a land of hawks, deer, flannel, Timberlands, and substance instead of pigeons, poodles, silk, Guccis, and pretense. Transportation is more often by Evinrude and Ski-doo than by Honda or BMW. The space-black night sky is etched by high-intensity stars instead of mercury vapor street lamps. The glass-brittle silence is shattered by the sound of crickets and loons instead of squealing tires and sirens. And, the banging of garbage cans in the wee hours is by raccoons instead of sanitary engineers. This, then, and not some West Village party, is wild New York.

Right(left) Junction with **Woodhull Road:**

000.6 Right. *Annie's Corner (315-392-2442). This consign-*
ment shop, the contents of which run from garage sale
items to collectibles and antiques, is in a new steel garage
down the driveway behind the house.

Entering Woodhull.

001.0 Right. *C & R Hardware (315-392-4021).*

001.2 Right. *Bonnie's Country Store (315-392-6571). Gro-*
ceries, fishing tackle, topo maps, souvenirs, gifts, ice, etc.

Road splits at a "Y". Bear right onto Bardwells Mill
Road (CR 72) to continue to Kayuta Lake Campground.
(Road to left becomes N. Lake Road.)

Left. Buffalo Head Restaurant (315-392-2632).
Large, rustic, family-oriented restaurant with
three fireplaces. Full breakfast menu. Lunch and
dinner share the same menu featuring steaks and
seafood as well as burgers, sandwiches, and
salads. Entrees from $3 to $25, with most $8-$15.

000.1   *Left.* **Garramone's Restaurant** *(315-392-2052). Fine Italian-American dining in a deceptively-plain building with pretty mauve and pink decor. Family-owned business serving lunch and dinner with daily specials. Prime rib, steaks, chops, seafood, sandwiches, wings. Everything homemade including pastas, sauces, breads, and pizza. Entrees $5-$16. Cocktail lounge.*

001.0   *Right.* **Be Creative** *(315-392-5462). Large variety of crafts, party and hobby supplies. Teddy bears, crystals, yarns, ribbons, lace, etc.*

002.2   *Left.* **Kayuta Lake Campground** *(315-831-5077). Three-tenths of a mile down* **Campground Road,** *with 138 sites under the pines on the Black River and Kayuta Lake. Pretty, tidy campground with partial and full hookups, beach, boat ramp, canoe and rowboat rentals, tennis, mini-golf, arcade, playground, etc. Store, dump station, and propane. Mid-May through mid-October. $16.50-$18.50/night.*

End of coverage of Woodhull Road and Bardwells Mill Road.

177.6   Right(left) **Little House of Crafts** (315-392-5570). Unfinished pine craft items. Novelties, cut-outs, angels, picture frames, serving trays, boxes, plaques, small lamps, etc.

177.7   Right(left) **Lures & Fins** (315-392-5570). Fishing equipment and supplies. Rods, reels, tackle, live bait, hunting supplies, ammo, and licenses.

177.9   Right(left) **Keith's Taxidermy** (315-392-2078).

178.3   Left(right) **Scouten's Auto Services** (315-392-6303). Complete car repair.

178.5   Left(right) **Log Cabin**. Snack bar featuring ice cream, hot dogs, barbecues, etc.

178.9   Left(right) **The Wigwam** (315-392-4811). Food, burgers, wings, pizza, and antiques.

180.9   Left(right) **Andy's Service** (315-392-3917). Auto repair service.

181.0   Right(left) **Bywood Inn** (315-392-3287).   Closed at time of publication.

182.4   Right(left) **Early Adirondack Living Museum**.   Museum depicting early 1900 Adirondack logging, canoeing, etc. Collection of period equipment and tools (pike poles, peaveys, crosscut saws, broad axes, etc.), canoes, including a genuine Algonquin birchbark, and more. Also an impressive, hand-hewn spruce beam, 11" x 11" x 50' long, which started out at least 2' in diameter. Owned and operated by a man who has done and seen it all: hunter, fisherman, trapper, logger, guide, retired forest ranger, who has published a book, *What Happened Was*, which relates this Adirondack man's Adirondack adventures. Ask to see his trap collection. Also antique and gift shop.

182.5   Left(right) **Old Time Trading Post** (315-392-FISH). Fishing and camping supplies in a new building (it was formerly in an old school bus). Tents, sleeping bags, lanterns, stoves, compasses, knives, pots and pans, tarps, rope, pickaxes, shovels, rods and reels, antique rods and reels, ammo, hides, and more.

183.5   Entering(leaving) **Woodgate**.

Woodgate is the site every December (usually the second Thursday) of Snowmobile Shootout, snowmobile drag races between various manu-facturers' machines. It is a prelude to Old Forge's Snodeo. Call 315-896-3963 for information.

Right(left) **Woodgate Post Office** (315-392-4999). ZIP 13494.

183.6   Left(right) Flashing light at junction with **Hawksbill Road** (sometimes called Hawkinsville Road or Hogsback Road) to the left and **Bear Creek Road** to the right. Turning left(right) onto **Hawksbill Road** yields the following:

> *000.1   Right. **Woodgate Free Library** (315-392-4814).*
>
> *002.8   Right. Junction with **Round Lake Road**, down which 0.2 mile on the right is **Creekside Gifts and Antiques** (315-392-4639). A generous assortment of new, consignment, and hand-crafted gifts and collectibles relevant to the Adirondacks, and some antiques. Handmade Adirondack twig furniture, primitives, kitchenware, lamps, lanterns, and candles. Also gourmet jams and jellies; quilts, blankets, and placemats; and stuffed animals. Large Christmas collection as well as Thanksgiving and Halloween items.*
>
> *Hawksbill Road continues to Hawkinsville and Boonville. End of coverage.*

Right(left) **Rob's Adirondack Diner** (315-392-2709). Newly refurbished interior, big fireplace, and pink and rose decor create a bright and cheerful diner open for breakfast and lunch daily. Everything cooked to order, with homemade soups and desserts. Omelets highly recommended.

183.8   Leaving(entering) **Woodgate**.

184.3   Entering(leaving) **Adirondack Park**.

Adirondack Park, established in 1892, encompasses almost six million acres of mountains, rivers, streams, brooks, lakes, ponds, and wetlands. Forty-six of the billion-year-old mountains make up the "high peaks" region in the northeastern part of the park. Forty-two of the high peaks are more than 4,000 feet high, with Mt. Marcy, at 5,344', the highest point in New York State. The Adirondacks' brooks, streams, and rivers feed the Mohawk, Hudson, and St. Lawrence Rivers, Lake Champlain, and Lake Ontario.

The park is unique in the United States from a management point of view. About the size of Vermont, it is a protected area which includes state and private lands. The state lands are contained in the Adirondack Forest Preserve and comprise 2.5 million acres, or 42 percent of the park. There are five categories of land use, from wilderness to intensive use areas, in the preserve. Some allow only activities such as hiking, canoeing, cross-country skiing, etc., while others support public camp grounds, beaches, and boat launching ramps. The other 3.5 million acres not in the forest preserve are occupied by homes, general businesses, and industry such as logging, manufacturing, mining, and agriculture. The Adirondack Park Agency, established in 1971, works to balance private and public interests within the park.

Fifty million people live within a six-hour drive of the park, and every year millions come as day-trippers, or to stay in hotels, motels, inns, B&B's, cabins, cottages, motor homes, campers, tents, and in sleeping bags under the stars. They engage in year-round outdoor activities such as hiking, biking, canoeing, kayaking, white water rafting, fishing, hunting, trapping, cross-country and downhill skiing, snowshoeing, motor boating, snowmobiling, and leaf peeping. Route 28's path through the Adirondacks offers participation in all these activities. The Adirondacks' high peak region is about an hour's drive from Route 28 either via NY 30 north from Blue Mountain Lake, or via I-87 and NY 73 north from Warrensburg.

Hiking, biking, snowmobiling, canoeing and cross-country skiing trails and routes in the Adirondacks are shown on area maps. An excellent collection of seven maps, *The Adirondack Series of Maps*, is published by Adirondack Maps Inc. (see Appendix C, *Additional Information),* and can be found in area stores carrying such items.

184.6   Right(left) **Matteson Vinery and Produce** (315-392-5600). Produce, maple syrup, jellies, crafts, balsam pillows, Christmas wreaths, and Christmas trees. Open Memorial Day to Labor Day and the Christmas season.

Right(left) **Chain Saw Carving** (315-429-9069). Beautiful north country sculptures created by a chain saw artist with a magical touch. Bears, cubs, etc.

184.8   Left(right) **Camp Russell** (315-392-3290).   Boy Scouts of America Camp. The sight of the scouts' tent village pitched in the cool, brown, pine-grove shadows made this former tent camper warm and toasty all over, even without my down bag.

185.0   Entering(leaving) **White Lake**.

185.2   Right(left) **White Lake Inn** (315-392-5439). Casual, fine-food restaurant with a view of the lake. Bar, big screen TV, jukebox, and electronic dart board. Open for lunch and dinner, with daily specials. Menu features prime rib, steaks, seafood, chicken, chops, pasta ($7-$16). Also appetizers, soups, salads, sandwiches, pizza, burgers, wings, etc. Salad bar on weekends.

185.4   Leaving(entering) **White Lake**.

185.7   Right(left) **White Lake Polaris-Mercury** (315-392-3013). Snowmobile, ATV, jet ski and outboard motor sales, service, and parts and accessories.

186.3   Right(left) **Stumble Inn** (315-392-2088).   Restaurant and bar. Restaurant open for lunch daily except Monday, and for dinner on weekends.   Steaks, Italian food, specials, salad bar, pizza, and finger foods.   Lunch $2-$5, dinner $6-$13.   Nice non-smoking dining room.   Video games and pool table.

Left(right) **White Lake Lodge and Cabins** (315-392-3493, 942-2862). Rustic, honey-colored, log-cabin-styled lakefront cabins and lodges providing flexible accommodations for two to 16 people. Beach, swimming, docks, fishing, and complimentary paddle boat usage.   Cabins with no kitchens ($75/night) to apartments with kitchens and two bedrooms ($125/night) to lodges with eight bedrooms and two baths ($1500/week). June through Labor Day. A wooded, camp-like getaway.

187.1   Short, extra lanes to the right in both directions. If you're slowly driving a big rig, you may want to pull to the right out of the traffic lanes to allow following traffic to pass.

188.0   Right(left) Access to **state land**.

188.1   Left(right) Trailhead **parking** area. Snowmobile trail to **Brandy Lake** (3.0 miles), **Round Pond** (4.5), **Moose River Road** (6.0) and **Round Lake Road** (6.5).

189.0   Entering(leaving) **Otter Lake**.

189.3   Right(left) **Adirondack Grocery** (315-369-3112). Groceries, Citgo gas, kerosene, propane exchange, videos, newspapers, and fishing, hunting, and snowmobiling supplies.

189.4   Right(left) **Iron Horse Tavern** (315-369-9920). Food and spirits and a pool table. Menu features burgers, wings, finger foods, etc. Also fish fry, steaks, prime rib, etc. on Fridays and Saturdays. $3-$15. Access to new Brandy Lake snowmobile trail.

189.7   Left(right) **Standard Supply Company** (315-369-6530). Gift shop, souvenirs. Interesting and unique inventory of balsam pillows, incense, jewelry, sweats and T's, figurines, chinaware, woodenware, maple syrup and candy, toys, cards, postcards, local Otter Lake books, stationery items, and more. Family-owned business since 1914, and in the same store since 1921.

Right(left) **Point of View Antiques** (315-369-2625). Antique store owned by an excellent artist with an appreciation for fine things, reflected in the quality and flavor of much of her antique inventory. The store, on the old rail line and formerly a country grocery store and post office, is full of dolls, china, glassware, tableware, kitchen utensils, green glass, jewelry, ladies' hats and finery, books, prints, tools, sleigh bells, furniture, and more. Historical and charming.

190.4   **Oneida/Herkimer** county line, **Forestport/Webb** town line. Leaving(entering) **Otter Lake**.

190.5   Left(right) **Kowalik's Hotel** (315-369-6440). Run by the same proprietor for almost 50 years, this hotel offers a bar, lunch, dinner, and rooms with a genuine Adirondack flavor. Homemade meals, soups, big sandwiches, and Friday night fish fry. Lunch $3-$5, dinner entrees $8-$18, with $8-$9 specials. Piano in dining room. Rooms $45-$50/couple.

190.7   Right(left) Perfect example of an Adirondack still pond. Photographers, reach for your cameras.

191.3   Crossing the **Moose River**.

Designated Bike Route.

193.1   Left(right) Paved **parking** area.

194.3   Right(left) **Nelson Lake Trailhead parking**, offering access to the **Black River Wild Forest**.

194.4   Left(right) **Parking** area, conservation easements, **Hancock Timber Resource Group**. Hiking trail to **Gull Lake** (0.48 mile). One-half mile down a dirt/gravel road is a **parking** area for **Ha De Ron Dah Wilderness** and **Middle Settlement Lake**. Hiking trail to **Ha De Ron Dah** (0.74 mile).

195.3   Right(left) **Singing Waters Campground** (315-369-6618). One hundred forty-two sandy sites, tenting to full hookups, under a cover of pines and hardwoods on the banks of the Moose River. Tennis courts, basketball court, swimming, canoeing, fishing, grocery store, and dump station. A pleasant, green, and woodsy campground. $17-$25/night.

197.1   Right(left) Paved **parking** area.

197.3   Left(right) Footpath access across wooden bridge to **state land**.

197.4   Right(left) **Whitewater Challengers Rafting Center** (315-369-6699, 800-443-RAFT). White water rafting trips for both the inexperienced and experienced of all ages. Full and half-day, guided and unguided trips. Canoe, kayak, and mountain bike rentals, bike deliveries, and bike/rail trips. Canoe and kayak instruction, adventure/lodging packages, and adventure/dining packages. Open April through October.

Also **Old Forge Outfitters**. Fishing and camping equipment and supplies, clothing, books of local interest, and more. Tourist info.

198.2   Left(right) Junction with **Jones Road**. Two-tenths of a mile down Jones Road is **parking** for access to state land and snowmobile trail #6.

199.6   Right(left) **Mountainview Motel** (315-369-6139). Comfortable, attractive, and nicely-furnished eleven-unit motel with a swimming pool. Doubles $48; $80 for a family room with one double and three singles.

199.9   Right(left) Junction with **Birch Street**, down which are:

*000.0   Left. Junction with **Forge Street**. Turning left onto Forge Street takes you to:*

*000.0   Right. **Van Auken's Inne and Restaurant** (315-369-3033). Lovely 1891 Victorian hotel with 12 guest rooms, all with private bath, television, and telephone. Four dining rooms for fine dining, a fireplace, a player piano, and a bar. Thickly-carpeted stairways, tin ceilings, and natural wainscoting. Building was formerly next to the train station, but it was constantly catching fire from the burning embers emitted by the steam locomotives, so in 1905 it was jacked up, placed on rollers and moved across the road and behind the train station, out of harm's way. Rooms $45-$85/two, lunch $2-$8, dinner entrees $11-$21. Open Mother's Day weekend through mid-October, and again from the second weekend in December through the end of March.*

*Left. **Morin's Collision** (315-369-3396). 24-hour towing.*

Left. **Front Line Automotive** *(315-369-AUTO).*
Auto repair shop.

000.1   Left. **Tote's Tea House** *(315-369-3231). Bar and*
weekend entertainment.

000.2   Left.   **Old Forge Sport Tours** *(315-369-3796).*
Snowmobile and personal watercraft rentals.

End of Forge Street coverage.

000.1   Right. **Moose River House** *(315-369-3104). A restored,*
1884 Victorian bed and breakfast under large pine trees
on the banks of the Moose River. The house, furnished in
antiques and wicker, boasts a formal parlor, living room
with a fireplace, sun room, and porches. The living room
and dining room, as well as three of the four guest rooms
(two with private bath), have river views. You can canoe,
kayak, hike, cross-country ski, snowshoe, and mountain
bike directly from the property. Canoes and kayaks
available for a fee. Rooms $65-$95/couple, with full
breakfast.

End of Birch Street coverage.

Right(left) **Adirondack Scenic Railroad** (315-369-6290). Hour-
long train rides along the scenic Moose River in vintage open-
window passenger cars. Train robberies are staged on Tuesdays
during July and August. Rail/bike trips and return canoe trips also
can be arranged. New for 1998 is round trip service from Utica to
Old Forge. Ride the train from Utica to Thendara aboard
heated/air-conditioned cars, plus a cafe car. Gift shop and
museum; handicapped accessible; open May through October. A
wonderful experience for the entire family.

200.1   Entering **Thendara**.

Left(right) Access to **state land**.

200.3   Right(left) **Steak House Restaurant** (315-369-6981). Restaurant and cocktail lounge. Dinner menu features steaks and seafood, chicken, and chops, $10-$17. Sunday barbecue, $7-$15.

Right(left) **Moose River Trading Company** (315-369-6091). Adirondack Outpost Number One. Upscale camping equipment and traditional Adirondack products. Locally-made, hand-pounded, black ash Adirondack pack baskets; custom-made knives; traditional fishing equipment including handmade graphite fly rods; also flies and wooden-framed nets. . Tee shirts, sweat shirts, jewelry, books, coffees, jams, maple syrup, and much more, all with an Adirondack flavor or theme.

200.4   Right(left) **Brussel's Thendara Garage** (315-369-3755). Auto repairs.

200.6   Left(right) **Country Club Motel** (315-369-6340). Twenty-seven well-kept units in neat and tidy brick and frame building on manicured lawns studded with pine trees. Each comfortable unit has a small refrigerator and a microwave oven, a wreath on the door and an Adirondack chair out front. Inviting in-ground pool. $40-$85/couple. Adjacent to the Thendara Golf Club (open to the public).

Right(left) **Sunset Inn** (315-369-6836). This Best Western motel has 52 units, some with whirlpool baths. Tennis court, heated indoor pool, whirlpool, and sauna. Continental breakfast and premium cable channels; $45-89/couple.

Left(right) **Nineteenth Green Motel** (315-369-3575). Thirteen tidy and attractive units with individual refrigerators and microwave ovens. Snowmobile from your front door. Comfortable, clean, with friendly proprietors; $50-75.

200.7   Right(left) **Knotty Pine Restaurant** (315-369-6859). Adirondack style fine dining, casual atmosphere, and a lounge. Traditional cuisine, specializing in prime ribs, steaks, seafood, chicken, and chops. Large wine selection by the bottle and glass. Varnished knotty pine interior with a stone fireplace and comfortable furnishings create a warm, cozy ambiance. Entrees $10-$20, and the kitchen is open until 10 PM on weekends.

Left(right) Junction with 5th Street, down which 0.4 mile is the **Thendara Golf Club** (315-369-3136), a semi-private, eighteen-hole, professionally-designed golf course on rolling hills. The front nine opened in 1921. Open May through Columbus Day weekend, $20/eighteen. Free, cross-country skiing with set track in the winter. Restaurant offers breakfast and lunch ($3-$9) daily, Friday fish fry, and Saturday prime rib dinner. You may have to ask the deer if you can play through.

201.0   Right(left) **Thendara Mini Mall**:
Fetterman's Butcher Block (315-369-3006). Fresh meats, deli products, salads, sandwiches, party platters, etc.
Browns Apparel and Factory Outlet (315-369-2006). Name-brand family apparel, sportswear, outerwear, and Adirondack souvenir apparel.
Thendara Post Office (315-369-6525). ZIP 13472.

Left(right) **Farm Restaurant and Museum**. Local landmark decorated with such interesting and authentic Adirondack antiques and memorabilia that it is also known as a museum. Open for breakfast and lunch, $3.50-$7.

Right(left) **Smith Marine** (315-369-3366). Ski-Doo snowmobile and Sea-Doo jet ski sales, service, accessories, and clothing. Mountain bike sales and service.
Also, **Snow Mobile Depot** (315-369-2280). Snowmobile clothing, helmets, and parts.

Left(right) **Black Bear Inn**. Closed at the time of publication.

201.1   **Thendara/Old Forge** line.

Old Forge

Old Forge is an oasis in the middle of the Adirondacks, boasting much natural beauty as well as resort activities for the entire family. It is the only settlement along Route 28 within the Adirondack Park large enough to have its population (1061) listed in an atlas. At 1700 feet above sea level, it surrounds Old Forge Pond, the western-most body of water of the Fulton Chain of Lakes, where deeply forested mountains accentuate a necklace of lakes created by the damming of the middle branch of the Moose River. Outdoor activities include snowmobiling, canoeing, boating, water skiing, biking, mountain biking, hiking, downhill and cross-country skiing, snowboarding, ice skating, white water rafting, swimming, fishing, hunting, golf, miniature golf, water wars, and more. Attractions include a water park, sightseeing boat rides on the Fulton Chain of Lakes, the Forest Industries Exhibit Hall, and the Arts Center/Old Forge, which features art shows, plays, musical performances, and ballet. The town also offers a movie theater, a comedy club, an arcade, unique shops, and a great variety of restaurants. It even has a town beach, town docks, and a covered bridge.

Old Forge is touted as the largest snowmobile area east of the Rockies. People come from hundreds of miles away to enjoy the pleasure of using Old Forge's 500 miles of marked and groomed snowmobile trails. Most lodging establishments are open all year to support the snowmobilers. Old Forge requires the purchase of a $40/week or $60/season ($75 after November 15) snowmobile permit for all machines operated on any property other than the machine owner's property. Permits are available at the Tourist Information Center (315-369-6983). All snowmobiles must be registered and, if operated on the town of Webb/Inlet trails and/or roads, the owner must carry liability insurance. Snowmobile season starts immediately after the close of big game hunting season in early December with Snodeo Weekend, Old Forge's annual snowmobile season kick-off festival. The season lasts until the end of March or beginning of April, depending upon snow cover. Snowmobiles may be rented at Old Forge Sport Tours on Forge Street in Thendara, 315-369-3796.

Many snowmobile trails were recently opened to hikers and mountain bikers. Mountain bikes can be rented at Whitewater Challengers in Okara Lakes, a few miles south of Old Forge. The Adirondack Scenic Railroad in Thendara, two miles south of Old Forge, will deliver bikers and their bikes to Carter Station to ride on the town of Webb's 100-mile Mountain Bike Trail System.

Old Forge lies at the western end of the Fulton Chain of Lakes canoe route, extending (with two carries) for 16 miles to the eastern end of Eighth Lake. Old Forge also offers 11 miles of easy canoeing through wilderness and wildlife on the slow-moving North Branch of the Moose River. Canoe and kayak rentals are available at Tickner's and Rivett's Marine. For the more daring, Whitewater Challengers in Okara Lakes and Adirondack River Outfitters in Old Forge offer white water rafting on the more difficult sections of the Moose River below Old Forge.

Leaf peepers, note: Old Forge autumn foliage colors are at their most magnificent around the last few days of September and first few days of October.

The Old Forge Tourist Information Center (315-369-6983), should be the first place you stop when arriving in Old Forge. It offers volumes of information about lodging, dining, activities, and attractions in and around Old Forge, and is a great source of brochures, guides, maps, trail maps, rules and regulations, etc. It is also the local Snowmobile Information Office.

Lodging is at a premium during the peak tourist and snowmobile seasons along Route 28 in the Adirondacks, so reservations are strongly suggested. If you find yourself in Old Forge without a reservation, call the Tourist Information Center. They can tell you up-to-the-minute area lodging availability.

As the seasons in Old Forge change, so do the shop hours. If you are coming to visit a specific shop, it is best to phone ahead to ensure the shop is open.

Not all streets in Old Forge have name signs. Also, some Old Forge street names and addresses may change due to implementation of 911 emergency telephone service.

To experience the full flavor of the hamlet of Old Forge, take a walk. A round-trip walk from the Old Mill Restaurant to the Forest Industries Exhibit Hall is a bit more than three miles long, and will give you a full-bodied taste of Old Forge while giving your full body excellent exercise.

201.1   **Thendara/Old Forge** line.

Crossing the Middle Branch of the Moose River.

The Middle Branch of the Moose River offering wonderful exploring by canoe.

Right(left) **The Old Mill** (315-369-3662). A charming, fine-dining restaurant overlooking the Moose River and featuring the warmth of wood. The board and batten, post and beam building has vaulted ceilings, a stone fireplace, and a wood-burning stove, and the golden varnished wood interior simply glows. There is even a porch for dining outside. Steaks, seafood, homemade soups, and bread. Dinner entrees $11-$16.

Left(right) **Mountain Music** (315-369-6869). Audio equipment, string instruments, tapes and CD's, and cellular phones.

Right(left) **Blue Spruce Motel** (315-369-3817). Thirteen rooms with refrigerators and free HBO, $40-$85/couple. Also one efficiency. Heated pool.

Right(left) **Christy's Motel** (315-369-6138). Fifteen units, some with refrigerators, an efficiency unit, and a handicapped-accessible unit. Heated pool and free HBO. $35-$86 depending upon room and season.

Left(right) **Nice 'n Easy** (315-369-3020). Convenience store, ATM, **Subway** sandwich shop, Mobil gas (the only gas station in town), and worms.

Right(left) **George's Liquors** (315-369-3371).

Right(left) **George's Thing** (315-369-3022). Gifts, cards, flowers, collectibles, Adirondack souvenirs, jewelry, clothing, glass figurines, candles, stained glass crafts, and more.

Left(right) **C & S Service**, although the sign says C & H, (315-369-3678).   Complete auto service, open Tuesday through Saturday.

201.3   Right(left) **Albo's Just Desserts Bakeshop** (315-369-6505). Cheese cakes, carrot cakes, decorated birthday and wedding cakes (on 30-minute notice!), Italian biscotti, German stollen, cookies, muffins, breads, and rolls. Open every day in summer; weekends otherwise.

Right(left) **Adirondack Supply** (315-369-6300).   Parts Plus automobile parts store.

Right(left) **Old Forge Glass and Car Wash** (315-369-3435). Auto glass repair shop and car wash.

Left(right) **Twigs**.   Gifts, books, tobacco, cigars (some hand rolled), and pipes. Locally made crafts, hand-painted flower pots, hand-carved wooden ties, and second-hand books. Loon tables; bear tables; hand-carved, fish-shaped fishing pole racks. An eclectic collection of Adirondack and whimsical crafts not seen elsewhere.

Left(right) **Nutty Putty** (315-369-6636).   Eighteen holes of miniature golf, the oldest in Old Forge.

Left(right) **Meyda Stained Glass Studio** (315-369-6636). Beautiful stained-glass lamps of all shapes and sizes. Mirrors, windows, jewelry boxes, gifts, and custom work. An impressive collection of colorful craftsmanship.

Right(left) **Di Orio's Big M Supermarket** (315-369-3131). Wonderful breads, ATM.

201.4   Left(right) **Twin Oaks** (315-369-6439).   Gifts and branded collectibles. Soft stuffed animals, miniature villages, scenes of local Old Forge buildings, dolls, crafts, fabric, knitted goods, crockery, pottery, weather vanes, and wind chimes. Also candles, aromatherapy candles, T-shirts, sweatshirts, throws, pillows, balsam pillows, lamps, shades, a Christmas corner, and more.

Right(left) **The Fabric Hutch** (315-369-6878). A shop featuring Adirondack gifts, stuffed animals, coffee mugs, pot pourri, candles, knick-knacks, cards and notes, Christmas cards, dish towels, frames, candle holders, tiny wind chimes, sun catchers, T's, sweats, pillows, throws, bead crafts, candy sticks, Pez dispensers, and more.

Right(left) **Spring Street Shops** (315-369-6376):

Scooper's Ice Cream Extravaganza. Old-fashioned-style ice cream shop. Hard and soft ice cream, yogurt, and homemade desserts. Seasonal.

The Muffin Patch, offering:

A **restaurant** with a warm, cozy atmosphere. Breakfast featuring pancakes, waffles, French toast with fresh strawberries or blueberries, omelettes, etc., with all fresh ingredients, real maple syrup, and home fries ($3-$9). Even the plants in the windows and the smiles on the staff's faces are real. Lunch and dinner offer sandwiches on fresh homemade breads, soups, and salads, and chicken, steak, and barbecued pork dinners ($3-$9). Friday fresh haddock dinner ($8). Open for dinner during summer months only.

Also, a **bakery** offering muffins, cinnamon rolls, specialty breads, bagels, and turnovers. Seasonal.

Also, a **gift shop** featuring T-shirts, sweatshirts, local crafts, wind chimes, plush bears, postcards, tapes, maple syrup, etc. Seasonal. **JC & Co**. (315-369-4420). Full-service hair salon for men and women.

Left(Right) **Moose Country Cabins** (315-369-6447). Old Adirondack cabins in a secluded, woodsy, Adirondack setting. Various cabin and housekeeping cottage plans from one bedroom and one bath to two bedrooms, living room and kitchen, all with heat and porches. Picnic area with grills and tables. Can snowmobile right from your cabin's door. From $47/couple.

Junction with **Spring Street**:

*000.0   Right. Junction with **Riverside Drive**:*

> *000.0   Left. **Tickner Canoe Rental/Tickner's Adirondack Canoe Outfitters** (315-369-6286). Canoe and kayak rentals on the Moose River, by the hour, day, week, etc. One- to six-hour trips available on the quiet Moose River from Tickner's dock, return shuttle service provided. Or float downriver by canoe, and return via the historic Adirondack Scenic Railroad. Souvenir shop.*

Open Memorial Day weekend through Columbus Day. A perfect way to experience the Adirondacks.

End of Riverside Drive and Spring Street coverage.

201.5   Left(right) **Cricket on the Common** (315-369-3894). Branded collectibles and gifts, Adirondack gifts, cards, gourmet coffee and tea, specialty foods, candy, and more.

Left(right) **Keyes Pancake House** (315-369-6752).   Family dining.   Breakfast served all day ($3-$8), lunch of burgers, sandwiches, clubs, spaghetti, fish platter, etc., ($2-$8), and dinner of chicken, veal, scallops, shrimp, chopped round steak, etc. ($7-$8).

Right(left) **The Broom Man** (315-369-6503). Straw crafts, gifts, and Amish crafts.   Also brooms, baskets, door snakes, rugs, potholders, placemats, candles, hex signs, cedar buckets, butter churns, furniture, etc. Teddy bears with a theme, plush rabbits, pigs, cows, and more.

Left(right). **Radio Shack** (315-369-3493).   Electronics and computer store.

Left(right) **Adirondack Bead Works** (315-369-4490). Handmade jewelry and mobiles; beads and beading supplies. Also, next-day photo development and dry cleaning.

Left(right) **Head First Salon** (315-369-2553). Hair salon.

Right(left) **Old Forge Post Office** (315-369-3414). ZIP 13420.

Left(right) **Town of Webb Historical Association** (315-369-3838).

201.6   Junction with **Gilbert Street**. Turn right(left) here for **Nicks Lake Public Campground and Day Use Area** and **McCauley Mountain Ski Area** and chairlift:

000.1   Turn right at stop sign onto **Railroad Avenue**.

000.2   Turn left at stop sign onto **Joy Tract Road**.

001.0   Turn left onto **Bisby Road**.

001.1   Right.   **Black River Wild Forest Bisby Road trailhead parking**.   Hiking and snowmobile trails to **Nicks Lake** *(1.0)*, **Humphrey Hill** *(1.2)*, **Nelson Lake Trail Around Nicks Lake** *(1.3)*, **Nelson Lake** *(6.2)*, **Remsen Falls Lean-to** *(6.9)*, and **Remsen Falls & Nelson Lake Loop** *(18.5)*.

001.6   Left.   Junction with **McCauley Mountain Road**, down which 0.6 mile is **McCauley Mountain Ski Area** *(315-369-3225)*.   Summer chairlift rides from Memorial Day through Labor Day (closed Tuesdays and Wednesdays), and weekends through Columbus Day.   Winter brings downhill skiing on 14 novice to expert trails on 633' of vertical drop and a longest run of 3/4 mile. Also cross-country skiing on 20km of set track.   Average snowfall of 281" and 65 percent snowmaking coverage yields a season spanning from mid-December through the end of March. Ski school, lodge, cafeteria, bar, and fireplace. **Sporting Propositions Ski Shop** *(315-369-3144)* has downhill and cross-country ski and snowboard rentals.   Mountain biking is under consideration, but plans were not complete at the time of publication.

Right.   Entrance to **Nicks Lake Public Campground and Day Use Area** *(315-369-3314)*.   More than 100 tent and trailer sites, picnicking, rowboating, canoeing, boat launch, swimming, fishing, and hiking.   Also, showers, playground, and dump station.   Reservations 800-456-CAMP. Early May through late October.

End of Gilbert Street to Bisby Road coverage.

Left(right) **Gallery-North** (315-369-2218). Fine art and custom framing.   Original art, Adirondack-themed wildlife art, watercolors, limited edition prints, carvings, posters, old black and white and contemporary color photographs, gifts, books, note paper, and more.

Left(right) **Moose River Company** (315-369-3682).   Outdoor supplies and guide service. Camping, hiking, hunting, and fishing supplies, including canoes, guns, ammo, clothing, maps, prints, etc. Complete guide service and wilderness trips for hiking, backpacking, fishing, deer and bear hunting, winter camping, ice fishing, etc., with transportation by hiking, mountain biking, canoeing, horseback riding, and seaplane flying. Visit the remote Adirondacks with Moose River Company's assistance.

Right(left) **Hand of Man Gallery** (315-369-3381).   Handmade artwork and fine crafts for the discriminating, with many items by local artists and many with an Adirondack theme. Outstanding pencil line drawings are almost as real as photographs.   Pottery, jewelry, glassware, burl vases, totem carvings, and watercolors. Also, baskets with antler handles, furniture, leather works, window decorations, dream-catcher gourds, and more.

Left(right) **Allen's Jewelers** (315-369-6660).   Fine jewelry and gifts. Watches, jewelry, glassware, etc.

201.7   Left(right) Junction with **Adams Street**:

> *Turning left onto **Adams Street**, driving one-tenth of a mile and turning right onto **Garmon Avenue**, and then driving a few hundred feet takes you to **Village Cottages** (315-369-3432) on the right. Eight one- and two-bedroom cottages with fully-equipped kitchens available year 'round for the weekend, week, month, or season. Swimming pool, fireplace, basketball court, and swings. $50-$85/couple.   Home-like accommodations in a quiet, family setting.*

Right(left) **Foley Lumber and Hardware** (315-369-3233).   Home center.

Left(right) **Adirondack Gazebo** (315-369-2469). Vintage gifts and jewelry.

Left(right) **Candy Cottage**. Fudge, candy, jelly beans, fresh hot popcorn, coloring books, gifts, souvenirs, stuffed animals, postcards, etc.

Right(left) **The Clipping Station** (315-369-3900). Beauty salon.

Left(right) **Antiques and Articles** (315-369-3883, 369-3316). Furniture, Adirondack furniture, artifacts, collectibles, jewelry, toys, glassware, china, silver, deer heads, clothing, photos, postcards, records, many books, and much more. A browser's delight.

Left(right) **Sporting Propositions** (315-369-6188). Ski and bike shop. Skis, snowboards, and toboggans; equipment, accessories, and clothing. Bike sales and service. Rentals of mountain bikes, downhill skis, cross-country skis, snowboards, Sled Dogs, and tents.

Right(left) **Carol's Liquors** (315-369-6737).

Right(left) **The Old Forge Woodmaker** (315-369-3535). Wooden furniture, Adirondack chairs and twig furniture, rockers, beach chairs, bar stools, lamps, crockery, wind chimes, mobiles, and gifts.

Right(left) **The Village Wick** (315-369-3363). Candles, jewelry, Native American items, flags, and gifts.

Left(right) **Magic Mountain Miniature Golf and Gift Shop** (315-369-6602). Eighteen holes of miniature golf. Also, beach wear, beach towels, inflatable rafts and toys, candy, and slush puppies.

Left(right) **ARO Adventures** (800-525-RAFT). Serious, full-day, white water rafting on a 14-mile, class 5 section of the Moose River. Also adventure rafting on the Hudson and Black Rivers, and family rafting on the Sacandaga River. Season is beginning of April to end of October, depending upon the rivers.

Right(left) **Herron Realty** (315-369-6910). Century 21 office.

Left(right) **The Ferns**:
Conscious Cotton Boutique (315-369-4403). Cotton apparel. Ladies' dresses, T-shirts, sweats, jewelry, printed shirts, hats, beer mugs, and bird houses.
Tropical Paradise (315-369-6602). Indoor miniature golf. Open seven days year round.
Walt's Diner (315-369-2582). Serving fresh home cooking for breakfast, lunch, and dinner. Specialties include omelettes, homemade soups, overstuffed sandwiches, and homemade pies. No entrees over $8.
The Ferns Pasta House (315-369-2582). Italian/American cuisine prepared by an Italian chef. Chicken and veal Parmigiana, chicken riggs, beef, pasta, daily specials, and more. Serving lunch and dinner. Dinner entrees $7-$13.

Right(left) **The Adirondack Express** (315-369-2237). Local weekly newspaper.

Right(left) **The Brewery Shop** (315-369-2705). Memorabilia for lovers of Saranac, Matt's, or Utica Club beer. T-shirts, glasses, tankards, mugs, steins, trays, crystal, paddles, tents, golf towels, posters, umbrellas, coolers, bags, hammocks, director chairs, Adirondack chairs, and bottle suits.

Left(right) **Mountain Peddler** (315-369-3428). Gift shop. Lamps and shades, clocks, pottery, bears, collectibles, candles, jewelry, T-shirts, cards, postcards, and more. Also an Adirondack room and a Christmas room.

Right(left) **The Sweat Shop** (315-369-4402). Souvenir sweat-shirts, T-shirts, jackets, nightshirts, etc. Also aromatherapy products.

201.8   Right(left) **The Fulton Chain** (315-369-2260).   Gift shop. Wooden items created in the Fulton Chain woodshop. Camp signs, toys, nutcrackers, ornaments, decoys, and gift items. Christmas and Adirondack items.

Right(left) **Wildwood** (315-369-3397). A blend of new and old relating to the Adirondacks and its history. Antiques and crafts, books and prints, maps and postcards. Adirondack twig furniture, guide baskets, snowshoes; wooden loons, geese and decoys; wooden souvenirs and gifts. Also a fainting couch, chairs, old Adirondack hardware, china, glassware, and painted saws. An Adirondack attic.

Left(right) **Old Forge Parts** (315-369-3611). NAPA auto parts.

Left(right) **Adirondack Coin Laundry**.

Right(left) **Greco's Pizza** (315-369-2480). Pizzeria. Specialty pizzas, strombolis, salads, subs, wings, fish fry, finger foods, etc. Delivery available.

Left(right) **Helmer's Fuel** (315-369-3134). Propane by weight/-volume.

Left(right) **Rainbow Zen**. Interesting collection of unique Central American, South American, and Balinese imports. Sweaters, dresses, T-shirts, tie-dyes, caps, jewelry, and personal enhancements. Much more. Eclecticism at its best.

Right(left) **The Artworks** (315-369-2007). A cooperative of Adirondack artists. Regional arts and crafts including watercolors, pottery, stained glass, photography, jewelry, fabrics, baskets, folk art, etc. Closed April.

Left(right) **Tow Bar Inn** (315-369-6405). Bar and pool table.

Left(right) **The Maple Diner**. Closed at time of publication.

Junction with **Crosby Boulevard**.

Making a left onto **Crosby Boulevard** to the north yields:

*Right. **Old Forge Library** (315-369-6008).*

Making a right onto **Crosby Boulevard** to the south yields:

*000.0   Right.   **Nathan's Adirondack Bakery** (315-369-3933). Freshly baked bagels, bialys, donuts, muffins, breads, rolls, cakes, pies, cookies, and pizza. Open about 5 AM to 6 PM seven days during the summer, weekends only off-season.*

*Junction with **Park Avenue** at stop sign at "T". Make a left and follow Park Avenue for one-tenth of a mile to **South Shore Road**. Make a right onto South Shore Road and continue northeast. South Shore Road follows the south shores of First through Fourth Lakes from Old Forge to Inlet. It passes through beautiful forests and by scenic ponds and lakes. Deer often graze along its shoulders. Also a designated bike route.*

*000.2   Left.   **Rivett's Marine Recreation and Service** (315-369-3123). Boat rentals, sales, and service. Experience the Adirondack Mountains from the reflective surface of the Fulton Chain of Lakes. Water ski, explore lagoons, visit islands, or eat lunch at a waterside restaurant; it's all available with a boat. Rivett's offers rentals of everything from pedal boats, canoes, and rowboats to pontoon boats and power boats with from 10 to 150 horsepower engines. Flexible rental arrangements from hourly to weekly. From Old Forge to Inlet, 14 miles of watery adventure await.*

*Right.   **Central Adirondack Family Practice** (315-369-6619). In the Town of Webb Professional Offices. Private doctor's office, the only one in Old Forge. Hours are 9-5, seven days, and 9-9 in the summer. Calling ahead is recommended since doctors are not always in. Nearest* *hospitals are in Utica (52 miles to the south) and Saranac Lake (89 miles to the north).*

Left. **Pine Knoll Motel and Cottages on the Lake** *(315-369-6740). On a pine-shaded knoll overlooking Old Forge Pond, with private beach and dock. Motel units, some lakefront, some with kitchenettes, all with refrigerators. Three cottages, two with fireplaces, one lakefront. Snowmobile from your door. $60-$70. In summer, cottages rent by the week only.*

002.2   Right. **Twin Pond.**

A fawn, already used to traffic, grazes alongside the road.

005.6   Right. **Trailhead parking** *for hiking and cross-country ski trail to* **Limekiln Lake**.

005.9   Left. Junction with **Petrie Road***:*

000.5   Left. **Timber Lane Lodge** *(315-369-3485). In a lovely wooded setting on the shores of Third Lake* *are three new two- and three-bedroom lakefront houses and an apartment with heat and all amenities, and a two-bedroom cottage with fireplace, offering lodging for six to eight people. Swimming, fishing, boat dockage, and gorgeous sunsets. $415-$750/week. Fall through spring, $55-$150/night, two night minimum.*

000.7   Left. **Fourth Lake Picnic Area** *(315-369-3224). Public fishing, picnic tables, fireplaces, hibachis, and boat launching. Launch site and parking for* **Fulton Chain Canoe Route***, and for campers boating the one-third mile to* **Alger Island Campsite** *(315-369-3415) in the middle of Fourth Lake which offers 15 lean-tos, a picnic area with tables, fireplaces and hibachis, lake-water pump, and outhouses.*

End of Petrie Road and South Shore Road coverages.

201.9   Right(left) **Old Forge Hardware** (315-369-6100).   Large hardware and general store, the place in Old Forge to find whatever you need. Adirondack pack baskets, snowshoes, outdoor clothing, toboggans, sleds, and canoes. Fishing and camping supplies, furniture and Adirondack furniture, bedding, kitchenware, china, glassware, and appliances. Souvenirs, large selection of books, topo maps, artist supplies, and much, much more. Also baskets, baskets, baskets.

Right(left) Junction at a "Y" with **Fulton Street**, which goes straight ahead while Main Street (Route 28) bears to the left:

Going down **Fulton Street** *a few hundred feet and turning right onto* **Lamberton Street** *takes you to the* **Forge Motel** *(315-369-3313) on the left. Overlooking Old Forge Pond, 61 units with patios and Adirondack chairs. Some units with air conditioning. Heated pool in summer, direct access to Old Forge's snowmobile trails in winter. $70-$81/couple.*

*Continuing down **Fulton Street** another few hundred feet takes you to a "T" at the **Town of Webb Public Beach** on the shores of Old Forge Pond. Lifeguard, floats, swing set, picnic tables, and rest rooms. Beach is open to the public from Memorial Day to Labor Day; admission is free for children aged 14 and under, $1 for adults. Also green, grassy public park with free tennis courts, benches, and boat docks. You can dock your boat free for up to 10 days.*

End of Fulton Street coverage.

Left(right) **Forge Pharmacy** (315-369-6276). Pharmacy, gifts, souvenirs, and cards.

Left(right) **Old Forge Department Store** (315-369-6609). Ace hardware store. Fishing and camping supplies, sporting goods, clothing, T-s and sweats, toys, gifts, and souvenirs.

Left(right) **Sassy Scissors Salon** (315-369-6235). Beauty salon.

Right(left) **Adirondack Family Buffet** (315-369-6846). Bright, cheerful, buffet-style restaurant serving all-you-can-eat breakfast ($5), lunch ($6) and dinner ($8). Lower prices for children. Deli, bakery, and sandwiches.

Right(left) **The Back Door** (315-369-6846). Lounge. Bar menu, happy hour, and weekend entertainment.

Left(right) **The Strand Theater** (315-369-6703). Art Deco movie theater. Call for 24-hour info.

Right(left) **Community Bank, NA** (315-369-2288, 2764). 24-hour ATM.

202.0   Left(right) **Arcade** and **Adirondack Pizzeria** (315-369-6028). Large arcade housing video games, pinball machines, bowling machines, pool tables, etc. Also pizza, wings, finger food, subs, salads, torpedoes, and ice cream. Picnic tables under a canopy.

Pizzeria open daily Mother's Day through Columbus Day, then weekends only from December through late March. Arcade open summer months only.

Left(right) **Souvenir Village** (315-369-3811). Souvenirs, candy, pottery, T-shirts, sweatshirts. Indian souvenirs, and beach articles.

Left(right) **Forge Corner**. Antiques.

Left(right) **Adirondack Bank** (315-369-3153). 24-hour ATM.

Right(left) **Clark's Beach Motel** (315-369-3026). Overlooking Old Forge Pond, 42 units, some with lake view, some with screened porches. Indoor heated pool and a game room; $39-$65.

Left(right) **McDonald's** (315-369-3966).

Left(right) **Town of Webb Police** (315-369-6515), and New York State Police (315-369-3322).

Right(left) **Slicker's** (315-369-3002). Food and spirits. Pizza, burgers, sandwiches, and soup. Weekend entertainment.

202.1   Right(left) **Old Forge Tourist Information Center** (315-369-6983). This information center is tied with Cooperstown for being the best information center along Route 28, and offers complete data on lodging, dining, activities, and attractions such as snowmobiling, canoeing, biking, cross-country skiing, etc., in and around Old Forge. Also snowmobiling permits issued here. A must stop.

Right(left) **Old Forge Covered Bridge**, crossing the Middle Branch of the Moose River at the dam forming the Fulton Chain of Lakes.

Right(left) **Old Forge Community Playground**. Dock, benches, and picnic tables.

202.2   Left(right) **Trails End** (315-369-2632). Restaurant and lounge.

Left(right) **Forge Lanes Bowling** (315-369-2631). Bowling alley.

Left(right) **Mountain Stop** (315-369-3525). Convenience store and propane cylinder exchange.

Right(left) **Pied Piper** (315-369-3115). Drive-in. Chicken wings, chicken specialties, hot dogs, ice cream, etc.

Left(right) **Lion King Chinese Restaurant** (315-369-2102). Lunch $3-$5. Dinner mostly $5-$10. Daily until 11 PM. Take out.

Left(right) **Enchanted Forest/Water Safari** (315-369-6145). Largest water park in New York State. Experience the thrills of the White Cobra, Wild Waters, or Killermanjaro. Or swim in the surf in the wave pool, float down a river, or take the little ones to their own pond. Twenty-three water rides, 14 amusement rides, circus shows, and Storybook Lane. Heated water, games center, concession stands, and gift shop. This park has something for everyone. Admission price (adults $17, children aged 2-11 $15) includes all rides, shows, and attractions, including unlimited water rides. Mid-June through Labor Day.

202.3 Right(left) **Water's Edge Inn & Conference Center** (315-369-2484). Also **Riley's Lounge & Restaurant.** Sixty-one rooms in three stories in a contemporary inn on the shores of Old Forge Pond. Balconies, library with fireplace, indoor pool, and sauna. Rooms are $65-$99/couple; suites $99-$150. Riley's offers fine dining on steaks, seafood, veal, chicken, Italian favorites, and chef's originals; $9-$19 for most entrees.

Left(right) **Calypso's Cove** (315-369-2777). Family amusement center. Miniature golf, batting cages, go-carts, arcade, bumper boats, pizza, and more. Free admission; one ride $4, ten rides $35, open until 11 PM. Mid-June through mid-September.

Right(left) **Old Forge Lake Cruises** (315-369-6473). Narrated cruises of four lakes aboard the *Clearwater II* and the *Uncas,* $9. Three- to three-and-one-half-hour rides aboard the mail boat as it makes its rounds of lakeside and island-based houses and camps. Also, various combination packages including a scenic lake cruise, lunch, and rail ride. Sit back, relax and learn about the Old Forge area while absorbing the magnificent, natural, mountain and lake scenery. An Old Forge tradition for more than 25 years.

202.4   Right(left) **Club 28** (315-369-2446). Bar and lounge, comedy club, karaoke, dancing, pizza, and snacks. July through Labor Day: two live comedians every Friday and Saturday night, karaoke Tuesdays and Thursdays and after the comedians perform on weekends. Occasional summer bands. The rest of the year features karaoke on Friday and Saturday evenings. Fun and entertainment after the sun goes down.

As an aside, the word "karaoke" is of Japanese origin and is made up of two words: "kara" meaning "empty", and "oke" meaning "orchestra". As you sing, you add your voice to that empty orchestra.

Right(left) **Over the Rainbow**. Eighteen-hole mini-golf and Water Wars, a two-party arena in which you sling-shoot water balloons at your opponent, who is protected by a wire mesh. The mesh causes the balloons to break and your opponent to get soaked. Six balloons, $1; 15 balloons, $2, 24 balloons, $3. Great fun! Experience shows that many parents won't let their children play Water Wars. They say that it is an adult game, just so they can play it themselves. Reminds me of electric trains. Also souvenirs, scarves, T-shirts, etc. April through Labor Day.

Right(left) **Over the Rainbow**. Produce stand and garden center. Fruits, vegetables, eggs, milk, flowers, perennials, and baskets.

202.6   Right(left) **Arts Center/Old Forge** (315-369-6411). Year-round art exhibitions, workshops and classes. Summer concerts, theatrical performances, and lectures. Craft fair, antiques fair, auction, clothesline art sale. Pottery studio, darkroom, and art library. Annual events include four major exhibitions. Memorial Day through July 4 is an Adirondack theme exhibition. Late July through early August is the Central Adirondack Art Show which exhibits about 275 regional artworks. Late August through September is the Adirondack National Exhibition of American Watercolors, which has about 1,000 entries from across the country. The autumn show is the Northeast Quilts Unlimited, which also attracts national entries. This is an earnest, active, and multifarious art center. Its greatest endowments are its natural surroundings and its devoted staff. Wheelchair accessible.

Right(left) **Front Porch Gift Shop** (315-369-2210). Quality gifts for home and garden. Wind chimes, bird feeders and houses, wooden birds, candles and candle holders, wreaths and baskets, gift baskets, specialty gourmet items, and Christmas ornaments and decorations. Memorial Day through Labor Day, and weekends through the foliage season.

202.7   Right(left) **Holly Woodworking Giftshop** (315-369-3757). Wooden gifts and decorative home accessories, much of which is made in its woodworking shop. Lamps, clocks, candle holders, sconces, mirrors, boxes, bowls, cheese trays, wine racks, mug stands, napkin holders, key racks, etc. Also moccasins, jewelry, wind chimes, Southwestern pottery, stationery, candles, plush toys, specialty foods, and maple syrup. Regional, nature, and wood-carving books. Owned by the same proprietors for 40 years.

Right(left) **The Narrows** (315-369-6458). Newly-renovated housekeeping cottages overlooking First Lake Channel. Eight cottages sleep up to five, and one sleeps up to seven. Three are winterized. All have full kitchens, heat, showers, TVs, outside fireplaces, and picnic tables, and all furnishings except towels and bed linens. Swimming area, sun deck, boat and fishing dock, canoes, rowboat, and paddle boat. $460-$525, Saturday to Saturday. Shorter stays available off-season.

202.8   Left(right) **Northeastern Loggers' Association Forest Industries Exhibit Hall** (315-369-3078). Three-floor building beautifully made of various wooden materials interprets logging industry and the beauty of wood. Displays include a short history of wood, a model contemporary small sawmill, a slice of a 329-year-old tree, and a display of 25 wooden birds, each carved from a different wood. Interesting insight into an Adirondack industry.

202.9   Left(right) **KOA Campground** (315-369-6011, 800-562-3251). Some 250 sites for tents to RV's with full hookups, 131 heated cabins which sleep four, and 15 heated two-room cottages with cooking and restroom facilities which sleep six. Lake swimming, fishing, boat and bike rentals, lounge, arcade, playground, nightly movies, camping supplies, and laundry. Sites $22-$31, cabins $42, cottages $100. Open all year. Linen rental available if you forgot your sleeping bag.

30 Old Forge to Inlet

The section of Route 28 from Old Forge to Raquette Lake is among the most scenic along its 282-mile length. Mountains and lakes have arranged themselves into a three-dimensional tapestry of seemingly-embraceable pattern, color, and texture. You almost want to run your hand over the landscape and feel its warm, fuzzy nap as you would a patch of moss on the forest floor. Pervasive nature fills all the senses, replacing our preoccupation with man's artificial and image-based world with overwhelming beauty. Here in the Adirondacks man remains a bit player to the leading-role performance of nature.

There are many housekeeping cottages along Route 28 in the Adirondack Park. As mentioned in the introduction, "housekeeping" usually means fully furnished with kitchens and supplies, but no maid service, linens or towels, and often no soap or paper products. These cottages usually rent during the summer by the week only, and at other times by the night with a two-night minimum. Lodging can be at a premium in the Adirondacks during the peak tourist and snowmobile seasons, so reservations are strongly suggested. If you do get caught in the Old Forge area without a reservation, call the Tourist Information Center on 315-369-6983 for up-to-the-minute lodging availability.

Route 28 east of Old Forge is often older and narrower than Route 28 west of Old Forge, so wide-shoulder designated bike routes come and go as the road changes from old to new to old again.

202.9   Left(right) **KOA Campground** (315-369-6011) east of Old Forge. See *Chapter 29: Old Forge* for description.

206.7   Right(left) **Fulton House Cottages** (315-369-6626). On Fourth Lake.   Five heated, housekeeping cottages, some winterized, sleeping from five to 12 people. Sunny lawn, acres of woods, sandy beach, docks, canoes, sailboat, and paddle boat. $650-$1200/week. Shorter stays possible off season.

Left(right) Junction with **Rondaxe Road**, up which 0.2 mile on the left is **Fulton Chain Wild Forest Rondaxe Mountain Trailhead Parking**. Hiking trail to the southwest to **Bald Mountain** and the old fire tower (1.0). Across the road is the trailhead to the northeast to **Scenic Mountain** (2.1).

*Three miles up Rondaxe Road is **Adirondack Woodcraft Camps** and the **Adirondack Woodcraft Ski Touring Center** (315-369-6031). A nature camp for boys and girls on 400 wilderness acres with two lakes offering outdoor education, sailing, canoeing, kayaking, and windsurfing. In winter the Ski Touring Center maintains more than six miles of groomed and track-set cross-country ski trails for beginner to expert. Open weekends, the center also offers equipment rentals and night skiing. Rustic winter lodging includes a four-person housekeeping cabin ($50/night), a two-person loft and a four-person cabin, both with bath in nearby building ($30/night), and dormitory-style cabins for up to 10 people, also with bath in nearby building, $50-$100/night/cabin.*

207.7   Right(left) **Daiker's Inn** (315-369-6954). Large, rustic bar and restaurant on a bluff overlooking Fourth Lake and across the road from snowmobile trail #5. Dock for arrival by boat. Sixty-year old building is decorated in trophies, beer mugs, and big moose heads. The restaurant sports a large, U-shaped bar, outdoor bar, dance floor, large-screen TV, a baby grand piano, and live music. Don't miss the miniature of the bar and restaurant as it looked in 1972. Sandwiches, chicken in the basket, pizza, wings, finger foods, etc., $4-$9. Famous for its steak sub sandwich. A car/boat/snowmobile road house.

Right(left) **Daiker's Brookside Lodging** (315-369-3054). Four motel units, seasonal efficiencies, and beach on Fourth Lake, with a hiking trail and snowmobile trail #5 across road. Motel units $35-$55.

207.8   Right(left) **Hyla's Four Seasons** (315-369-6779). Housekeeping cottages. Open all year.

Right(left) **Le Bon Air** (315-369-3053). Housekeeping cottages.

209.4   Right(left) **Mountain Side Lodge and Motel** (315-357-4371). Ten-unit motel with lodge and bar. Breakfast. Snowmobile trail #5 directly across street. Friendly little place to stay. $55 to $60/double.

209.5   Right(left) **Mingo Lodge** (315-357-3143). Weekly apartment rentals. Fireplaces. Access to snowmobile trail #5.

209.6   Right(left) **Ledger's Lakefront** (315-357-5342). Three immaculate, private, housekeeping cottages on the shores of Fourth Lake. Manicured lawns with umbrella tables and chairs, outside fireplace, gradual sand beach, two boat docks, and a protected boat slip. Boathouse with a large picnic table and chairs for picnicking even in inclement weather. Heated cottages with fully-furnished kitchens (even microwave ovens) house from two to five people. Summertime $475-$600/week; after Labor Day $75-$90/night. Memorial Day weekend through Columbus Day. Lovely accommodations in a gorgeous setting.

Right(left) **The Lanterns** (315-357-5461). Warm and cozy restaurant and bar in a rustic, Adirondack-brown building. Varnished knotty-pine interior accented by a collection of lanterns. Full dinner menu, $8-$15.

209.7   Right(left) **The Turner Camps** (315-357-4221). Oldest, continuously family-run housekeeping cottages in the area. Eight spotless, rustic, heated cottages with contemporary amenities (some have dishwashers, some have microwave ovens) and various configurations accommodating from three to eight people. Sand beach and boat docks; rowboat, canoe, and sailboat rentals. Sunday afternoon get-acquainted deck party and Wednesday night community campfire. Weekly rentals only during the summer ($310-$570) with two-night minimums in June and September. Authentic Adirondack ambiance since 1914.

Right(left) **Country Lane Gifts** (315-357-2895). Gift and Christmas shop. China, porcelains, figurines, miniature cuckoo clocks, cedar boxes, dried flower arrangements, cards, and audio tapes. Beautiful, locally-crafted corn husk dolls, "T"s and sweats, Indian items, and sheepskin moccasins. A refined gift shop with a feminine flavor.

Left(right) Hiking trail to **Vista Trail** (0.2), **Bubb Lake** (0.5), **Sis Lake** (0.9), **Moss Lake** (2.3), **Big Moose Road** (2.9).

209.8   Right(left) **Palmer Point** (315-357-5594). Old Adirondack boating and cottage colony on a point of land with a 180-degree view of Fourth Lake. Five heated cottages housing from two to six persons ($200-$370/couple/week) on five quiet, wooded acres. One of the cottages is a converted icehouse, another a 1900 boathouse with slab bark exterior and wainscoted interior. Boat rentals include canoes, Sunfish, sloops, pontoon boats, motorboats, bowriders, etc. Fuel dock, sailing lessons, gradual sandy beach, and unique footbridge over boat channel. Well-behaved pets allowed. Mid-May through Columbus Day.

210.2   Right(left) **The Kenmore** (315-357-5285). A family-oriented cottage colony on Fourth Lake established in 1901. Fourteen heated housekeeping cottages housing four to 12 persons in wooded and lakefront settings. Five winterized cottages, each with a wood stove or fireplace. Sandy beach, sandy volleyball court, basketball court, horseshoe pits, campfire area, and free rowboat and canoe usage. Good dockage facilities, across from snowmobile trail #5. $480-$900/week, $160-$180/night in the winter with three-night minimum.

210.3   Right(left) **Alexander's Lakeside Cottages** (315-357-5451, 736-7604). Off same driveway as the Kenmore. One-, three- and four-bedroom heated cottages, the large one with an Adirondack fireplace. Dock, swimming, campfire ring, picnic tables, Adirondack chairs, and sandbox. $410-$790 in summer, 15 percent off-season discount. Extra charge for pets. Mid-May through mid-October.

211.0   Left(right) **Village Peddler** (315-357-6002).   An eclectic collection of pottery, candles, wind chimes, collectibles, coffees and teas, kitchen items, blankets, stuffed animals, toys, and more.

Entering(leaving) **Eagle Bay**.

Right(left) **The Donut Shop** (315-357-6421). Homemade donuts, subs, barbecue, and ice cream. Walk-up windows and picnic tables. Open Memorial Day through Columbus Day.

Left(right) **Village Tub**. Coin laundry.

211.1   Right(left) **Eagle's Nest Motor Inn** (315-357-3898). Restaurant, bar, and motel. Five motel rooms ($44-$64), three sleeping cabins ($38-$48) and one three-person housekeeping cottage, $325-$350/week.   Restaurant features pizza, wings, basket suppers, combo platters, and late-night menu. Suppers and platters $5-$7. Pool table, video game, and juke box. On snowmobile trail #5. Closed mid-March to mid-May.

Left(right) **Big Moose Yamaha** (315-357-2998). Yamaha, Arctic Cat, and Boston Whaler dealership. Snowmobile, boat, jet ski, outboard engine, and chain saw sales and service. Snowmobile trailers and used snowmobiles.

Left(right) **Hard Times Cafe** (315-357-5199). Casual, rustic restaurant and bar serving all three meals. Fireplace with wood stove and a piano. Breakfast of pancakes, waffles, omelets, and biscuits and gravy, $2-7. Lunch of chili, burgers, shrimp and pasta salad, club sandwiches, and nacho bravo, $3-$7. Dinner entrees include burger plate, chicken, shrimp, scallops, and steaks, $6-$16. Try its Mile High Pie, made with three different flavors of ice cream between a vanilla wafer crust, chocolate wafer crust, and graham cracker crust, and topped with hot fudge and whipped cream. Closed mid-March to end of April and two weeks in November.

Right(left) **The Tavern** (315-357-4305). Bar with a fireplace, pool table, and dart board serves burgers for lunch, and sometimes homemade soup in the winter.

Left(right) **Tim's Super Duper** (315-357-4311). Full supermarket with produce, fresh meats, butcher, and deli. Also a liquor store and an ATM.

211.2   Right(left) **Eckerson's Restaurant** (315-357-4641). The sign appropriately states fine dining and cocktails. Plush, soft, elegantly appointed restaurant in a natural, rustic locale. Comprehensive menu offering steaks and chops, chicken, duck, veal, spaghetti and meatballs, eggplant Parmigiana, vegetarian medley, shrimp, frog legs, crab legs, lobster tails, and more. Most entrees $9-$16. Midtown Manhattan in the mountains. Closed a couple weeks in November and three weeks in April.

Left(right) Junction with **Big Moose Road**, which leads to **Big Moose Lake**, the site of the 1906 murder of Grace Brown, a pregnant 20-year old, on which Theodore Dreiser based his 1925 novel, *An American Tragedy*. Chester Gillette, who was said to have had designs on another woman, took the mother-to-be for a boat ride, allegedly clubbed her with a tennis racket, upset the boat, and swam to safety while Grace drowned. In 1907 he was tried and convicted at the Herkimer County Courthouse in Herkimer, and executed.

Driving up **Big Moose Road** yields:

*000.8   Right. **Cascade Lake Trailhead**. Hiking trail to **Cascade Lake** and **Cascade Falls**, with continuation to **Chain Ponds**, **Queer Lake**, and more.*

001.2   Right. **Cascade Lake Trailhead Parking**, *offering hiking and cross-country skiing access to the* **Pigeon Lake Wilderness Area**.

002.0   Left. **Fulton Chain Wild Forest Moss Lake Trailhead Parking**. *Hiking trail circumscribing* **Moss Lake**, *with five trailside campsites and three boat-access lakeside campsites. Trail around* **Moss Lake** *(2.5); to* **Bubb Lake** *and* **Sis Lake** *trail (0.7),* **Vista Trail** *(2.7), and* **Route 28** *(2.9)*.

003.1   Right. **Pigeon Lake Wilderness Windfall Pond Trailhead Parking**. *Hiking trail to* **Cascade Lake, Cascade Falls, Queer Lake, Chain Ponds, Constable Lake, Chub Pond, Mays Pond, Pigeon Lake,** *and beyond to* **West Mountain** *and* **Raquette Lake**.

003.7   Left. **Camp Goreham** *(315-357-6401). YMCA camp.*

004.1   Right. **Covewood Lodge** *(315-357-3041). Wilderness lodging in the Adirondack great camp tradition. On the shores of Big Moose Lake and built from local trees and stones, a colony of housekeeping cottages and lodge apartments of various configurations from cozy for two, to extended family sized with seven bedrooms, four baths, and two fireplaces. All cottages are heated, have a fireplace, an outside grill, and floodlights for animal watching. Two beaches, two rec rooms, water skiing, sailing, windsurfing, pool table, table tennis, and more. Lodge rooms from $90/night/two to a housekeeping cottage for 12 people for $1600/week. Open all year.*

005.0   Right. **Dunn's Boat Service** *(315-357-3532). On Big Moose Lake. Sales, service, and rentals. Plus 1½-hour historic boat tours of Big Moose Lake.*

005.1   Right. **Big Moose Inn** *(315-357-2042). A resort country inn offering fine lodging and dining (restaurant open to the public) on Big Moose Lake, a one-mile by five-mile* *lake nestled between the Fulton Chain Wild Forest and the Pigeon Lake Wilderness. The lodge has 16 guest rooms (shared and private baths), one with a gas-fired fireplace and one with a Jacuzzi, but no telephones or televisions ($40-$150/couple). Numerous hiking and biking trails are nearby, and the inn offers its guests complimentary canoes to explore the lake. Elegant lakeside dining with an excellent menu (dinner of chicken, veal, lamb, fruit of the sea, filet of beef Oscar, Alaskan king crab legs, etc., $14-$30) and an extensive wine list. Living room with big fireplace, easy chairs, and recliners; porch and deck overlooking the lake; docks with Adirondack chairs and a gazebo. Closed December until the 26th, and the month of April. Cozy, elegant accommodations in the heart of the wilderness.*

005.6   *Right. Junction with unnamed road, down which 1.5 miles on the right is* **The Waldheim** *(315-357-2353). Fifteen one- to five-bedroom cottages at the end of the road on 300 acres along the north shore of Big Moose Lake. Established in 1904 and built from trees growing on the property, the Waldheim (German for "Forest Home") provides a vacation for everyone in the family by operating on the full American plan, with three meals provided every day. A much-appreciated tradition is the woodboy who comes by every morning to start a fire in your fireplace. Many families come here year after year. Some families are on their fifth generation of visitors, and others return for family reunions. Refrigerators, fireplaces, daily cleaning service, beach, canoe rentals, hiking trails, and weekly trail-hike picnics. $505-$648/adult/week, $57-$112/adult/day, two-day minimum. Call for children's rates. End of June through Columbus Day. A rare, traditional Adirondack camp experience.*

End of Big Moose Road coverage.

Right(left) **Village Square** (315-357-3818). Souvenirs and gifts. Jewelry, clothing, moccasins, beach towels, beach toys, cards, postcards, and firewood.

Right(left) **Eagle Bay Post Office** (315-357-3401). ZIP 13331.

Right(left) **Adirondack Ice Cream** (315-357-3232). Ice cream, yogurt, ice cream pies, hot dogs, and soda. Seasonal.

211.3   Right(left) **Eagle Bay Villas** (315-357-2411). Twelve cottages and five motel units set on expansive lawns overlooking Fourth Lake and its islands. Motel units have their front porches literally on the water. Boat access, big sand beach, tennis court, basketball, badminton, swing set, and shuffleboard. Some units open all year. Lodging/horseback riding packages available. Motel rooms and efficiencies, $60-$68/couple; cottages $295-$880/week.

Herkimer/Hamilton county line, **Webb/Inlet** town line, leaving(entering) **Eagle Bay**.

Hamilton County's population of 5,279 makes it the least-populous county in New York State. In an area of 1,721 square miles (just slightly smaller than the state of Delaware), there are just three people per square mile, a density less than any state other than Alaska. Are we still in New York?

211.4   Left(right) Intersection with **Uncas Road**. In the snow-free months, **Uncas Road** provides an easy, dirt-road mountain bike ride to **Brown's Tract Pond** and **Raquette Lake**. In the winter snowmobilers replace the bikers. The round trip from Eagle Bay to Brown's Tract Pond is about 14 miles and to Raquette Lake and back is about 20 miles.

Down **Uncas Road** are the following:

*000.1   Right. Junction with **North Star Road**, down which 0.1 mile on the left is **North Star Motel** (315-357-4131). Nine-unit motel plus a housekeeping cottage and mobile home away from Route 28's traffic. Motel rates are $35-*

$55/couple. Cottage and mobile home are $55-$90/night for four to six people. Call for weekly rates.

*Right.   **Adirondack Saddle Tours** (315-357-4499). Guided horseback riding tours to wilderness mountains, lakes, and waterfalls, from one hour to all day. Three-day pack trips to fishing holes and high peaks. Children welcome. Reservations recommended. Custom trips available. Season is from the time it dries up in the spring until the snow gets too deep in the fall. Lodging/riding packages with Eagle Bay Villas.*

End of Uncas Road coverage.

211.5   Right(left) **Clark's Marine Service** (315-357-3231). On Fourth Lake; sales, service, parts, and accessories. Marina, launching ramp, and worms. Rentals of canoes and pedal boats; fishing, ski and party boats; water skiing packages.

211.6   Left(right) Intersection with **North Star Road,** down which 0.1 mile on the right is **North Star Motel** (see description on Uncas Road a few paragraphs back).

212.3   Left(right) Hiking and cross-country ski trail around **Black Bear Mountain,** 6.0 miles.

212.4   Right(left) **Rocky Point Lakeside Lodges** (315-357-3751, 800-442-2251). New, three-bedroom three-bath town homes with fireplace for sale and rent (two night minimum to 3-month seasonal). Sandy beach, tennis courts, fitness center, indoor pool, Jacuzzi, and island gazebo with fireplace. Rates for one to six people are from $160-$260/ night for two nights; $60-$180/night for one month. Call for other rates.

212.7   Right(left) **Crosswinds** (315-357-4500). A charming cottage colony directly on the shores of Fourth Lake. Modern, well-maintained, two-bedroom housekeeping cottages with knotty-pine interiors. Wide, sandy beach, manicured grounds, seawall, and dock.   Rates are $495-$545/week/two, depending upon season. Open mid-June through Columbus Day.

212.8   Right(left) **Sunset Beach** (315-357-2692).   Five heated, two-bedroom housekeeping cottages with screened porches, picnic tables, and grills, and one of the nicest beaches on Fourth Lake. Also one efficiency motel unit with a couch, sink, two-burner stove, and refrigerator.   All units nicely separated affording comfortable privacy.   Cottages sleep from four to six, $325/week/four. Efficiency unit $195/week. Season is Memorial Day to Columbus Day.

213.0   Left(right) **Black Bear Trading Post** (315-357-2222). Adirondack-themed craft and gift shop. Adirondack pack baskets, carved and dressed Adirondack guides, etc. Open Memorial Day weekend through Columbus Day.

213.0   Right(left) **Stiefvater's Motel and Cottages** (315-357-2222). Motel units and cabins (with up to five bedrooms) on the shores of Fourth Lake.   Shallow sandy beach, outdoor fireplace, docks, paddle boats, canoe, rowboat, barbecues, picnic tables, lawn furniture, horseshoes, badminton, and more. Also a rec hall with a fireplace and an arcade. An Adirondack country getaway with a warm and friendly atmosphere.   Motel rooms $50/night/two, cabins $350-$900/week. Open Memorial Weekend through Columbus Day.

Right(left) **Hazen's Lakeside Cottages** (315-357-2121). Seven heated housekeeping cottages, sleeping two to eight people in one to three bedrooms, on the shores of Fourth Lake. Beach, dock, tetherball, and fire rings; free rowboat, pedal boat, and canoe. About $350-$490/week. Open July 4 through Columbus Day.

Right(left) **Nelson's Housekeeping Overnight Cottages** (315-357-4111). Eight heated, family-oriented housekeeping cottages, sleeping up to eight, on Fourth Lake. Sandy beach with a dock and a fireplace; basketball, volleyball, children's play area and unobstructed sunset views.   Also four motel units, some with refrigerators. Cottages $375-$550 per week; motel units $50-$55

per night. In the same family for more than 45 years. Open
Memorial Day through Columbus Day.

Right(left) **Fourth Lake Fishing Access**. Boat launching site and
parking lot.

213.1   Entering **Inlet**.

Inlet to
Raquette Lake

213.1   Entering **Inlet**.

Inlet is a little town with big opportunities. If you've made it this far into the middle of the Adirondacks, I suspect you are enough of a nature and outdoors lover that you will certainly find something fun and interesting to do here. Inlet offers snowmobiling, canoeing, kayaking, boating, water skiing, biking, mountain biking, hiking, picnicking, camping, cross-country skiing, snowshoeing, swimming, fishing, hunting, ice skating, horseback riding, golf, and seaplane rides. If you don't have the equipment, Inlet shops rent boats, bikes, canoes and kayaks, camping equipment, cross-country skis, snowshoes, and ice skates.

Inlet is a major paddle sports and mountain biking center. The Fulton Chain Canoe Route runs adjacent to Inlet, with the carry between Fifth and Sixth Lakes crossing Route 28 at the eastern end of the hamlet. In June, Inlet hosts the Black Fly Challenge, and in September the Adirondack Mountain Bike Festival, both major mountain bike races.

Inlet and Old Forge share and maintain a 500-mile network of marked and groomed snowmobile trails, for which they require the purchase of a $40/week or $60/season ($75 after November 15) snowmobile permit for all machines operated on any property other than the machine owner's property. Permits may be obtained from the Inlet Chamber of Commerce, 315-357-5501. All snowmobiles must be registered and, if operated on the town of Webb/Inlet trails and/or roads, the owner must carry liability insurance. Snowmobile season starts immediately after the close of big game hunting season in early December with Snodeo Weekend, Old

Forge's annual snowmobile season kick-off festival. The season lasts until the end of March or beginning of April, depending upon snow coverage.

213.2   Left(right) **Arrowhead Trading Post** (315-357-2140).   Indian crafts, gifts and souvenirs, specializing in items crafted by Adirondack and Native American artisans.   Clothing, jewelry, Adirondack pack baskets, moccasins, and maple syrup.   Chain saw-carved bears, hand-carved totem poles, antler lamps, and more.

Left(right) **Loose Caboose** (315-357-3200).   Take-out wings, pizza, fried chicken, barbecued ribs, soups, and salads.

Right(left) **Mary's Gift Shop**.   Adirondack gifts and souvenirs. Rings, cedar boxes, Indian toys, T-shirts, sweatshirts, figurines, plush toys, postcard sunglasses, Indian pottery, moccasins, books of local interest, maple syrup, and more.

Left(right) **Tamarack Cafe and Movie House** (315-357-2001). Family restaurant with attractive, Adirondack-themed interior serving breakfast and lunch, plus dinner in July and August. Pancakes, eggs, omelets, and eggs Benedict; sandwiches, burgers, and grill items; pasta with homemade sauce, and chicken Parmigiana, etc., all at reasonable prices (usually $3-$7). Famous for hot turkey sandwiches made with fresh, oven-roasted turkey, and homemade pasta sauce.   Closed November and April.   The Movie House is open in July and August.

Right(left) **Mary's White Pine Bakery**.   Donuts, breads, bagels, pies, turnovers, muffins, etc.   Open July and August.

Left(right) **The Wine Shop** (315-357-6961).   Liquors and wines.

Right(left) **Founders Keepers** (315-357-5116).   Souvenir shop. T-shirts, coffee mugs, sunglasses, frisbees, and more.

Right(left) **Rainbow Zen**.   An eclectic collection of imports, "T"s, souvenirs, and much more.

Left(right) **Burkhard Evans** (315-357-5901).   Real estate.

Left(right) **Hodel's Trustworthy Hardware** (315-357-2341). Hardware, paints, etc. Fishing bait and tackle, and camping supplies. Books, maps, and audio tapes. Custom T-shirt and sweatshirt printing. Also, an arcade with video games and the like.

Right(left) **Arrowhead Public Park.** Beach, picnic tables, children's playground, tennis courts, canoe launch, public boat docks, and restrooms.

Right(left) **Inlet Police Department** (315-357-5091).

Right(left) **Inlet Chamber of Commerce Information Office** (315-357-5501). Upstairs in the Inlet Municipal Building. Tourist information, snowmobile permits, and cross-country ski trail maps.

Right(left) **Northern Lights**. Hamburger, hotdog, and pizza stand with umbrella tables.

Right(left) **Inlet Post Office** (315-357-2012). ZIP 13360.

Left(right) **Inlet Gift Center.** Tastefully presented gifts, jewelry, and clothing. Moccasins, soaps, candles, ceramics, porcelain, stuffed animals, wind chimes, flags, cards, postcards, and more.

Right(left) **Inlet Public Library** (315-369-6494).

Right(left) **Ara-Ho Outfitters** (315-357-3306, 888-859-7676). Sales and rentals of hiking, camping, and backpacking gear. You can rent sleeping bags, tents, cooking gear, utensils, etc. Equipment advice, licensed guide service, gifts, books, T-shirts, hats, sweats, booties, walking sticks, topographical maps, etc. Open May through October.

Left(right) Formerly Coasters, closed at time of publication.

Right(left) Junction with **South Shore Road,** which follows the south shores of Fourth through First Lakes of the Fulton Chain southwest to Old Forge. On South Shore Road are:

Right. **Inlet Marina** *(315-357-4896). Boat and motor sales, service, rentals, gas, and live bait. Mercury sales & service.*

000.1   Right. **Marina Motel** *(315-357-3883). North-country-looking complex offers 16 motel units and three cottages on a knoll overlooking the hamlet of Inlet. Game room, free Disney Channel, and some king-sized beds. Snowmobile or cross-country ski from the parking lot, and the public beach is just steps away. Motel units $45-$58/couple. Cottages $350-$425/week for two to six people.*

000.2   Left. *Junction with* **Loomis Road** *(no street sign), down which one-tenth of a mile is the* **Fern Park Recreation Area**, *trailhead for Inlet's 20 kilometers of cross-country (X-C) ski trails and two kilometers of lighted X-C ski trails. The longer trails go to South Shore Road, Limekiln Road, Limekiln Lake Public Campsite, and Eagle Cove. The park also offers a warming hut, lighted skating rink under a pavilion, baseball field, basketball court, nature trails, picnic tables, and restrooms. Additional X-C ski trails nearby. See the Inlet Chamber of Commerce Information Office for an X-C ski map.*

000.3   Right. **Inlet Ski Touring Center** *(315-357-6961). Sales and rentals of cross-country skis, snowshoes, ice skates, and related equipment.*

000.5   Right. **Holl's Inn** *(315-357-2941, 733-2748). Experience the elegance of the past at this last of the old Fourth Lake hotels. Established in 1935 on more than 150 acres, this many-windowed inn offers modest to deluxe accommodations in three buildings. The sun room, sun porch, cozy furnishings and large, stone fireplace enhance the already wonderful natural Adirondack ambiance. Tyrolean-themed bar, canoes, rowboats, tennis court, shuffleboard, and table tennis. Hotel rooms, with private bath and including three meals a day, are $85-$120/person/night (two-night minimum), or $540-*

$700/person/week, double occupancy. Also three- and four-bedroom housekeeping cottages housing six to 10 people, $1,200-$1,400/week. Lakeside dining room open to the public. Open July to Labor Day.

End of South Shore Road coverage.

Left(right) **Inlet Department Store** (315-357-3636). Department store and Ace Hardware store. Souvenirs, clothing, "T"s and sweats, shoes, sandals, and beach toys. Boating, gardening, fishing, hunting, and camping equipment and supplies, and much more. Also an ATM.

Left(right) **Kalil's Supermarket** (315-357-3603). Small but complete supermarket with fresh produce, fresh meats, and a deli.

213.3 Right(left) **Screamen Eagle** (315-357-6026). Bar, pool table, video games, and video rentals; subs ($3-$8), and pizza. Also **Kirsty's** (315-357-5502). Restaurant serving breakfast ($2-$6), appetizers, cold and hot sandwiches, pasta, burgers, and salads, ($3-$7).

Right(left) **The Awesome Years** (315-357-5604). Crafts, homemade jellies, stuffed animals, helium balloons, and more.

Right(left) **Pedals & Petals** (315-357-3281). A unique bike and flower shop. Bicycle sales, service, and accessories. Bike, bike trailer, and bike baby trailer rentals by the hour, day, or longer. Fresh cut and potted flowers, dried flowers, balloons, massage oils, fragrances, soaps, and gifts. Floral delivery and wire service.

213.5 Right(left) **Fifth Lake**.

Left(right) **Lakeview Antiques**. Outdoor and indoor furniture, antiques, grandfather clocks, lamps, and accessories.

213.6 Left(right) **Mountainman Outdoor Supply Co.** (315-357-6672). Canoe, kayak, cross-country ski, and snowshoe sales and rentals. Hiking, camping, cross-country skiing equipment; gear, clothing, backpacks, boots, carabiners, and books. Daily rentals as well as fully outfitted canoe trips for two to 10 days including canoes, paddles, life vests, tents, sleeping bags, cooking gear, etc. Guided tours, sunset tours, canoe and kayak lessons, and shuttling. A paddle sports center for beginner to expert.

Right(left) **Canoe carry** between Fifth and Sixth Lakes, down which 0.1 mile is the Fifth Lake launching site.

213.7   Right(left) **J.R. Adirondack E-Z Mart** (315-357-4288). Convenience store and Citgo gas. Fresh homemade pizza, fresh pastries, homemade soups, Italian specialties, and more.

213.8   Right(left) Coin laundry and $1 hot showers. An oasis for canoeists, hikers, and campers. Showers seasonal.

Leaving(entering) **Inlet**.

213.9   **Caution**: Crosswalk for canoeists and kayakers making the half-mile carry between Fifth and Sixth Lakes.

Left(right) **Sixth Lake Road**, down which one-tenth of a mile is a canoe launching site just above the Sixth Lake dam. This is the east end of the Fifth Lake/Sixth Lake canoe carry.

214.0   Left(right) **Bird's Seaplane Service** (315-357-3631). Sightseeing seaplane rides, amphibious charters, airline connections, and hunting, fishing, and camping trips.

Right(left) Junction with **Limekiln Road**. Turning right yields:

000.4   *Right.* ***The Ole Barn*** *(315-357-4000). Large, 30-year-old, country-styled restaurant open for lunch and dinner (most entrees $6-$14) in the summer and on weekends, dinner only the rest of the year. Interesting newspaper menu, enclosed porch, large bar, pool table, and entertainment. Popular with the locals and snowmobilers. Closed April and November.*

Left. A natural Adirondack pond at the side of the road.

001.4   *Right.* **Limekiln Lake Public Campsite** *(315-357-4401). Tent and trailer camping on 271 sites. Picnicking, beach swimming, fishing, hiking, canoeing, small boat launch, boat rentals, showers, and dump station. Reservations 800-456-CAMP (2267). Mid-May through Labor Day.*

001.5   *End of Limekiln Road at the Limekiln Lake* **Department of Environmental Conservation** *Ranger Headquarters and the entrance to the* **Moose River Recreation Area** *(315-357-4403, 518-863-4545), a 50,000-acre wild forest with a maze of abandoned logging roads providing access for primitive camping, hiking, fishing, hunting, and snowmobiling. There are 140 free camping sites at seven different locations throughout the area, plus roadside camping areas for R/Vs and parking lots for day visitors. This is a rough, remote area unsuitable for vehicles of more than one ton capacity. During hunting season, all vehicles must have either four-wheel-drive or appropriate tire chains. Call for rules and regulations prior to entering. The season usually runs from Memorial Day weekend to the end of deer season in early December. Entry by foot is always allowed, and there are more than 25 miles of hiking trails in the area.*

End of Limekiln Road coverage.

214.2   Right(left) **Inlet Golf Club** (315-357-3503). Eighteen-hole par-70 golf course, restaurant, pro shop, and bar. Greens fees $20 for 18 holes, cart rental $20. Mulligan's Restaurant (315-357-4310) offers breakfast and lunch, $3-$6. A manicured, emerald jewel set among the uncut emerald mountains. If you stop on a sunny day for lunch on the deck with its multi-greened view you won't want to leave. Mid-May through Columbus Day.

214.4   Right(left) **Cinnamon Bear** (315-357-6013). Bed and breakfast in an old two-story colonial with a tin roof and antique and period furnishings. One of only a few B&Bs along Route 28 in the

Adirondacks. Four large rooms sharing two bathrooms, living room, dining room, fireplace, TV, and a VCR with a family-oriented tape library. Coffee and hot water always on. Across the road from Sixth Lake and on snowmobile trail "A". Canoe and kayak rentals arranged. Rates are $65/couple including a "mountain" breakfast. Open all year.

214.6   Left(right) **Drake's Inn** (315-357-5181). Restaurant and sports bar, neat and cozy with red and white tablecloths. Breakfast ($2-$4), lunch (soups, sandwiches, fried mushrooms, fried zucchini, pizza, chili, etc., $2-$7) and dinner (from spaghetti and meatballs to rib eye steak and shrimp scampi, $8-$13). Fresh haddock Friday nights, $9. Friendly, relaxed, and comfortable.

Left(right) Junction with **Seventh Lake Road**:

000.0   Left(right) ***Clayton's Cottages*** *(315-357-3394). Rustic, family oriented, lakeside, housekeeping cottage colony with 14 one- to three-bedroom winterized cottages. All cottages have a porch or a balcony, a picnic table, a charcoal grill, and all but one have a fireplace. Huge lawn, sandy beach, docks, rowboats, fireplace, swing set, volleyball, and evening bonfires. Wheelchair accessible right to the water. Rates are 310-$640, depending upon season and number of people.*

Left(right) **The Gift Cottage**. Gifts for all seasons. An eclectic collection of Adirondack, Americana, and Victorian gifts, much of it handmade. Stationery, jewelry, stuffed animals, baskets, twig and straw items, picture frames, candles, soaps, Christmas items, and more. Open July through September.

214.9   Left(right) **Willis Lodges** (315-357-3904). Ten two- and three-bedroom cottages with covered decks, picnic tables, and charcoal grills on 12 lakeside acres on Seventh Lake. Safe, gradual swimming area, lakeside fireplace, docks, basketball, badminton, tetherball, swings, horseshoes, shuffleboard, and croquet. Built, operated, and well maintained by the same proprietor for more than 40 years. $400 to $550 per week. Nightly rate $55/couple, off season only. Mid-May through mid-October.

215.0   Right(left) **Deer Meadows Motel and Cottages** (315-357-3274). Attractive motel and cottage complex with cottages for two to 16 people on the shores of Seventh Lake. Sand beach, row boats, game room, volleyball, and horseshoes. Inlet and Old Forge snowmobile trails are immediately behind the motel and can be hiked in the summer. Motel rooms $48-$55/couple. Cottages $60-$85/couple, $320-$650/week for up to eight people. Duplex (for up to 16 people) $830-$1220/week. Comfortable, cozy Adirondack lodging.

215.2   Left(right) **Payne's Air Service** (315-357-3971, 357-2079). Scenic sea-plane rides. Fly-in hunting, fishing, and camping trips. Charter service to anywhere.

215.4   Right(left) **T & M Horseback Riding** (315-357-3594). Horseback riding, paintball war games, and slatball. Three-quarter hour, two-hour, half-day, and overnight horseback rides, Western and English, mid-June through Columbus Day. Refereed war games (age 15 and over) with all equipment (mask, goggles, guns, paint balls, paint grenades, smoke grenades, etc.). Target range and new and used gun sales. Open year-round.

215.6   Left(right) **Seventh Lake House** (315-357-6028). Restaurant offering elegant dining in a bright and airy atmosphere. Contemporary American cuisine, large international wine list, and attentive staff. Bar, fireplace, and a rear deck overlooking a large lawn and Seventh Lake. Entrees $11-$22, reservations recommended. Open all year. The restaurant also hosts on the first Sunday in May the Fire & Spice Festival, a spicy food competition with entertainment and fun.

215.9   Left(right) **Lakeside Lodge** (315-357-4768, 834-6132). Lovely lakefront housekeeping cabins and tourist rooms. Two housekeeping cabins, each with two bedrooms, can accommodate from four to six people at $490-$500/week. Five lodge rooms with one shared bath, $50-$55/couple/night. Beautiful deck over the lake, boat dock, and swimming. Warm, homey accommodations with handmade quilts on the beds. Grandmother's place in the Adirondacks. Mid-June through the week after Labor Day.

216.8   Left(right) **Parking** area providing an outstanding view and a photo opportunity of beautiful **Seventh Lake, Goff Island,** and the mountains beyond. For safety reasons I recommend stopping at this narrow parking area from a westbound direction only.

217.3   Route 28 dips to almost lake level, crosses a lagoon of **Seventh Lake** fed by **Buck Creek,** and rises again on the other side. From the middle of the crossing the lake on one side of the road and the lagoon on the other offer two contrasting but beautiful Adirondack scenes.

217.4   Left(right) **Seventh Lake Fishing Access Parking Area and Boat Launch** with wonderful Seventh Lake views. Much of Seventh Lake's shoreline is state land, making it one of the quietest lakes in the Fulton Chain.

Right(left) Opposite the boat launch is the **Buck Creek** end of the **Seventh Lake Inlet/Uncas Road/Buck Creek snowmobile trail,** also used by mountain bikers, hikers, and cross-country skiers. This trail also branches off to **Mohegan Lake** and **Sagamore** (4.2 miles). From here to the far end of the trail at the junction of **Seventh Lake Inlet** and Route 28 by **Eighth Lake Public Campground** is 6.7 miles, and to return full circle via Route 28 to here is 8.7 miles.

218.5   Left(right) **Cathedral Pines Trail.** A 0.1 mile-long trail to a memorial.

218.8   Left(right) A little lagoon with old stumps, grasses, and brush, all amid quiet water. A beautiful example of Adirondack wetlands.

219.4   Right(left) Seventh Lake Inlet end of the **Seventh Lake Inlet/Uncas Road/Buck Creek snowmobile trail,** which also goes to **Mohegan Lake** and **Sagamore.** See Buck Creek above.

Seventh Lake Boat Launch on the left, and Buck Creek on the right.

A lagoon on Seventh Lake, perfect for exploring by canoe.

Left(right) **Eighth Lake Public Campground** (315-357-3132).
Some 125 tent and trailer sites with no hookups. Facilities for
picnicking, beach swimming, hiking, fishing, and boat launching.
Handicapped accessible, showers, and dump station. At the back
end of the main road through the campground is a hiking and
snowmobile trailhead to Bug Lake and Uncas Road. Reservations
800-456-CAMP (2267). Mid-April through mid-November.

219.7   **Eighth Lake** on the left.

223.9   Junction with unsigned road on left to the hamlet of **Raquette
Lake**, and with **Sagamore Road** on the right to **Sagamore**.

Raquette Lake to Blue Mountain Lake

The junction of Route 28 and Sagamore Road is the beginning of a 13-mile, circuitous trail used for hiking, mountain biking, and snowmobiling. From this junction it goes south on Sagamore Road, past Great Camp Sagamore and Mohegan Lake, and down the Uncas Road trail (or the Buck Creek trail, an even longer trip) to Route 28 across from the Eighth Lake Public Campground, and back to here via Route 28.

223.9   Junction with unsigned road on the left to the hamlet of **Raquette Lake**, and with **Sagamore Road** on the right to **Great Camp Sagamore**.

Turning left(right) onto unsigned **CR 2** (sometimes called Main Street) takes you to the hamlet of **Raquette Lake**:

*000.4   Left. **Whimsical Wood Furniture and Fantasies** (315-354-4116). An eclectic collection of Adirondack twig furniture, local crafts, artifacts, souvenirs, and other recycled and indescribable items. This shop in a shed is almost a museum, representing a survivalist spirit of making the most from the least. The shop's proprietor makes much of the eclectic merchandise on display, and embodies this Adirondack spirit. It doesn't get any more Adirondack than this.*

Right. Large brick building (called the "Raquette Lake Mall" by some locals) housing the following:
***Raquette Lake Post Office** (315-354-4291). ZIP 13436.*

Raquette Lake Tap Room and Liquor Store *(315-354-4581)*. *Tap room features soups and sandwiches.*
Raquette Lake Supply Co. *(315-354-4301)*. *Fresh meats and produce, fresh bakery, groceries, clothing, T-shirts, sweats, camping supplies, maps, books, film, and souvenirs.*
Laundry. *On the rear of the building, clockwise beyond Raquette Lake Supply Co.*

Right. *Raquette Lake Supply Co.* *Mobil gas station and ice.*

Right. *Boat launching ramp* *and public docks.*

Right. *Raquette Lake Navigation Company* *(315-354-5532).* *Narrated scenic, dining, and moonlight entertainment cruises aboard the W. W. Durant on Raquette Lake. Lunch, dinner, and Sunday brunch cruises. View the lake's 99 miles of shoreline, most of which are forever wild. Drink in the fall foliage or the summer stars. See the Adirondack Great Camps of W. W. Durant, Connecticut governor Phinneas Lounsbury, publisher Robert Collier, and the Carnegie family, all built in the late 19th century. A unique Adirondack experience. Reservations required for dining cruises. Memorial Day through the end of October.*

Right. *Raquette Lake Marina* *(315-354-4361).* *Fishing boat, pontoon boat, and canoe rentals; gasoline, and bait. Mid-May through mid-October.*

000.5 *Left.* *Raquette Lake Public Library* *(315-354-4005).* *Established in 1922, Raquette Lake's library was damaged and its books burned in the fire of 1927. It has been housed in its current brick building since 1937. It is nestled under tall pine trees and has a large, carved bear and cub standing on the front lawn. The library houses a collection of Adirondack books and a computer with Internet access.*

Raquette Lake Library's pet carved bears.

002.0   *Continuing up the hill, making a left onto **Brown's Tract***
         ***Road** (the eastern end of **Uncas Road** from **Eagle Bay**)*
         *and driving about two miles takes you to **Brown's Tract***
         ***Pond Public Campground** (315-354-4412).   Ninety tent*
         and trailer sites, no hookups.   Picnicking, swimming,
         fishing, hiking, boat launch, boat rentals, and dump
         station.   No power boats allowed.   Camp with the loons
         while fishing for perch, bullhead, and small mouth bass.

Reservations 800-456-CAMP (2267). Mid-May through Labor Day.

*Near the campground entrance, between **Upper Pond** and **Lower Pond**, is a small bridge over a stream, by which you can launch your canoe for a scenic, two-hour trip down **Brown's Tract Inlet** to **Raquette Lake** hamlet. This launching point, and the **Eighth Lake** launching point one mile southwest on the Eighth Lake/Brown's Tract canoe carry, are on either side of a divide. The water from Eighth lake flows eventually into Lake Ontario, while the water from Brown's Tract Inlet flows eventually into the St. Lawrence River. It's all downhill from here.*

002.8   *Right. **Trailhead**, just east of **Upper Pond**, to **Beaver Brook**, **Shallow Lake**, and **Sucker Brook Bay**.*

End of coverage of CR 2 to Raquette Lake and Brown's Tract Ponds.

Turning right(left) onto **Sagamore Road** offers a beautiful forest drive along a dirt road to:

003.5   *Left. **Great Camp Sagamore** (315-354-5311, 354-4303). Once the wilderness retreat of the Vanderbilts, this original Adirondack great camp was built in 1897 on 1,526 acres of wilderness, and is a perfect example of Adirondack architecture. Sagamore is comprised of a main lodge, a dining hall, playhouse, guest cottages, boathouse, blacksmith shop, carpenter shop, school, store, and ice house. Two-hour tours are available daily during summer and weekends through Columbus Day. Week-long and weekend lodging programs cover virtually every aspect of the Adirondack experience. Snack shop, book store, hiking, skiing, swimming, canoeing, boating, and more. An outstanding, one-of-a-kind retreat along Route 28.*

End of Sagamore Road coverage.

224.2   Right(left) **South Bay Tavern** (315-354-4223). Small, rustic, and unassuming, this full-service restaurant in Raquette Lake serves breakfast ($3-$5), lunch ($2-$6), and dinner of spaghetti, steaks, Friday fish fry, etc., ($8-$18).

Right(left) **Bird's Marine** (315-354-4441). Boat, motor, canoe and trailer sales, service and accessories, and gas. Water taxi service and mail boat tours. Rentals of pontoon boats, fishing boats, runabouts, canoes, motors, and trailers. Water skiing, water ski lessons, and water ski package rentals. Snowmobile parts and service. Open for boating and snowmobiling seasons.

224.5   Left(right) Expansive, beautiful view of Raquette Lake's **Otter Bay** as the road crosses a little stream. For the next few miles Route 28 hugs the south shore of Raquette Lake, offering an abundance of soothing views of the lake and the mountains, each one different from the one before. A couple of miles ahead Route 28 crosses **South Inlet**, where the view of the lake is especially pretty, as is the view of the inlet itself. South Inlet offers great exploring by canoe.

225.3   Left(right) **Tony Harper Pizza** (315-354-4222). Pizza, subs, wings, etc., in a dark brown, rough pine, north-country building. Dock on the lake for visiting customers and pizza pick-up. Will deliver to camps, cabins, boats, etc. Open July and August, and occasional weekends in June and September.

225.4   Left(right) **Risley's Rush Point Cottages** (315-354-5211, 429-9239). A former estate that is now a colony of housekeeping cottages. The eight cottages, sleeping from four to 10, are in what once were the lodge, the ice house, the boat house, etc., and most have a wood-burning stove. Gentle swimming area, swimming dock, boat slips, two canoes, and children's play area. Evening campfires and marshmallow roasts, and the children can "camp out" in two lean-tos. Most pets allowed. Rates are $530-$580 per week, by reservation only. Open late June to early September. Unwind in an Adirondack chair, listen to the loons, and watch both sunrise and sunset from Rush Point.

225.8   Left(right) **Burke's Marina** (315-354-4623). Marina on Raquette Lake offering boat, outboard motor, and trailer sales, service, accessories, and supplies. Dockage, boat rentals, tackle, and gifts. Mobil automotive gas station plus a gas dock.

Right(left) **Burke Towne Restaurant** (315-354-5066). Small, quaint restaurant serving all three meals. Dinner of haddock, New York strip steak, ham steak, etc., $8-$9. Pizza, wings, and homemade breads and pies. Mid-May through October.

Left(right) **Burke's Cabins** (315-354-4623). Four one-bedroom and five two-bedroom cabins overlooking the marina and Raquette Lake, $40-$50 nightly, $240-$300 weekly. Early May through mid-October.

228.0   Left(right) **Golden Beach Public Campground and Day Use Area** (315-354-4230). State campground. Tent and trailer camping on 205 sites. Picnicking, swimming, fishing, boat launch, and dump station. Golden Beach is also the launch point for boats for the four-mile trip to **Tioga Point Campsite** (accessible by boat only) on the eastern shore of Raquette Lake. Tioga Point has nine tent sites and 15 lean-tos with fireplaces and picnic tables. Campers must bring their own drinking water. Tioga Point has a trailhead for hiking and snowmobiling to Lower, Middle, and Upper **Sargent Ponds** and to **North Point Road** southwest of **Deerland**.

231.2   **Utowana Lake**.

As you continue east, Route 28 starts to undulate again as it climbs up and down the hills south of Utowana and Eagle Lakes. In mid-September, yellow and orange wild flowers sprinkle the roadside with color, seemingly as a preview of the fall foliage season, which is already beginning to show itself in the trees. As you get closer to the hamlet of Blue Mountain Lake, you'll catch glimpses through the trees of the 3,759-foot peak of Blue Mountain.

233.3   Right(left) **Trailhead parking** for trail to **Grassy Pond** (0.5 mile) and **Wilson Pond** and its lean-to (2.8).

236.0   Left(right) **Blue Mountain Lake**.

236.1   Left(right) **The Hedges on the Lake** (518-352-7325, 761-3115). This family resort is the recipient over many years of numerous newspaper and magazine accolades. Perfectly maintained, rustic, Adirondack-styled buildings on green lawns overlooking Blue Mountain Lake and its islands, with Blue Mountain in the background. Two main lodges with lounges, fireplaces, and a library, plus eight lakefront cottages housing from three to eight people. Modified American plan includes breakfast, with homemade breads and pastries, and dinner. Coffee hour each evening includes coffee, tea, hot chocolate, cookies, cake, and popcorn. Self-service coffee and tea served all day in the dining room lighted by an array of Tiffany lamps. On 12 acres, the resort offers swimming and diving areas and a beach for small children, plus complimentary canoes, kayaks, paddle boats, and rowboats. $138-$158 per couple per night. Mid-June through Columbus Day. True Adirondack charm and luxury.

236.2   Entering **Blue Mountain Lake**.

Blue Mountain Lake is another outdoors Nirvana. It offers boating, water skiing, fishing, biking, hiking, and all the other activities normally found on or near an Adirondack Mountain lake. Although all the land surrounding the lake is privately owned, there are two boat launching ramps in town, plus a public beach and canoe launching site. The lake is home to largemouth bass, lake trout, brook trout, and whitefish. Hiking trails lead to Slim Pond south from Route 28 and to Chub Pond, Castle Rock, and Upper Sargent Pond from the end of Maple Lodge Road, and to the summit of Blue Mountain Lake from NY 28N/NY 30 north of the hamlet. And, the Northville-Lake Placid Trail crosses Route 28 at the Lake Durant Public Campground three miles south of the hamlet. Take a two-hour, three-lake, narrated historical boat tour. Canoe on more than 100 miles of connected and semi-connected (canoe carry necessary) waterways. Bike the 10 miles from Blue Mountain Lake to Indian Lake along wide-shouldered Route 28 on the state's first designated bike route. There is much to do in Blue Mountain Lake.

In addition to the lodging, restaurants, outfitters, and merchants described on the next few pages, Blue Mountain Lake is home to Blue Mountain Lake Guide Service (518-352-7684), providing guided outdoor experiences from white water rafting to pond fishing and big game hunting to ski touring. The service also has a remote, secluded hunting lodge accommodating six people. Design your own Adirondack experience.

For tourist information, contact the Blue Mountain Lake Association (518-352-7659).

236.5   Left(right) **Prospect Point Cottages** (518-352-7378). Five rustic housekeeping cottages, linens and towels provided, on the shores of Blue Mountain Lake. Beach and dock. $625-$675/week for four to six people. Off-season $75/night/couple, two night minimum. Pets allowed.

236.6   Right(left) Junction with **Durant Road (CR 19)**.

236.7   Left(right) **Blue Mountain Lake Boat Livery** (518-352-7351, 305-666-5773). Boat sales, rentals, repairs, and tours; and live bait. Two-hour, three-lake (Blue Mountain, Eagle, and Utowana) narrated cruises in historic, 1916 boats. Three cruises daily, Memorial Day to Labor Day, then once a day after Labor Day, reservations requested. Rental pontoon boats, fishing boats, ski boats, canoes, kayaks, and a large sailing fleet. Deep water boat **launching ramp**; $5 launch fee. Open May through Columbus Day.

236.8   Left(right) **Public Beach** (518-352-7768). Early July through Labor Day. Also public canoe **launching site**. Restrooms across road.

Right(left) **Blue Mountain Lake Post Office** (518-352-7654). ZIP 12812.

Right(left) **The Cedarwood** (518-352-7675). Gifts in various mediums: clay, metal, wood, glass, paper, cloth, etc. Also books, cards, jewelry, and baskets. Seasonal.

Right(left) **The Adirondack Lakes Center for the Arts (ALCA)** (518-352-7715). Performances, exhibits, concerts, films, workshops, lessons, programs for youngsters, craft sales, and a Fall Festival. Gift and craft shop (daily Memorial Day through Columbus Day, weekdays through year end) offering local and regional Adirondack crafts, jewelry, and more. Call for program.

Right(left) **Blue Mountain Lake Inn** (518-352-7600) and **Hudson River Rafting Company** (518-251-3215, 800-888-RAFT). Rustic, mostly-original, turn-of-the-century bed and breakfast retaining much of its original boarding house character. Six bedrooms, two baths, living room, dining room, and kitchen. Also three cabins. $30-$35/person, including continental breakfast. Memorial Day weekend through Columbus Day. Also canoe rentals and white water rafting trips on the Hudson River.

236.9 Left(right) **Curry's Cottages** (518-352-7354, 7355). Eight red, rustic, heated, Adirondack housekeeping cabins (linens provided, but no maid service) either on or overlooking the lake, housing two to six people each. Large lawns; excellent private, sandy beach; boat launch; dock; and complimentary canoe and rowboat. $400-$750/week during the summer; shorter stays acceptable after Labor Day. May through September.

237.1 Left(right) **Potter's Motor Lodge and Resort** (518-352-7331, 888-352-7331). Twelve beach and forest housekeeping cottages, a 10-unit motel, and a restaurant perfectly located on the eastern shores of Blue Mountain Lake. Fireplaces, porches; one cottage even has a whirlpool bath and a game room with a pool table. Natural, shallow sandy beach, docks, tennis courts, and a basketball court. Canoes and rowboats for rent. The charming restaurant offers fine dining in rustic elegance and serves three meals a day, with American-style dinner entrees costing $10-$19. A liquor store is also on the premises. Cottages accommodate three to eight people, $475-$1250. Motel rooms $45-$85/couple. Memorial Day through mid-September.

Right(left) **The Station Country Store** (518-352-7318). Groceries and Citgo gas. Deli, subs, hot dogs, ice cream, ice, and firewood.

Junction of **Route 28** with **NY 28N** and **NY 30**. Route 28 turns right(left) to follow NY 30 south to **Indian Lake**. NY 28N and NY 30 north continue straight ahead toward **Long Lake** and **Tupper Lake**.

Route 28 coverage continues in Chapter 33, *Blue Mountain Lake to Indian Lake*.

NY 28N/NY 30 North

Bike route follows NY 28N/NY 30 north toward **Long Lake**.

000.0   Left. **LaPrairie's Lakeside Cottages** (518-352-7675). Two heated housekeeping cottages (linens and towels provided) on the lake housing from five to nine people, each with handmade quilts on the beds, private sandy beach, dock, and charcoal grill. The larger cottage has a fireplace. Open May through September, $600-$900/week.

Left. **Steamboat Landing** (518-352-7323). Deck rooms, cabins, and suites accommodating from two to five people at the former steamboat terminus and landing on the shores of Blue Mountain Lake. The seven deck rooms, sharing two baths, are on the third floor of the solid, century-old boathouse where the steamboats were hauled and stored for winter. The third floor deck overlooks the marine railway and provides magnificent views of Blue Mountain Lake. The suites and cabins have private baths, some have fireplaces, some have magnificent views, and all except the one-room cabins are housekeeping units. Private dock. Rustic, quaint, charming, and historic. $45-$80/night, $350-$450/week. Open May through October.

000.1   Left. **Blue Mountain Outfitters** (518-352-7306). Canoe and kayak sales and rentals; camping, fishing, and hiking equipment, supplies, and clothing. Hourly rentals, customized guided trips, canoe camping outfit rentals, shuttle service, etc. Bait and tackle, maps, books, film, and postcards. May through mid-October.

000.2   Right. **Blue Mountain Designs and Crafts** (518-352-7361). Craft gallery featuring clocks, rustic furniture, stained glass, pottery, Adirondack items, pocketbooks, clothing, watercolors, photos, books, sun catchers, wooden toys, cards, jewelry, and more. Warm and cozy atmosphere with soft music. An Adirondack tradition for more than 25 years. May through December.

000.6   Left. Junction with **Maple Lodge Road,** which clings to the mountainside northeast of **Blue Mountain Lake**. The road provides gorgeous views of the lake and the surrounding mountains, and ends at the hiking trailhead to **Castle Rock** and the snowmobile trail to **Upper Pond**:

001.0   *Left.* ***Hemlock Hall*** *(518-352-7706). Lodge, motel, and cottages in the forest on a mountainside overlooking Blue Mountain Lake. The lodge has a huge porch with rough-hewn Adirondack furniture and a magnificent view of the lake. Two fireplaces, including a three-sided corner one, melt early morning chills. Bay window seats, varnished wainscoting, and tongue-and-groove woodwork in the ceiling help make the lodge as impressive as its setting. All rooms have private baths except for some lodge rooms. Cottages, some with fireplaces and porches, accomodate up to six. Main dining room serves meals family-style. Private beach, Sunfish, canoes, paddle boats, rowboats, kayaks, and game room. $78-$145 per couple, including two meals a day and use of all facilities. Memorial Day through Columbus Day. A superb Adirondack lodging experience.*

001.2   *End of road at* ***Minnowbrook Conference Center****. Trialhead for trails to* ***Chub Pond*** *(0.8 mile),* ***Castle Rock*** *(1.7), and* ***Upper Sargent Pond*** *(4.3).*

End of Maple Lodge Road coverage.

001.3   Left. **Adirondack Museum** (518-352-7311). A must stop if you are anywhere within 50 miles. This outstanding museum depicting the history of the Adirondacks is my favorite museum in the world. Twenty-three exhibit areas of genuine artifacts depicting Adirondack life in the past. Stage coaches and buggies; boats and guide boats; a locomotive and a plush, private, rail passenger car; Adirondack logging, mining, and living exhibits. A log hotel, an Adirondack cottage, log cabins, wood-burning stoves, ice harvesting tools, and much more, plus spectacular views of Blue Mountain Lake. Also a cafeteria, a refreshment deck, and a gift shop featuring books, paintings, Adirondack memorabilia, crafts, souvenirs, and more. Memorial Day weekend through mid-October. The museum also hosts a number of annual events such as the No-Octane Regatta Weekend (non-powered boat races), Rustic Furniture Fair, the Adirondack Museum Antiques Show, an Author's Evening, field trips, Monday evening lectures, and more. A wonderful Adirondack experience.

001.4   Right. **Trailhead parking** for **Blue Mountain** summit and the old fire tower, built in 1917, which has been reopened for hikers' sightseeing pleasure (2.0 miles); junction with **Northville-Lake Placid Trail** (3.3); and **Tirrell Pond lean-to** (3.6).

End of NY 28N/NY 30 coverage.

Blue Mountain Lake to Indian Lake

This Route 28/NY 28N/NY 30 junction marks the northernmost point of Route 28. Driving Route 28 in a clockwise manner (as this book was written), from this point it no longer heads north and east, as it has been doing ever since Barneveld, but now heads south and east all the way to its northern terminus at its junction with US 9 north of Warrensburg.

Route 28 between Blue Mountain Lake and Indian Lake is a 10-mile-long designated bike route. This route, on the wide shoulder of the highway, was first opened in 1976, and is the forerunner of similar routes elsewhere along Route 28 and other routes in the state. As you ride to Indian Lake there are numerous opportunities along the way to stop at rest areas, trailhead parking areas, a stretch of old Routes 28 and 30, and the Lake Durant Public Campground.

237.1   Junction of **Route 28** with **NY 28N** and **NY 30**. Route 28 turns right(left) to follow NY 30 south toward **Indian Lake**. NY 28N and NY 30 north continue straight ahead toward **Long Lake** and **Tupper Lake**.

237.5   Crossing the divide between the **St. Lawrence** and the **Hudson Rivers**. Blue Mountain Lake waters and waters from other lakes, rivers, and streams north of this divide eventually find their way to the St. Lawrence River. Waters from Lake Durant just a few miles south, and other waters south of this divide, make their way to the Hudson. Lake Durant waters reach the Hudson while it is still an Adirondack wild river a mere 10 miles east of the lake.

Right(left) **Mountain Motel** (518-352-7781). Four motel rooms and two mini-suites accommodate up to six people. All guests have access to a fully-equipped communal kitchen with refrigerator and microwave. Pets and children welcome. $40-$60 per couple; children under six are free. Friendly, relaxed, family-run lodging.

237.6   Left(right) **Red Truck Clayworks** (518-352-7611). Fine crafts. Pottery, woodenware, wovenware, baskets, candles, paintings, photographs, dried floral arrangements, and clothing. Also ice cream and yogurt. June through Labor Day.

238.0   Leaving(entering) **Blue Mountain Lake**.

Right(left) Junction with **Durant Road (CR 19)**:

000.2   *Left. Junction with an unsigned road, down which one-tenth of a mile is **trailhead parking** for trail to **Rock Pond** (.75 mile), **Cascade Pond Lean-to** (2.8) and **Stephens Pond Lean-to** (4.3). One-tenth of a mile past the parking area on the shores of Lake Durant is a site suitable for launching a canoe.*

End of Durant Road coverage.

238.7   Left(right) **Parking** area with picnic tables and an unobstructed view of **Lake Durant** across the road. One of the nicest parking areas along entire Route 28. My favorite place to stop for lunch.

Across Route 28 from the eastern end of this picnic area is the western end of a mile-long section of old Route 28/30 which offers hiking and Lake Durant fishing access. The old road is built on fill, with Lake Durant directly on the south side and wetlands on the north. Bird watchers may be rewarded by ducks congregating west of the western end of the road. You can also launch a canoe from this old road.

The wetlands between Route 28/NY 30 and Old Route 28/NY 30.

Right(left) South end of **Old Route 28/30**.

239.7   Right and Left. **Trailhead parking** for hiking the **Northville-Lake Placid Trail**. Right (south) parking lot for **Stephens Pond** (3.1 miles), **Cedar River Flow** (12.1) and **Cedar Lakes** (21.6). Left (north) parking lot for **O'Neil Lean-to** (3.3), **Tirrell Pond Lean-to** (4.3) and **Long Lake** (17.7).

240.1   Right(left) **Lake Durant Public Campground** (518-352-7797, 800-456-CAMP for reservations). Sixty tent and trailer sites, many of them lakefront. Picnicking, swimming, hiking, fishing (tiger muskies and bass), a boat launch, and a dump station. Mid-May through Columbus Day.

241.8   Right(left) **The Forest House** (518-352-7776). Fine dining in a casual Adirondack atmosphere, open for breakfast buffet and dinner Tuesdays through Sundays. Varied American dinner cuisine of chicken scampi, chicken marsala, saltimbocca, filet of salmon, shrimp scampi, etc., $10-$17.

Right(left) **The Forest House Lodge** (518-352-7030). A pretty and homey bed and breakfast. A bright, white clapboard house with flowers on the enclosed porch and a well-cared-for green lawn.   Original wood finishings, fireplace, full or queen-sized beds, full breakfast. $55/couple.

241.9   Left(right) **Pumpkin Mountain Gun Shop**. Guns, ammo, bait, tackle, camp wood, and worms.

242.5   Left(right) **Trailhead parking** for hiking and snowmobiling to **Rock Lake**, 0.5 mile.

244.0   Left(right) **Trailhead parking** for hiking and snowmobiling to **Rock River**, 3.0 miles.

244.1   Right(left) **Trailhead parking** for hiking and cross-country skiing to summit of **Sawyer Mountain**, 1.1 miles.

245.7   Left(right) The **Adirondack Guide Boat Shop** (518-648-5455). Rustic furnishings, wooden boat restoration, and new boat construction.

246.4   Right(left) Junction with **Cedar River Road (CR 12)**, up which you will find:

002.4   Right. *Wakely Lodge Golf Course (518-648-5011). The beauty of this public golf course in a pristine setting surrounded by Adirondack peaks and home to deer and frogs will relax you, but the nine holes with obstacles like trees, hills, a lake and the Cedar River may threaten that relaxation. Driving range, pro shop, clubhouse with bar serving lunch of soups, sandwiches, burgers, etc., ($2-$5). Greens fees $9/9 holes, $15/18, carts $8/$14. Swing with the wildlife. May through late September.*

004.6   Right. *Snowshoe Hill Cottages (518-648-5207). On a quiet forest hillside under the pines, balsams, and maples, three private, heated, housekeeping cottages sleeping from four to seven. One has an outdoor fireplace, another a* *screened porch.   Simple, tidy, and woodsy, $60/couple. Call for weekly rates.*

014.1 *End of the road at **Wakely Dam**, the Cedar River **Department of Environmental Conservation** Ranger Headquarters, and the entrance to the **Moose River Recreation Area** (518-648-5055, 518-863-4545), a 50,000- acre wild forest with a maze of abandoned logging roads providing access for primitive camping, hiking, fishing, hunting, and snowmobiling. There are 140 free camping sites at seven different locations throughout the area, plus roadside camping areas for R/Vs and parking lots for day visitors.   This is a rough, remote area unsuitable for vehicles over one ton capacity.   During hunting season all vehicles must have either four-wheel-drive or appropriate tire chains.   Call for rules and regulations prior to entering. The season usually runs from Memorial Day weekend to the end of deer season in early December.   Entry by foot is always allowed, and there are more than 25 miles of hiking trails in the area.*

End of Cedar River Road coverage.

246.5   Right(left) **Cedar River Golf Club** and **Cedar River House** (518-648-5906). Golf course and motel. Nine-hole golf course ($10/9 holes, $15/18; cart $9 and $15). Also a six-unit motel ($35/night), swimming pool, small pro shop, and snack bar. End of May through Columbus Day.

247.4   Right(left) **Cummins Sport Shop** (518-648-0261). Fishing tackle, live bait, feed, grain, birdseed, flowers, and plants. Locally-made camp chairs.

Right(left) **Cedar River Sports** (518-648-5143).   Ski-doo snowmobile and trailer sales, parts, and service.

247.6   Bike route ends.

Hamlet of **Indian Lake.**

34 Indian Lake to North Creek

Indian Lake calls itself the white water capital of New York State. It is the starting point for exciting canoe, kayak, and raft trips down the Hudson River Gorge. It is also a year-round playground for many other outdoor activities. Indian Lake hosts snowmobile races in January, a Winter Festival (snowshoe races, sledding races, fireworks, and more) in February, a Spring Fling and town-wide flea market in May, library book sale in August, a pig roast and a car and truck show in September, a Halloween parade in October, and more. Some 300 miles of snowmobile trails (no permit required) and 100 miles of cross-country ski trails help folks work up a sweat in wintertime. (Trail maps and guides are available at the Chamber of Commerce Information Office in the hamlet.) In spring, it's the white water rafting, canoeing, kayaking, and fishing which bring people out. Summer offers camping, hiking, biking, swimming, boating, and golf. The fiery leaves of autumn play host to leaf peepers for strolling, hiking, or canoeing in a sunburst-colored wonderland. Indian Lake is a friendly, unassuming, little town for residents and visitors to do what they most love to do: enjoy nature and play outdoors.

Indian Lake is situated at the Route 28/NY 30 intersection, and, like most of the settlements along Route 28, doesn't have enough inhabitants to be listed in an atlas. However, it is the only settlement along Route 28 to have a song written about it. In 1968 the Cowsills popularized a song written by Tony Romeo called "Indian Lake". It made it to #83 on Billboard Magazine's top songs for that year.

247.6   Hamlet of **Indian Lake**.

Right(left) **Bear Trap Inn** (518-648-5341). Bar and restaurant serving lunch and dinner. Cozy dining room with a fireplace with woodstove, pool table, and jukebox. Chicken, fish, shrimp, clams, burgers, and steaks; and homemade lasagna, chili, and pizza; $4-$12. Nacho platters and frozen Margaritas are local favorites. Take out available. Deer and bear often visit the back yard.

Left(right) **Adirondack Trail Motel** (518-648-5044). Ten double units, open year-round; $45-58/couple.

248.0   Left(right) **1870 Bed and Breakfast** (518-648-5377). Family-run rooming house for more than half a century. Five spotless bedrooms with private and shared baths in a lovely home. Large porch with rocking chairs, flower boxes, fireplace, trim lawns, fruit trees, flower garden, raspberry patch, and hiking trail. Tastefully decorated, comfortable, and homey. Your grandmother's home in the Adirondacks. $55-$65/couple with breakfast.

248.1   Left(right) **Indian Lake Health Center** (518-648-5707). Open Monday through Friday, 9-5, and Saturday 2-5. Drop-ins Phone active 24 hours a day.

Left(right) Junction with **Pelon Road**, down which a short walk on the left is the **Indian Lake Town Hall** (518-648-0223) and the **Indian Lake Public Library** (518-648-5444).

Right(left) **Indian Lake Museum**. Open 7-9 PM, summers only.

248.2   Right(left) **Big Dog's Ice Cream** (518-648-0265). Soft ice cream, Ben & Jerry's hard ice cream, frozen yogurt, and hot dogs. Memorial Day daily through Labor Day, then weekends through Columbus Day.

248.3   Right(left) **Key Bank** (518-648-5711).

Left(right) **Indian Lake Post Office** (518-648-5252). ZIP 12842.

Right(left) **Pats Pizzeria** (518-648-6319). Pizza, white pizza, pizza by the slice, calzones, hot and cold hero sandwiches, soup, salads, fresh fruit salad, and cannolies. Tuesday through Friday dinner specials $7-$8. May through early November.

Left(right) **Exquisite Beauty Spa** (518-648-0276). Full service salon: hair, nails, manicures, pedicures, piercing, massage, and tanning.

Right(left) **Lake Theater** (518-648-5950). Memorial Day through Labor Day and weekends through Columbus Day. Also open other festival weekends.

Left(right) **Eldridge Automotive** (518-648-0086). Automobile repair shop.

Right(left) **Marty's Tavern** (518-648-5832). Mexican restaurant and tap room. Mexican (not Tex/Mex) cuisine featuring chili in a bread bowl, nachos, enchiladas, quesadillas, fajitas, etc. On the light side, $3-$8, entrees $6-$12. Children's menu. Tap room has pool table, foosball, and large-screen TV. Restaurant open Thursday through Sunday.

248.4   Left(right) **E. Townsend Chevrolet-Oldsmobile-Geo** (518-648-5544). Dealership.

Right(left) **Indian Lake Chamber of Commerce Information Office** (518-648-5112). Tourist information.

Right(left) **Grandma's Things** (518-648-5589). Locally made crafts. Handmade quilts, pillows, quillows (lap robes which fold up into their own pockets to form pillows), racks, dolls, baskets, and more. Useful, interesting, and fun things.

Left(right) **Oak Barrel Restaurant and Tavern** (518-648-5115). Two dining rooms grace this comfortable and cozy restaurant. The front room is bright and cheerful with a garnet stone fireplace, while the rear is subdued and private. Lunch ($3-$7) and dinner (mostly $9-$15) are served from April through mid-November. Wings, burgers, pizza, spaghetti, chicken, veal, steaks, shrimp, trout, crab legs, and lobster. Vegetarian and low-fat dishes, salad bar, homemade pizza, and desserts. The tavern is the home of the "Old Nassau Bar" and sports a TV and pool table. Something for everyone, even the children.

Left(right) **Oak Barrel** (518-648-5115). Liquor store.

Left(right) **Grand Union** (518-648-5664). Supermarket.

In the left rear of the parking lot between the liquor store and the Grand Union are:

> *Jane & Cathy's (518-648-5908). Breakfast, lunch, and dinner. Casual dining in a bright dining room with large windows and decorated by local art. Specials for all three meals. Homemade soups, pie ala mode, and fifty-cent coffee. Dinner $4-$9.*

> *Village Laundromat (518-648-0222). Laundry, dry cleaning, drop-off, home pick-up, and delivery.*

Right(left) **Cycle N Recycle** (518-648-6385) Second floor second-hand shop and bike rentals. Up the outside stairway around the corner on NY 30. Also the **Bagel Boy**. Bagels and donuts, breakfast bagels, sandwiches, and coffee.

Right(left) Intersection with **NY 30** south to **Sabael** and **Speculator**. Turning right(left) onto NY 30 south yields:

000.0 *Left.* **Pick-it Patch** *(518-648-5660). Cards, newspapers, magazines, postcards, notions, gifts, souvenirs, ceramics, fuzzy animals, candy, and books.*

> *Left.* **Softserve Ice Cream** *(518-648-5660). Ice cream stand, with tables, serving cones, flurries, sundaes, shakes, floats, splits, and sodas. May through Columbus Day.*

000.1 *Right.* **King's Collision and Automotive Center** *(518-648-6327). Automotive repairs and 24-hour towing.*

000.5   Right. **Indian Lake Motel** *(518-648-5859). A charming colony of rough cedar-sided buildings on green lawns under the pines. Motel rooms, efficiencies, and a private chalet with two units, picnic table, grill, and swing set. Entire chalet can house up to 14 people. Towels and linens provided for efficiencies and chalet. Continental breakfast. On snowmobile trail. Motel $40-$47/couple, $210/week. The efficiencies and two chalet units (one with one bath, the other with two) are $48-$70 for two/night and $210-$335/week. Dogs accepted.*

Right. *Junction with* **Ski Hut Road** *and* **Indian Lake Ski Center** *(518-648-5611). On* **Crow Hill**, *a ski center with three slopes, a T-bar lift, a large ice skating rink, and cross-country ski trails. Free to the public.*

000.9   Left. **Parking** *area with scenic view, which is fading due to the growing trees in the foreground. Visit soon or the view will be gone.*

002.0   Left. **Point Breeze Motel** *(518-648-5555). Six motel units and four housekeeping cottages with beach on Indian Lake. Half-log siding exteriors with knotty pine interior give these units a ski lodge appearance. Cozy, comfortable, and neat accommodations with homemade patchwork quilts and frilly pillowcases. Motel rooms $46-$54/couple; cabins for two to four, $355-$385/week. Memorial Day through Columbus Day.*

Left. **Papa Tom's** *(518-648-5623). Genuinely woodsy and rustic north country log cabin restaurant and tavern serving burgers, grinders, sandwiches, and sides for lunch ($3-$5) and meatloaf, lasagna, pork chops, and strip steak for dinner ($5-$12). Specials. Smoking and non-smoking dining rooms. Pool table. Open every day until midnight.*

002.9   Right. **Furnell's Housekeeping Cottages** *(518-648-5505). Five housekeeping cottages housing four to six people in quiet, scenic setting on 65 acres. Screened porches, and* *picnic tables. Memorial Day through Labor Day. Call for rates.*

004.0   Left. **Twin Coves on Indian Lake** *(518-648-5332, 203-743-0653). Quiet and secluded housekeeping cottages on the lake with a private beach. The nine heated cottages are of various configurations and accommodate up to eight people. Open by reservation only from the last weekend in June through Labor day, and weekends in the fall by special arrangement. No pets. Call for rates and availability.*

Entering **Sabael**.

Left. **Sandy Beach Camps** *(518-648-5406). Five heated housekeeping cottages and a beach on Indian Lake. The cottages accommodate from two to six people, and range from $350-$520/week. Open from the last week in June to the first week in September.*

Left. **Smith's Cottage** *(518-648-5222). A lodge with seven bedrooms, 2½ baths, kitchen, living and dining rooms, and two sun porches, plus 11 housekeeping cottages sparsely scattered about the hillside overlooking Indian Lake. The lodge houses 14 ($210/night or $1040/week) and the cottages from two to eight ($45-$160/night or $220-$798/week). All units are heated. Canoe, rowboat, and motorboat rentals. Pets allowed at $7/day, prior approval required. Mid-May through mid-October.*

004.1   Left. **The Lake Store** *(518-648-5222). Meats, groceries, deli, soda fountain, sweats, some general merchandise, and souvenirs.*

004.7   Left. **Sabael Post Office** *(518-648-5791). ZIP 12864.*

004.9   Right. **Squaw-Brook Motel** *(518-648-5262). Attractive, woodsy motel with eight heated units on landscaped* *grounds. Swimming pool, sun deck, screened cabana, and picnicking facilities for outdoor cooking. Hunters have less than a quarter-mile walk to state hunting grounds. May through November. $42-$47/couple.*

007.0   Right. **Trailhead parking** *for* **Snowy Mountain** *hiking trail, 3.4 miles, across Route 28 from parking lot.*

009.0   Left. **Timberlock on Indian Lake** *(518-648-5494). An Adirondack resort since 1899 and surrounded by wilderness, Timberlock describes itself as "rustic but not rough." A wonderful step back in time, the resort offers various-sized, non-electric cabins with wood stove heating, and propane lighting and water heating. There is a large log lodge, a children's lodge, and one-half mile of Indian Lake shore front. Activities include canoeing, kayaking, row boating, motor boating, water skiing, swimming, fishing, tennis, horseback riding, archery, children's playground, and more. Adult rates are $560-$700/person/week or $93-$116/person/day. Open June through October.*

Beautiful Indian Lake and some of its islands.

011.7   Left. **Indian Lake Islands Public Campground** *(518-648-5300). Parking area and boat launch for boat-access camping on Indian Lake. There are 55 tent sites and six picnic areas with tables and fireplaces on the islands and along the shores of Indian Lake, and accessible by boat only. One of the few remaining opportunities to truly get away from it all.*

011.9   Right. **Lewey Lake Public Campground** *(518-648-5266). More than 200 sites for tents and R/V's, some handicapped accessible. Picnic area, beach, hiking, fishing, biking, canoeing (rentals available), boating, and boat launches on Lewey Lake and Indian Lake. Dump station.*

End of NY 30 south coverage.

Junction of Route 28 and **NY 30** in the middle of Indian Lake. Continuing south on Route 28.

Designated bike route begins on east side of Indian Lake and continues for the 12-mile descent from the Adirondack Mountains to North River.

Left(right) **Pine's Country Store** (518-648-5212). General store and ServiStar Hardware store. Downstairs is a hardware store, and upstairs is a general store with clothing, T-shirts, sweats, and more. The first place to look for what you need.

Left(right) **Adirondack Mountain Sports** (518-648-0215). Arctic Cat snowmobile dealership. ATV's and jet skis.

248.5   Right(left) **Stewart's Shops** (518-648-5992). Convenience store, Mobil gas, and an ATM.

Left(right) **Springs General Store** (518-648-6105). Sporting goods. Boats, paddles, fishing tackle, hunting gear, camping supplies, toboggans, snowshoes, Adirondack pack baskets, Adirondack chairs, swings, books, maps, T-shirts, sweats, souvenirs, maple syrup, knives, ammo, and worms.

Left(right) **Adventure Sports Rafting Company** (518-648-5812). White water day rafting on the Hudson and Moose Rivers.

248.6   Left(right) **Mary Kay's Original Oil Paintings**. Paintings and ceramic gifts.

248.8   Right(left) **State Police** (518-648-5757).

Left(right) **Byron Park** on the shores of **Adirondack Lake**. Public dock and fireplace.

248.9   Right(left) **Geandreau's Cabins** (518-648-5500). Six well-maintained, country-looking housekeeping cabins with screened porches. The cabins are heated, sleep from four to six, and linens and towels are provided; $410-$450/week. Picnic area and playground, and pets are welcome. Cross-country ski from the premises. Canoes and rowboats available.

249.0   Leaving(entering) **Indian Lake**.

Left(right) **Byron Park Recreation Area** (518-648-6483). Public beach at the site of the Lake Adirondack Dam. Rest rooms. July through Labor Day.

249.2   Right(left) **Lone Birch Motel** (518-648-5225). Accommodations to fit everyone's preference. Four motel rooms with two double beds each; three condo units that sleep four to six; and a chalet-style cottage with sleeping loft, spiral staircase, and deck, sleeping up to eight. Heat, A/C, cable, and linens. Picnic areas with tables and grills, access to snowmobile and cross-country ski trails. Motel rooms are $45-$48/couple. Condos and cottage are $65-$70/couple, two-night minimum, and $400-$450/week for three persons. Comfortable, contemporary lodging with all the comforts of home.

249.6   Right(left) Grave of Reuben Rist, first settler of Indian Lake, 1836.

249.8   Left(right) Junction with **Chain Lakes Road**, a dirt road along the banks of Lake Abanakee and the Indian River:

*000.6   Right.   **Indian Lake Public Beach** (518-648-5335). Parking area and bath house. Swimming in Lake Abanakee.*

*000.7   Right.   **Lake Abanakee** on the right and a small pond on the left.   **BOATERS NOTE**: the dam across the Indian River which forms Lake Abanakee and toward which the current flows is just one-third mile downstream.*

*001.0   Right.   Dam across **Indian River** forming **Lake Abanakee**. Above the dam is beautiful, quiet Lake Abanakee. Below the dam is white water. A sign states that a white water release occurs between 10 AM and noon daily.*

001.3   Right. White water canoe launching site. A Department of Environmental Conservation sign for the Indian River Waterway Access Site notes: "Caution: Dangerous rapids downstream. If you are unsure of your ability or your watercraft, you should utilize the services of a river outfitter. A list of river outfitters is available at the Indian Lake Town Hall." This is the launching site for Hudson River Gorge canoe, kayak, and rafting trips. The Indian River empties into the Hudson River 2½ miles downstream.

End of coverage of Chain Lakes Road.

249.9   Right(left) **Parking** area with magnificent views of **Lake Abanakee.**

250.0   Left(right) Homemade quilts, crafts, and maple syrup for sale in private home.

Continuing east from Indian Lake to North River, Route 28 descends quickly from the Adirondack Mountains.   For the next 10 miles the roadside mer-chants are few and the views magnificent. You could say there is nothing at all along this 10-mile stretch of road, unless you count the scenery, the natural mountain flora, and the marvelous views. Around every bend and over every hill crest lies a different Adirondack postcard scene. If you come to the Adirondacks from the east to escape the rat race of the everyday world, you're lucky to have such a pleasant ride for the return trip home. And just because you leave the mountains doesn't mean you leave nature. At the bottom of the major descent, Route 28's journey southeast is joined by the mighty Hudson River, here in its adolescent stage, often displaying its moods as white water.

Speaking of white water, the Hudson River Gorge is one of the best white water rivers in the country.   Its watery thrills, heightened by spring snowmelt, are amplified by the rugged and pristine Adirondack wilderness. A number of white water outfits in Indian Lake, North River, and North Creek run rafting trips down this famous stretch of water.   If you're physically fit, adventurous, and looking for excitement, give one of them a call. Outrageous water through outrageous forest yields an outrageous Adirondack experience.

251.1   Left(right) **Indian Lake Real Estate** (518-648-5349).

254.5   Designated bike route.

256.4   Beautiful view of the mountains as you start down a hill. Along this stretch of Route 28 sections of Old Route 28 branch off Route 28, some for a short distance and some for a few miles, and come back out to Route 28 again. These loops provide interesting excursions into the past.

260.6   **Hamilton/Warren** county line, **Indian Lake/Johnsburg** town line, entering(leaving) village of **North River**.

Right(left) Junction with **Thirteenth Lake Road**, which climbs from 1060 feet above sea level to more than 1800 feet, toward Siamese Ponds Wilderness Area:

001.4   *Right. **North Country Sports** (518-251-4299). Fishing tackle, guns, licenses, etc.*

003.2   *Right. Junction with **Beach Road**, down which is **Thirteenth Lake** and:*

003.9   *Right. Junction with **Old Farm Road** to **Old Farm Clearing** and the **Siamese Ponds Wilderness Area** (518-623-3671). About 112,000 acres (175 square miles!) of mountains, lakes, ponds, streams, and wildlife. This area is rugged, remote, and little visited. Recreational facilities include 33 miles of marked hiking trails (many of which are also excellent cross-country ski trails), primitive tent*

000.8.   *Trailhead parking. At this lot begins the trail to **Peaked Mountain Pond** (2.5 miles) and **Peaked Mountain** (3.0). The lot also provides access to **Thirteenth Lake** and 21 tent sites, some reachable by foot and some only by boat.*

sites, and four lean-tos. Hiking, cross-country skiing, snowshoeing, fishing, hunting, and trapping are all allowed in the wilderness area.

*004.3   Left. **Garnet Hill Lodge and Cross-Country Ski Center** (518-251-2821) and **Loghouse Restaurant**. At 2,000' elevation in the middle of the Adirondacks adjacent to the Siamese Ponds Wilderness Area, the drive up the road makes you think you're approaching Shangri La. The dark brown log lodge with its red trim is massive. The interior pine walls and exposed log beams are all of varnished wood, accented by red garnet fireplaces, Adirondack twig furniture, and breathtaking views of the mountains and Thirteenth Lake. Twenty-seven guest rooms in four impressive buildings. Huge enclosed porch, TV/reading room with fireplace, lounges, hot tub, sauna, pool table, table tennis, tennis courts, and beach. Cross-country skiing and mountain biking on more than 50 kilometers of trails, 2km of which are lighted. Ski and bike downhill and ride the shuttle bus back. Ski lessons, ski shop, and ski and mountain bike rentals. Also a fly fishing school, naturalist programs, and more. Lodging is $140-$220/couple,   breakfast   and   dinner   included. Representative dinner entrees are seafood grille, steak au poivre, chicken stir-fry, and artichokes Barigoule. A perfect place to treat yourself to an outstanding Adirondack experience.*

End of Thirteenth Lake Road coverage.

Right(left) **Towne Grocery** (518-251-2677). Groceries, ice cream, soft drinks, candy, tobacco, newspapers, greeting cards, film, maps, etc.

Left(right) **Warren County Canoe Access Site** and picnic area alongside the Hudson River.

260.9   Right(left) **North River Post Office** (518-251-3311). ZIP 12856.

Right(left) **North River Guest House** (518-251-4643, 413-566-0239). A Civil War-period home, furnished with antiques, and having four bedrooms sleeping up to seven, a shared bath, dining room, living room, and kitchen. Rates are $400-$700/week. Add 20 percent for holidays. Well-behaved pets welcome.

261.2   Left(right) **Warren County Canoe Access Site** and picnic area alongside the Hudson River.

261.3   Right(left) Junction with **Barton Mines Road**:

> *000.0   Left. **Jasco Minerals** (518-251-3196). Mineral, fossil, crystal, and jewelry shop with items from around the world. Local and imported garnet a specialty. Local Gore Mountain red garnet is New York State's gemstone. Custom gold and silver jewelry. Stones, stone carvings, coral, gifts, etc.*

> *005.0   **Highwinds Inn** (518-251-3760, 800-241-1923). A lovely, 1933 home offering gracious accommodations in four bedrooms, each with an outstanding view and a private bath. Glassed-in dining room, fireplace, full breakfasts, gourmet dinners, and 25 kilometers of trails for hiking, mountain biking, or ski touring. Rates are $140-$170 per couple, breakfast and dinner included. Special mid-week rates. Bed and breakfast sometimes available. Also available are wilderness cabins for roughing it in the mountains. The cabins offer propane heating and cooking (or dine at the inn), outdoor toilets, and water must be carried in. They are a mile and one-half walk/ski from the inn, can accommodate six people each, and are $75 per cabin per night.*

> ***Gore Mountain Garnet Mine and Mineral Shop** (518-251-2706). Guided tours of an open pit garnet mine. Also a shop offering gem stones, jewelry, etc. Last weekend in June through Labor Day.*

End of Barton Mines Road coverage.

261.4   Right(left) **Whitewater Challengers** (518-251-3746, 800-443-RAFT).   White water rafting trips covering three miles on the Indian River and 13 miles on the Hudson River through the Hudson River Gorge, and ending here.   Also canoe, kayak, and equipment sales and rentals.   Kayak clinics, shuttle buses, and gift shop.   Also plan to offer overnight Hudson River Gorge camping trips.   April through Columbus Day.

263.1   Left(right) **Warren County Canoe Access Site** parking area alongside the Hudson River.

263.4   Railroad tracks cross the road diagonally and caused my small, top-heavy motor home to sway unexpectedly.

263.9   Right(left) **Riverwood** (518-251-2798).   Bar and restaurant. Woodsy and homey bar with a fireplace, TV, aquarium, pool table, dart board, and horseshoe pits.   Appetizers, finger foods, chili, pizza; big, homemade specialty sandwiches on home-baked breads and rolls ($4-$7).   Occasional live entertainment.   One of the few restaurants directly on Route 28 between Warrensburg and Indian Lake.

265.3   Left(right) Junction with **Main Street** to **North Creek** business district.   See Chapter 35, *North Creek,* for North Creek's business district coverage.   See Chapter 36, *North Creek to Warrensburg*, for continued Route 28 coverage.

35

North Creek

Although North Creek was bypassed by the rerouting of Route 28 in the early 1960's, it remains the only cluster of stores and shops along the 35 miles of Route 28 between Warrensburg and Indian Lake. But its real claim to fame is that it is a ski town. Or, perhaps its real claim to fame is as a white water rafting town. Or, maybe it's famous for its canoeing and kayaking. Or perhaps the mountain biking. Or the hiking. Or even the leaf peeping. Whatever the outdoor recreation, North Creek offers it in spades.

North Creek has lately seen growth, and it's getting more charming by the minute, attracting even more growth. It is still a small community in which almost everybody knows almost everybody else. And, unlike some other small communities along Route 28 which focus on their pasts, North Creek is facing the opposite direction, focusing on its future, and moving resolutely toward the twenty-first century.

Each year in mid-September North Creek hosts Teddy Roosevelt Bull Moose Days, re-enacting Roosevelt's original motorcade from Newcomb to the North Creek train station, where Theodore Roosevelt first learned that, due to the assassination of President William McKinley, he had become president of the United States. Also in September, Gore Mountain Ski Area hosts a Sports Fair featuring various sports equipment and accessories offered by Warren County sporting goods dealers. In October, Gore Mountain Ski Area hosts an International Fall Foliage Festival with chairlift rides, a crafts show, music, dancing, children's programs, food and drink, and more.

For tourist information and lodging assistance in North Creek and the Gore Mountain region, call the Gore Mountain Region Chamber of Commerce Accommodation and Visitors Bureau on 518-251-2612 or 800-880-GORE.

The Town of Johnsburg Historical Society has laid out a walking tour of the hamlet of North Creek. The tour is less than a half-mile long. It begins at the North Creek Railroad Depot on Railroad Place and ends at the Bottoms Up Building at the corner of Main Street and Wade Avenue. Tour descriptions are available from the chamber of commerce office on Main Street and the historical society office at the junction of Route 28 and NY 8 in Wevertown. Also, the historical society has published a book, *River, Rails and Ski Trails*, on the history of the town of Johnsburg. It is available at the North Creek Deli & Marketplace on Main Street.

000.0   North end of **North Creek's Main Street** at its junction with **Route 28**.

000.4   Left. Junction with **Railroad Place**, down which a few steps is:

> The **North Creek Railway Station**, where Vice President Theodore Roosevelt first learned of the assassination of President William McKinley on September 14, 1901, and that Roosevelt had become president of the United States. Planning to commence operation on September 1, 1998, is the **Upper Hudson River Rail Road** (518-251-5334), running eight-and-one-half mile, hour-and-one-half-long, round-trip tourist excursions between here and Riverside Station in Riparius.

Right. **Copperfield Inn** (518-251-2500, 800-424-9910). Fine colonial-styled inn with 24 rooms and seven suites. A marble foyer, high ceilings, brass chandeliers, and elegant furnishings belie the inn's Adirondack Park location. Amenities include a full-service restaurant (dinner entrees $14-$27), lounge, heated pool, Jacuzzi, tennis court, health center, and ski shuttle bus to Gore Mountain. Rooms have either two queen- or one king-sized bed, TV, VCR, and Sony Playstation, $110-$195/couple/night. The suites, with varied features, may have two rooms, a whirlpool tub, a fireplace, a patio, a balcony, or more, and are $125-$325/couple.

Room and suite rates include breakfast. The new **Trapper's Tavern** is a re-creation of an Adirondack lodge, with exposed rough-hewn beams, a river stone fireplace, twig furniture, deer-antler chandeliers, and a carved, wooden bear. It has a bandstand, and is a popular gathering place for visitors and locals alike. Luxury accommodations in the Adirondacks.

Right. **Trimmers Full Service Salon** (518-251-0815). In Copperfield Inn.

Left. **Donato's** (518-251-5159). Casual, country Italian restaurant serving Italian favorites and specialties, traditional and gourmet pizza, and more. Open for lunch and dinner, with dining room, takeout, and delivery service. Most entrees $7-$12.

Left. **Smith's Restaurant** (518-251-9965). Since 1924. Serving breakfast, lunch, and dinner, and offering traditional chicken, beef, lamb, pork, and seafood dinners, as well as German-style knockwurst, sauerbraten, sauerkraut, and spätzle. The food is prepared with all fresh ingredients, and all baked goods are prepared on the premises. One or two turkeys are also roasted every day. Plate-filling entrees are $8-$14. Open seven days year 'round.

Left. **Hudson River Trading Co.** (518-251-4461). Co-op antique store and framing shop. Rustic furniture, antiques, north country products, and more. Hours vary by season; open seven days from Independence Day through Labor Day.

Right. **North Creek Chamber of Commerce** (518-251-2612). Tourist info.

Right. **Reflections**. Gift shop.

Right. **Whitewater World** (800-WHITEWATER). Four to five hours of white water rafting on 13 tumultuous miles of the Upper Hudson through the middle of awesome, rugged, and unspoiled wilderness. Daily April through June, weekends September through mid-October. Tuesdays, Thursdays, Saturdays, and

Sundays in summer, depending on the water level. Also, two-day overnight trips.

Left. **Sheer Style Salon** (518-251-5311).

000.5   Left. **Mountain Drugs and Sundries** (518-251-3777). Pharmacy, cards, postcards, books, toys, games, etc.

Left.   **North Creek Deli & Marketplace** (518-251-2977). Market, deli, on-site bakery, and general store.   Farm-fresh vegetables, soups, salads, subs, coffee, soft ice cream, and maple syrup. Books, gifts, Adirondack products, bird houses, clothing, dry goods, footwear, moccasins, cookwear, plush toys, sleds, and more. Also travelers' info.

Right. **Grand Union** (518-251-4669). Supermarket.

Right. **Adirondack Spirits** (518-251-3898). Wine and liquor.

Right. **Mountain & Boardertown** (518-251-3111). An outdoors store with excitement. This unique store has a stream running through it, and indoor thunder storms erupt every 55 minutes. Featured are skis, snowboards, snowshoes, in-line skates, skateboards, wake boards, mountain bikes, BMX bikes, freestyle bikes, hiking and climbing gear, flat water and white water paddling equipment, boots, clothing, accessories, gadgets, books, maps, and more. Challenging activities include an indoor climbing wall, plus interactive games for downhill ski racing, snowboarding, skateboarding, waterskiing, and jet skiing. Ski, snowboard, and bike rentals, plus a shuttle service to and from Gore Mountain. Also the **Saloon and Grill**, serving breakfast, lunch, and dinner, plus live entertainment. And more to come.

000.6   Left. **Morwood IGA Market** (518-251-2775). Supermarket.

Left. **Marsha's Family Restaurant** (518-251-5750). Serving breakfast, lunch, and dinner seven days a week. Home-cooked specialties include Texas-style French toast, waffles, fresh roasted turkey, and chicken cordon bleu. Sandwiches, burgers, steaks, daily specials, seniors menu, and children's menu. Dinner entrees $8-$13. Beer and wine also served.

Right. **Air Land Motor Parts** (518-251-2514). Parts Plus auto store.

Left. **Alpine Motel** (518-251-2451). Private baths, double beds, phones, cable TV, and A/C. Seventeen units in the middle of the village, $35-$55. Ski season is high season.

Left. Junction with **Circle Avenue**, down which a few steps on the left is the **North Creek Post Office** (518-251-2121). ZIP 12853.

Left. **Braley & Noxon Pro Hardware** (518-251-2855). Hardware and housewares.

Left. **Residents Committee to Protect the Adirondacks** (518-251-4257).

Left. **P J's Jewelry Shoppe** (518-251-2582). Jewelry, gifts, souvenirs, videos, and fax.

000.7   Left. **Key Bank** (518-251-2441). 24-hour ATM.

Left. **Tech Services Company** (518-251-2250). Computer sales and service.

Right. **Broderick Real Estate** (518-251-0103).

Junction with **NY 28N**. Turning right on NY 28N south takes you in 0.1 mile to **Route 28**.

Turning left onto **NY 28N** north (**Bridge Street**) and walking a few steps takes you to the following:

> Left. ***Four Seasons Floral Shop*** *(518-251-3119). Fresh cut, dried, and silk flowers; house plants, stuffed animals, gifts, food baskets, and wire service.*

*Right. **North Creek Laundromat** (518-251-3133). Same day wash-dry-fold drop-off service.*

*NY 28N continues north to **Minerva** and **Newcomb**. End of NY 28N north coverage.*

000.8   Left. **Bacon's Service Center** (518-251-3638). Auto service and 24-hour towing.

Right. **Town of Johnsburg Library** (518-251-4343). Entrance on right side of the town hall.

Right. **Town of Johnsburg Town Hall** (518-251-3011).

000.9   Left. **Goose Pond Inn** (518-251-3434). This country bed and breakfast, built in 1894, occupies a large, yellow clapboard house with a slate roof. Outside are a large tree in the front yard from which hangs a double swing, and the namesake goose pond. Inside there are four guest rooms, each with a queen-sized bed and private bath, and furnished like a country gift shop with soft, casual, and comfortable furniture. The guest living room has a fireplace with a wood-burning stove, and there are two dining rooms, a game room, a sauna, and a hot tub. Open year round, rates are $70-95/couple including full gourmet breakfast.

001.8   Junction with **Route 28** at south end of North Creek.

End of North Creek Main Street coverage.

North Creek to Warrensburg

265.3   Left(right) Junction with **Main Street** to **North Creek** business district. See Chapter 35, *North Creek*, for North Creek business district coverage.

265.5   Junction with **Ski Bowl Road**. Turning left(right) onto Ski Bowl Road takes you to North Creek's **Main Street** and business district.

Turning right(left) down **Ski Bowl Road** are:

*000.0   Left.   **North Creek Health Center** (518-251-2541). Emergency care facility. Member of Hudson Headwaters Health Network. Open Mondays through Wednesdays and Fridays 9-5, Thursdays 9-8, Saturdays 9-12.*

*000.2   **North Creek Ski Bowl** (518-251-5120).   Beginner's ski slope with T-bar lift and warming hut, open free to all on winter weekends and school holidays. **Schaefer Hiking Trail** to **Burnt Ridge** and the fire tower at the summit of **Gore Mountain** (4.5 miles).   The trail ends in winter at Burnt Ridge at the edge of Gore Mountain ski slopes. Children's playground, pavilion, picnic tables, baseball diamond, basketball court, and tennis courts.   Also **Dr. Jacques Grunblatt Memorial Beach** south of the ski bowl.*

*001.0   Stop sign.   Turn left for **Route 28**.*

*001.2   Junction of southern end of **Ski Bowl Road** with **Route 28**.
End of Ski Bowl Road coverage.*

265.9   Left(right) Junction with **NY 28N** north to **North Creek** business district, 0.1 mile.

266.1   Right(left) Junction with south end of **Ski Bowl Road** (see above).

266.2   Left(right) Junction with **Peacefull [sic] Valley Road** to **North Creek's Main Street.**

266.6   Right(left) Junction with **Peaceful [sic] Valley Road** to **Gore Mountain Ski Area:**

*000.2   Right.   **Valhaus Motel** (518-251-2700).   Comfortable accommodations in an unspoiled setting between two streams, just down the road from Gore Mountain Ski Area. Twelve units, $40-$65/couple, plus a one-bedroom apartment available by the week or longer.   Nice, quiet motel with free coffee and donuts in the morning.*

*000.5   Right. **Gore Mountain Ski Area** (518-251-2411). Opened in 1964, this family-oriented ski and snowboard area has 49 trails on 2,100 vertical feet.   Uphill service is by nine lifts, including a triple chair, two quad chairs, and New York State's only gondola.   Eleven kilometers of cross-country and telemark trails are split between the base level and Burnt Ridge up on the mountain. Lodge with cafeteria and cocktail lounge, ski shop, downhill and cross-country ski and snowboard rentals, and lessons. May through Columbus Day brings weekend mountain biking (Fridays through Sundays from Independence Day to Labor Day, Saturdays and Sundays other times) with lift service, bike rentals, and a two-and-one-half mile skyride to the 3,600' peak of the mountain.*

*000.9   Right.   **Inn on Gore Mountain** (518-251-2111).   Ski chalets on the pine-studded side of Gore Mountain.   Four chalets housing 16 rooms sleeping up to four in each room*

($49-$75/couple). Large restaurant with stone fireplace, wood-burning stove, knotty-pine bar, and a casual, ski-lodge atmosphere. Varied menu offers soups, salads, starters, sandwiches, and burgers, as well as dinner entrees of shrimp, chicken, pasta, and steaks (11-$14). Banquet room. Restaurant open seven days during winter, otherwise Thursdays through Sundays.

*002.5   Right.   **Northwind   Lodge**   (518-251-2522,   888-NY-GETAWAY). Rustic, scenic, and quiet motel with 11 units (most non-smoking); with a full-service, non-smoking, Alpine-style restaurant and bar. Also a gazebo and a private, outdoor pool surrounded by a wall of pine trees, all on two and one-half landscaped acres. Restaurant open for breakfast with a Texas flair ($3-$6) and dinner of steaks, seafood, and heart-healthy entrees ($7-$16). More than 20 different beers and a nice wine list. $45-$70/-couple.   Weekend lodging packages. Chocolate chip cookies on your pillow as you turn in.*

*003.9   Junction with **NY 8**. Turning left takes you immediately to:*

*Left.   **Black Mountain Ski Lodge and Motel** (518-251-2800).   Twenty-five rooms, a swimming pool, and an Alpine-styled ski lodge with large fireplace and game room, all in a dark brown wooden building with yellow trim and a bright interior. Rooms $47-65/couple, mini-efficiencies (with small refrigerator and microwave) $138-$168/couple for two days. Dining room open for breakfast. Neat, tidy, and well-maintained.*

End of Peaceful Valley Road coverage.

266.9   Right(left) **The Summit at Gore Mountain** (518-251-4180, 800-220-0333). One-, two-, and three-bedroom townhouse rentals. Fireplaces, and some Jacuzzi's. Price range for one bedroom is $300-$400 for two nights. Three nights for the price of two in non-holiday weeks. Call for other rates.

267.1   Left(right) Junction with southern end of **Main Street**.

Left(right) **Cunningham's Ski Barn** and **Hudson River Rafting Company** (518-251-3215, 800-888-RAFT). A ski shop since 1934, offering downhill and cross-country (X-C) skis, clothing and accessories, plus a full-service ski shop. Ski and snowshoe rentals, X-C lessons. Thirty kilometers of groomed X-C trails. Also, white water rafting trips on the Hudson.

267.2   Right(left) **Steven's Auto Repair** (518-251-2521). Motor vehicle repair shop.

267.4   Left(right) **Stewart's Shops** (518-251-9903). Convenience store, gas, picnic tables, and ATM.

267.5   Left(right) **Nice 'n' Easy** (518-251-3667). Deli, groceries, fast food, Mobil gas, and ATM.

267.5   Right(left) **Gore Village** (518-251-4141, 800-666-3757). Luxury town homes with three bedrooms and two and one-half baths, fireplace, some with Jacuzzi's, accommodating up to eight people, available for rental at $250-$500 per couple for three nights (non-holiday periods). One-night stays as available.

267.6   Leaving(entering) **North Creek**.

269.7   Left(right) **Gore Mountain Lodge** (518-251-5268). Under new ownership, 12 motel units and a bar with a fireplace and a pool table. New owner serves light fare foods through the summer and, when last contacted, was planning to re-open the full restaurant. Motel rooms $60/couple.

270.0   Left(right) **Old Farmhouse Rocker Shop**. Gifts, quilts, and more in private home.

270.4   Left(right) **White Pine Restaurant** (518-251-2233). Rustic building with woodsy, barnside interior serving breakfast, lunch, and dinner. Exposed-beam ceiling, wooden floors, pine tables, and vinyl-covered pine armchairs, and vinyl and chrome counter stools.

Varied menu with soup and salad bar. Wednesday night all-you-can-eat spaghetti and meatballs; Friday night all-you-can-eat fish fry. Sunday morning breakfast buffet, $6. Gift shop. One of the few restaurants directly on Route 28 between Warrensburg and Indian Lake. Comfortable and relaxed atmosphere.

271.1   Entering /leaving **Wevertown.**

271.2   Left(right) **Town of Johnsburg Historical Society** (518-251-5811).

Right(left) **Pearsall Realty** (518-251-2422).

271.3   Flashing traffic light at junction with **NY 8**:

Making a left(right) onto **NY 8** east yields:

*000.1   Right.   **Wevertown Post Office** (518-251-3791) ZIP 12886.*

*Continuing east on NY 8 a few miles takes you to a canoe launching site on the **Hudson River**. Beyond the Hudson, NY 8 can take you to **Riparius**, **Loon Lake**, **Chestertown**, **Dynamite Hill Ski Area**, **US 9**, and **I-87 (Northway)** Exit 25.*

End of coverage of NY 8 east.

Making a right(left) onto **NY 8** west takes you to:

*000.8   Left.   **Cabins at Mill Creek** (518-251-4238). One cabin with two bedrooms, fireplace, kitchen, and a bath, $90/night.*

*001.3   Entering **Johnsburg**.*

*001.5   Left.   **Mosher's Corner Country Diner**. Going west, the last diner until Speculator, 32 miles away. Serving breakfast, lunch, and dinner daily, except for 3 PM close* *on Sundays and Mondays. Reasonably priced with most dinners $7-$9; dinner specials $6. Knotty pine throughout; rear porch with mountain views.*

001.6   *Left.* **Johnsburg Post Office** *(518-251-2238). ZIP 12843.*

Right. **Johnsburg Public Market** *(518-251-3943). General merchandise, groceries, soft ice cream, and beverages. Also daily homemade breakfasts; burgers, pizza, subs, sandwiches, onion rings, etc.; chicken, shrimp, clam, and fish dinners.*

002.0   *Leaving* **Johnsburg***.*

003.7   *Right.* **Black Mountain Ski Lodge and Motel** *(518-251-2800). See description on Peaceful Valley Road earlier in this chapter.*

Right. *Junction with* **Peaceful Valley Road***, which goes past* **Gore Mountain Ski Area** *and back to* **North Creek***.*

End of coverage of NY 8 west.

271.3   Right(left) **Beaver Brook Outfitters** (518-251-3394, 888-454-8433). All-season sport shop in an old church offering quality equipment. Camping and fishing equipment, packs, hiking boots, snowshoes, outdoor wear, and wet and dry flies. Books, guidebooks, and maps. River rafting for fun or for fishing. Two- and three-day rafting trips on the Hudson for fishing and camping, with rower and all equipment provided, freeing guests to concentrate on fishing, photography, etc. Guided stream and pond fishing. Canoe, downhill ski, snowboard, and snowshoe rentals. Ski tuning shop.

271.4   Right(left) **Mill Creek Public Fishing Stream**.

271.5   Leaving(entering) **Wevertown**.

272.1   Left(right) **Dillon Hill Trading Post** (518-251-3576). Tavern with a pool table.

272.9   Right(left) **Mountainaire Adventures** (518-251-2194, 800-950-2194).   A bed and breakfast in a converted farm house with four double rooms with private baths, plus a handicapped-accessible, two-story, three-bedroom, housekeeping chalet for up to 10 people. Hot tub, sauna, and game room. Arranged adventures include eco and historic tours; fishing trips; canoeing, kayaking, rafting, X-C skiing, cycling, backpacking adventures, and more. Also canoe and bike rentals.   Bed and breakfast $55-$75/couple, including an all-you-can-eat, cooked-to-order breakfast. Chalet $590-$800/six people/week. Call for other rates.

275.7   Left(right) **Hansel Gretel Craft Shop**. Country wood crafts and gifts in a small building set beneath pine trees. Signs, baskets, bird feeders, paintings on slate roof shingles, stitchery, and quilting.

276.7   Crossing **Glen Creek**, entering **The Glen**.

276.9   Right(left) **Wildwaters Outdoor Center** and the **Glen House B&B** (518-494-4984, 800-867-2335). A one-stop shop for rafters, canoeists, and kayakers who don't have their own equipment and who need a place to stay. Also, one- to two-day rafting trips on the Hudson, and one- to five-day kayaking and canoe clinics on the Hudson.   The Glen House has nine rooms and four baths at $45/room, two to three people per room.

Johnsburg/Thurman town line.

277.0   Right(left) Junction with **Glen-Athol Road**:

*000.0   Left.   **Warren County Canoe Access Site** immediately under the bridge over the Hudson.*

*003.1   Left.   **Daggett Lake Campsite** (518-623-2198). Camping, water skiing, hiking, mountain biking, fly fishing, and more. Sixty wooded sites for tents and R/V's, with no- to full-hookups, $18-$24/night/two. Some 700 acres with an*

85-acre private lake with two water skiing slalom courses. Hire the ski boat and its driver for water skiing or beginner to advanced water skiing lessons. Five miles of hiking trails, plus a separate five miles of mountain biking trails. Also swimming, fly fishing for trout, canoeing, and row boating. All activities available to campers and non-campers alike. Canoe, row boat, and paddle boat rentals; store, and laundry. Open mid-April through mid-October.

*End of **Glen-Athol Road** coverage.*

277.1   Crossing the **Hudson River. Thurman/Chester** town line.

277.2   Left(right) Junction with **Friends Lake Road (CR 8)**:

*000.2   Right. **Stuff & Things**. Antiques and clothing.*

*000.8   Right. Junction with **Atateka Drive**, down which is:*

*001.7   Right.   **Circle B Ranch** (518-494-4074). Horseback riding stable. Guided, one-hour rides, $17. Group rates for 10 or more people. Hay rides and sleigh rides. Open all year.*

End of Atateka Drive coverage.

*004.1   Left. **Friends Lake Inn and Nordic Ski Center** (518-494-4751). This inn, built in the 1860's, offers gracious country lodging, dining, and cross-country skiing. Well-known for its restaurant and its huge 14,000-bottle wine cellar, the inn has two lovely dining rooms, each with a fireplace and beautiful southern yellow pine and chestnut woodwork; a bar; and a private dining room in the wine cellar. Fourteen air-conditioned guest rooms, each beautifully decorated and appointed. Queen-sized beds, tasteful furniture, window seats, and some Jacuzzi's. One room received the Waverly Country Inn Room of the Year Award. Amenities include large grounds with a gazebo, a double swing, Adirondack chairs, a fishpond, a hot tub,* *and a beach on the lake. The full-service ski touring center includes a warming hut with wood stove, ski rentals, 32 kilometers of groomed cross-country ski trails, plus snowshoe trails.   Lodging $135-$325/couple, including breakfast and dinner. Other lodging/meal plans available. Restaurant open to the public for dinner, $19-$25. Lovely.*

End of Friends Lake Road coverage.

278.0   Chester/Warrensburg town line.

The Hudson River in its adolescence north of Warrensburg.

280.4   Right(left) Junction with **Hudson Street Extension/Golf Course Road,** which runs along the **Hudson River** to **Warrensburg.** Down Hudson Street Extension/Golf Course Road are the following (see descriptions on Hudson Street in Chapter 37, US 9 Through Warrensburg):

*02.1   Right. **Warren County Recreational Day Use Area** (518-623-2877).*

*002.3   Right. **Cronin's Golf Resort** (518-623-9336).*

*003.4   Left. State of New York **Department of Environmental Conservation** Headquarters (518-623-3671).*

*003.7   Right. **Echo Lake Road** to the **Warren County Fish Hatchery** (518-623-2877).*

*003.8   Right. **Morry Stein Park and Beach at Echo Lake** (518-623-9511).*

*004.7. Junction with **Elm Street** and **Main Street** in the center of **Warrensburg**.*

End of Hudson Street Extension/Golf Course Road coverage.

281.1   Right(left) **Cozy Cabin Stove and Fireplace Shop** (518-623-4349).

281.5   Right(left) **Country Carvings**. Chain saw carvings.

281.7   Left(right) **Fine Finish Antiques** (518-623-2428). Furniture, antiques, and collectibles. Also furniture refinishing and chair caning.

281.8   Right(left) **House on the Hill** (518-623-9390, 800-221-9390). A perfectly lovely, non-smoking bed and breakfast for the whole family in an ornate eighteenth-century house with a wrap-around porch. About 175 acres with hiking, biking, and cross-country ski trails provide room to roam. Inside are five guest rooms with private and shared baths, all exquisitely decorated in antiques, genuine art, and handiwork. Two rooms have Jacuzzis. The one in the honeymoon suite is double-sized. Full, made-to-order breakfasts in a charming dining room. Satellite TV. Ducks, geese, and rabbits abound on the property. A perfectly exquisite place to relax. $99-$149/couple.

282.1   Northern end of **Route 28** at its junction with **US 9**. Traveling in a northerly direction this intersection is known as the "Gateway to the Adirondacks".

End of coverage of Route 28. See Chapter 37, *US 9 Through Warrensburg*, for coverage of **US 9** through **Warrensburg** to **New York's Northway (I-87)** exit 23.

The end of the road.

37

US 9 Through Warrensburg

Warrensburg (formerly Warrensburgh) is located just above the confluence of the Schroon and Hudson Rivers. It is thought to have been settled in 1784. Settlers originally came for the abundant water power and the forests for lumber. Sawmills, grist mills, and tanneries were soon established. Later, the railroad brought nature lovers to the area and boarding houses were built to accommodate them. Today the boarding houses have been replaced by campgrounds, motels, and B&B's, and the current nature lovers come by car and recreational vehicle instead of by train. Annual events include an Arts, Crafts, and Collectibles Festival in July, the Warren County Fair in August, and the World's Largest Garage Sale and Fall Foliage Festival in October. History and architectural buffs can take the Architectural Heritage Tour of the village's historic buildings, some of which date from before 1800. Other Warrensburg attractions include the Warren County Recreational Day Use Area with its hiking and cross-country ski trails, the Warren County Fish Hatchery, and Morry Stein Park and Beach at Echo Lake.

282.1   Junction of **Route 28** with **US 9** at the northern end of Route 28. Turn right(left) from Route 28 onto US 9 south. Coverage continues of US 9 south through Warrensburg to I-87.

Left(right) **Discoveries** (518-623-4567). New and used treasures. A cornucopia of unusual and very old things which have withstood the test of time because they were well designed and well built. Most items are from the fifties and before. Jewelry, cameras, clocks, photographs, frames, lamps, kitchen utensils, chinaware, glassware, silverware, baskets, gemstones, rings, toys, tools, fishing rods, children's clothes, plush toys, sporting goods, drafting kits, locks, furniture, books, and much more.   Also custom silver jewelry creations. Almost a museum.

Left(right) **Professional Auto Craft** (518-623-3811). Body shop and 24-hour towing.

282.2   Left(right) **Maltbie Chrysler Plymouth Dodge** (518-623-3405). New and used car dealership.

283.4   Right(left) **Queen Village Campground** (518-623-3184). Roomy campground under big pines has swimming pool. Seasonal sites only.

283.7   Left(right) **Gaby's Restaurant & Tavern** (518-623-4307). North-country rustic on a massive scale. This large restaurant and tavern boasts huge exposed beams, a big stone fire ring, wooden furniture and booths, and is accented by a stone and carpeted floor. The restaurant offers fine dining on steaks, chops, seafood, Italian favorites, and more, while the tavern offers sandwiches, burgers, and such. Dinner entrees $11-$18. Also occasional entertainment. Impressive.

283.8   Left(right) **North Country Lodge** (518-623-2162). A bed and breakfast with special appeal to movie lovers. Each room is decorated to honor a specific movie. Hence, the lodge has a *Maltese Falcon* room, a *Birds* room, a *High Sierra* room, etc. Each room has a private bath and a TV, and some have VCRs. Film library includes foreign and American classics. Rates are $58-$80, continental breakfast included. A 15 percent discount is offered Monday through Thursday.

284.0   Entering **Warrensburg**.

284.1   Left(right) **Route 9 Motel** (518-623-2955). Six motel rooms, and six efficiencies with microwave, refrigerator, and sink. Motel rooms $45-$55, efficiencies $55-$65. Fresh flowers by every room, morning complimentary coffee, and pets welcome. Recently remodeled and like new.

Left(right) **Nemec's Sportshop, Farm & Garden Center** (518-623-2049).   Hunting, fishing, and camping equipment and supplies. Hunting and fishing licenses and live bait. Hardware, and garden and pool supplies. R/V supplies and a propane filling station. Pure maple syrup, horse tack, and pet food and supplies.

284.3   Left(Right) **Hometown Oil** (518-623-3613).   Automotive diesel fuel and kerosene.

Left(right) **Smith's Garage** (518-623-4174).   Automotive repair shop.

284.4   Right(left) **Warrensburg Car Care Collision Center** (518-623-2135). Body shop and 24-hour towing.

Left(right)   **Hagie's   Mainstreet   Menu**   (518-623-4393). Sandwiches, subs, homemade soups, and coffee. Lunch specials such as a cheeseburger sub, chicken Parmigian sandwich, Cajun chicken, etc. Dinner specials in the warmer months, $5-$6. Soft ice cream April through October.

Left(right) **Warrensburg Car Care Accessory Shop** (518-623-4847). Auto accessories, performance parts, bed liners, NASCAR memorabilia, gifts, etc.

Left(right) **Warren Ford Mercury** (518-623-4221).   Used car dealer.

284.5   Right(left) **Warrensburg Fruit**.   Farm stand.   Corn, apples, tomatoes, lettuce, eggs, honey, jellies, maple syrup, and homemade bread and pies, etc.

Right(left) **Rodney's Family Restaurant** (518-623-3246). Breakfast, lunch, and dinner ($2-$8).

Right(left) **Bob Griffin & Sons** (518-623-2559). Auto service and tires.

Right(left) Junction with **Fourth Avenue**.

Right(left) **Heck of a Pizza** (518-623-2329). Traditional red pizzas, broccoli and spinach white pizzas, pizza rolls, and strombolis. Open Wednesday through Sunday.

284.6   Right(left) **Wilson's Auto Parts** (518-623-2881). NAPA store.

Right(left) **Rob's Diversified** (518-623-4061). Second-hand furniture, appliances, TV's, etc.

Left(right) Junction with **Raymond Lane**, up which a short walk is **Oscar's Smokehouse** (518-623-3431). Meats, cheeses, sausages, homemade wursts, and jerky.

Right(left) Junction with **Third Avenue**.

284.7   Left(right) **Warrensburg Post Office** (518-623-4641). ZIP 12885.

Left(right) **E. L. Kreinheder** (518-623-2149). Quality antiques, lamps, furniture, china, linens, etc. New, used, and out-of-print books. Tastefully presented.

Right(left) **Bent Finial Manor** (518-623-3308, 888-802-6006). A stunning, 1904 Queen Anne bed and breakfast with round rooms, angled rooms, stained-glass windows, and a huge, wrap-around porch. Inside are three fireplaces, a grand staircase, a grand piano, and grand Corinthian columns. Twenty-three different kinds of wood accent the interior. Seven guest rooms furnished in antiques, and five baths. A proud, beautiful, sophisticated, Victorian lady. $100-$135/couple with full breakfast.

Right(left) Junction with **Second Avenue**.

284.8   Left(right) **Bluebird Bakery** (518-623-3301). Eclairs, pastry, cookies, and popovers.

Left(right) **Jack's Liquors** (518-623-3366).

Right(left) **Bill's Restaurant** (518-623-2669).   Homecooked breakfast, lunch, and dinner at reasonable prices.   Burgers, homemade biscuits, strawberry shortcake, real mashed potatoes, and friendly staff. Breakfast $2-$5, dinner $6-$8.

Right(left) Junction with **First Avenue**.

Left(right) **Higgins Sales and Service** (518-623-9769). Kawasaki generators, Husqvarna snowblowers, lawnmowers, chain saws, and more. Will service almost anything.

Left(right) Junction with **Hackensack Street**.

Left(right) **Fieldhouse Antiques**. In weathered barn in the rear. Larger than it looks.

Right(left) **Hollywood Limousines** (518-623-4527). Limo rentals.

284.9 Right(left) **The Store** (518-623-2786). Gift shop, antiques, and designer and vintage clothing.

Right(left) **Marco Polo's** (518-623-2786). Italian food. Pizza, pizza by the slice, subs, and Buffalo wings. Meatballs, eggplant, and sausage Italian dinners ($4-$9). Cheese cake, cannolis, Italian ices, soft ice cream, and beer and wine. Open late.

Right(left) **Corner Auto Care** (518-623-9895). Auto repairs and tires.

Left(right) **Jacobs & Toney IGA** (518-623-3850). Supermarket and Mobil gas. "Meat store of the North". Fresh meat; deli; produce; home baked rolls, breads, cookies, etc.; sandwiches and cold beer. The home baked chocolate truffles are outrageously delicious. Try to get them just as they come out of the oven. Mmmmmouthwateringly delicious.

Left(right) **LD's Pharmacy** (518-623-2993).   Postcards, magazines, etc. Trailways bus depot.

285.0   Traffic light at intersection with **Adirondack Avenue** on the left(right) and **Hudson** and **Elm Streets** on the right(left). Hudson Street offers the following:

> *000.0   Left. **Merrill Magee House** (518-623-2449). Listed on the National Register of Historic Places, this 1832 inn offers bed and breakfast accommodations and fine dining. Accommodations include a family suite (children welcome) with two bedrooms, sitting room, and bathroom; and a romantic guesthouse with 10 guestrooms, each with a private bath, fireplace, and contemporary amenities but no TVs. The guesthouse also has a sun room with a Jacuzzi. The restaurant has two dining rooms and a porch. Tavern, TV room, fireplaces, and swimming pool. Antique furnishings include a melodian and a doll-house miniature of the inn. Flower, herb, and vegetable gardens provide fresh ingredients and cut flowers for the restaurant. Accommodations $105-125/couple. Restaurant open to the public for lunch and dinner (dinner entrees $15-$27.) Various lodging/dinner plans are available.*

> *Right. **This and That Shop** (518-623-2786). General line of antiques and collectibles.*

> *000.9   Left. **Morry Stein Park and Beach at Echo Lake** (518-623-9511). Operated by the town of Warrensburg and open to the public. Beach with lifeguard, floating dock, bathhouse, picnic tables, grills, pavilion, volleyball court, and basketball net. Handicapped accessible. Open daily, 11-5. Season corresponds with the local school summer vacation.*

> *001.0   Left. **Echo Lake Road** to the **Warren County Fish Hatchery** (518-623-2877). Visitor center, self-guided hatchery tours, pavilion, picnic tables, barbecue grills, volleyball court, playground, and rest rooms. Open free to public.*

001.3   *Right. State of New York **Department of Environmental Conservation** Headquarters (518-623-3671). Regional offices.*

As Hudson Street continues north it becomes Hudson Street Extension/Golf Course Road.

002.4   *Left.   **Cronin's Golf Resort** (518-623-9336).   A beautifully-situated, public eighteen-hole golf course with gently undulating fairways overlooking the Hudson, with the majestic Adirondacks beyond. Fifteen housekeeping cottages with screened porches and eight motel rooms. Pro shop, pool, restaurant open for lunch and bar open late with occasional entertainment.   Scenic, family oriented, and cordial. Operated by the same family since 1945. $50/couple/night. Eighteen holes $16-$18, cart $22. Representative golf/lodging package offers two days of unlimited golf and two nights double occupancy for $200. Other packages available. Golf season is early April through October, lodging from May through Columbus Day.*

002.6   *Left. **Warren County Recreational Day Use Area** (518-623-2877). Three-quarter-mile, self-guided nature trail through the forest and along the banks of the Hudson River, becomes a cross-country skiing trail in winter. Canoe access site and picnic area. Peaceful quiet among the pines.*

004.7   *Junction of **Golf Course Road** with Route 28.*

End of Hudson Street Extension/Golf Course Road coverage.

Right(left) **Floyd Bennett Park**, a tiny, triangular area with a bandstand and two benches.

Left(right) **Rite Aid Pharmacy** (518-623-3805). Drug store and drive-through pharmacy.

Right(left) **Tamarack Shoppe** (518-623-3384). Antiques, fine gifts, jewelry, carvings, baskets, linens, lace, and more.

Right(left) **Brown's Shoe Store** (518-623-9566). Shoes, shoe repairs, and jewelry.

Right(left) **Glens Falls National Bank** (518-623-3036). 24-hour ATM.

Left(right) Junction with **Mountain Avenue**.

285.1   Left(right) **Evergreen Bank** (518-623-2666). 24-hour ATM.

Right(left) **Warrensburg Chamber of Commerce** (518-623-2161). Tourist info.

Left(right) **Grand Union** (518-623-3114). Supermarket.

Left(right) **Radio Shack** (518-623-3315). Electronics, computers, phones, etc.

Left(right) **Adirondack Family Health Center** (518-623-3911). A Community Health Plan (CHP) HMO facility.

Right(left) **Le Count** (518-623-2480). Real estate.

Left(right) Junction with **Emerson Avenue**.

Left(right) **Donegal Manor** (518-623-3549). An Irish-flavored bed and breakfast and an antique shop. One Victorian suite and one efficiency suite, plus a one-bedroom apartment accommodating up to six, all with private bath. Wrap-around porch, fireplaces, antique furnishings, and full breakfasts. Built in the 1820's, Donegal Manor is the only house still standing in which James Fenimore Cooper stayed while writing *The Last of the Mohicans*. Antique store has a general line, with oaken furniture, depression glass, jewelry, coins, bric-a-brac, and the "the good, the bad, and the ugly." $85-$125 per couple.

Right(left) Junction with **Stewart-Farrar Street**:

000.1   *At the end of Stewart-Farrar Street, at its junction with
Elm Street, is the* **Richards Library** *(518-623-3011), a
privately-endowed library in a gorgeous building
constructed of local stone, donated to the town by the
Richards sisters. Sarah, the librarian, relates the story of
the stone having some fool's gold in it, and she once found
a young boy at the rear of the library chipping away at the
building to retrieve some of the fool's gold, which he
thought was real. Strong focus on local history. Closed
Saturday afternoons and Sundays.*

285.2   Left(right) Junction with **Pasco Avenue**.

Right(left) **Cumberland Farms** (518-623-9857).   Convenience
store and Gulf gas. Propane and firewood.

Right(left) **Video Broker II** (518-623-3175).   Video sales and
rentals, games, etc.

285.3   Right(left) **Warrensburg Town Hall** (518-623-4561).

Right(left) **The Pillars**, a collection of shops:
Lilly's Place (518-623-3194). Breakfast and lunch. International
cooking, baked specialties, and desserts.   A charming little
restaurant with patio dining under umbrellas.
New Beginnings Styling Salon (518-623-3645).
Courtly Music Unlimited (518-623-2867).   Specializing in
recorders, recorder music, and recorder instructional tapes.
Budget Baby Kids and More (518-623-4861).   Children's
clothing.
This, That and In-Between (518-623-4153). Variety store, clock
shop, floral shop, handmade crafts and collectibles. Clothing,
housewares, kitchenware, jewelry, furniture, books, dolls, and
stuffed animals. Clocks and clock repairs. Christmas shop. Full
flower shop, including Teleflora wire service.

285.4   Right(left) Gas, car wash, and kerosene down driveway.

Right(left) **Warrensburg Getty** (518-623-2069). Getty gas and garage.

Right(left) Intersection with **Richards Avenue (NY 418)** at traffic light. Turning right leads you to:

*000.0   Left.   **Warrensburg Health Center** (518-623-2844). Urgent care facility seven days a week.   Walk-ins accepted.*

*Right.   **Warrensburg Laundry & Dry Cleaning** (518-623-3101).*

*Junction with **Elm Street.***

*Right.   **Riverside Gallery** (518-623-2026).   Art gallery and framing salon.   Original artwork, prints, and more, tastefully presented in a charming space alongside the Schroon River.*

*Right.   **Barbara Ann-tiques**.   Behind the Riverside Gallery in a lovely setting on the banks of the Schroon River. Quality antiques in wonderful condition. Furniture, china, glassware, mirrors, and prints, plus an entire room of antique linens and lace. Memorial Day weekend through early October.*

End of Richards Avenue coverage.

Right(left) **Engle Park**. A little park with benches and one picnic table. Enjoy a picnic or take-out pizza lunch while watching the world of Warrensburg go by.

Right(left) **Joanne's Beauty Salon** (518-623-3988).

Right(left) **OJ's TV and Appliance** (518-623-3900). Sales and service.

285.5   Right(left) **Charles Shoes** (518-623-2477). Shoe store.

Right(left) **TJ's Outlet** and **The Sewing Basket** (518-623-3381). Variety store. Adirondack crafts, gifts, clothes, craft supplies, sewing supplies, fabrics, thread, notions, and postcards.

Right(left) **Second Time Around** (518-623-2029). Books, CD's, tapes, quality used clothing, and wedding dresses.

Right(left) **Heidi's Clip Joint** (518-623-2818). Barber and beauty shop.

Left(right) **Warrensburgh Museum of Local History** (518-623-3660). In old VFW/IOOF building. Open Tuesday through Saturday afternoons.

Right(left) Junction with **Herrick Avenue**.

Right(left) **The Beary Best Shoppe** (518-623-2703). Children's clothing up to size 14; accessories, furniture, toys, and maternity clothing.

Right(left) **Perfect Grinds** (518-623-4149). Coffee bar and eatery. Specialty and gourmet coffees, teas, espresso, and cappuccino. Soups, salads, bagels, and sandwiches. Library and outdoor deck. Entertainment Friday and Saturday nights. Open late.

Left(right) **Potter's Diner** (518-623-2158). Open for breakfast and lunch seven days, with counter and table service. Eggs, pancakes, hot dogs, burgers, subs, soups, salads, club sandwiches, hot open sandwiches, and more. Home-baked raisin toast is a favorite. $1-$6.

Right(left) **Posies** (518-623-2211). Flowers and gifts.

Right(left) **Sweet Peas Market** (518-623-2769). Produce market. Jellies, pies, and flowers. Open Mother's Day to Halloween and Christmas season to sell trees.

Right(left) **Ray's Liquors** (518-623-2001).

Right(left) **Tax Express** (518-623-1040). Tax preparation service.

Left(right) **Stewart Shops** (518-623-9848). Convenience store, gas, and ATM.

Left(right) **Subway** (518-623-2598). Sandwich shop.

Left(right) **Dragon Lee Restaurant** (518-623-3796). Chinese restaurant.

Traffic light at junction with **Horicon Avenue** and **Water Street**. Making a left(right) onto Horicon Avenue leads you to:

000.5   Right.   Warrensburg Travel Park (518-623-9833). Family campground with 150 shady sites nestled under pines and supporting all types of camping. Swimming pool, tennis court, pavilion, table tennis, swing sets, and canoe and rowboat rentals. $17-$22/two people. May through mid-October.

003.0   Right.   Schroon River Campsite (518-623-2171). Beautifully landscaped campground on the Schroon River. Some 300 field and forest sites, from tent sites to full-hookup RV sites, on 350 acres. Beach, heated pool, store, game room, and shuffleboard table. Canoe, rowboat, and bike rentals. Much more. Mid-may through September. $21-$23/night.

End of Horicon Avenue coverage.

285.6   Right(left) **Brew & Stew** (518-623-9845). "Best damned food in town." Casual restaurant serving three meals a day. Known for their burgers, club sandwiches, and homemade french fries. Pool table, foosball, and pinball. Breakfast and lunch $2-$8, dinner $6-$13.

Left(right) **Witz End Tavern**. Bar with a pool table.

Right(left) **Miller Art and Frame** (518-623-3966). Art and frame shop featuring local art and genuine Adirondack antiques. Pack baskets, tools, skis, tables, chairs, cupboards, dishes, jewelry, glassware, lamps, pictures, and more.

Right(left) **Cathy's Curio**. Handmade crafts gift shop. Dolls, Adirondack furniture, paintings, stuffed animals, wreaths, Christmas ornaments, and giftware.

Right(left) **Inspirations Doll Shoppe and Artisans Gallery** (518-623-4602). Porcelain doll shop and porcelain doll making studio. Completed dolls, doll kits, greenware, doll parts, pieces, and accessories. Modern doll repair. Also vintage hats, china, silver, fabrics, and lace.

Right(left) **Cleverdale Antiques** (518-623-4368). Uncluttered presentation of 19th century country and Victorian furniture and accessories.

285.7   Right(Left) **Warren Ford Mercury** (518-623-4221). Dealership.

Right(left) **Cooper Antiques and Collectibles** (518-623-4696). General line of antiques including furniture, pottery, china, tools, Turkish prayer rugs, bronze statues, and more.

Right(left) **Rafter J Western World** (518-623-2325). Hats, boots, leather jackets, jeans, shirts, belts, and more.

Right(left) **D & G Hardware & Variety** (518-623-3592). Hardware, videos, and coins.

Left(right) **Warrensburg Chamber of Commerce Information Booth** (518-623-2519). Tourist information.

Right(left) Junction with **Judd Bridge**.

285.8   Right(left) **Exit 23 Auto Sales** (518-623-3798).

Right(left) **The Chimney Store** (518-623-4033).   Chimneys, carpentry, wood stoves, vacuums, power tools, and lamps.

Right(left) **Winslow & Sons Power Equipment** (518-623-3740). Sales, service, parts, and rentals.

285.9   Crossing the **Schroon River**. **Warrensburg/Lake George** town line. The Schroon empties into the Hudson less than three miles west of here.

286.0   Left(right) **Rainbow View Campground** (518-623-9444). Family campground with 100 sites on a 17-acre peninsula surrounded by the Schroon River. Pool, sandy beach, playground, mini-golf, half-court basketball, adult and children's volleyball courts, and a bacci ball court. Pool table, pinball, and video games. May through mid-October. $20-$26/night.

Right(left) Junction with **Prosser Road**:

> *Left.* ***Super 8 Motel*** *(518-623-2811, 800-800-8000). Thirty-two room log motel on the side of a hill with beautiful views. $53-$80/couple.*

Left(right) **McDonald's** (518-623-3323). Hamburgers, etc.

Right(left) **Rondack Realty** (518-623-9929). Real estate.

286.1   Left(right) **Exit 23 Mobil** (518-623-9492). Mobil gas and snack shop.

286.2   Traffic light at junction with **Diamond Point Road**. Turn left and drive a few hundred feet for **I-87** (**Northway**) Exit 23. I-87 goes north toward **Montreal** and south to **Albany** and **New York City**.

End of coverage of **Warrensburg**.

Driving **US 9** south from its junction with **Diamond Point Road** yields:

*000.0   Left. **Foodmart** (518-623-3707).   Convenience store, Citgo gas, and diesel fuel. Some debit cards accepted.*

*000.1   Right. **Brunetto's Restaurant** (518-623-1041). Casual dining in a relaxed, unpretentious atmosphere, warmed in winter by a stone fireplace.   The menu of seafood specialties, steaks, chicken, pasta, etc., varies daily depending upon availability of fresh ingredients, and ranges from $14-$22. Open at 5 PM Tuesday through Sunday in summer, Thursday through Sunday otherwise.*

*Left. **Exit 23 Truck Stop** (518-623-3736). Truck repairs and service.*

End of coverage of US 9 south.

If you've been on Route 28, New York's Adventure Route, since Kingston, or have traversed the highway in the opposite direction, your eyes, ears, heart, and mind have experienced a beautiful slice of Americana unparalleled anywhere else in the country. I hope you've taken the time for some exciting adventures along the way. Maybe you've even fallen in love with the road the way I have and already have plans for another Route 28 adventure. Whatever your travel plans for the future, I wish you a wonderful trip. Thanks for coming along.

Appendix A: Annual Events

Annual events are usually held at the same time each year, but life is a sea of changes. Call ahead to ensure that the event that interests you is still being held when indicated.

Andes (607-746-2281)
July: *Strawberry Festival.*
September: *Lumberjack Competition*, Bobcat Ski Area (914-676-3143).
September: *Andes Gun Show* (914-676-3589).

Arkville (607-746-2281)
June: *Arkville Fire Department Community Fair* (914-586-3264).
September and October: *Fall Foliage Runs on the Delaware and Ulster Rail Ride* (914-586-3877, 800-225-4132).

Barneveld (315-896-3963)
February: *America's Greatest Heart Run and Walk.*

Blue Mountain Lake (518-352-7659)
March: *Mardi Gras Benefit*, Adirondack Lakes Center for the Arts (518-352-7715).
June: *No-Octane Weekend Regatta*, Adirondack Museum (518-352-7311).
July: *Annual Auction*, Adirondack Lakes Center for the Arts (518-352-7715).
August: *Author's Evening*, Adirondack Museum (518-352-7311).
September: *Rustic Furniture Fair*, Adirondack Museum (518-352-7311).
September: *Antiques Show*, Adirondack Museum (518-352-7311).
December: *Christmas Party*, Adirondack Lakes Center for the Arts (518-352-7715).
December: *North Country Family Christmas*, Adirondack Museum (518-352-7311).

Cooperstown (607-547-9983)
February: *Winter Carnival.*
May, Memorial Day weekend: *General Clinton Canoe Regatta*, Cooperstown to Bainbridge (607-967-8700).
June: *Antiquarian Book Fair*, Clark Sports Center (607-547-2800).
June through August: *Weekend Farmers' Market.*

July: *Independence Day Celebration and Fireworks.*
July: *The Farmers' Museum Junior Livestock Show* (607-547-1450).
July: *Gala Weekend at Glimmerglass Opera* (607-547-2255).
July or August: *National Baseball Hall of Fame Induction Weekend* (607-547-7200).
July and August: *Foot Stomping Bluegrass and Country Music and Chicken Barbecue*, Friday evenings at The Farmers' Museum (607-547-1450).
August: *Glimmerglass Triathlon* (canoe, bike, run), Glimmerglass State Park (607-547-8662).
September, Labor Day weekend: *Outdoor Arts and Craft Show*, Clark Sports Center (607-547-2800).
September: *Senior Invitational Golf Tournament*, Leatherstocking Golf Course at The Otesaga (607-547-5275).
September: *Harvest Festival*, The Farmers' Museum (607-547-1450).
December: *Christmas events.*

Delhi (607-746-6100)
April: *Delaware Academy Book Fair* (607-746-2103).
June: *Delhi Chamber of Commerce 10K Run and 10K Bike Time Trial.*
June through September: *Farmers' Market.*
July or August: *Catskills Farmlife and Foodways Festival,* Delaware County Historical Association (607-746-3849).
October: *Harvest Festival.*

Fleischmanns (914-254-5856, 800-724-7910)
May, Memorial Day Weekend: *Out of the Attic Village Yard Sale.*
July: *Quilt Show and Exhibit.*
July or August: *Fleischmanns Open Tennis Tournament.*

Fly Creek (607-432-4500, 800-843-3394)
August: *Cider Making in the Country and Antique Engine Show*, Fly Creek Cider Mill (607-547-9692).
September: *Applefest Weekend*, Fly Creek Cider Mill (607-547-9692).
October: *Samplers Weekend*, Fly Creek Cider Mill (607-547-9692).

Forestport (315-896-3963)
June: *Forestport Summer Festival.*

Highmount (914-340-3566)
July and August: *Belleayre Conservatory Summer Concerts*, Belleayre Mountain Ski Center (914-254-5600, 800-942-6904).
October: *Fall Festival*, Belleayre Mountain Ski Center (914-254-5600, 800-942-6904).

Herkimer (315-866-7820)
July: *Youth Fishing Derby* (315-866-3303).
August: *A Summer Evening*, with a parade, entertainment and crafters (315-866-3303).

Hurley (914-340-3566)
July, second Saturday: *Old Stone House Day*.
August, third Saturday: *Corn and Craft Festival*.

Indian Lake (518-648-5112)
January: *Snowmobile Races*.
February: *Winterfest*.
May: *Town Flea Market*.
May: *Memorial Day Parade*.
June: *Whitewater Sunday*.
July, Independence Day holiday: *Community Festival and Fireworks*.
August: *Great Camp Benefit, Library Book Sale*.
September: *Pig Roast*.
September: *Car Show*.
October: *Halloween Party and Parade*.

Inlet (315-357-5501)
May: *Fire and Spice Festival* (315-357-6028).
June: *Capecelatro Inlet Fishing Derby*.
June: *Techniques of Alcohol Management Seminar*.
June: *Father's Day Picnic*.
June: *Black Fly Challenge Mountain Bike Race*.
June through August: *Bingo*.
July and August: *Sailing Races*.
July, Independence Day: *Ping Pong Ball Drop and Fireworks*.
July and August: *Saturday Evening Band Concerts*.
July: *Bogg Walk Flowers and Birds Presentation*.
July: *Arts in the Park Craft Fair*.

July: *Pet Show.*
July: *Meet the Author Night.*
August: *Charity Golf Tournament.*
September: *KenDucky Derby.*
September: *Fall Festival.*
September: *Adirondack Mountain Bike Festival.*
December: *American Snowmobilers "Battle of Old Forge".*

Margaretville (800-586-3303)
July, Independence Day holiday: *Margaretville Fire Department Field Days.*
August: *Margaretville Memorial Hospital Auxiliary Antique and Flea Market.*
August: *Margaretville Chamber of Commerce Street Fair.*

Milford (607-432-4500)
May or June: *Milford Railroad Day* (607-432-2429) and *French and Indian War Reenactment* (607-286-7038).
July: *Outdoor Cooperstown Antique Show*, Wood Bull Antiques (607-286-9021).
July: *Rotary Club Antique Market.*

North Creek (518-251-2612, 800-880-GORE)
May: *Hudson River White Water Derby.*
August: *Adirondack Gem, Mineral, and Jewelry Show*, Gore Mountain Ski Area.
September: *Teddy Roosevelt Bull Moose Days.*
September: *Sports Fair*, Gore Mountain Ski Area.
October: *International Fall Foliage Festival*, Gore Mountain Ski Area.

Old Forge (315-369-6983)
March: *Annual Snocross*, McCauley Mountain (315-369-6983).
May, Memorial Day weekend: *Polka Festival.*
June: *Father's Day Weekend Classic Car Show.*
July, Independence Day holiday: *Craft Fair, Band Concert, and Fireworks.*
July: *Top 'Vette Adirondack High Peaks Road Tour and Show* (315-942-6420, 315-942-2352).
July: *Antique Boat and Woodie Car Show.*
July and August: *Free concert on the beach on Sunday evenings.*

August: *Central Adirondack Art Show*, Arts Center/Old Forge.
August: *Author's Fair*, Old Forge Library (315-369-6008).
August: *Fox Family Bluegrass Fest.*
August or September: *Adirondacks National Exhibition of American Watercolors*, Arts Center/Old Forge (315-369-6411).
September: *Adirondack Canoe Classic*, Old Forge to Saranac Lake (800-347-1992).
September: *Oktoberfest.*
October: *Annual Antique Show*, Arts Center/Old Forge (315-369-6411).
October-November: *Northeast Quilts Unlimited Exhibition*, Arts Center/Old Forge (315-369-6411).
October: *Moose River Festival,* white water events.
November: *Holiday Bazaar*, Arts Center/Old Forge (315-369-6411).
December: *Snodeo Weekend*, snowmobile rodeo.

Oneonta (607-432-4500, 800-843-3394)
June or July: *National Soccer Hall of Fame Induction Weekend* (607-432-3351, 800-545-3263).
July: *Hometown Fourth of July*, Neahwa Park.
September: *Spalding Cup Soccer Tournament* (women).
September: *Mayor's Cup Soccer Tournament* (men).
September: *Grand and Glorious Garage Sale.*

Phoenicia (914-679-8057)
June, first full weekend: *White Water Slalom* canoe and kayak races.
October, first weekend: *Esopus Level White Water Races.*

Raquette Lake (518-624-3077)
January, February, or March: *Ice Harvest* (weather dependent).
February: *Winter Carnival.*
February: *Raquetteers Snowmobile Club Poker Run.*
July, Independence Day holiday: *Canoe and Paddleboat Races, music, and fireworks.*
July: *Fireworks Cruise* (315-354-5532).
July: *Grand Tour* at Sagamore (315-354-5311).
July and August: *Full-Moon Cruises* (315-354-5532).
August: *Craft Show, Bake Sale, Book Sale, and Ambulance Fund Auction.*
August: *Moonlight Boat Parade.*
September: *Labor Day Party.*

September: *Volunteer Fire Department Clam Bake.*
October: *Mountain Music and Dance Weekend* at Sagamore (315-354-5311).
October and November: *Hunter's Dinners.*

Remsen (315-896-3963)
August: *50's and 60's Car Show and Block Dance.*
September: *Barn Festival of the Arts.*

Richfield Springs (315-858-1050)
June: *Friendship Craft Fair*, Spring Park.
July: *Firemen's Field Day and Sidewalk Bazaar.*

Roxbury (607-746-2281)
September: *Catskill Mountain Harvest Fair and Fiddler's Festival* (607-363-7908).

Thendara (315-369-6983)
August: *Clothesline Art Sale*, Adirondack Scenic Railroad (315-369-6290, 315-369-6411).

Warrensburg (518-623-2161)
February: *Sled Dog Races.*
July, Independence Day holiday period: *Arts, Crafts, and Collectibles Festival.*
July: *Smokeaters Jamboree.*
July and August: *Street Dances* at the Bandstand at Floyd Bennett Park.
August: *Warren County Fair.*
October: *World's Largest Garage Sale and Foliage Festival*, and *Las Vegas Night.*
December: *Christmas in Warrensburgh.*

Woodgate (315-896-3963)
December: *Snomobile Shootout.*

Woodstock (914-679-6234)
May: *Renaissance Fair.*
July: *Library Fair.*
August: *The Craft Fair in Woodstock.*

Appendix B: Equipment Rental Sources

Bikes and mountain bikes
Cycle N Recycle, Indian Lake (518-648-6385).
Garnet Hill Lodge and Cross-Country Ski Center, North River (518-251-2821).
Gore Mountain Ski Area, North Creek (518-251-2411).
Mountain & Boardertown, North Creek (518-251-3111).
Mountainaire Adventures, Wevertown (518-251-2194, 800-950-2194).
Overlook Mountain Bikes, Woodstock (914-679-2122).
Pedals & Petals, Inlet (315-357-3281).
Sporting Propositions, Old Forge (315-369-6188).
Withworth Ski Shop at Ski Plattekill, Roxbury (607-326-2845).
Whitewater Challengers Rafting Center, Okara Lakes (315-369-6699, 800-443-RAFT).

Boats
Belleayre Mountain Day Use Area, Pine Hill (914-254-5600).
Bird's Marine, Raquette Lake (315-354-4441).
Blue Mountain Lake Boat Livery, Blue Mountain Lake (518-352-7351, 305-666-5773).
Burke's Marina, Raquette Lake (315-354-4623).
Clark's Marine Service, Eagle Bay (315-357-3231).
Dunn's Boat Service, Big Moose (315-357-3532).
Inlet Marina, Inlet (315-357-4896).
Knott's Motel, Goodyear Lake (607-432-5948).
Palmer Point, Old Forge (315-357-5594).
Raquette Lake Marina, Raquette Lake (315-354-4361).
Rivett's Marine Recreation and Service, Old Forge (315-369-3123).
Sam Smith's Boatyard, Cooperstown (607-547-2543).

Rowboats and canoes are also available for rent at many campgrounds.

Camping equipment
Ara-Ho Outfitters, Inlet (315-357-3306, 888-859-7676).
Blue Mountain Outfitters, Blue Mountain Lake (518-352-7306).
Mountainman Outdoor Supply Co., Inlet (315-357-6672).
Sporting Propositions, Old Forge (315-369-6188).

Campers
Guido's R/V's and Garage, Mohawk (315-866-0680).

Canoes and/or kayaks
Beaver Brook Outfitters, Wevertown (518-251-3394, 888-454-8433).
Bird's Marine, Raquette Lake (315-354-4441).
Blue Mountain Lake Boat Livery, Blue Mountain Lake (518-352-7351, 305-666-5773).
Blue Mountain Lake Inn, Blue Mountain Lake (518-352-7600).
Blue Mountain Outfitters, Blue Mountain Lake (518-352-7306).
Clark's Marine Service, Eagle Bay (315-357-3231).
Mountain Sports, Barneveld (315-896-4421).
Mountainaire Adventures, Wevertown (518-251-2194, 800-950-2194).
Mountainman Outdoor Supply Co., Inlet (315-357-6672).
Palmer Point, Old Forge (315-357-5594).
Raquette Lake Marina, Raquette Lake (315-354-4361).
Rivett's Marine Recreation and Service, Old Forge (315-369-3123).
Tickner Canoe Rental/Tickner's Adirondack Canoe Outfitters, Old Forge (315-369-6286).
Whitewater Challengers Rafting Center, Okara Lakes (315-369-6699, 800-443-RAFT).
Whitewater Challengers Rafting Center, North River (800-443-RAFT).

Cars and trailers
B & D Motors, Margaretville (914-586-3253).
Enterprise rent-a-car, Oneonta's Southside (800-RENT-A-CAR, 800-736-8222).

Erie Canal boats
Collar City Charters, Troy (518-272-5341, 800-830-5341).
Mid-Lakes Navigation Co., Skaneateles (315-685-8500, 800-545-4318).

Ice skates
Inlet Ski Touring Center, Inlet (315-357-6961).

Personal watercraft
Old Forge Sport Tours, Old Forge (315-369-3796).

Sailboats
Blue Mountain Lake Boat Livery, Blue Mountain Lake (518-352-7351, 305-666-5773).
Palmer Point, Old Forge (315-357-5594).

Skis/Snowboards
Adirondack Woodcraft Ski Touring Center, Old Forge (315-369-6031).
Beaver Brook Outfitters, Wevertown (518-251-3394, 888-454-8433).
Belleayre Mountain Ski Center, Highmount (914-254-5600).
Belleayre Ski Shop, Highmount (914-254-5338).
Bobcat Ski Center, Andes (914-676-3143).
Cunningham's Ski Barn, North Creek (518-251-3215).
Friends Lake Inn and Nordic Ski Center, Chestertown (518-494-4751).
Garnet Hill Lodge and Cross-Country Ski Center, North River (518-251-2821).
Gore Mountain Ski Area, North Creek (518-251-2411).
Inlet Ski Touring Center, Inlet (315-357-6961).
Mountain & Boardertown, North Creek (518-251-3111).
Mountainman Outdoor Supply Co., Inlet (315-357-6672).
Ski Plattekill, Roxbury (607-326-3500).
Potter Brothers Ski Shops, Kingston (914-338-5119).
Sporting Propositions Ski Shop, at McCauley Mountain in Old Forge (315-369-3144).
Sporting Propositions Ski Shop, Old Forge (315-369-6188).

Snowmobiles
Alder Creek Snowmobile Rentals, Alder Creek (888-942-3526).
Old Forge Sport Tours, Thendara (315-369-3796).

Snowshoes
Beaver Brook Outfitters, Wevertown (518-251-3394, 888-454-8433).
Cunningham's Ski Barn, North Creek (518-251-3215).
Inlet Ski Touring Center, Inlet (315-357-6961).
Mountainman Outdoor Supply Co., Inlet (315-357-6672).

Tents and camping supplies
Ara-Ho Outfitters, Inlet (315-357-3306, 888-859-7676).
Mountainman Outdoor Supply Co., Inlet (315-357-6672).
Sporting Propositions Ski Shop, Old Forge (315-369-6188).

Tubes for tubing

F.S. Tube Rental, Phoenicia (914-688-7633).
Rubber Ducky Tube Rentals, Phoenicia (914-688-2018).
Town Tinker Tube Rental, Phoenicia (914-688-5553).

VCRs

Video-Fax, Richfield Springs (315-858-1607).
Video Plus, West Hurley along NY 375 (914-679-8993).
Wild Bird Crossing, Barneveld (315-896-4608).

Water skiing

Bird's Marine, Raquette Lake (315-354-4441).
Blue Mountain Lake Boat Livery, Blue Mountain Lake (518-352-7351, 305-666-5773).
Clark's Marine Service, Eagle Bay (315-357-3231).
Daggett Lake Campsite, Thurman (518-623-2198).

Appendix C: Additional Information

Books

Aprill, Dennis. *Good Fishing in the Adirondacks: From Lake Champlain to the Tug Hill.* Backcountry Publications, Woodstock, VT.

Burroughs, John. *In the Catskills.* Riverby Books, West Park, NY.

Christman, Henry. *Tin Horns and Calico, A Decisive Episode in the Emergence of Democracy.* Hope Farm Press, Saugerties, NY.

Crocker, John D. *Tales of the Courthouse Square.* Available at the Delaware County Historical Association's bookshop in Delhi.

Dieffenbacher, Jane. *Middleville, New York: The Story of a Village.* Steffen Publishing, Holland Patent, NY.

Draheim, Paul. *Herkimer Sesquicentennial 1807-1957.* Available at the Herkimer County Historical Society.

Ehling, William P. *Fifty Hikes in Central New York.* Backcountry Publications, Woodstock, VT.

Evers, Alf. *The Catskills: From Wilderness to Woodstock.* Doubleday & Company, Inc., Garden City, NY.

Evers, Alf. *Woodstock: History of an American Town.* The Overlook Press, Woodstock, NY.

Farb, Nathan. *The Adirondacks.* Rizzoli International Publications, Inc., New York, NY.

Fried, Marc B. *The Early History of Kingston & Ulster County, N.Y.* Ulster County Historical Society, Marbletown, NY.

Folwell, Elizabeth. *The Adirondack Book.* Berkshire House Publishers, Lee, MA.

Goodwin, Tony. *Classic Adirondack Ski Tours.* ADK Mountain Club, Lake George, NY.

Greater Milford Historical Association. *Time Once Past.* Available from the Milford Free Library Association.

Hamlin, Loren. *What Happened Was.* Early Adirondack Living Museum, Route 28, Woodgate, NY 13494.

Hayes, John, and Wilson, Alex. *Quiet Water Canoe Guide: New York. Best Paddling Lakes and Ponds for Canoe and Kayak.* Appalachian Mountain Club Books, Boston, MA.

Herkimer County Historical Society Staff. *Herkimer County at 200.* Purple Mountain Press, Ltd., Fleischmanns, NY.

Ingersoll, Ernest. *Handy Guide to the Hudson River and Catskill Mountains: 1910.* J.C. & A.L. Fawcett, Inc., Astoria, NY.

Jamieson, Paul, and Morris, Donald. *Adirondack Canoe Waters, North Floe.* ADK Mountain Club, Lake George, NY.

Johnsburg Historical Society. *River, Rails and Ski Trails. The History of the Town of Johnsburg.* Contact the Town of Johnsburg Historical Society (518-251-5811) concerning availability.

Kinney, Kathryn. *The Innkeepers' Register: Country Inns of North America 1996.* Independent Innkeepers' Association, Marshall, MI.

Kubik, Dorothy. *A Free Soil—A Free People: The Anti-Rent War in Delaware County, New York.* Purple Mountain Press, Ltd., Fleischmanns, NY.

LaBastille, Anne. *Woodswoman: Living Alone in the Adirondack Wilderness.* Penguin Books, New York, NY.

LaBastille, Anne. *Women and Wilderness.* Sierra Club Books, San Francisco, CA

LaBastille, Anne. *Woodswoman III.* West of the Wind Publications, Westport, NY.

Lamy, Marge. *Cross Country Ski Inns: Northeastern U.S. & Quebec.* Snow Vacations Books, North River, NY.

Long Lake Department of Parks, Recreation & Tourism. *Woods and Waters: A Guide to Long Lake and Raquette Lake.* Available from the Long Lake Department of Parks, Recreation & Tourism, Box 496, Long Lake, NY 12847, 518-624-3077.

Martin, J. Peter. *Adirondack Golf Courses: Past and Present.* Adirondack Golf, Box 492, Lake Placid, NY 12946.

McAllister, Lee, and Ochman, Myron Steven. *Hiking the Catskills.* The New York - New Jersey Trail Conference, New York, NY.

McKibben, Bill; Halpern, Sue; Hay, Mitchell; and Lemmel, Barbara. *Twenty-Five Bicycle Tours in the Adirondacks: Road Adventures in the East's Largest Wilderness.* Backcountry Publications, Woodstock, VT.

McMartin, Barbara. *Fifty Hikes in the Adirondacks.* Backcountry Publications, Woodstock, VT.

Michaels, Joanne, and Barile, Mary-Margaret. *The Hudson Valley and Catskill Mountains: An Explorer's Guide.* Countryman Press, Woodstock, VT.

Michaels, Joanne, and Barile, Mary. *Let's Take the Kids. Great Places to Go with Children in New York's Hudson Valley.* St. Martin's Press, New York, NY.

Milener, Eugene D. *Oneonta: The Development of a Railroad Town.* Available at the Huntington Memorial Library in Oneonta.

Mulligan, Tim. *The Traveler's Guide to the Hudson River Valley: From Saratoga Springs to New York City.* Random House, New York, NY.

Nealy,William. *The Mountain Bike Way of Knowledge.* Menasha Ridge Press, Inc., Birmingham, AL.

Nestle, David F. *The Leatherstocking Route: From Mohawk to the Susque-hanna by Interurban.* Available at the Richfield Springs library.

Ostertag, Rhonda, and Ostertag, George. *Hiking New York.* Falcon Press Publishing Company, Inc., Helena, MT.

Penny, Richard. *The Whitewater Sourcebook.* Menasha Ridge Press, Birmingham, AL.

Proskine, Alec C. *No Two Rivers Alike. Fifty-Six Canoeable Rivers in New York State.* Purple Mountain Press, Ltd., Fleischmanns, NY.

Proskine, Alec C. *Adirondack Canoe Waters: South and West Floe.* ADK Mountain Club, Lake George, NY.

Quinn, George V. *The Catskills: A Cross-Country Skiing Guide.* Purple Mountain Press, Ltd., Fleischmanns, NY.

Raitt, John E. *Delaware County and the Three Courthouses.* Reporter Company, Inc., Walton, NY. Available at the Delaware County Historical Association's bookshop in Delhi.

Roberts, Harry. *The Basic Essentials of Backpacking.* ICS Books, Merrill-ville, IN.

Schildge, Sue. *Famous Adirondacks Restaurants & Recipes.* Schildge Publishing Company, Plattsburgh, NY.

Steuding, Bob. *The Last of the Handmade Dams: The Story of the Ashokan Reservoir.* Purple Mountain Press, Ltd., Fleischmanns, NY.

Timm, Ruth. *Raquette Lake: A Time to Remember.* North Country Books, Utica, NY.

Titus, Robert. *The Catskills: A Geological Guide.* Purple Mountain Press, Ltd., Fleischmanns, NY.

Vanderstigchel, Armand C., and Birkel, Robert E., Jr. *Adirondack Cookbook.* Vanders and Birkel Publishing, Farmingdale, NY.

Wadsworth, Bruce. *An Adirondack Sampler: Day Hikes for All Seasons.* ADK Mountain Club, Lake George, NY.

Van Zandt, Roland. *The Catskill Mountain House.* Rutgers University Press, New Brunswick, NJ.

The *Forest Preserve Series of Guides to Adirondack and Catskill Trails* available from the Adirondack Mountain Club (ADK), Lake George, NY (800-395-8080):
High Peaks Region by Tony Goodwin.
Northern Region by Peter O'Shea.
Central Region by Bruce Wadsworth.
Northville-Placid Trail by Bruce Wadsworth.
West-Central Region by Arthur W. Haberl.
Eastern Region by Carl Heilman II.
Southern Region by Linda Laing.
Guide to Catskill Trails by Bruce Wadsworth.

Publishers and Distributors

The following publish and distribute books about upstate New York. Contact them for their catalogs.

Hope Farm Press and Bookshop, 252 Main St., Saugerties, NY 12477 (914-246-3522).

North Country Books, Inc., 311 Turner St., Utica, NY 13501 (315-735-4877).

Purple Mountain Press, Ltd., Main Street, Fleischmanns, NY 12430 (914-254-4062, 800-325-2665).

Maps and Guides

Adirondack Great Walks & Day Hikes. A Guide to Exploring "The Northeast's Last Great Wilderness". Adirondack Regional Tourism Council, P.O. Box 51, West Chazy, NY 12992-0051 (518-846-8016).

Adirondack Waterways. A Guide to Paddling "The Northeast's Last Great Wilderness". Adirondack Regional Tourism Council, P.O. Box 51, West Chazy, NY 12992-0051 (518-846-8016).

The Adirondack Series of Maps. A series of seven excellent maps published by Adirondack Maps Inc., P.O. Box 718, Keene Valley, NY 12943 (518-576-9861):
The Adirondack Park.
Adirondack Canoe Map.
The Adirondacks: Central Mountains.
The Adirondacks: High Peaks Region.
The Adirondacks: Lake George Region .
The Adirondacks: Northwest Lakes.
The Adirondacks: West-Central Wilderness Area.

Bikeways of the Adirondack North Country. Adirondack North Country Association, 183 Broadway, Saranac Lake, NY 12983 (518-891-6200).

Fulton Chain of Lakes. Boating Information. Fulton Chain of Lakes Association, Inc., P.O. Box 564, Old Forge, NY 13420.

Mountain Bike Trails. Central Adirondacks. Tourist Information Center, Old Forge, NY 13420 (315-369-6983).

Mountain Bike & Hiking Trail System Map. Tourist Information Center, Old Forge, NY 13420 (315-369-6983).

Town of Inlet Cross Country Ski Map.   Town of Inlet Chamber of Commerce Information Office, Inlet, NY 13360 (315-357-5501).

Whitewater Rafting and Canoe Access Sites. Warren County Tourism, 795 Municipal Center, Lake George, NY 12845 (518-761-6366).

Index

About the Author

Rob Scharpf was born in Kingston and lived in the Kingston and Woodstock area for nearly half a century, during which time he often traveled Route 28 in pursuit of hiking, skiing, camping, canoeing, and fishing. After a 30-year career with a major computer manufacturer, he and his dog Rip departed Kingston aboard Rob's sailboat *Uncle Wiggily*, bound for Florida. Upon reaching Florida unscathed, Rob spent more than two years researching and writing this guide to his favorite road so other people can share the enjoyment and adventure of Route 28. Rob and Rip currently live in Melbourne, Florida.

To Our Readers

In today's world things seem to change faster than we can think, and Route 28 is no exception. As you use this book you will perhaps notice things which differ from the information provided herein. Please write me in care of the publisher to let me know about any inaccuracies, changes, or updates which affect the information in this guide. I would also appreciate knowing if you have suggestions for improvements or enhanced coverage. And of course I would like to know those aspects of the guide which most appeal to you and which helped you the most. Thank you.

_____

_____

_____

_____

_____

_____

_____

_____

_____

_____

Mail to:
Big Pencil Publishing
P.O. Box 410675
Melbourne, FL 32941-0675

Order Form

For copies of *Route 28: A Mile-by-Mile Guide to New York's Adventure Route*, please complete the following:

Name: _____

Address: _____

City: _____

State: _____ ZIP: _____ - _____

The cost per book is $19.95.

Quantity:_____ @ $19.95 each = $_____

Florida residents please add 6% sales tax
   ($1.20/book) $_____

Please add $4.00 shipping for the first
book and $2.00 for each additional book: $_____

Total amount enclosed: $_____

Please mail this completed form to:
   Big Pencil Publishing
   P.O. Box 410675
   Melbourne, Florida 32941-0675

Thank you for your order.

To Our Readers

In today's world things seem to change faster than we can think, and Route 28 is no exception. As you use this book you will perhaps notice things which differ from the information provided herein. Please write me in care of the publisher to let me know about any inaccuracies, changes, or updates which affect the information in this guide. I would also appreciate knowing if you have suggestions for improvements or enhanced coverage. And of course I would like to know those aspects of the guide which most appeal to you and which helped you the most. Thank you.

_____

_____

_____

_____

_____

_____

_____

_____

_____

_____

Mail to:
Big Pencil Publishing
P.O. Box 410675
Melbourne, FL 32941-0675

Order Form

For copies of *Route 28: A Mile-by-Mile Guide to New York's Adventure Route*, please complete the following:

Name: _____

Address: _____

City: _____

State: _____ZIP: _____ _____

The cost per book is $19.95.

Quantity:_____ @ $19.95 each = $_____

Florida residents please add 6% sales tax
   ($1.20/book) $_____

Please add $4.00 shipping for the first
book and $2.00 for each additional book: $_____

Total amount enclosed: $_____

Please mail this completed form to:
  Big Pencil Publishing
  P.O. Box 410675
  Melbourne, Florida 32941-0675

Thank you for your order.

BPP02

To Our Readers

In today's world things seem to change faster than we can think, and Route 28 is no exception. As you use this book you will perhaps notice things which differ from the information provided herein. Please write me in care of the publisher to let me know about any inaccuracies, changes, or updates which affect the information in this guide. I would also appreciate knowing if you have suggestions for improvements or enhanced coverage. And of course I would like to know those aspects of the guide which most appeal to you and which helped you the most. Thank you.

_____

_____

_____

_____

_____

_____

_____

_____

_____

_____

Mail to:
Big Pencil Publishing
P.O. Box 410675
Melbourne, FL 32941-0675

Order Form

For copies of *Route 28: A Mile-by-Mile Guide to New York's Adventure Route*, please complete the following:

Name: _____

Address: _____

City: _____

State: _____ZIP: _____ _____

The cost per book is $19.95.

Quantity:_____ @ $19.95 each = $_____

Florida residents please add 6% sales tax
   ($1.20/book) $_____

Please add $4.00 shipping for the first
book and $2.00 for each additional book: $_____

Total amount enclosed: $_____

Please mail this completed form to:
   Big Pencil Publishing
   P.O. Box 410675
   Melbourne, Florida 32941-0675

Thank you for your order.

BPP01